CLINT—
ENJOY
Mark

Too Good to Be True

Other books by Jan Harold Brunvand

The Truth Never Stands in the Way of a Good Story
American Folklore: An Encyclopedia
The Baby Train
Curses! Broiled Again!
The Mexican Pet
The Choking Doberman
The Vanishing Hitchhiker
The Study of American Folklore
Readings in American Folklore

Too Good to Be True

The Colossal Book of Urban Legends

Jan Harold Brunvand

W. W. Norton & Company

New York · London

Printed in the United States of America
First Edition

The text of this book is composed in Weiss
with the display set in Journal Ultra and Radiant Bold
Composition by Julia Druskin
Manufacturing by Courier Companies, Inc.
Book design by Chris Welch
Chapter opening illustrations as well as illustrations on
the following pages by Michael Wood: 31, 62, 112, 117, 142, 148, 208,
233, 240, 267, 278, 293, 310, 318, 328, 345, 420, 435, 440, 473

Library of Congress Cataloging-in-Publication Data

Brunvand, Jan Harold.
Too good to be true : the colossal book of urban legends / Jan
Harold Brunvand.
p. cm.
ISBN 0-393-04734-2
1. Urban folklore—United States. 2. Legends—United States.
3. Urban folklore. 4. Legends. I. Title.
GR105.B715 1999
398.2'0973'091732—dc21 99-17562
CIP

W. W. Norton & Company, Inc., 500 Fifth Avenue, New York, N.Y. 10110
www.wwnorton.com

W. W. Norton & Company Ltd., 10 Coptic street, London WC1A 1PU

6 7 8 9 0

Scholar Jan Brunvand calls tales of fatal
Pop Rocks candy & hook-handed
molesters this kind of "legend."

Question: What is urban?
(Topic on Jeopardy, *October 24, 1997)*

Contents

A Note on Texts and Sources

The letters quoted in this book came from readers of my five previous urban legend collections (1981 to 1993) and of my syndicated newspaper columns (1987 to 1992) who responded to my invitations published there to contribute stories they had heard. In quoting urban legends from these letters, I have sometimes made slight changes in punctuation, spelling, or usage in order to present a consistent style throughout the book. Occasionally I have inserted information from the longer letter in order to clarify points mentioned in the stories themselves, but I have not combined story texts, deleted details, or added anything to the plots of the stories. I give the name of the writer, his or her location, and the date of each letter quoted; however, some of my contributors may have changed their names or moved since writing to me. The stories selected, in every instance, are typical of a wider tradition represented by other versions of the same legends in my files.

Besides the people named in notes to individual legends, I wish to thank the following for material supplied, services rendered, and general support of my work on this book: David Baker, Mac Barrick, Mike Bell, Meg Brady, Simon Bronner, Rich Buhler, Mary Carroll, Terry Chan, Tad Cook, Neal Coulter, Norine Dresser, Bill Ellis, Gary Alan Fine, Joe Goodwin, Harriet A. Hall, Mary Anne Hill, Ann Jarvis, John Johansen, R. R. Kohout, Janet Langlois, Jens Lund, Bill McNeill, Joey Meyer, Barbara and David Mikkelson, C. Claiborne Ray, Michael Richerson, David Rockhill, Peter Samuelson, Cynthia Scheer, John Schleppenbach, Sharon Sherman, Steve Siporin, Paul Smith, David Stanley, Steve Terrell, Barre Toelken, Patricia Turner, Eugene G. Weinberg, Valerie Westcott, Dan Wilson, William A. Wilson, Sue Wolfe, and Ed Zotti.

A special thanks to my tactful, wise, and expert editor Amy Cherry, whose eagle eye for detail is legendary. Without her, I would have let many embarasing misteaks get into print.

Introduction

True Stories, Too Good to Be True

Urban legends (ULs) are true stories that are too good to be true. These popular fables describe presumably real (though odd) events that happened to a friend of a friend. And they are usually told by credible persons narrating them in a believable style because they *do* believe them. The settings and actions in ULs are realistic and familiar—homes, offices, hotels, shopping malls, freeways, etc.—and the human characters in urban legends are quite ordinary people. However, the bizarre, comic, or horrifying incidents that occur to these people go one step too far to be believable.

For example, in some well-known ULs people do things like fill cars with cement, microwave their pets, get bitten by poisonous snakes concealed in imported garments, lose their grandmother's corpse from the car roof, buy a Porsche for a mere $50, mistake a rat for a stray Chihuahua, sit on an exploding toilet, steal a package that contains only a dead cat, get caught in the nude by a gas-meter reader, or snag a tablecloth in a pants zipper, just to mention a few typical plots. All of these things could conceivably happen, but it is thoroughly unlikely that they really did happen in all the different times and places that the legend-tellers describe.

Urban legends are also too neatly plotted to be believed. Nothing is extraneous; everything in the story is relevant and focused on the conclusion. Thus, they're too weird and coincidental to be absolute truth, especially considering that the same stories are attributed to many different settings, yet each telling of an urban legend is presumably about something that really happened to a friend of a friend—a FOAF, as we folklorists say. In short, ULs are just too darn *good*—that is, polished, balanced, focused, and neat—to be true.

But it's not really truth or fiction that defines an urban legend. As with any folklore—and these stories are definitely part of our modern folklore—the defining qualities are oral repetition and variation. As folk stories are repeated from person to person, and even to some degree in printed circulation, they constantly change in minor details while retaining a consistent narrative core. Here's an example taken from published sources sent to me by Charles D. Poe of Houston, Texas, an inveterate collector of the echoes of folklore in print and one of my favorite correspondents since I got into the UL business. For years Poe has been regularly sending me four-by-six envelopes stuffed with photocopies of dozens of bizarre published items, which he has liberally highlighted in glowing colors and to which he has added inked comments in red in the margins. In my "Poe file," I found these three accounts of something witty that different American astronauts supposedly said:

- Was it, as one 1978 source claimed, Apollo 15 astronaut David Scott who remarked about his thoughts before launch, "You just sat there thinking that this piece of hardware had 400,000 components, all of them built by the lowest bidder"?
- Or was it Walter Schirra who, according to a 1980 report, phrased the idea, "Just think, Wally, everything that makes this thing go was supplied by the lowest bidder"?
- Or was it really Gus Grissom who posed the quip as a question, according to a 1973 source: "How would *you* feel, taking off, sitting up there on top of fifty thousand parts, knowing that every one had been let to the lowest bidder?"

By permission of Rick Detorie and Creators Syndicate

For the purposes of folklore research, it doesn't really matter if any of these men ever said anything like this; perhaps it's just an astronauts' joke, and they've all expressed this idea from time to time as a prank on interviewers. What's interesting here is that we observe how a tale gets recycled and revised, and we see how *any* version of the story serves to illustrate the astronauts' human situation perched atop a technological marvel of modern engineering that was built by fallible fellow humans.

No one is certain who coined the term "urban legend," but folklorists interested in modern oral narratives have been studying them for about half a century. Their work continues in the ongoing studies by members of the International Society for Contemporary Legend Research (ISCLR) as well as in reports by scores of interested journalists, broadcasters, and devoted hobbyist collectors of ULs who communicate nowadays largely via print and the Internet.*

Among nonfolklorists who have been fascinated by urban legends is the renowned Nobel Prize–winning novelist Gabriel García Marquez (author of *One Hundred Years of Solitude* and *Love in the Time of Cholera*). In an essay titled "Lost Stories," published in 1989 in the English edition of *Granma*, a Cuban newspaper, García Marquez discussed plots that are "passed down from generation to generation and country to country, with slight modifications along the way." That's exactly how urban legends behave; but why does he call them "lost stories"?

García Marquez explained that he had been unable to trace the origins of many wonderful stories that he had heard repeatedly. So, just as I did while I was writing a syndicated newspaper column from 1987 through 1992, he asked readers to help him locate some of them. I don't know whether García Marquez got the huge response that I have enjoyed from my writings, but I do know that it is seldom possible to deduce the actual origins of folk stories.

García Marquez made this intriguing suggestion: "There ought to be an anthology of these stories that are repeated all over the world and which, according to those telling them, were verified by eyewitnesses." We can attempt this by tracing a few of the variations of one story that García

* For detailed information on urban legend research, see my book *The Truth Never Stands in the Way of a Good Story*, published by the University of Illinois Press in 2000.

Marquez mentioned, about a man who discovered a large diamond inside the stomach of a fish he caught. The *Motif-Index of Folk-Literature,* a standard folklore reference source, indicates that finding some amazing contents inside a fish is an old idea found in folklore worldwide. There's even a biblical prototype for this theme: In Matthew 17:24–27, Jesus directs a disciple who lacks the money for a temple tax to go catch a fish. The fisherman is told, "When thou hast opened his mouth, thou shalt find a piece of money: that take, and give unto them. . . ." Proving the extraordinarily adaptive nature of folklore, even in modern times, here is how the amazing-contents-of-a-fish theme shows up in a version of an urban legend called "The Kentucky Fried Rat." I got the story from a California reader:

> This woman was showing off her new wedding band, and when she took it off to show a friend the inscription inside the band, it fell through an open sewer grate. To their horror, the two friends saw the ring swallowed by a large rat.
>
> Sometime later this same woman was eating at a fried chicken place, and she bit into a large piece of meat. Her teeth struck something hard, and it turned out to be her lost ring!

To me, that sounds like an episode that Garbriel García Marquez could have used in one of his novels.

At any rate, this book, I hope, represents the kind of anthology of ULs that the Nobelist yearned for. I've selected one or more good, representative examples of hundreds of major urban legends, mostly those that are well known in the United States, but also some from abroad. I've chosen to include both legends whose specific texts are not quoted in my previous collections and the full versions of stories that I have previously only summarized or paraphrased. I've also included in each chapter a box with one story about which I know little or nothing, as a "no comment" example. (Perhaps these are the truly "lost" stories.) Finally, I have added some "true" urban legends and a selection of UL parodies.

To illustrate how ULs have penetrated our contemporary popular culture, and to demonstrate the wide range of styles in which they are transmitted, I chose my sample texts from a broad range of sources, including oral tradition, written versions, newspapers, advice columns, tabloids, literature, folklore studies, and even some texts from radio or television broadcasts and from the so-called information superhighway. A few of the selected stories came from celebrities, but most came from just normal folks. My largest and best single source of stories has been through conversation—the mail and E-mail that flows steadily from my faithful and generous readers. When no specific source is cited, it means that I have phrased a common story in my own words.

My groupings of stories here is by typical themes. I've retained the traditional titles for the individual stories, and in the notes to each story I summarize my earlier findings before updating the information. This compilation, although large, still merely samples the vast archive of urban legend texts, studies, and background information I've compiled and have written about in books and in my newspaper column since taking up research on this genre nearly 20 years ago. To locate the specific pages where individual legends are discussed in my books, readers should consult "A Type-Index of Urban Legends," in *The Baby Train* (Norton, 1993), pp. 325–47.

Besides printed works on urban legends, the Internet has become a prolific source of UL texts and discussions of same. An excellent entry to this material that is linked to other related sites is the "Urban Legends Reference Pages" (www.snopes.com). Internet distribution of urban legends had become so pervasive by late 1998 that an "Anti–Urban Legend" letter started to circulate there. It contained explanations such as "There is no kidney theft ring in New Orleans"; "Neiman Marcus doesn't really sell a $200 cookie recipe"; and "Craig Shergold in England is not dying of cancer at this time and would like everyone to stop sending him their business cards." These statements refer to well-known urban legends discussed in this book.

1

Jumping to Conclusions

If you wanted to invent new urban legends, you might start by imagining ways that people could be led astray by jumping to conclusions. Your UL characters could completely misinterpret, say, a faithful wife's unexpected behavior, or a beautiful secretary's intentions, or a pet's sudden death. The poor schnook in your legend could then end up destroying his own new car, or disrobing for his office's surprise birthday party, or sending her dinner guests to the hospital for an unnecessary stomach pumping. To prove not only that this principle governs some legends, but also that the stories themselves are much better than mere plot summaries, see the tellings of "The Solid Cement Cadillac," "Why I Fired My Secretary," and "The Poisoned Pussycat at the Party."

All of the legends in this chapter—and many more—center on the natural human tendency to jump to conclusions even when the evidence is ambiguous. A couple of hot new stories follow this same logic, or illogic, if you will. Number one: A guy gets a new computer and calls the manufacturer's technical support to complain that his cup holder is stuck. Cup holder? He mistook the function of the built-in CD-ROM tray. (I give the full story in the introduction to Chapter 14, "Baffled by Technology.") Number two: A new secretary told to order more fax paper for the office calls the supplier and asks them to fax her a few dozen sheets until the larger order can be filled.

Did many of the classic urban legends actually start that way? Frankly, my friends, I don't know. After nearly two decades of collecting and studying this vibrant genre of modern folklore, I'm still pretty much in the dark about how such tales originate. It was the same with Bill Hall, a columnist for the *Lewiston (Idaho) Morning Tribune*, who wrote this a few years ago:

> It's a question as eternal as where dirty jokes come from: Where do those untrue stories of amazing things that allegedly happened to someone in your town come from? . . . The same stories surface and resurface over the years [and] . . . most of the people who spread the phony stories believe them to be true.

But if Bill Hall and I—and other journalists and folklorists—are unsure about the ultimate origins of urban legends, we agree on the likely process of how they develop in oral tradition, and this too involves faulty reasoning. Somehow a story gets started, and then, as Hall perceptively wrote:

> It's a funny yarn so it passes quickly from person to person. And each one accidentally embellishes it a bit—jumping to the conclusion, for instance, that it happened to someone right here in this town.

That Bill Hall heard urban legends way out in Lewiston, Idaho, hardly a metropolis, proves how widespread these stories are nowadays. And his apt observation of how "jumping to conclusions" works in the stories proves that human psychology operates similarly on modern legends wherever they are told. The human impulse in Bill Hall's example is to make the stories more personal and local; in my view, we should also note the impulse to formulate theories even on bad premises.

Folklorists call the process of story reinvention in oral tradition "communal re-creation," but describing it as simply passing stories along with an occasional teller jumping to the wrong conclusion will work just fine, too. You can easily imagine that's what was going on in the invention and development of the following specimens.

"Miracle at Lourdes"

An Irish Catholic woman, because of poor health, traveled to France in order to visit the famous shrine to the Blessed Virgin Mary at Lourdes. The spring water there is renowned for its miraculous healing powers.

The woman became very tired during the long wait at the grotto for the blessing of the sick to begin. And since there happened to be an empty wheelchair among the crowds of pilgrims, she sat down in it for a rest.

As a priest finally approached to give the healing blessing, the woman stood up from the chair to meet him. And immediately when the people saw her rising, everybody started to claim that it was a miracle.

Crowds gathered around her, and they started to push and shove, wanting to touch her. In all this commotion, and with all the pushing and shoving, the woman fell and broke her leg. So the poor woman came home from Lourdes with a broken leg.

"The Brain Drain"

One scorching day a woman pulled into a parking spot at a supermarket and noticed that the woman in the next space was slumped rigidly over her steering wheel holding one hand up to the back of her head. She felt concerned for the other woman, but went on with her shopping. When she returned to her car with her groceries, the other woman was still sitting in the same position—hand up to the back of her head and bent over her steering wheel.

So the first woman tapped on the window and asked if the other woman needed any help. Was she feeling all right?

"Please call 911," she gasped, "I've been shot and I can feel my brains coming out!"

Then the first woman noticed a grey sticky substance oozing out between the other woman's fingers, so she ran back into the store, phoned for help, and notified the store's manager.

When the paramedics arrived they carefully pried the woman's fingers from the back of her head, examined the injury, and checked the rest of the car. Then they started laughing. The paramedics explained that a canister of Pillsbury Poppin' Fresh® biscuit dough on the top of her grocery bag in the back seat had exploded in the heat. The metal lid on the tube had struck the woman on the back of her head, and the top biscuit had shot out and stuck to her hair.

The sales receipt in the woman's groceries showed that she had sat there for one and a half hours before anyone had stopped to offer help. The manager gave her a new can of biscuit dough.

This story became popular during the long, hot summer of 1995 and continued to circulate through the following year. A "joke" version developed on the Internet, beginning "Beware the Dough Boy. My friend Linda went to Arkansas last week to visit her in-laws. . . ." The comedian Brett Butler, among other media personalities, delighted in retelling "The Biscuit Bullet Story," sometimes as a supposedly true story. The "leaky brain" motif occurred in several old, traditional folktales, one of which may have mutated into the modern legend. I provide a complete history in The Truth Never Stands in the Way of a Good Story.

"The Solid Cement Cadillac"

A cement-truck driver cut through his own neighborhood one day while delivering a load of ready-mix, and he was surprised to see a new Cadillac convertible standing in his driveway. He parked his truck, sneaked up to the kitchen window, and spied his wife inside talking to a strange man.

Suspecting that his wife was cheating on him, the driver backed his truck up to the Caddy and dumped the full load of wet concrete into it. The Cadillac sank slowly to the pavement like the mother of all low riders.

That evening the man came home and found his wife hysterical, with the now-solid Cadillac being towed away. Through her tears she explained how that morning the dealer had delivered the new car that she was going to give her husband for his birthday. She had been scrimping and saving for years to buy him his dream car.

Technically, this legend should be titled "The Solid Concrete *Cadillac," since cement is merely the grey powder that, when mixed with aggregate [sand and gravel] and water, hardens into concrete. But "cement" is the folk term for the finished product. This story has circulated in many communities for decades, sometimes claimed to have happened locally as long ago as the 1940s. In an alternate version, the car was won in a lottery. An authenticated instance of an actual concrete-filled car was reported in the* Denver Post *in August 1960, but the car was a DeSoto, and there was no jealousy motive involved. A*

1970 article in Small World, *a magazine for Volkswagen owners, claimed that a prototype of the legend, involving a garbage-truck driver emptying his load into a Stutz Bearcat, was told in the 1920s, but we have no concrete proof of when and where this story originated.*

"The Package of Cookies"

Who's Sharing What with Whom?

A woman was out shopping one day and decided to stop for a cup of coffee. She bought a little bag of cookies, put them into her purse, and then entered a coffee shop. All the tables were filled, except for one at which a man sat reading a newspaper. Seating herself in the opposite chair, she opened her purse, took out a magazine, and began reading.

After a while, she looked up and reached for a cookie, only to see the man across from her also taking a cookie. She glared at him; he just smiled at her, and she resumed her reading.

Moments later she reached for another cookie, just as the man also took one. Now feeling quite angry, she stared at the one remaining cookie—whereupon the man reached over, broke the cookie in half and offered her a piece. She grabbed it and stuffed it into her mouth as the man smiled at her again, rose, and left.

The woman was really steaming as she angrily opened her purse, her coffee break now ruined, and put her magazine away. And there she saw her own bag of cookies. All along she'd unknowingly been helping herself to the cookies belonging to the gracious man whose table she'd shared!

From The Pastor's Story File, *Number 1, November 1984, credited to a United Church of Christ minister from West Virginia who heard it from a missionary to Japan at a church conference. The chain of retellings, plus the certainty of other ministers adding the story to their repertoires, indicate one way that this popular legend has spread. Known in England since the early 1970s as "The Packet of Biscuits," the story has endless variations. Sometimes the shared food is a Snickers or a Kit Kat candy bar, and often there is considerable social distance between the participants: a punk rocker and a little old lady, for instance, or a pair of high- and low-ranking military officers. British science-fiction author Douglas Adams incorporated the story into his 1984 book* So Long, and Thanks for All the Fish. *Another version of the story provided the plot of* The Lunch Date, *an Oscar-winning short film of 1990, and the legend separately inspired* Boeuf Bourgignon, *an independent Dutch film first shown in Europe in 1988. Ann Landers published a letter containing a Canadian version of this story in her November 11, 1977, column. In the May 25, 1998, "Metropolitan Diary" feature in the* New York Times *a reader reported yet another "Package of Cookies" incident with the same old familiar details, but this time supposedly having happened to the reader's aunt. Obviously, this is too good to be true, so to avoid embarrassing her, I am not repeating the name of the contributor.*

"The Tube on the Tube"

A man working in a small office on an upper floor of a Manhattan skyscraper was exasperated one day when the lone fluorescent tube in his light fixture burned out. Rather than bothering the maintenance crew,

who always gave him a hard time about fixing anything, he went out and bought a new tube and replaced the burned-out one himself.

Then he had the problem of disposing of the old tube: it was too long to leave in the wastebasket, and he didn't want it there for the janitor to find. So he decided to carry the tube out of the building at quitting time and leave it in a Dumpster.

But he still had not found a Dumpster by the time he got to his subway station, so the man, holding the fluorescent tube upright—like a shepherd's staff—hoping to disturb as few people as possible, boarded his homeward-bound car. As he rode, several other people got on, saw no open seats, and grabbed hold of the tube, believing it to be a pole in the subway car.

When the man reached his stop, several other hands were still gripping the tube, so he shrugged, released his own grip, and quietly left the car.

Although this is hardly a popular urban legend—I've heard it just a few times with little variation—it's one of my favorite stories. My invented title fits London's "tubes" better than New York City's subways, but I have no evidence that it was ever told in England. In fact, several people told me they believe they read it in the "Life in These United States" section of Reader's Digest. *That's no guarantee that the story has any truth to it, of course, and its details seem highly unlikely.*

"The Surpriser Surprised"

Version #1: "Why I Fired My Secretary"

Two men sat at the club, and one said, "Say, how is that gorgeous secretary of yours?"

"Oh, I had to fire her."

"Fire her? How come?"

"Well, it all started a week ago last Thursday, on my 49th birthday. I was never so depressed."

"What has that got to do with it?"

"Well, I came down for breakfast and my wife never mentioned my birthday. A few minutes later, the kids came down and I was sure they would wish me a Happy Birthday, but not one word. As I say, I was most depressed, but when I arrived at the office, my secretary greeted me with 'Happy Birthday,' and I was glad someone remembered.

"At noon time she suggested that it was a beautiful day and that she would like to take me to lunch to a nice intimate place in the country. Well, it was nice and we enjoyed our lunch and a couple of martinis. On the way back, she said it was much too nice a day to return to the office, and she suggested that we go to her apartment where she would give me another martini. That also appealed to me, and after a drink and a cigarette, she asked to be excused while she went into the bedroom to change into something more comfortable.

"A few minutes later, the bedroom door opened and out came my secretary, my office staff, my wife and two kids, with a birthday cake, all singing 'Happy Birthday.'

"And there I sat with nothing on but my socks."

Anonymous photocopies—Xeroxlore—of this classic spicy tale are sometimes headlined "The Boss" or "The 49th Birthday"; folklorists sometimes call it "The Nude Surprise Party." The story has been around since at least the 1920s. Ann Landers first printed a version sent to her by a reader in a 1976 column, and she liked the story well enough to reprint it twice more, in 1993 and 1996. Another version made the rounds in newspapers in 1982 via reprints of a Los Angeles Times *business column reporting stories told at a local conference of realtors. In the March 1997 issue of* Reader's Digest *yet another variation appeared, billed as a true story that happened to the former boss of a reader from San Diego.*

Version #2: "The Engaged Couple"

A young couple, engaged to be married, had scheduled a premarital counseling session with a minister. But they failed to show up, so the next morning the minister called the bride-to-be's home.

"She's in the hospital," the young woman's mother told the minister. "She would probably like to tell you herself why she didn't make it to her session yesterday."

So the minister went to the hospital, and there he found the young woman in traction with a broken leg and collarbone. But, as she explained the situation, the accident had left her feeling more embarrassed than pained.

She said that her parents had been out of town for the weekend, and they asked her to house-sit. So she and her fiancé decided that this would be a perfect chance to "practice for their honeymoon." So as soon as her parents left, the couple set about practicing in her parents' bedroom.

Not long afterward the phone rang. It was her mother, in a panic. She said she had left the iron on in the basement, and would they please turn it off?

The fiancé playfully picked her up and carried her to the top of the basement stairs. Both of them were still naked. When she switched on the lights, shouts of "Surprise! Surprise!" came from the basement. Her parents were standing at the bottom of the stairs, along with relatives, in-laws, and friends. It was a surprise wedding shower.

The shock was too much for the fiancé, and he dropped the girl and fled up the stairs and out of the house. She rolled down the stairs and lay there naked, while her family gaped. Her grandmother reached for her heart medicine. Everyone was too shocked even to cover the girl.

Sent to me in 1987 by a woman in Fort Wayne, Indiana, who heard it from her niece to whom it was told by a minister. The typical ending has the boy carrying the girl piggy-back down the stairs; after the lights come on, usually it's said that "The girl went crazy, and the boy left town." Among the shocked guests, often, is their minister, but this time he's involved otherwise in the story. "Practicing for their honeymoon" is a euphemism unique to this telling. A discreet version was incorporated into an episode of Newhart *in November 1982: Bob's wife, wearing a filmy nighty, descends the stairs to their rendezvous beside the fireplace, and guests at the planned surprise party take flash photos of her shocked response when the lights come on. There's a related legend of nudity involving a dog and peanut butter that has been very popular lately. You can find it in the introduction to Chapter 5, "Sexcapades."*

Version #3: "The Fart in the Dark"

Once upon a time there lived a man who had a maddening passion for baked beans. He loved them, but they always had a very embarrassing and somewhat lively effect on him. Then, one day, he met a girl and fell in love. When it was apparent that they would marry, he thought to himself, "She is such a sweet and gentle girl, who will never go for this kind of carrying on." So he made the supreme sacrifice and gave up eating beans. They were married shortly thereafter.

Some months later his car broke down on the way home from work, and since they lived in the country he called his wife and told her that he would be a little late because he had to walk home. On his way, he passed a small cafe and the odor of freshly baked beans was overwhelming. Since he still had several miles to walk, he figured that he would work off the ill effects before he got home, so he stopped at the cafe. Before leaving he ate three large orders of baked beans.

All the way home he putt-putted, and after arriving he felt reasonably safe that he had putt-putted his last. His wife seemed somewhat agitated and excited to see him and she exclaimed delightedly, "Darling, I have the most wonderful surprise for dinner tonight." She then blindfolded him and led him to his chair at the head of the dining table. He seated himself and just as she was ready to remove the blindfold, the phone rang. She made him vow not to touch the blindfold until she returned, then went to answer the phone.

Seizing the opportunity, he shifted his weight to one leg and let go. It was not only loud, but ripe as rotten eggs. He took the napkin from his lap and vigorously fanned the air about him. Things had just returned to normal when he felt another urge coming on him, so he shifted his weight to the other leg and let go again. This was a true prize winner. While keeping his ear on the conversation in the hall, he went on like this for ten minutes until he knew the phone farewells indicated the end of his freedom. He placed his napkin on his lap and folded his hands on top of it, smiling contentedly to himself, and was the very picture of innocence when his wife returned, apologizing for taking so long.

She then asked him if he had peeked, and he, of course, assured her that he had not. At this point she removed the blindfold, and there was his surprise—twelve dinner guests seated around the table for his birthday dinner.

This version is another anonymous piece of Xeroxlore that elaborates on earlier earthy tellings with fairy tale–like language and structure. The legend gained some respectability from its inclusion in Carson McCullers's 1940 book The Heart is a Lonely Hunter. *More recent versions of the story set the action in a darkened car with a double-dating couple seated in back who overhear the girl's flatulence; the same variation inspired a short film shown in 1997, entitled* The Date.

"The Hairdresser's Error"

A woman hairdresser in a big city is the last person in the shop one evening, just tidying up the place before going home. A distinguished-looking man in a three-piece suit taps on the door and begs her to reopen the shop and cut his hair. He explains that he has an important business meeting in the morning and needs to look neat for it. After some pleading, plus offering to pay double her usual price, the man convinces the hairdresser to let him in, against her better judgment, and to give him an after-hours haircut.

The hairdresser has pinned a sheet around his neck and turned to get her comb and scissors. When she turns back towards him, she notices a rhythmic motion under the middle of the sheet in the area of the man's lap, and she panics, thinking she may have a sexual deviant or worse in the chair.

She grabs a hair dryer and beans the man as hard as she can, knocking him unconscious; then she dials 911 and screams for help. When the police arrive they find the man still out cold with the hairdresser standing guard, still wielding her weapon. They remove the sheet and find—that he had only been cleaning his glasses. When the man recovers consciousness, he promises to sue the hairdresser for an unprovoked attack.

I heard this story from several locations in 1986, and also have heard of prototypes from England. In some versions the hairdresser holds a straight razor to the man's throat and whips off the sheet. In one from New Zealand the hairdresser takes a swipe at the lump in the middle of the sheet with a hairbrush, and the man shouts, "I was only cleaning my spectacles, you idiot!" In 1989 a bookstore clerk in Minneapolis assured me that the incident had actually occurred in St. Paul. In 1996 I heard from United Airlines pilot Capt. David L. Webster IV of "The Flight Attendant's Error": a female attendant asks the captain to speak to a man in the coach section who seems to be masturbating under a blanket. The captain checks, only to find that he has been trying to get a roll of film unjammed from his new camera.

"The Stolen Wallet"

A New York City office worker is on his regular jogging route in Central Park early one morning before going to work when he is bumped rather hard by another runner. Instinctively, he reaches for his wallet and discovers that it is not in his pocket.

Determined not to be a victim, the man races back to the supposed pickpocket, grabs him vigorously, shakes him, and snarls through clenched teeth, "Give me that wallet!"

The other man, highly intimidated, hands over a wallet.

When the office worker arrives at work and has washed up and changed clothes, he is just telling his coworkers about the incident when his telephone rings. It's his wife on the phone, saying that she hopes he can borrow money for lunch, because he had forgotten his wallet on the dresser that morning.

In variations of this story the confrontation takes place on a bus or subway, and the stolen item may be a watch. At least with a wallet the unwitting thief can identify his victim from its contents and return the stolen goods! The wallet version was incorporated into the 1975 film The Prisoner of Second Avenue, *starring Jack Lemmon, based on a Neil Simon play. I have a report of a keynote speaker at a conference claiming that he himself had been the unwitting thief the night before and concluding his anecdote saying, "And now if [John Doe], who is also at this conference, will come forward, I'd like to return his wallet." A version published in* New York *magazine in 1987 has a Spanish-speaking vic-*

tim crying "¡Es mio! ¡Es mio!" to the uncomprehending English-speaking thief. A version published in Germany in 1967 ends with the thief exclaiming, "Mein Gott, ich bin ja ein Taschendieb!" (My God, I'm a pickpocket!) A "Moon Mullins" comic strip of 1935 proves that the stolen-watch version goes far back, but European versions are even older, as the following example demonstrates.

An Englishman managed to get aboard a crowded car one evening and was obliged to stand on the back platform. He was very nervous and imagined that one neatly dressed little man avoided his eyes. Reaching down for his watch, he found it missing. Just after that the little man got off the car. The Englishman followed quickly and the little man began to run. The Englishman finally caught him in a yard hiding behind a pile of wood. He said in a commanding voice: "Watch! Watch!" The little man promptly handed over a watch.

Safe at home the Englishman found his own watch on his dresser where he had carelessly left it in the morning and a strange watch in his pocket. Very much upset by what he had done, he advertised in the papers and in due time the little man appeared. The Englishman began an elaborate apology, but the little man shut him off. "It's quite all right," he said, "what worried me that night was that I was carrying 3,000 rubles and I was afraid you would demand those."

This account is from Louise Bryant, Six Red Months in Russia: An Observer's Account of Russia Before and During the Proletarian Dictatorship *(originally published in 1918), p. 270.*

"The Mexican Pet"

A couple from New York are on vacation in Florida. One day they take a rented boat out on the bay to go fishing. Off in the distance across the water they see something small bobbing in the waves, and as they move closer they see that it's a pathetic-looking little dog clinging for dear life to a piece of driftwood. The poor creature is shivering and evidently scared out of its wits. It whines and squeaks pitifully as they fish it out of the sea and bring it aboard.

The couple take the little dog home, dry it off, and feed it, and they run an ad in a local paper: "Found—small dark brown hairless dog with long tail. No collar." But nobody responds to the ad, and they take the little dog home with them when they return to New York.

The second day after they have returned home, coming back from work in the evening, they find that their new pet has had a fight with their cat, chewing the kitty's fur up pretty badly (in some versions, killing and partially *eating* the cat). They take both pets (or just the survivor) to the

Lane Yerkes. From *Smithsonian*, vol. 23, no. 8.

vet, who takes one look at their new pet and asks them, "Have you ever heard this dog bark?"

"No," they admit, "it never does bark exactly; it just sort of squeaks."

"The reason for that," explains the vet, "is that this is not a dog. It's a Haitian rat!"

(In other versions the vet immediately kills the new pet, then explains what it really is.)

This little parable, with its obvious reference to illegal Haitian refugees arriving on the Florida coast, started circulating in the early 1990s. In San Francisco at the same time the lost "dog" turned out to be a Chinese rat, referring to the West Coast smuggling of illegal Asian immigrants. The earlier version that gave the legend its name, however, was about a "Chihuahua" adopted by an American couple vacationing in Mexico. In 1987 the Rumor Control Center of Baltimore, Maryland, was flooded with calls about a Norwegian rat that had arrived on a freighter and was adopted by a couple who believed it to be a Chihuahua. Besides Central and South American rats, other folkloric species mentioned are Himalayan beach rats, swamp rats, "Wampus" rats, and "Coco" rats. European versions of the story describe a Dutch couple adopting an "Egyptian Pharaoh Rat" or a Spanish couple returning from vacation in Thailand with a pet rat that looked like a Yorkshire terrier. The tabloids have exploited this legend under such headlines as "Our New Puppy Is a Killer Rat!" As recently as August 1996 a reputable news agency circulated a widely printed story about a Ukrainian couple who had adopted a pet that resembled a bull terrier puppy but turned out to be a Pakistani rat.

"The Hare Dryer"

As told by Johnny Carson

There's a story going around. I told it yesterday to Peter and Freddy. They had heard it. I thought it was a real story, but apparently it's one of those stories that makes the rounds and comes up every few years, and my neighbor, whom I play tennis with, Howard Smith, told it to me. About the lady whose rabbit died? (To audience) Have you heard it? (Chorus of "nos" with perhaps a few "yeahs.") It's a funny story.

Now the way they told it, this neighbor of their's—apparently had—the people who lived next door—the little daughter, had a rabbit, and the guy who lived next door had a Rottweiler dog. And one morning his Rottweiler comes in and it's got the rabbit in its mouth, and the rabbit is dead. (Laughter) And the guy doesn't know what he's gonna do; he knows the little girl loves her rabbit. So—apparently the rabbit, there's no blood on it, but the neck, he thought, had been broken by the dog.

So he takes the rabbit and he cleans it up. He even takes a hair, a hand uh (Ed McMahon: hair dryer) a *hair* dryer. Fluffs it all up very nice, takes it over and puts the rabbit back in the cage, thinking the people will get up the next day and see the rabbit and think it just—the rabbit maybe died of a heart attack or something, and won't realize that the guy's dog had killed the rabbit.

Ed: Right.

Johnny: All of a sudden he hears a scream . . . he runs out next door, and the lady is there. He says, "What's wrong?"

She says, she's almost hysterical, she says, "My little daughter's rabbit died yesterday, and we buried it, and it's *back!*" (Extended laughter. Camera zooms back to show Ed and Johnny laughing heartily.)

Now I don't know if that's true, but that is a great story.

Ed: Great, oh . . .

Johnny: Apparently the dog had dug it up, you know, he puts it back, and you see that lady the next day . . . (Gestures of shock and dismay)

Ed: Oh!

Johnny: It's like Friday the 13th.

Tonight Show, *January 1989. This legend had become so popular the previous year that I dubbed 1988 "The Year of the Rabbit." Here Johnny repeats on air a "true" story that he had heard from a neighbor and had earlier told to a couple of* Tonight Show *staff members. His performance now was for Ed McMahon, the studio audience, and his vast television audience. Oddly, Johnny muffed the key term "hair dryer" and failed to exploit the obvious pun that I've used as the title for the legend. But his delivery, timing, gestures, and facial expressions were perfect, as usual. Surely many who heard him tell it had heard the story before, and doubtless many, many other people repeated the story the next day.*

As told by Michael Landon to Johnny Carson

(Just introduced as the first guest, sits, runs his hands through his hair, shakes his head.) Oh, boy—what a week I had!

Johnny: Yeah?

Michael: I had a *terrible* experience. You know I moved in to the ranch.

Johnny: Oh, you finally moved into your place?

Michael: Moved to the ranch; I'm in this smaller place until they finish the other. Wanna move in, get the kids used to it, get to know the neighbors. Well, I've got the *nicest* neighbors, right. And I've got—you know all the pets I've got—I've got parrots, I've got dogs, I've got horses.

The next door neighbor family—it's a husband, wife, and two kids, they have one pet—a rabbit. Right? Beautiful rabbit.

They go away skiing for a weekend. And I go out to get the paper Saturday morning. My dog, Albert, is sitting by the front steps, and he's got the rabbit in his mouth. (Laughter)

Now what do I do? I get the dog, I take it in the house, the kids start to . . . "Oh my God," I said. "Look, we cannot tell them. These are our new neighbors. You can't tell them that my dog killed their rabbit."

I'm gonna live a lie. I take the rabbit in the kitchen, I wash the rabbit off—he's got a lot of dirt on him. I blow-dry the rabbit. (Laughter) I sneak into his yard, and I put the rabbit back into the hutch.

Monday morning, I go out to get the paper, there he is. Waves. He's a wonderful guy. I say, "How was the weekend?" I'm playing it cool, "Skiing good?"

"Yeah, powder, beautiful," he said. "But, boy, a weird thing happened over the weekend."

I said, "Oh, what was that?"

He said, "Well you know that rabbit I had?"

"Rabbit? Oh, yeah, you have a rabbit, yeah."

He said, "Well the strangest thing happened." He said, "The rabbit died on Friday, and the family and I went out and buried it." (Laughter) Said, "I came home and this morning it was in the hutch again. Clean as could be."

Believe it or stuff it!

Johnny: (echoing) or stuff it! We'll be right back. (Extended laughter. Camera zooms back, and fades to commercial break)

Tonight Show, *April 1989. Despite having told his own version of the same story just three months earlier, Johnny gave no hint that he'd heard this one before. Landon adroitly converted the legend to a supposed personal experience story, then dropped his serious demeanor at the end to repeat a line from a skit, "Believe It or Stuff It," that Johnny had just performed. Although this telling has all the earmarks of a scripted comedy routine, Landon's manner was convincing and innocent throughout. One "folk" version of "The Hare Dryer" describes a baby-sitter who washes the dead bunny in Woolite, then hangs it by its ears in the shower to dry.*

"The Air-Freighted Pet"

As told by Paul Harvey

Joe Griffith of Dallas informs our For What It's Worth Department . . . of the airline baggage handlers who retrieved an animal carrier in the luggage bay of an airliner. . . .

But the dog in it was dead.

With visions of lawsuits dancing in their heads they advised the woman passenger that her dog had been mis-sent to another destination. . . .

Promised they would find it.

They disposed of the dead dog.

Meanwhile they set out to search animal welfare agencies for a look-alike live dog.

They found one.

An airline baggage handler put the substitute dog in the animal carrier with the lady's name and address on it—delivered it to her front door.

She took one look and said, "That's not *my* dog!"

She said, "My dog is dead; I was bringing it home for burial."

April 30, 1987

Paul Harvey's For What It's Worth *(1991), edited by Paul Harvey, Jr., p. 67. In his trademark telegraphic style, Paul Harvey retells what he describes in this book as a "truth-is-funnier-than-fiction" story sent in by a listener. There are many other baggage-handler versions of this popular legend, varying as to place, description of the pet, and reaction of the owner. In July 1988 the* Willamette (Oregon) Week *free newsweekly reported that former Marine Lt. Col. Oliver North, star of the Iran-Contra hearings, had told the same story during a lecture in Portland, Oregon. Rural and foreign prototypes for the "resurrected pet" theme go back at least to the 1950s, and these stories probably gave rise to "The Hare Dryer" legend quoted above.*

"The Poisoned Pussycat at the Party"

A woman had just put the final touch on her preparations for an elegant buffet dinner in her palatial home by adding as the centerpiece to the table a large baked salmon. The doorbell rang as the first guests arrived, and the woman turned away from the table for a moment. Then, hearing the maid answer the ring, she turned and took one more look at the buffet.

To her horror, she saw that her cat had jumped up on the table and was nibbling at the salmon. She snatched the cat from the table, tossed it out the back door, and hurriedly put a lemon slice and some parsley over the bite marks. Then she composed herself and went out to the entry to greet her guests.

The party was a great success, and everybody complimented her on the meal, the salmon in particular. But later as the house got stuffy, the maid opened the back door to let in some air and was horrified at what she saw. The maid tiptoed in and whispered in her boss's ear, "Your cat is lying dead out on the back porch!"

The hostess had no alternative but to admit to all of her guests that the cat had earlier eaten some of the salmon and was now dead, presumably from food poisoning. She even had to telephone a few couples who had departed the party early. The hostess and all of her guests rushed to a hospital to have their stomachs pumped.

The morning after the disastrous dinner party the woman's neighbor came over to offer her apologies. She explained that during the party last night she had accidentally backed her car over the cat, killing it. "I knew you were having a big dinner, and I just didn't want to spoil your good time, so I left your cat's body on the back porch."

This story has been a staple of joke books, newspaper columns, and oral tradition for at least 60 years. The main dish at the party is generally seafood—a fish casserole, shrimp salad, salmon mousse, or the like. Even in modern versions mentioning pizza, the suspect topping is anchovies. In Europe the preferred version of the story is that a family picks wild mushrooms and tests some of them on their dog or cat; I heard this one in Romania in 1981. A version in which the mushroom-fed cat seems to be having convulsions was published in a German tabloid in 1981 with its variant conclusion referred to in the headline, "Katze warf Junge—Familie ins Krankenhaus!" (The [pregnant] cat had kittens, but the family went to the hospital!) A transitional American version has the hostess skimming off some scum from atop a can of mushroom soup required in her recipe, then feeding the skimmed scum to her dog. Several stories, plays, and movies have incorporated the poisoned-pet legend, the most recent being the 1989 film Her Alibi *in which the cat is thought to have died from eating contaminated stew.*

"The Bug under the Rug"

As told by Alex Thien

A friend of mine says a man and wife enjoyed travel more than anything. With the new welcome to Americans from the Soviet Union, they decided to visit Moscow.

In their room at an old, classic hotel not far from Red Square, she said, "I'm still nervous about all this. Are you sure this room isn't bugged?"

"There's no reason why it should be," he said, "but I'll look around."

He inspected the walls and flower vases. He didn't find a thing. But as he walked across the room, he noticed a lump beneath the carpet. He pulled it back and found a metal plate. Just to be sure, he took out the screws. They went to bed.

"Did you sleep well, new comrades?" the desk clerk asked as they were checking out the next morning.

"Just great," they said.

"Is good to know this for commissar of hotel report," the clerk said. "Peoples in room below yours had only bad things to say."

"How's that?"

"Chandelier fall on them at night."

From Alex Thien's column, "Wary Americans check hotel room," Milwaukee Sentinel, *March 19, 1990. The hotel clerk's mangled English is typical of such travelers' tales. The Cold War version of the above* glasnost-*era legend was told in Dick Beddoes's* Pal Hal *(1989), p. 190, a book about Canadian hockey-team owner Harold Ballard. This time it's told about hockey star Frank Mahovlich and his wife staying in a Moscow hotel during a 1972 series of games played against the Soviets. All very well, except that the* Little, Brown Book of Anecdotes *(1985), edited by Clifton Fadiman, attributes the incident to Canadian-born hockey player Phil Esposito "in the early 1970s." Mahovlich and Esposito did play together on Canadian teams that competed in Russia. Probably earlier than any of these versions set in the Soviet Union is one in which the fearful couple are honeymooners who think their friends may have bugged their room as a wedding-night prank.*

2

Classic Dog Tales

Most traditional dog stories are of the overblown superheroic genre, and excruciatingly sentimental, as well. It's the "man's best friend" pattern: Rin Tin Tin once again saves the day or Lassie rescues little Timmy for the umpteenth time. (At least Wishbone, the dog hero of PBS, has a sense of humor—*and* wears cute costumes—while he's fighting alongside the Three Musketeers or playing the title role in *Robin Hood.*)

Here's a typical tear-jerker dog legend from Wales. The story is inscribed thus on a stone erected at the supposed site of the incident near Mount Snowdon:

> GELERT'S GRAVE
>
> In the 13th Century, Llewelyn, Prince of North Wales, had a palace at Beddgelert. One day he went hunting without Gelert
>
> "THE FAITHFUL HOUND"
>
> who was unaccountably absent. On Llewelyn's return, the truant stained and smeared with blood, joyfully sprang to meet his master. The prince alarmed hastened to find his son, and saw the infant's cot empty, the bedclothes and floor covered with blood. The frantic father plunged his sword into the hound's side thinking it had killed his heir. The dog's dying yell was answered by a child's cry. Llewelyn searched and discovered his boy unharmed. But near by lay the body of a mighty wolf which Gelert had slain. The prince filled with remorse is said never to have smiled again. He buried Gelert here. The spot is called
>
> BEDDGELERT

I wouldn't want to argue with a proud Welshman about the truth of this touching tale, which has been often repeated in books and articles and is told to every tourist. But, unfortunately, there's no proof that such an event ever happened, and prototypical stories about a variety of misunderstood helpful animals go back before the Middle Ages and were recorded first in the Middle East. One nineteenth-century English folklorist called Gelert "a mythical dog" and referred to the story as being "primeval [and] told with many variations." Recently, a brave Welsh historian dubbed the Gelert story "moonshine, or more exactly, a clever adaptation of a well-known international folktale."

The Llewelyn and Gelert legend was retold in the New World, where it evolved into "The Trapper and His Dog," a Northwoods variation of the same plot, much reprinted. As late as 1989 the legend re-emerged in a court of law as what we might call "the Gelert defense." In *The People of the State of Illinois v. Robert Gene Turner,* according to the case summary of Turner's appeal of his murder conviction, the defense lawyer had, in the original trial,

> told the jury about [the lawyer's] great-great-grandparents who lived long ago in rural Iowa. During an especially cold winter, the husband became ill and the wife had to take him 20 miles to the nearest doctor. She left her baby at home, under the protection of their faithful dog. When she returned, the home was a shambles and the dog lay bloody and near death. Because she could not find the baby, she assumed the dog had killed it and in a fit of anger she shot the dog. Only then did she hear the baby cry, and when she found the baby, there lay nearby a dead wolf. Though it appeared to her that the dog killed the baby, it had in fact saved the baby from the wolf.

The prosecutor began his response by commenting, "This is not a place for stories and quite frankly I don't believe the wolf story. . . ." The defendant's appeal was denied. (*North Eastern Reporter,* 2d series, vol. 539, p. 1204, pointed out to me by lawyer K. L. Jones of Oak Park, Illinois.)

The Gelert story and its direct spinoffs are traditional "rural" legends. What we get of the story in *urban* legend form, after further transformations along the way, is "The Choking Doberman," which emerged in the early 1980s as another true dog story that was too good to be true. The prince's palace became an ordinary home, and the wolf was changed to a burglar. The impulsive slaying of the dog was replaced by a trip to the vet, and the dog doc makes an emergency telephone call to the cops. A prime example of how this "new" urban legend is told is the first legend of this chapter, which, by the way, is just as much a "jumping-to-conclusions" story as are those in Chapter 1.

In general, urban legend dogs are more often victims than heroes (likewise the UL cats, gerbils, birds, and even babies). The pooches get cooked, crushed, and sometimes fooled into jumping out of an upper-story window. They get blamed for barging in where they are not invited and scolded for causing messes that they never created. Even a pet dog's lifeless body gets no respect in the world of urban legends.

Read on for all of these themes, and notice, please, that I saved one of the most disturbing dog tales for the next chapter, where poetic justice is the overall operative theme.

LOST DOG

Description:

3 legs

Blind in left eye

Missing right ear

Tail broken

Neutered . . .

Answers to name of "Lucky"

"The Choking Doberman"

Elizabeth Bunn: Jordan and I were at dinner with friends of ours, Mike and his wife Shar. . . . His wife is a nurse, and she's from the Upper Peninsula. OK, so we were out to dinner with them, and they live in Rosedale Park [a Detroit neighborhood]. And I'm not entirely sure how it came up in discussion. But they have dogs; they have two dogs, and she was pregnant at the time, and I think we were talking about dogs and security . . . and break-ins in Detroit, and they knew that we had dogs. . . . [Discussion of her two dogs and their personalities]

And then Shar says, "Oh, God, you're not going to believe this story," that she heard from her sister who still lives in St. Paul, and her sister had told her of an incident that happened to a neighbor of her sister's, an elderly woman who lived alone, I think was a widow. This woman had a Doberman Pinscher, in part for companionship and part for protection. And the woman came home one day, and the Doberman Pinscher was gagging [laughter]. Which anyone who has dogs knows is actually a common phenomenon. But whatever the dog was gagging on, it was stuck in his throat, and the woman got real concerned. So she took the dog to the vet, thinking the dog was going to choke to death.

So she got to the vet, and the vet said, "No problem, he's just got something caught in his throat and we'll get it out, but you might as well go home while we do it, because I don't know how long it's going to take."

So the woman goes home, and as she's entering her house the phone is

RUSTY THAT CRAZY-ASS DOBERMAN PINSCHER

By Ivan Brunetti

ringing. And so she grabs the phone, and it's the vet. And the vet says, "Don't ask any questions, the police are on their way, just leave your house immediately." So the woman has no idea what's going on, but does as instructed and leaves the house. And the police do shortly arrive, and the police go immediately downstairs in the cellar, I guess where the dog was normally kept . . . they somehow knew to go right to the cellar where they found a guy [laughter] in shock, I mean frozen in shock with three fingers missing!

[Janet Langlois: *Oh!* {laughs and groans}]

Bunn: . . . and the moral of the story, or the whatever of the story, was that the vet . . . that the Doberman Pinscher had eventually gagged up or thrown up three fingers. The vet had pieced together that it was a burglar and called the police and called the woman, and that was it.

Langlois: Amazing! Do you remember what your response was when you first heard it?

Bunn: Well, I totally believed it 100%, as did Jordan, and we were both just sick; it's so disgusting, and yet so vivid! And I think part of it is . . . I grew up with dogs, and there's very few dogs I'm really scared of, but Doberman Pinschers are . . . I'm just very very frightened of Doberman Pinschers. I've heard a lot of Doberman Pinscher stories. . . .

[In retelling the story later] I do know that I chopped off a person in the telling. I did not say "a friend of mine's sister's neighbor." . . . I said "a friend of mine's neighbor when she lived in St. Paul." . . .

Langlois: Can you locate the time when you first heard it?

Bunn: It would have been about April, May, or June of '81.

As told by Elizabeth Bunn, a Detroit labor lawyer, interviewed in 1983 by Dr. Janet Langlois, Professor of English at Wayne State University. Extracts from Tape No. R1983(1), Wayne State University Folklore Archive, Detroit, Michigan. I wrote an analysis of this legend for my book, The Choking Doberman, *and even worked out a genealogical chart of the legend's development for* The Mexican Pet. *The most distinctive modern motif that has entered is the telephone call warning the victim of an intruder hiding in the house. The same plot device occurs in "The Baby-Sitter and the Man Upstairs," included in Chapter 10. It's also notable that a veterinarian saves the day, both in "The Choking Doberman" and in "The Mexican Pet" legend of Chapter 1.*

"The Swiss Charred Poodle"

What Can You Believe?

Our recent series on Famous Fables & Legends of Our Time & Our Town drew such a thunderous lack of response that we have decided to accede to popular request and drop dead with yet another (will the last one to leave please turn off the presses?).

Actually, what inspired me to fly in the face of such unanimous opposition was the surfacing of the Chinese Poodle story on the front page of my very own beloved newspaper; *The Chronicle,* if memory serves. Like all deathless fables, the Chinese Poodle is on a 10-year cycle, so I guess it was due again. I printed it first in '39, with a Chinatown setting. I heard it again in '49, from New York, and in '59 it "occurred" in Honolulu.

This time, a couple of years overdue [1971], it was circulated by the Reuters news agency from Zurich via Hong Kong, and goes:

"Hans and Erna W., who asked the Zurich newspaper *Blick* not to publish their full names, said they took Rosa to a restaurant and asked the waiter to give her something to eat. The waiter had trouble understanding the couple but eventually picked up the dog and carried her to the kitchen where they thought she would be fed.

"Eventually the waiter returned carrying a dish. When the couple removed the silver lid they found Rosa."

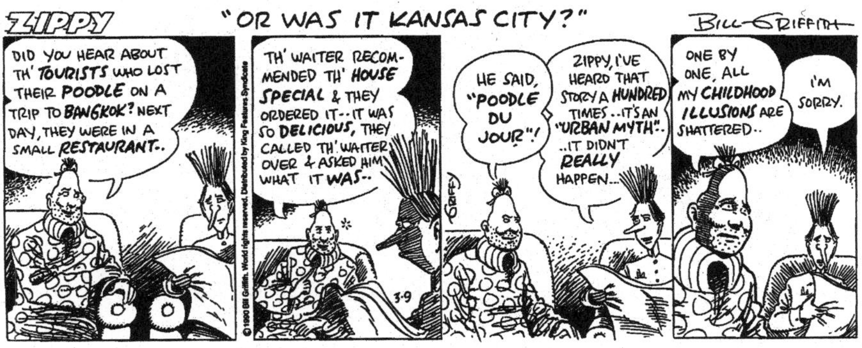

Reprinted with special permission of King Features Syndicate

When you first read that, you immediately smelled a rat, or at least a roast poodle, right? The tipoff is that Hans and Erna W. didn't want their names published, the telltale sign of your true fable. People involved in these fabrications never want their names published.

Among the rat-smellers when the Roast Rosa story broke was S.F.'s Robert Reynolds, U.S. representative for the Hong Kong Tourist Association. "That story had so many holes in it we didn't even bother to issue a denial," he says. "First of all, that alleged Swiss couple couldn't have been tourists because pets are quarantined for six months before they're allowed into Hong Kong. And in the second place, pets are forbidden in Hong Kong restaurants, just as they are here."

However, I should add that the Roast a la Rosa fable engendered some lively dialogue that day at Harvey Wallbanger's pub on Sansome. "Now there's the original Chinese Doggy Diner," said Jack Geyer, publicist for the L.A. Rams. "Nope," disagreed P. K. Macker, "it's chow mein." "You're both wrong," decided Pat Short, owner of Wallbanger's. "That's a Swiss charred poodle."

From Herb Caen's column in the San Francisco Chronicle, *September 12, 1971. Caen captured perfectly the typical discussion of "The Dog's Dinner" legend, although, of course, he may have invented all or part of his report. Quoting one's cronies in a bar is a traditional device used by newspaper columnists. The actual news item Caen quoted was circulated by Reuters, a frequent source of doubtful stories; their report claimed that Rosa had been served "garnished with pepper sauce and bamboo shoots." In other versions of the story the couple finish their multi-course meal, then ask about the dog and are told, "Dog was dish number eight." Or they recognize the dog's collar on the serving dish. Sometimes the horrified couple drop dead on the spot; more often, they sue the restaurant. The legend is told among the deaf community as an illustration of how sign language may be misunderstood by hearing people. When the legend was alluded to in the comic strip "Zippy" in 1990, the weird clown for whom the strip is titled said the incident happened in Bangkok, but he is told that "It's an old 'Urban Myth' . . . It didn't really happen." Zippy laments, "One by one, all my childhood illusions are shattered."*

"Not My Dog"

A certain shaggy-dog story that's been circulating for nearly 75 years hounds me, and I'll be doggoned if I can figure out whether I'm barking up the wrong tree when I call it a legend.

This is the "Lassie Come Home" of animal legends that keeps reappearing after I've decided it has gone forever:

The story begins when someone is invited to visit the home of a person who is usually wealthier or socially superior. The uncomfortable visitor is unsure about etiquette, and matters are made worse when a large, lively, dirty beast of a dog follows the caller into the house.

While the caller tries to respect social amenities, the dog tracks mud in, gobbles the snacks, and paws the furniture. The conversation becomes strained.

As the caller rises to leave, the hostess, with one eye on the wreckage, remarks icily, "Don't forget to take your dog!"

"My dog?" the caller says. "I thought it was yours!"

People telling this story always supply some corroborating details. For example, a version published in 1991 in a Salt Lake City, Utah, newspaper gave the names of newlyweds, "the youngest couple on the block," who had purchased a "snug old bungalow" and spent heavily to remodel and decorate the place.

When their next-door neighbor, "an ancient eccentric" and former socialite came to call, she was followed into the house by a big, black Labrador.

When the dog chased the newlyweds' pet Siamese, the room was trashed, and as the aghast visitor rose to leave, the hostess begged, "Please, don't leave your dog."

Punch line: "My dog? My dear young woman, I thought that beast was yours."

But there are too many other versions of the story circulating to credit this as absolutely 100% true and original.

The earliest version of "Not My Dog" I've found was in Lucy Maud Montgomery's 1924 children's book, *Emily Climbs.* I suspect Montgomery, author of *Anne of Green Gables,* was adapting a story she'd heard, perhaps on Prince Edward Island, Canada, where she grew up.

Emily, the young heroine, mistakes "a fairly large, fluffy white dog" for her hostess's pet chow, Chu-Chin, when she calls on Miss Janet Royal, a "brilliant, successful woman." The dog, covered with mud, and certainly *not* a chow, follows her into the elegant parlor and makes a mess.

As she leaves, Emily is asked, "Hadn't you better take your dog?"

Punch line: "I—I thought he was yours—your chow."

Time passes . . . then the story shows up in *House of Ill Fame,* a 1985 book by Simon Hoggart, a columnist for the *Observer* (London). Hoggart tells it about a Member of Parliament who, while "doing the rounds of his constituency," is invited into one home for tea. He is followed in by a large dog which, to everyone's surprise and embarrassment, "suddenly cocked its leg and peed on the floor."

You guessed it: The dog does not belong to the hosts.

A couple of years pass . . . and the story shows up again, this time in Ed Regis's 1987 book *Who Got Einstein's Office?* In this version, said to have occurred at Princeton in 1946, the famous mathematician Julian Bigelow called on his distinguished colleague John von Neumann and was followed into the house by a Great Dane.

It doesn't take a genius to figure out the rest of the story.

And again . . . this time in *Uncommon Genius,* a 1990 book by Denise G. Shekerjian about winners of the MacArthur "genius awards." (This story seems to have an attraction for geniuses!) Shekerjian recalls an interview she had with a University of California anthropologist in Berkeley during which a "big old mangy dog . . . a bearlike creature . . . a big, smelly animal," etc., followed her inside.

She concludes, "I asked her if we could let her dog outside for a while, just until we finished."

"My dog?" she says. "You mean he's not your dog?"

Could such an incident actually happen? I have no reason to doubt any of these published accounts, but has it also happened to what we might call "ordinary people" who don't write books or articles about it?

Well, it *did,* in fact, also happen to a man in Ashland, Ohio, who wrote me in 1990 about one time in 1970 when his family was visiting friends in Florida. A beagle hound followed them into the friends' home, climbed on a chair, and started eating from a plate.

It was not either family's dog, of course, and so, wrote the man, "The dog got the bum's rush."

I need mention also the lady from Middletown, Rhode Island, who wrote me about the time when she lived in California around 1975. Her mother's supervisor came to visit, followed into the house by a large dog . . . and so forth.

I have other accounts, but the best variation on the story I have was sent to me in 1991, marked "for your 'Not My Dog' file." It came from Debbi Brennan of Moss Beach, California, who wrote that she kept goats in the 1960s. One time a new neighbor asked to have her female goat bred with Brennan's male goat.

The neighbor arrived leading the goat and followed by a little girl who closely watched the mating, asking several questions which were answered "truthfully but tactfully."

Afterwards Debbi invited the neighbor to have a cup of tea, and asked if her little girl would like a cookie. Punch line: "That's not my little girl. She just followed me in from the gate."

By then, the child had wandered off. I wonder if she had a big shaggy dog tagging along.

Expanded from my newspaper column "Urban Legends" for the week of July 1, 1991. When I announced in June 1992 that my syndicated column was to be discontinued, I heard from Jacob and Helen Schneider of Westerville, Ohio, who wrote that it seemed like their last chance to report their experience of a dozen years before. Invited to dinner with other members of their daughter's high school drill team, they were followed into the hosts' home by "a huge black dog." The dog sniffed at all the potluck dishes set out on the table, and the host finally asked, "Jake, how long have you had that dog?" It was not, of course, the Schneiders', nor the hosts', and the incident spawned a catch phrase still used between the couples: "Remember that dog!?"

My conclusion: this is truly an experience that repeats itself, and it has generated an oft-retold story. So, in my dogged search for the truth, I'll call it "almost a legend."

"The Licked Hand"

There was a girl who had a dog that would lie under her bed. Whenever she wanted to know if everything was okay, she would put her hand under the bed. If the dog licked her hand, that meant everything was all right.

One night the girl was home all alone, and she was in bed. She heard a noise like a dog panting. She put her hand under the bed and the dog licked it. Later that night she wanted to get something to eat. She went down to the kitchen. When she got to the kitchen she heard, "Drip, drip, drip." She went over to the sink, but the tap wasn't dripping. In the sink, though, there was a bloody knife.

After she saw the knife, she backed up and backed into the fridge. Again she heard, "Drip, drip, drip." She opened the fridge door, and out swung her butchered dog. On the dog there was a note that said, "Humans can lick, too."

From Simon J. Bronner, American Children's Folklore *(1988), pp. 150-51, as told by a fourteen-year-old girl in Logan, Utah, in 1984, who heard the story told at a slumber party. Indeed, often a slumber party is the scene in which the plot occurs as well; all the girls except the hostess of the party are killed, and the killer's taunting message is found written in blood on the kitchen or bathroom wall. This handwriting-on-the-wall motif recurs in "AIDS Mary," quoted in Chapter 5. Bronner quotes a second text in which "The Licked Hand" is combined with "The Baby-Sitter and the Man Upstairs," quoted in Chapter 10.*

A further shock occurs in a few versions in which the girl's feet *are licked rather than her hand. Sometimes the protagonist is a blind woman whose Seeing Eye dog licks her hand. A college variation of the story is "The Roommate's Death," given in Chapter 22.*

"The Crushed Dog"

A young American scholar, fresh from his dissertation, won a prestigious fellowship to do postdoctoral research at an institute (art history, I think) in England. The institute was housed in a famous old castle in the countryside. He arrived at night and, awed by his surroundings, was taken to his room, which looked like something out of a movie about the Tudors.

He decided to get into bed and do some work there, but as he tried to fill his pen (this was some years ago), the ink bottle slipped from his hand. Reaching out to grab it, he splashed ink all over a priceless tapestry that hung over the bed. He was so mortified that he immediately dressed, repacked, and sneaking out of the castle, walked back to the train station, and went back home to America.

Twenty years later, the man, by then a famous scholar, was invited back to the institute. Though he still remembered with pain his earlier exit from that place, he figured that, the English being what they were, the episode would never be mentioned. He accepted.

When he arrived, he was shown into the director's office and told that the director would be there to greet him in a moment. Tired from his travels, he put down his suitcases and pitched himself into an overstuffed chintz chair, whereupon he heard a little yelp.

He got up and found a small bit of dead fur. He had sat on the director's little dog and killed it. He picked up his suitcases, snuck out of the castle, walked back to the train station, and went back home to America.

Sent to me in March 1996 by Joan Acocella of New York City, who heard it from a professor, who had heard it from another academic. Other versions of this popular tale of a sleeping dog lying down for good retain the hapless-outsider theme, but may include just one of the embarrassing episodes, or may describe the dog's death first and the inkspill second. Southern California musicians have attributed the accident to a local bass player, a houseguest of a well-to-do jazz fan. Kingsley Amis elaborated on the ink spilling in a hilarious scene in his 1954 novel, Lucky Jim. *The crushed-dog portion of the story appeared in Tom Robbins's 1980 novel,* Still Life with Woodpecker. *Other published versions include S. J. Perelman's early* New Yorker *story, "Don't Blench! This Way to the Fantods," reprinted in his 1975 book,* Vinegar Puss; *William Gaddis's 1952 book,* The Recognitions; *and Terry Southern's 1958 book,* Flash and Filigree. *The dog is variously described as a tiny terrier, a Pomeranian, or—as in 1984 in the* Old Farmer's Almanac*—a Chihuahua. Stephen Pile in his 1979* The Incomplete Book of

Failures *attributed the story to England "in the late 1900s"* [sic], *but provided no documentation and titled the chapter in which it appears, "Stories We Failed to Pin Down."*

"The Dog in the High-Rise"

As told by Truman Capote to Lawrence Grobel

Dogs have figured in two personal incidents in your life and one macabre but humorous story, about a friend of yours you set up on a date with a woman who lived at the Dakota and had a Great Dane . . .

I didn't set him up to meet her. This guy had a crush on this girl, a very well known model. He arranged to take her to dinner and the theater. When he arrived at her apartment in the Dakota the maid answered the door and said the young lady was getting dressed, would he go into the living room and make himself a drink. So he went into this big room that had French windows which were open. He saw this enormous Great Dane lying on the floor, playing with a ball. It was obvious that the dog wanted him to play with him. So he goes over, picks up the ball, and bounces it against this big plain white wall. The dog jumps up and grabs it, runs back and hands it to him. He throws it against the wall again and this goes on for about five minutes. Suddenly he throws the ball and it glanced against the wall and went out the window. The dog took one look and followed it right out the window! There was this horrible crash. At just this moment, the girl came into the room saying, "Oh, I'm so terribly sorry, we're going to be late for the theater." He was just speechless with horror and didn't know what to do or say. She kept saying, "Hurry, hurry, hurry—the elevators in this building are slow." So they went to the theater and he didn't say a word. She became more and more mystified. Here was this guy who was supposed to have a fabulous crush on her and he wouldn't even speak to her. During the intermission she said, "I don't understand what's the matter with you, but you're making me frightfully nervous and I'm going home." Then she said, "I forgot to feed my dog. Did you see my dog?" "Yes," he said, "I did. And I must say he looked awful hungry and despondent." She walked out, went home, and the dog was in the courtyard. Along with John Lennon.

From Lawrence Grobel, Conversations with Capote *(1985), pp. 68–70. Capote (1924–84) told this story repeatedly in interviews and lectures and on television talk shows, including the* Tonight Show, *with Johnny Carson. A particularly detailed version written by Capote appeared in* Ladies' Home Journal *in January 1974. Carson himself repeated the story in his opening monologue in November 1985, and many other people—some celebrities, some not—have retold the story, both with and without crediting it to Capote. The story also inspired a "lite" beer TV commercial and an episode of* The Jeffersons *in the 1980s. Whether "The Dog in the High-Rise" was original with Truman Capote is impossible to determine, but it should be noted that the Australian-born novelist Sumner Locke Elliott was reported telling it as a personal experience as early as 1974, and another version titled "Fetch!" appeared in* Boys' Life *in January 1975, later reprinted in a reader for middle school classes.*

"Fifi Spills the Paint," aka "Kitty Takes the Rap"

I recently heard about a friend of a friend—a FOAF—who is an interior decorator with a thriving business on Chicago's wealthy North Shore. He had just finished painting an elegant home in Wilmette, and was going around with a can of touch-up paint, making sure everything was perfect.

He finished the last brush stroke, stepped back to admire his work, and kicked the paint can over onto the priceless Oriental rug. What to do?

At that moment the client's yappy, snappy, obnoxious toy poodle, Fifi, trotted into the room. Thinking quickly, the decorator scooped her up and dropped her into the puddle of paint, at the same time exclaiming loudly, "Fifi! Bad Dog! What have you done?"

I was attending a seminar in Trial Advocacy, sponsored by the Association of Trial Lawyers of America, held on Nov. 11–16, 1989, in Washington, D.C. One of the featured speakers was a famous Texas trial lawyer, Jack Zimmermann.

Mr. Zimmermann has a wonderful Texas twang, and he gave his speech with a great deal of colorful language. He was speaking on the rules of evidence, and their use in trials. He was critical of the tendency of prosecutors to rely on circumstantial evidence. Then he told a story, which he said was from his boyhood. He said that he and his brother—aged about 8 and 10—had been left in charge of the house while their mother went out to run an errand. She had left a Dutch apple pie cooling on the kitchen table.

The boys were specifically told to keep an eye on the pie, and to make sure that no one touched it or ate any of it. But the pie smelled wonderful, and eventually the aroma became irresistible. Jack reasoned that if he and his brother only took a little bit from the corners of the pie, and then smoothed it over, their mother would never know the difference.

Unfortunately, the boys were unable to stick to their plan, and they ended up eating almost half of the pie. They knew that they could never hide or disguise what they had done. And, just then, Jack heard his mother's car pull into the garage.

Suddenly Jack got an idea. He grabbed the family cat, and he shoved its face into the pie. The cat's face became covered with bits and pieces of the pie filling and the crumb crust.

Jack's mother walked into the kitchen and saw the cat looking up at her, and she didn't hesitate for a moment. She grabbed the cat, and threw him out the back door into a stream right behind the house (which everyone called "the river").

At this point, Mr. Zimmermann ended his story, saying, "Now that wasn't the last cat to be sent up the river on crummy circumstantial evidence!"

"Fifi" was sent to me in 1986 by Susan Levin Kraykowski of Crystal Lake, Illinois. After I published her story in a newspaper column and in Curses! Broiled Again!, *several professional painters wrote to inform me that this is a traditional ploy well known among painters as a way to shift blame for spillages. The variation, "Kitty Takes the Rap," was sent by Jim Goodluck of Cleveland, Ohio; I paraphrased it in* The Baby Train *and also mentioned a letter that Jack B. Zimmermann of Houston sent me in 1990 in response to my query. Zimmermann wrote, "For criminal defense attorneys, this story is the perfect explanation of how seductive, yet how weak, circumstantial evidence can be." But, he continued, "I confess I learned the story from another trial lawyer—one of Colorado's greatest courtroom attorneys, Len Chesler of Denver." Another version of the story involving two young girls and some spilled berry cobbler appears in Toni Morrison's novel* The Bluest Eye, *published in 1972.*

"Take the Puppy and Run"

So this elderly lady constituent unfolded this complaint to State Sen. Roy Goodman:

Seems she had a Great Dane. She cherished this Great Dane. When he died, this distressed lady knew not how to get rid of her beloved pet, so she rang the ASPCA. Budget cuts prevented them from collecting him, they said. Bring him over and they'll organize a proper burial, they said. Right, but how, she said. In a suitcase, they said.

She was little and frail. The suitcase was large and heavy. Observing her struggling along the street a stranger offered to carry this cumbersome load. The panting lady stopped, thanked the stranger, and turned the handle over to him. The instant he grasped it, this happy thief ran like hell.

Only in New York, kids, only in New York.

Oh Well, in That Case

A friend of mine agreed to look after a couple's aged dog while they went on a two-week vacation. Murphy's Law—the dog died. My friend didn't know what to do with it, as the couple wouldn't return for another week, and a stiff German shepherd was hardly the conversation piece she'd always dreamed of.

She called the ASPCA who told her they could dispose of the body if she could get it to their center. Problem number two: What cab driver in New York is going to let someone take a huge dog in his cab, let alone a dead one? She decided to stuff the dog into a steamer trunk and take it on the subway.

Anyone who has tried to get the dead weight of a German shepherd down subway steps quickly realizes that it's not easy. Seeing her struggle, a young man offered to help her. This is unusual in New York, but she thought it very kind—right up to the time the subway doors closed, with her on the inside and him on the platform, laughing and carting the trunk away.

I would have given anything to see the expression on his face when he opened the trunk to admire his loot.

Janet M. Nordon

Version one is from Cindy Adams's column in the New York Post *for January 27, 1987; version two from the "Only in New York" feature edited by John Sullivan in the* New York Daily News Magazine *for February 21, 1988. The latter was repeated as proof that "crime still doesn't pay" in New York City on the* San Diego Union's *editorial page, no less, for March 4, 1988. Makes you proud of American journalism. Both versions display features of the breathless style and jazzy format of typical gossip columns. Several readers forwarded me these examples, saying they had heard variations of the same story told in a more conversational style, but—true to these columnists' claims—my correspondents heard the story "only in New York." This tale is an obvious localization of the venerable "Dead Cat in the Package" legend quoted in Chapter 3.*

3

Just Deserts

The late great *San Francisco Chronicle* columnist Herb Caen, who loved urban legends, wrote in 1971 with reference to them, "old-time newsmen claim there's no such thing as fables—'If enough people believe them, they're true'—and maybe that's right. I believed a lot of them once. I'm even ready for some more."

Many urban legends do indeed resemble fables. Like the ancient stories attributed to Aesop, they are short, snappy stories, usually with just a single episode, cast with stereotyped characters, and concluding with a moral that's either stated directly or implied.

The "truth" factor in fables and legends is not dependent on matching the incidents in the stories to a real-life origin. Instead, fables contain the truth of some universal meaning or moral.

Ancient fables might lead up to a moral like "Don't count your chickens before they hatch," or "Slow and steady wins the race." Modern urban legends lead up to morals like "Always check the back seat of your car," or "If it sounds too good to be true, it's probably not true." Somewhere between ancient and folk fables might be placed the usually comic stories with morals written by authors like James Thurber, two of whose original fables conclude "Don't count your boobies before they hatch" (from "The Unicorn in the Garden") and "A new broom may sweep clean, but never trust an old saw" (from his version of "The Tortoise and the Hare"). But, unsurprisingly, the fables of Thurber and other authors never passed into the oral tradition nor developed folkloric variations.

A good example of a modern oral story akin to an ancient fable was sent to me in 1991 by Jim Hutton of the *San Antonio Express-News*. He had heard it from his father, who had heard it in a conversation about greyhound racing in Texas:

At a greyhound race track somewhere in the United States, one of the dogs got fed up with endlessly chasing the mechanical rabbit around the track but never catching it. So the dog somehow figured out a better way to go.

One day when the starting gates opened, all the other greyhounds sprinted away, but this clever dog just turned and waited for the rabbit to come around the track. Unfortunately, when the waiting greyhound met the speeding metal rabbit head on, there wasn't much left of the dog.

I'll supply a moral for this sad story: Sometimes it's better to run with the pack than to follow your own path.

Or take this fable-like story that circulated by word of mouth and in the media during the time of the Exxon *Valdez* oil spill in Alaska:

During the cleanup, environmentalists spent a great deal of time, effort, and money to rescue and rehabilitate the oil-coated birds and animals. In order to commemorate their heroic efforts, a group of environmentalists arranged to publicly release a seal that they had lovingly cleaned up and restored to health.

The press and a large crowd of spectators gathered to observe the heartwarming release, and as the crowd applauded wildly, the seal swam happily out into the bay—where it was immediately eaten by a killer whale.

Moral: You never lose your place in the food chain.

A third example of a modern animal fable comes from syndicated humor columnist Dave Barry, who published it just before Christmas in 1991. Many readers who sent me clippings of the column recalled that they had also heard the story told, so it may be an authentic legend, or the story may have become one after Barry publicized it.

Barry, of course, said he was not making up "The Story of the Christmas Goat."

The goat was the pet of a family in Virginia, and one bitterly cold Christmas Eve they found their goat dead—frozen solid in a standing position. The family couldn't dig up the ground to bury their pet, nor could they find any agency during the holiday that would take the goat's body off their hands.

(If this problem of pet-corpse disposal seems familiar, it's because you just read "Take the Puppy and Run" in Chapter 2.)

As the family was driving around with the frozen goat awkwardly loaded into their station wagon, they passed a Nativity scene set up in front of a church, and they immediately saw the solution to their problem.

Barry claimed that the family added their dead goat to the assemblage of animals around the manger. "So it was a Merry Christmas after all, at least until the thaw came."

Here's my moral for this story: Always keep a stable relationship with your pet.

Urban legends differ from fables in that many legends with completely different plots have essentially the same moral. What is taught (among other lessons) in lots of urban legends is that "He/she/they got exactly what he/she/they deserved." And what "they" get is pretty gross—dead cats, dead grandmothers, a urine specimen, and worse. In only a few legends is *good* behavior rewarded; of course it's just as poetic that way, too. These brands of poetic justice are illustrated over and over again in modern legends, extending beyond the prime examples of just deserts included in this chapter.

"The Fallen Angel Cake"

Most everyone in town knows these two ladies, so they will remain anonymous for obvious reasons. [So reported a small-town Canadian newspaper in 1982.]

The first lady was to bake a cake for the church ladies' group bake sale, but she forgot to do it until the last minute. She baked an angel food cake, and when she took it out of the oven, the center had dropped flat.

Oh dear, there was no time to bake another cake, so she looked around the house for something to build up the centre of the cake.

She found it in the bathroom, a roll of toilet paper. She plunked it in and covered it with icing. The finished product looked beautiful, so she rushed it to the church.

She then gave her daughter some money and instructions to be at the sale the minute it opened and to buy that cake and bring it home.

When the daughter arrived at the sale, the attractive cake had already been sold. The lady was beside herself.

A couple of days later the same lady was invited to a friend's home where two tables of bridge were to be played that afternoon.

After the game a fancy lunch was served, and to top it off, the cake in question was presented for dessert.

After the lady saw the cake, she started to get off her chair to rush into the kitchen to tell her hostess all about it. But before she could get to her feet, one of the other ladies said, "What a beautiful cake!"

The first lady sat back in her chair when she heard the hostess say, "Thank you, I baked it myself." [The same story was published around 1980 in the Sydney (Australia) Morning Herald.*]*

"The Loaded Dog"

It Just Goes to Show, There Are No Lifeguards at the Gene Pool

From a radio program, true report of a happening in Georgia.

Guy buys brand new Grand Cherokee for $30,000 and has $400+ monthly payments.

He and a friend go duck hunting and of course all the lakes are frozen.

These two Atomic Brains go to the lake with the guns, the dog, the beer, and of course the new vehicle. They drive out onto the lake ice and get ready.

Now, they want to make some kind of a natural landing area for the ducks, something for the decoys to float on. In order to make a hole large enough to look like something a wandering duck would fly down and land on, it is going to take

a little more effort than an ice-hole drill.

Out of the back of the new Grand Cherokee comes a stick of dynamite with a short, 40-second fuse.

Now these two Rocket Scientists do take into consideration that if they place the stick of dynamite on the ice at a location far from where they are standing (and the new Grand Cherokee), they take the risk of slipping on the ice when they run from the burning fuse and possibly go up in smoke with the resulting blast. So, they decide to light this 40-second fuse and throw the dynamite.

Remember a couple of paragraphs back when I mentioned the vehicle, the beer, the guns, and the dog?

Yes, the dog: A highly trained black Lab used for retrieving, especially things thrown by the owner.

You guessed it, the dog takes off at a high rate of doggy speed on the ice and captures the stick of dynamite with the burning 40-second fuse about the time it hits the ice. The two men yell, scream, wave arms, and wonder what to do now.

The dog, cheered on, keeps coming.

One of the guys grabs the shotgun and shoots the dog. The shotgun is loaded with #8 duck shot, hardly big enough to stop a black Lab. Dog stops for a moment, slightly confused but continues on. Another shot and this time the dog, still standing, becomes really confused and of course scared, thinking these two Nobel Prize winners have gone insane. He takes off to find cover (with the now really short fuse burning on the stick of dynamite) . . . under the brand new Cherokee.

BOOM!

Dog and Cherokee are blown to bits and sink to the bottom of the lake in a very large hole, leaving the two candidates for Co-leaders of the Known Universe standing there with this "I can't believe this happened" look on their faces.

The insurance company says that sinking a vehicle in a lake by illegal use of explosives is not covered. He had yet to make the first of those $400+ a month payments.

This story was rampant on the Internet in nearly identical texts during late winter and spring 1997, when it was forwarded to me by several Internet friends. My title is borrowed from the classic version by Australian author Henry Lawson, written about 1899. Jack London penned his own treatment, "Moon-Face," in 1902, but the basic plot, involving an animal set afire, occurs in the Bible (Judges 15:4–5). Appropriately enough, there's a similar Aesopian fable called "The Burner Burnt." Another retold version is in New Zealander Barry Crump's hilarious 1960 book A Good Keen Man. *The animal in the story may be a rat, rabbit, raccoon, possum, hawk, coyote, or the like, and there is even a shark version. Underscoring the "Just Deserts" theme is the moral stated in a version published in a book titled* America's Dumbest Criminals *(1995): "that little coyote, although doomed, had at least managed to give them a small taste of what they deserved." Less preachy, and much funnier, is a version written in 1990 for the* Lewisburg (Tennessee) Tribune *by columnist Joe Murrey, who claimed that the hunters' dog was named Napoleon. Murrey's punch line, from the dog's tombstone, was "Napoleon Blown-apart."*

"The Plant's Revenge"

There was no way roommates David Grundman and James Joseph Suchochi could have known, on that winter morning in 1982, that their desert cactus-plugging expedition would one day be turned into an anthem by an Austin, Texas, rock band called the Lounge Lizards.

They also could not have known that their outing would eventually be documented for the world by urban-legend sleuth Jan Harold Brunvand.

And they certainly had no way of foretelling that Grundman would meet his ignominious end that day, literally at the hands of a giant saguaro.

Had they known all that, they might have gone, anyway. Such is the world view of cactus-pluggers—dumb shits who make sport out of blasting desert plants with firearms.

The facts of the case, according to Brunvand (who copped an account for his book *Curses! Broiled Again! The Hottest Urban Legends Going* from stories in the Phoenix newspapers), are simple: Grundman shoots saguaro limb. Saguaro limb falls and hits Grundman. Grundman dies. The cactus was approximately 25 feet tall, and likely well over 100 years old. Grundman—in his mid-20s at the time—was described by the Lounge Lizards in their song "Saguaro" as a "noxious little twerp."

An added wrinkle in this tale was some early confusion over Grundman's last words. The first news reports of the happy accident claimed that Grundman was yelling "Tim-ber!" at the time of impact, and had actually only managed to spout the first syllable, "Tim . . .," when the fatal blow came. Follow-up stories in the papers later speculated that the deceased more likely used his last breath to call out to his roommate, Jim.

From Dave Walker's article "When Cactus and Civilization Collide: Trifling with saguaros can be hazardous to one's health," in the Phoenix (Arizona) New Times, *March 3–9, 1993, p. 36. OK, I admit that my book* Curses! Broiled Again! *created a legend out of inconsistent news reports and a rock song, but there's also the parallel theme to the preceding story to consider: both stories illustrate how just deserts may be served up in the natural world. Plus there's a curious parallel story from Vermont in which a hunter shoots at a porcupine in a tree and the animal falls on him, puncturing him fatally with its quills. As with other people who have learned the story one way or another, I've become very fond of the account of Grundman's demise. Walker's lively summary appeals to me, too. The article was promoted on the cover of the* New Times *with this wonderful line: "Cactus Courageous: A pointed look at the saguaro, Arizona's signature succulent."*

"The Dead Cat in the Package"

In December of 1992 a friend of mine told me about two friends of a friend of hers. They worked at the Mall of America in Bloomington [a suburb of Minneapolis, Minnesota]. They got off work at about 7 p.m., and they went to their car to share a ride home. When they started the car it didn't seem to be running well, so they let it idle for a while, thinking it was just the cold weather. Then they noticed a bad smell coming from the engine, so they shut off the car and investigated. When they opened the hood, they discovered that a cat had climbed into the engine somehow while they were at work. The cat had gotten caught in a belt or something, and it was dead and mangled. The women found some sticks and poked the pieces of the dead cat loose.

They didn't want to just leave the cat there on the ground, so they put it in a shopping bag and started walking back towards the mall to throw it in the garbage. But before they got there, a woman ran by and swiped the bag, presumably thinking it was full of Christmas gifts or something. The two women thought that was pretty funny. They decided that they should report the incident to mall security, because next time the thief might steal something of value.

As they were walking to the security office, they noticed a big hullabaloo. They stopped to see what was going on, and they saw that a familiar someone—the dead-cat thief!—had fainted and she was being loaded into an ambulance. Then a bystander saw the shopping bag and told one of the paramedics that it belonged to the sick woman. So a paramedic put the bag on the woman's chest and secured it with a bungee cord. Of course, nobody had any firm details about what happened next, but my friend thought the thief probably had a pretty rough time of it when she woke up and the dead cat was still there.

I know I have heard or read this story before, but when I pressed my friend for details she kind of bit my head off. She was upset that I didn't believe the story, so I just dropped it. But it's been driving me nuts ever since. Was this a *Twilight Zone* episode or something, or was it just one of those stories you collect?

Sent to me in 1993 by Maria Westrup of Indianapolis. Many other readers, including several Midwestern newspaper columnists, confirmed that the old "dead cat" legend had found a new home at the gigantic Mall of America. And why not, since just about every other mall and department store in the United States, plus some abroad, have had the same story told about them? I've traced the version in which the cat-package is accidentally switched with one containing food—steaks, a ham, or the like—back to 1906, and both versions continue to pop up. It's an especially popular legend during the Christmas shopping season. Often the victims observe the thief faint twice, once when she feels into the bag to check on her loot, and again when she returns to consciousness while on the paramedics' stretcher and sees the dead cat staring her in the face. Ann Landers published a version in a letter signed "The Okie," in 1987, and she merely thanked her reader for "letting the cat out of the bag," evidently willing to believe the tale. An English music hall song, "The Body in the Bag," retells the legend, and this musical treatment has passed into folk-song tradition. Yevgeny Yevtushenko included a Russian version, in which the cat-package is switched on a commuter train, in his 1981 novel, Wild Berries. *That dead cat really gets around, and the thief always gets what he or she deserves.*

"The Runaway Grandmother"

One of the worst (or best) horror travel stories I've heard is of the American family traveling by Volkswagen through Spain. The two children were in the back seat of the car with Grandmother when she died. The parents decided to phone the American Embassy for advice, but first had to find a phone.

The children became hysterical with Grandmother still in the back seat, and there was no room in the front of the Volkswagen for all four of them. So the father wrapped the grandmother in a blanket and put her in the luggage rack on top of the car. (In emergencies you do what you have to do.)

They came to a filling station and all piled out of the car to make the phone call, leaving the keys in the car. They returned to find the car had been stolen, along with Grandmother and their luggage and passports. They never did find any of their possessions.

From a letter to the travel editor of the Washington Post, *December 23, 1990, from Wilfred "Mac" McCarty. Another letter published in that column on May 26, 1991, described a family from Frankfurt, Germany, who also lose their dead grandmother on a car trip in Spain. When Americans repeated this story, they were told that "this is a scenario that is commonly presented to first-year law students in Germany with instructions to determine and list all possible infractions of local and international law." Using families of different nationalities traveling in various foreign countries, "The Runaway Grandmother" is popular all over Europe, particularly in Scandinavia and Great Britain; it has migrated to Australia as well as to the United States. In American versions the family is motoring either in Mexico or Canada; in the latter setting, the grandmother's body is put either into a canoe on the car's roof or into a boat towed behind the car. Although the stolen corpse is the functional equivalent of the dead cat in the preceding legend, the grandmother story seems to have originated in Europe during World War II, whereas the cat story is older and of American origin. Elements of this widespread legend are echoed in sources ranging from John Steinbeck's* The Grapes of Wrath *to the film* National Lampoon's Vacation. *Novelist Anthony Burgess justified using this story in a 1986 book—*The Piano Players*—by making the unlikely claim that he had invented it in the 1930s. Whatever its source, "The Runaway Grandmother" legend offers an apt metaphor for the uneasiness modern people feel about aging and particularly death. Like a mortician in real life, the grannynapper takes the problem off the hands of the living.*

"The $50 Porsche"

The men in the insurance office propped their feet on the desks, puffed cigars and perused the classified ads. It was a Monday morning ritual. They were all talking about the eye-stopper.

Mercedes 280 SL For Sale. Sun Roof. Loaded. Burgundy, Leather Interior, Stereo. $75.

Their mouths watered. But their eyes moved on down the column. It had to be a misprint. No one, but no one, would sell that car for $75.

Finally, the talk turned to other things, and the car gradually was forgotten.

One salesman didn't forget it though. He kept looking at the ad, and finally he dialed the phone number listed.

A woman answered.

"I'm calling to inquire about the Mercedes," he said. "Is it still for sale?"

"Oh yes," she said. "It's still for sale."

"And the price is $75?"

"That's right—$75."

"Well, I'd like to come out and look at it."

He drove out to the address given him. It was a large, split-level brick home with a swimming pool and tennis courts. The manicured shrubbery and lawns bespoke the presence of a gardener.

An attractive blonde woman answered the door.

"I've come to see the Mercedes," he said.

She waved her hand at the double-car garage. "It's out there. Here's the keys. Just lift the door and crank it up."

The sight of that car took his breath away.

He could see his reflection in the hood. Its wheel covers gleamed. The interior was all plushy, shiny, tan leather and dark wooden paneling.

He tried the sunroof. He tried the stereo. Everything worked.

The engine ran like a dream. The car was perfect.

He went back to the door.

"The price is still $75?" he asked one more time.

"Yes, it is," the blonde said firmly.

His hand was shaking as he wrote the check.

But he couldn't leave without asking. "Lady, I just want to know why you're selling this car for $75. Nobody would sell that car for that."

She hesitated just a moment, but then she smiled just a little.

"I'll tell you," she said. "About five years ago, I met and married the perfect man. He was tall, well-built and good-looking. He was an engineer. He brought home about $200,000 a year and that's how we could afford this house and all you see here. Our marriage went well. Everything seemed fine.

"There was just one flaw. One of our neighbors was a beautiful, sexy woman. And last week, the two of them ran off together."

She paused and smiled again.

"He called me this week.

"'Now don't hang up, Honey, just don't hang up,' he said. 'You've been a good sport, and I know you're going to be a good sport about this, too. I know I did you wrong. You deserve better, and I'm sorry. But I just want you to do me a favor: Sell the Mercedes and send me half the money.'"

This beautifully elaborated version of a classic automobile revenge legend was written by Roger Ann Jones, managing editor of the Columbus (Georgia) Enquirer *for the October 10, 1983, edition. Ann Landers published a reader's version in a 1979 column, commenting "truth is stranger than fiction." When she reran that column in 1990 both she and I were inundated with letters from readers who recognized a legend they had heard. So Landers then published a comment from a reader who remembered back when the story featured a $20 Packard. My own files contain mostly $50 Porsches, but also prices running from a mere $10 up to $500 and cars including Cadillacs, BMWs, Karman Ghias, and Volvos. Often the husband has run off with his secretary. In England, the story has been documented back to the late 1940s; prices range from 5 to 50 pounds sterling for either a Rolls Royce or a Jaguar. Sometimes the terms of the Englishman's will specify that his widow sell the car and give the proceeds to his mistress. I heard singer John McCutcheon perform his own variation on* A Prairie Home Companion*; it began:*

One morning while reading the paper,
In search of a new set of wheels,
The classifieds had a most curious ad,
In their listing of automobiles.
What seemed like a wild stroke of luck:
"Corvette Stingray," it said,
"Low mileage—bright red,
83 model: 65 bucks."

"Dial R-E-V-E-N-G-E"

At the sound of the beep: A Dallas wife did this two weeks ago, but it shows Houston kind of genius. Learning her husband was on a three-week stay in the Caribbean with another woman instead of in London on business as he had said, the Mrs. quietly packed up her things, retrieved a number from directory assistance, dialed it and then left the line open for the Mr. to find when his trip was over. The number? That of the Hong Kong continual time and weather recording. . . .

One woman was visiting her out-of-town boyfriend, only to be abandoned as he supposedly went to visit his mother in the hospital. But when it was revealed that the mother was in perfect health and Mr. Two-Timing Rat actually was on a romantic rendezvous, this woman's solution was to call time and temperature in Tokyo, then leave the phone off the hook.

Version one was published in the Houston Post *some time in 1990; version two was in a* Chicago Tribune *article by Marla Donato headlined "Nifty ways to leave your lover," and published as a Valentine's Day item on February 12, 1993. I've collected references to this ploy—usually used to get rid of an unwanted live-in lover—going back to 1982. Foreign versions, such as a comical poem based on the legend published in the English journal* New Statesman *in 1986, usually mention calling the New York City number for the "speaking clock." The legend became the basis of a "Garfield" cartoon on Sunday June 2, 1996. Telephone company experts assure me that the trick would not work, since calls to the time and temperature service have an automatic cutoff after a specified period, usually one minute.*

"Revenge of the Rich"

As told by Paul Harvey

Our For What It's Worth Department hears from Hershey, Pennsylvania—where the woman in the Mercedes had been waiting patiently for a parking place to open up.

The shopping mall was crowded.

The woman in the Mercedes zigzagged between rows—then up ahead she saw a man with a load of packages head for his car.

She drove up and parked behind him and waited while he opened his trunk and loaded it with packages.

Finally he got in his car and backed out of the stall.

But before the woman in the Mercedes could drive into the parking space . . .

A young man in a shiny new Corvette zipped past and around her and HE pulled into the empty space and got out and started walking away.

"Hey!" shouted the woman in the Mercedes, "I've been waiting for that parking place!"

The college-ager responded, "Sorry lady; that's how it is when you're young and quick."

At that instant she put her Mercedes in gear, floorboarded it, and

Deseret News

crashed into and crushed the right rear fender and corner panel of the flashy new Corvette.

Now the young man is jumping up and down shouting, "You can't do that!"

The lady in the Mercedes said, "That's how it is when you're old and rich!"

Paul Harvey broadcast this story on May 22, 1987, but I quote the text from his 1991 book, For What It's Worth, *p. 1. After I published a version of "Old vs. Young" in a 1985 newspaper column I heard from readers who said they remembered the story with varying details from the 1960s and '70s. It's usually localized to a specific community, either American or European, but lacks the names of participants. An insurance adjuster wrote me saying he was convinced it had really happened until he checked back with his source, another adjuster. The source, of course, only knew the story from a FOAF. A similar incident was included in the 1991 film* Fried Green Tomatoes, *based on the novel by Fannie Flagg. This is another example of the numerous stories that Paul Harvey receives from his legions of listeners writing "from Main Street, USA." Journalist Dan Wilson analyzed some of Harvey's stories in the September/October 1997 issue of* Extra *and documented how this "broadcasting icon" not only fails to verify many of his supposed news items, but also injects "a conservative kick" into some of them.*

"Gag Me with a Siphon"

This guy had a big RV that he had converted to propane during the 1970s gas shortage. The conversion left a huge gas tank unused, so he modified it to use as a sewage holding tank instead.

One night, camped at an RV park, he heard a ruckus outside. He got up, threw on his robe, and emerged from the camper just as a car went screeching off into the night.

The guy went back inside for a flashlight and came back out to investigate. What he found was a five-gallon gas can, a siphon hose dangling from the spout of his former fuel tank, and on the ground evidence of somebody having been very, very sick.

Sent to me in 1989 by David Allard of Gag Harbor—I mean Gig *Harbor—Washington, who said he heard it about 1980. I first heard "The Unfortunate Gas Thief" in 1978 and first saw it published in a small-town Kansas newspaper in 1982 as something that happened to a man from Iola. Some versions of the story mention that the RV owner had not removed the "Unleaded fuel only" decal from the tank's spout. A version attributed to an unnamed motor-home owner in Seattle made the rounds of print and broadcast media in 1991 and '92. These tellings usually ended, "The motor home's owner declined to press charges. 'It's the best laugh I've ever had,' he explained to the cops." After* Road & Track *published the Seattle story in November 1991, readers wrote to inform the editors that it was merely an urban legend. As the Seattle version entered oral tradition, storytellers continued to elaborate details of the owner's reason for adapting his tanks and the thief's behavior after sucking on the misplaced siphon hose. Through all of these variations, the message is always clear: Served him right!*

"The Stolen Specimen"

A man coming out of a supermarket carrying his groceries noticed a pregnant woman get into her car, then suddenly slump over her steering wheel and begin shaking. She appeared to be crying or having some kind of convulsions.

Believing that she was starting to have her baby, the man dropped his grocery bags, ran over to the car, and tapped on the window, asking if the woman wanted him to call for help.

"No, no, I'm all right," the woman said. "I'm just laughing. You won't believe what just happened."

The woman explained that she was on the way to an appointment with her gynecologist, who had asked her to bring in a urine sample. But the only clean container the woman could find in the house was an old wine bottle.

So she had used the bottle for her specimen, and brought it with her. She left the bottle on the front seat of her car while she went into the supermarket to pick up a few items.

The pregnant woman had come out of the store just in time to see a man reach into her car, grab the bottle, and run away.

If the opening scene of this story sounds familiar, that's because it's also the way the legend of "The Brain Drain" (Chapter 1) begins: person in store parking lot offers to help woman in apparent distress. Both legends are resolved humorously, this time with another instance of someone stealing an undesirable item, like the dead cat, grandmother's corpse, or contents of an RV sewage tank. In an English version of "The Stolen Specimen," the woman—sometimes pregnant, sometimes not—is bicycling to the doctor's office with her sample in a Haig whiskey bottle, stowed in full view in the handlebar basket. Someone nabs it. A version was once told in Utah, back when restaurants still were required to dispense liquor only in "mini-bottles," and some drinkers bought their own minis in the state-owned liquor stores to bring to restaurants. At that time, the Utah woman in the legend carried her sample in a mini-bottle; how she managed to hit this tiny target was never adequately explained. Another instance of ingested urine appears in the box "Now Urine Trouble" in Chapter 22, and the same notion occurs in the old prank in which someone has apple juice in a specimen jar, then drinks it in front of witnesses, saying, "Looks a little thin; I'd better run it through again."

"The Videotaped Theft"

Dear Abby: Recently I attended the wedding of a good friend. Because I am a photojournalist by trade, she asked me if I would videotape her wedding, and I gladly agreed.

The wedding was beautiful and the reception went smoothly until the bride's father stopped the band to make an announcement. He said he had "lost" his wallet, which contained $1,500 with which he had intended to pay the band. He said if anyone found the money, it could be returned simply by leaving it in the men's lavatory, and no questions would be asked. No money was turned in.

The following day, I looked over the footage I had taken at the reception and was astonished to see that while filming a couple's conversation, in the background was the groom removing a wallet from the evening coat of the bride's father!

Now I don't know what to do. The couple is away for two weeks on their honeymoon. Should I tell my friend? Should I tell her father? Or should I just keep it to myself?

For the bride's sake, please do not use my name or address.

—No Name, No Address

Dear No Name: Call the bride's father and invite him to view the lovely video you took of his daughter's wedding—and you won't have to tell anybody anything.

"Dear Abby" column for October 30, 1991. Despite this anonymous, supposedly first-person report, virtually the same story has been around since 1982–83, when two sources published it; since then lots of people have sent me versions that they've heard, and Time *published yet another one in an article on big weddings in the July 7, 1986, edition. Among the variations, the couple are Jewish, Catholic, Polish, Italian, Iranian—you name it. The money may have been stolen from the bride or from her father, and the thief may be the groom's father or the groom himself. Sometimes the camcorder was left unattended and running on a tripod. The amount stolen varies from $1,500 to as high as $20,000, which seems like a huge sum for a person to carry around in cash. The bill—whether for the band, the caterer, or the reception hall—is then usually paid with a check, a credit card, or with cash borrowed from a relative attending the wedding. Sometimes people say the wedding was annulled; in other cases there's an early divorce. A few couples, according to the story, work things out and live happily ever after. They're probably the ones who are savvy to urban legends about poetic justice.*

"Urban Pancake"

An alert friend recently passed along this story:

The Modesto [California] couple drove their new BMW to the World Series home opener at Candlestick Park. They parked, found their seats. Then the stadium shook. The earthquake stopped the game.

They returned to the lot to discover that their new car was gone, stolen. They made their way home to Modesto, no easy trick in the confusion following the quake. Then began the frustrating process of recovering their car.

The authorities, of course, had other priorities. So the couple waited and waited for word on their missing vehicle.

Finally, weeks later, they received a call. Workers clearing the debris from the collapsed portion of the Nimitz Freeway had hoisted up one of the last sections of concrete to be removed. Beneath it was the BMW, squashed flat as a pancake.

Trapped inside was the car thief.

From Glenn Scott's column of December 29, 1989, "Wonderful tale; fact or fiction?" in the Modesto Bee. *The quake had occurred on October 17, 1989. Scott, who invented the title used here, commented in his column that the story "seems, as we say, too good to be true. Too poetic: the luxury car, the series, the theft and punishment." So he attempted to trace it with the California Department of Transportation and the Highway Patrol with no success. He also checked with me, explaining how and from whom he had heard the story: "in a bar, a cable TV ad salesman grabbed me and told the story. He'd heard it from a real estate agent at a party." And my answer? I had already heard it from about a dozen Californians living in the Bay Area or as far away as Fresno, who described luxury cars of several makes and models. In some versions of the story the owners receive notice of the accident from a state trooper who appears at their door with the crumpled license plate in his hand from their flattened car. Typically, there were many other rumors and stories surrounding this earthquake, but "Urban Pancake" was the best developed, most ironic, and neatest poetically justified one to rise from the rubble and tragedies of the event. It represents the ultimate level of a got-what-he-deserved story, and is often tinged with racism when the car thief is said, or implied, to be black.*

"The Will"

The quirky human-interest story was seized on by editors, repeated in news reports around the world, and had journalists in Spain scrambling for further details. Now some are muttering hoax. The wild-goose chase began when the German tabloid *Bild* published a heartwarming yarn about a good-natured Spaniard and a lonely Swede. According to *Bild,* Spanish Catholic Eduardo Sierra stopped at a Stockholm church while visiting Sweden on business. Noticing a coffin in front of the altar, he offered a prayer for the deceased, and entered his name in the blank condolence book nearby. A few weeks later, Sierra received word that he had become a millionaire. The dead stranger, a wealthy but friendless Swedish real estate agent named Jens Svenson, had bequeathed his estate to "Whoever prays for my soul." Eager to interview Sierra about his windfall, journalists plied the phones—to no avail. Neither the Swedish embassy in Madrid nor the Catholic diocese in Stockholm nor the Swedish press knew anything about the legacy—or Jens Svenson. Last week a German journalist acknowledged that she had altered the names—but claimed the story came straight from the lucky heir, who requested anonymity. After days of chasing false leads, some suspicious journalists wondered how many other facts in *Bild*'s report were fictitious. "I don't believe the man ever existed," sniffed disgruntled Madrid newswoman Isabel Flores. Truth or urban myth, the tale continues to spread. It may be too good to be true, but it is way too good not to be told and retold.

From Time's *International Edition of October 21, 1996. Except for dubbing the story a "myth" instead of "legend," this is a good account of how even a doubtful and unverified story may spread in the press and, sometimes, be debunked by journalistic effort.* Newsweek, *on the other hand, had simply published a paraphrase of the* Bild *item in its October 14 edition, and Chuck Shepherd's syndicated "News of the Weird" column used a similar retelling the following month. When I first published the New York City version I heard in 1986, in which a woman received a $10,000 bequest, I received letters from people who either confirmed the New York setting or claimed it had happened in Chicago and even in Honduras 15 years earlier. A column in the July 1990 issue of* Spy *magazine attributed the incident to Iphigene Sulzberger, "grand matriarch of the* New York Times,*" chiding the* Times *for not including the story in its 3,000-word obituary for Mrs. Sulzberger, but admitting that the tale was "possibly apocryphal." Another version, without a name this time, appeared in a 1992 guide to public toilets of Manhattan as a story heard fourth-hand and leading up to a paltry $500 bequest. Also in 1992, a* *woman wrote to the* Muncie (Indiana) Star *telling the story as she had heard it from her sister in Tucson; this time a male truck driver, city not mentioned, won a $50,000 inheritance for being the only person attending a funeral.*

"Promiscuity Rewarded"

Two IRS agents were traveling through a rural area when their car broke down. They walked to a nearby mansion and knocked on the door. A beautiful widow answered and said they were welcome to spend the night while her hired hands worked on the car.

Months later one of the agents received a package of legal documents. After surveying the contents, he quickly called the other agent.

"When we were up in the country," the first agent asked, "did you slip away in the night and go to that widow's bedroom?"

"Yes," the second agent admitted.

"Did you use my name?"

"Why, yes, but how'd you find out?"

"She died and left me her estate."

From the Reader's Digest *section "Laughter, the Best Medicine," August 1989, p. 70; contributed by Gaylen K. Bunker. While it sounds like merely a variation on the old traveling-salesman jokes, this story is based on an urban legend that's especially popular in Ireland, where it's called "The Kilkenny Widow." A version appeared in the Irish folklore journal* Béaloideas *in 1983, categorized with "Legends of Revenge"; I regard it more as a story of promiscuity rewarded. The Irish novelist Edna O'Brien claimed in a* New York Times *column on September 26, 1985, to have heard the story told in Rome, but she may have been simply remembering the gist of the Irish legend. Her version has the incident occur on a sleeper train and the* woman *involved giving a false name.*

4

Automania

Folklorist Richard M. Dorson was one of the first to identify and study American urban legends. In thinking about them, he noticed how many latched onto "the chief symbol of modern America"—the car. While I've quoted several car yarns already, there are many yet to come, even more than those parked in this chapter.

There are urban legends about virtually every aspect of cars and drivers, from assembly plants to road rage, from compact cars to vintage vehicles, and from freeways and rest stops to parking lots and garages. Car advertising, car dealers, car thefts, and car breakdowns are all subjects of urban legends, as are seat belts, car alarms, and traffic cops. No sooner is some new feature added to cars—like automatic transmission, for example—than a legend springs up concerning it (see "Push-Starting the Car" in Chapter 14). If I were to categorize legends solely by their contents, about one-third of the stories would be in the automobile section.

In the urban legend business, nothing piles up faster than generic car tales—odd stories about autos that may or may not be true. Some of these plausible but unverified accounts of supposed situations involving cars become genuine urban legends that "traverse the country," as Dorson put it. Other car tales are simpler and more localized, part of the anecdotal or joke repertoire of a community.

Here are some samples from my miscellaneous car-story file, all of them (in my humble opinion) too good to be true.

"Block that Ambulance"

An editorial in the *Syracuse (New York) Post-Standard* in 1990, criticizing New Yorkers' failure to yield to emergency vehicles, concluded with this ironic shocker: "Several years ago, a driver in the Bronx refused to yield to an ambulance responding to a reported heart attack. After slowing down the ambulance with his pigheadedness, the man reached home—only to find that the ambulance was on its way to help his own mother."

"Rotten to the Big Apple Core"

This was the headline in a 1991 British car magazine above the following item:

Britain's car theft problems pale into insignificance when compared with those faced by the good citizens of New York.

Car owners desperate not to have their cars broken into are, it seems, no longer bothering to replace the radio after it has been crow-barred from the facia [the dashboard]. Instead, they leave a board behind the windscreen stating "No Radio."

A pal of mine living in the Mad Apple left his board behind the windscreen one night. The next morning, he was horrified to find that his car's side window had been smashed.

"The note left on the front seat said, "Just Checkin."

"Have You Heard?"

In his letter a Texas reader asked me, "Have you heard the one about the guy who bought a used auto part and found his Social Security number engraved on it (his previous car having been stolen)? . . . How about the lady who totaled her car because it was possessed? The auto dealer had neglected to tell her about the verbal warning systems in the car, and the recording or whatever was faulty. All she heard was a garbled voice coming from her dashboard, so she ran it into a lightpost to destroy the demon."

"If You Can Beat Me"

Several readers sent me variations of a story about a beautiful blonde woman in (usually) a red Corvette who drives around challenging men to drag-races, promising a hot date to any guy who can catch her. Sometimes she is supposed to have a personalized license plate or a bumper sticker that poses the offer thus, "If you can beat me, you can have me."

"Dealing with 'Mr. Wiseguy' "

This was in the *Los Angeles Times* in 1991, identified there as an Urban Folk Tale (or UFT) and credited to the monthly bulletin of the local chapter of the California Society of Certified Public Accountants. CPAs, of course, would never ever, tell a legend. Wanna bet? Here's one:

The latest UFT . . . involves a motorist ticketed by a photo-radar system. Officials in Pasadena, which has such an apparatus, said they hadn't heard the story.

Anyway, the motorist receives a snapshot of his license plate, along with the ticket, in the mail.

"Mr. Wiseguy," goes the bulletin's version, "sends back a picture of a $40 check."

In return, Mr. Wiseguy receives a photo of a pair of handcuffs.

This time, he pays with real money.

"High Octane Revenge"

At one of those gas stations where you must pay first, then pump, a guy in a Mercedes 560SL cuts off a guy in a little Toyota saying, "Don't use that pump; I need to fill up fast."

The Mercedes driver takes off his gas cap and goes in to pay the cashier.

The Toyota driver takes off his own locking gas cap, locks it onto the Mercedes's open filler spout, and drives off, stranding the other guy at the pump.

"No Tag—You're It"

A man chooses "None" for his vanity license plate and never gets any tickets because when the people who process tickets at the Police Department see "None" in the license-plate-number space, they assume the car was unlicensed and cannot be traced.

Another man hears about this and chooses "No Tag" for his own vanity plate. But he gets all the tickets meant for cars without a legitimate plate.

This last tale reminds me of the man whose real complete name was R. B. Jones. When he entered military service his records were marked R(only) B(only) to clarify the situation—except that for his entire military career he was called Ronly Bonly Jones.

The latest full-sized urban legend about a car that was circulating on the Internet in the mid- to late 1990s was this:

The Arizona Highway Patrol came upon a pile of smoldering metal embedded into the side of a cliff rising above the road at the apex of a curve. The lab finally figured out that it was a car, and they reconstructed what must have happened.

It seems that a guy had somehow gotten hold of a JATO unit used to give heavy military transport planes an extra push for taking off from short airfields. He had driven his Chevy Impala out into the desert and found a long straight stretch of road. He attached the JATO unit to his car, jumped in, got up some speed, and fired off the rocket.

It appeared that he had hit the JATO ignition about three miles before the crash site. There was scorched and melted asphalt at that location, and the JATO would have reached maximum thrust in about five seconds, causing the Chevy to reach speeds in excess of 350 mph and continuing at full power for about twenty to twenty-five seconds. The driver most likely would have experienced G-forces similar to a dog-fighting F-14 under full afterburners.

The automobile remained on the straight highway for about two and one-half miles, fifteen to twenty seconds, before the driver applied and completely melted the brakes. His tires blew, leaving rubber on the road surface, and then the car became airborne for an additional one and one-half miles. It hit the cliff face at a height of about one hundred twenty-five feet, leaving a blackened crater three feet deep in the rock.

Only small fragments of bone, teeth, and hair could be extracted from the crater, and some fingernail and bone shards were removed from a piece of debris believed to be a portion of the steering wheel.

Most Internet versions of this implausible story concluded, "It only goes to show that speeding never killed anyone, but stopping did."

"Sticking Up for One's Rights"

A sweet, grandmotherly widow was convinced by her son to start carrying a small handgun in her purse for self-protection in these perilous times.

The first week she had the gun she came out of a shopping mall to the parking lot and found two men sitting in her car drinking beer and eating. With a firm, determined air she pulled the gun, advanced on the car, aimed it directly at the men, and ordered them out.

The men jumped out of the car and ran away in great panic. But when the woman got into the car, she found that her ignition key did not fit.

Then she noticed her own car, identical to theirs, parked one row over in the lot.

"The Hook"

I heard this story at a fraternity party. I heard this. This guy had this date with this really cool girl, and all he could think about all night was taking her out and parking and having a really good time, so he takes her out in the country, stops the car, turns the lights off, puts the radio on, nice music; he's really getting her in the mood, and all of the sudden there's this news flash comes on over the radio and says to the effect that a sex maniac has just escaped from the state insane asylum and the one distinguishing feature of this man is that he has a hook arm, and in the first place this girl is really, really upset, 'cause she's just sure this guy is going to come and try and get in the car, so the guy locks all the doors and says it'll be okay, but she says he could take his arm and break through the window and everything and she just cries and cries and goes just really frantic and the guy finally consents to take her home, but he's really mad 'cause you know he really had his plans for this girl, so he revs up the car and he goes torquing out of there and they get to her house, and he's really, really mad and he's not even going to get out of the car and open the door for her, and she just gets out on her own side of the car and as she gets out she turns around and looks and there's a hook hanging on the door.

Verbatim, as told in a breathless rush by an Indiana University undergraduate woman to her roommate in 1967. This was the first text published in the first issue of a journal largely devoted to urban legends edited by Indiana University professor Linda Dégh and her students at the Folklore Institute. In Indiana Folklore, *vol. I, no. 1 (1968), pp. 92–100, Dégh listed 44 locally collected texts of this legend going back to 1959. "The Hook" was printed in a "Dear Abby" column in November 1960 and continues to be one of the most popular American urban legends, one of the few that many people refer to by specific title rather than merely a descriptive phrase like "the one about the maniac and the teenagers." Numerous fiction writers have adapted the essential plot of the legend. Bill Murray told "The Hook" in his film* Meatballs, *and Gary Larson referred to the story in at least two of his "Far Side" cartoons. In 1992 the hook man appeared as the title character of the slick horror film* Candyman. *Perhaps because of the legend's improbably tidy plot, most tellers narrate the story nowadays more as a scary story than as a believed legend. Folklorists are divided about whether "The Hook" represents simply a warning story about staying out late in an unknown environment, or whether its details may signify sexual meanings, including symbolic castration of the threatening and deformed phallic symbol—the hook—outside the car at the same time that the boyfriend is trying to "get his hooks into the girl" inside the car.*

"The Severed Fingers"

A young couple were out together in a classic VW Beetle. Whilst parked in a deserted country lane, after some kissing and cuddling, they heard a noise near the exit to the lane. Looking up they saw, strung across the lane, a menacing group of Hell's Angels, all grinning and leering in a hideous manner, dressed in black leather and swinging tire chains, carrying knives and clubs. The gang advanced towards the car, blocking the exit to the lane.

The girl screamed, and the guy was shocked out of his senses. He started the engine and gunned it, driving straight at the intruders as fast as he could make the little car move. The bikers slashed at the car with their chains and grabbed at it with their hands as it sped past, but they were shaken off by the speeding Bug.

Gaining the safety of the main highway, the couple stopped to look for possible damage to their car. They saw, either:

Version A: Four severed fingers stuck in the air vents at the back of the car, cut off by the cooling fan.

Or:

Version B: A chain with four severed fingers caught in the chrome trim on the car.

Sent to me in 1987 by a reader in Reading, England, who was careful to point out that Hell's Angels are uncommon in England, that the air vents on a VW Beetle are too small for fingers to get through, and that other compact cars are much more common in England than VW Bugs ever were. Other readers pointed out that the Renault Dauphine model of the late 1950s and early 1960s did have wider rear ventilation slots. "The Severed Fingers" has, indeed, been documented back to 1960 in England, although usually without a specific car model mentioned. The story is also popular in Australia, where it was enacted in the 1979 film Mad Max. *In 1988 Phil Twyford, an Auckland, New Zealand, journalist, gave me copies of two versions sent to him after he published an article about modern legends. One of these had the fingers caught in the door frame of the car, while the other had them stuck in a bicycle chain that was caught on the "boot handle." The chain version seems to be better known in the United States. This legend is similar to "The Hook," and also to "The Robber Who Was Hurt," quoted in Chapter 15. Other severed fingers appear in "The Choking Doberman" (Chapter 2) while a severed head occurs in the next legend.*

"Decapitated Drivers and Riders"

Heads, heads—take care of your heads!" cried the loquacious stranger, as they came out under the low archway, which in those days formed the entrance to the coach-yard. "Terrible place—dangerous work—other day—

Bill Tidy

five children—mother—tall lady, eating sandwiches—forgot the arch—crash—knock—children look round—mother's head off—sandwich in her hand—no mouth to put it in—head of a family off—shocking, shocking!"

A classic WTS [Whale Tumour Story] tells of an extraordinary incident on the East Lancs Road (A580) [the highway number]. Apparently, a motorcyclist was riding behind a lorry which was carrying a load of thin steel plates. He decided to overtake the lorry, but as he moved out towards the centre of the road, one of the steel sheets became dislodged and decapitated him. However, his momentum carried him alongside the lorry, the lorry-driver glanced from his window, saw the headless motorcyclist passing, had a heart-attack, ran off the road and was killed.

The first story is told by Alfred Jingle in Chapter 2 of Charles Dickens's The Posthumous Papers of the Pickwick Club *(1836). The second, the modern automobile version of the former, is from Rodney Dale's* The Tumour in the Whale *(1978), p. 148. Although Dale's term "Whale Tumour Stories"—referring to a specific World War II British legend—never caught on as a name for such apocryphal anecdotes, his coinage "FOAF" became a standard reference in UL studies to the claimed sources of these incidents. In other versions of the decapitated motorcyclist story, the truck driver not only dies himself in the crash, but his truck plows into a crowd of people at the roadside, killing many more. In American variations on the theme of vehicular dismemberment, it may be a dog that loses its head while riding in a car with the window open, ears flapping in the breeze. The loss of Rover's head is so quick and neat that a child sitting next to it in the back seat continues to pet the dog for several miles before the tragedy is discovered.*

"The Killer in the Back Seat"

As told on Late Night with David Letterman

Version #1: 1982
David Letterman: What about "The Killer in the Back Seat?"
Jan Brunvand: Yeah, that's another car story, another horror story. There's

a woman driving home alone at night, she needs to stop for gas. She gets to a gas station, and the attendant fills the tank and takes her credit card. And he looks a little funny, and he says, "I'm sorry, lady, there's something a little funny about this credit card. Would you step into the station, let's check it against the numbers of . . ." discontinued cards or something. And she's puzzled by this, but she goes in. And as soon as she gets in the station, he locks the door and says, "There's a guy in the back seat with a meat cleaver!"

DL: Oh, a meat cleaver . . .

JB: Or a knife . . .

DL: Or a hook and a poisonous snake and a discount garment . . .

JB: Sometimes somebody follows her home on the freeway, flashing the lights behind her, and when she gets home the car's right behind her—the pursuing car—a man jumps out, opens the back door of the car and pulls this guy out. Says, "I flashed the lights to keep him from killing you."

DL: Now this one, up until the time I read your book, I believed.

JB: You believed it?

DL: Someone had told me that they were working in a store, working late one night, and that very thing happened. But more than likely, again, it never happened anywhere.

JB: The person who told you said it happened to whom? To himself?

DL: No, to a fellow employee.

JB: Yeah. We have here what we call the FOAF. The F-O-A-F, the "friend of a friend."

Version #2: 1984, DL briefly alluded to the same legend in an interview with JB.

Version #3: 1986

DL: Years ago I heard one that I think we discussed one time on this program before, and that is the woman—usually a woman—pulls into a filling station to get gas and the gasoline attendant fills up the tank and asks her to step out of the car. And he says, "There's a problem with your credit card." And I heard this as happening, again, to somebody I knew that they worked with. And it turns out that there's some kind of maniacal ax murderer in the back seat.

Version #4: 1987

DL: This is fascinating stuff. I remember, actually when I was a kid living in Indianapolis, I heard one of the classic stories about the woman pulls in for gas, and . . .

JB: [interrupting] You know what? . . .

DL: . . . the gasoline attendant says . . .

JB: You know, this is the third time you've told me that story. . . . I'm sorry I broke into it, maybe you've got a different ending. Let's hear how it ends.

DL: What say we have a number from the band now. . . . You seem to have been here five times now, so . . .

JB: I've probably worn out my welcome.

DL: You see everybody doesn't watch every night. I'm just trying to participate . . .

JB: That's true. You really *did* hear it?

DL: I'm trying to feign interest in this whole damn topic, and to tell you the truth, I don't give a rat's ass.

It appears that this is Letterman's favorite urban legend and one that he remembered spontaneously from his boyhood. My reaction to hearing it told repeatedly is a case study in how not *to listen to a storyteller; whoever says, "Stop me if you've heard this," doesn't really mean it. In the next segment of the program Letterman apologized for his comment, and I responded by saying I was glad to have his version of the legend to use in one of my books. The freeway-pursuit version of the legend dates from the mid-1960s, while the gas station versions come later, first mentioning a suspected counterfeit bill, then a faulty credit card. In the early 1990s, tellers of the legend began to claim that the hidden assailant was a gang member, often a racial minority, undergoing initiation. Numerous local law-enforcement groups repeated this story, warning women always to check the back seats of their cars. This, of course, is perfectly good advice for any driver, whether or not the incident ever really happened. "The Killer in the Back Seat" is the first story enacted in the 1998 slasher film* Urban Legend. *Publicity for the film explained that "Urban legends—modern day folktales that seem to arise spontaneously and spread by word-of-*

mouth—range from the silly . . . to the sinister." This definition was far superior to the depiction of a college folklore class shown in the film.

"The Hairy-Armed Hitchhiker"

The woman, an employee of the Fred S. James & Co., goes to her car after work. But when she gets there, she sees an elderly woman sitting in the back seat.

"I'm cold and wet," says the old woman, "and I need a ride home."

The old woman—she must be 85 or so—says she's sorry about getting into the car, but it was unlocked and she was so cold. "Please help me," she says.

"Why, of course," says the woman from Fred S. James. (Since we aren't certain of her real name, we will call her Jamie.) "But first I have to call my husband, so he'll know why I'm late."

The old woman has already told her she lives way out on Southeast 122nd.

So Jamie walks back to the office to make the call. It's a couple of blocks away, and she walks briskly because it's cold. It's already dark, and traffic is starting to thin out, leaving the city deserted.

She shivers. The poor old woman. How she got there is something of a mystery. The Fred S. James & Co., an insurance agency, is in the heart of downtown Portland, and that's a long way from 122nd Avenue.

She must be disoriented. Yes, that's it, says Jamie to herself. Oh, the poor dear.

Back inside her office she gets her husband on the phone and explains the situation to him.

"No way," he says. He is very upset. "No way are you giving a stranger a ride home."

Furthermore, he says, she should call building security. She doesn't want to, but she does.

Security tells her to call the police, because the car is parked on a city street, not in the company parking lot, which she does.

The police arrive at Jamie's car just as she does—two squad cars with flashing blue lights—and the little old lady is still sitting in the back seat, waiting for a ride.

But as the police quickly discover, the little old lady is actually a 25-year-old man, and he has a machete taped to his leg, and he is sitting on an ax. . . .

That's how it goes.

The first time I heard it was last week, when a letter arrived at the office. "I heard a chilling story," it began, "and thought the public should know it."

Unfortunately, the letter was unsigned, and as the writer explained, he or she "did not get it directly from the woman it happened to."

But it was obviously such a great story I thought I'd track it down.

So I called the Fred S. James & Co. A woman there spent a day checking around and called back.

"I'm sorry," she said, "but I can't find anyone who's heard anything about it."

Building security didn't know anything, so I called central precinct, which covers the downtown area, and talked with the sergeant who handles all the reports. He hadn't seen anything like that come across his desk, he said, but he'd ask around.

The next day he called to say he had struck out. "But it sure is a great story," he said. "Sort of chills your bones, doesn't it?"

Yes it does. It rings true. The only problem, apparently, is that it isn't.

A couple of days later I was talking with a friend. "Did you hear the story about the little old lady?" he said, and proceeded to tell the identical story—down to the machete taped to the man's leg and the ax he was sitting on.

It should be easy enough to track her down, he said. He had heard the story from his running partner that morning. It had happened to his running partner's secretary's sister-in-law.

It took a day to get in touch with the sister-in-law, who was more than helpful. Yes, she said, it was true.

However, there must be some misunderstanding, because it hadn't actually happened to her, but to her friend's daughter's coworker. Would I like her to get me in touch with them?

Yes, of course. But I already knew what was going to happen, because I was beginning to realize what we were dealing with here.

And that is more chilling, still, because what we have here is an urban myth for our city and our season—and therefore, in a way, truer than mere fact.

No need to explain here. But you will be careful, won't you, the next time you get out of work late and have to walk to your car in the dark?

And, you'll look carefully before you open the door, because maybe she'll be there and maybe she won't.

Oh, probably she won't, and you'll laugh at yourself for looking before you slide into the front seat. How silly of you.

But you'll always think about it now, won't you?

Column by Phil Stanford in the Portland Oregonian, *February 27, 1989. The details that give this urban legend either the title used above or the alternate title "The Hatchet in the Handbag" are missing here; otherwise, it's a classic version of this well-known story. On March 1st Stanford's column summarized letters and calls from readers, responding to his column, claiming that the incident had really happened in Las Vegas (in 1983); in Vancouver, Washington; in Sun City, Arizona; or in Pasadena, California. The story is actually much older and even more widespread than these claims. It circulated in English newspapers and in folklore in the mid–nineteenth century. An 1834 report, for example, has the disguised assailant riding in a horse-drawn carriage. Horse-travel versions were also collected in the United States as late as the 1940s and 1950s, with the newer versions, using automobiles, surfacing in the 1980s. The most recent versions tend to have the woman driver contrive her own escape from the disguised man without calling either her husband, a security guard, the police, or any other male helper. She simply asks the "old woman" to get out and check her taillights; then she drives away, finding [you guessed it] a hatchet in the handbag left behind. "The Hairy-Armed Hitchhiker" and other car-crime legends are frequently repeated in safety memos within companies or governmental agencies as warnings to drivers to be alert against attacks. In the spring of 1998 a new version of "The Hairy-Armed Hitchhiker" appeared in Columbus, Ohio, and was spread on the Internet. Supposedly, a woman shopping at Columbus's Tuttle Mall (actually called "Tuttle Crossing") found a flat tire when she returned to her car. While she was trying to figure out how to change the tire, a man came up and helped her, then he asked for a ride to his own car parked on the other side of the mall. Suspicious, the woman pretended to have other errands in the mall, and she closed her trunk, locked her car, and went back for a security guard. It was discovered that the tire had been deliberately deflated, and in a briefcase the man had left behind was found a coil of rope and a large butcher knife. One version of this legend concluded with the advice, "Learn to change your own tire!"*

"The Boyfriend's Death"

This story is about Peter Poore's grave, which is located in Shelburne, New Hampshire. Peter Poore was supposedly the last white man in the region to be killed by Indians, and legend has it that his grave is haunted.

The story goes that many years ago, a young couple drove to the deserted road near the site of the grave. They stopped the car and necked for a while. When they were ready to leave, however, the car would not start. The young man decided to go for help while the woman stayed alone in the car. After a while, the woman could hear rain falling on the car. More time passed, but her boyfriend still did not return. She decided to turn on the headlights to see if he was coming down the road. When she did, what she saw was her boyfriend hanging from a tree with a knife sticking out of his abdomen. What she had thought was rain was really his blood dripping onto the car. I first heard this story at least fifteen years ago.

Maria Gale, age 10 [speaking to a group of her fellow Navajo students]

MG: I got one. One of my sisters told me that there was a boy and a girl. They were going to the dance.

RD: Squaw dance.

MG: Then . . . they turned on the radio and the man said, "Watch out for this man that's a killer." And then he said, "It's a hairy one."

I: It's a what?

MG: A hairy one.

CY, RD, JD: A skinwalker.

MG: And then the gas got empty. And then the boy said, "Wait for me. Stay in the pickup and I'll go get some gasoline." So the girl went "OK," and then she went in the back. I guess the skinwalker killed the boy and then chopped off his head. And then the girl was sitting in the back and then she heard something on top of the car and she was scared. Then she didn't look up. She kept hearing that and then she saw her boyfriend's head chopped off. It was hanging down.

The first version was sent to me by Denise Day of Center Strafford, New Hampshire, in 1988. The second was tape-recorded by Navajo students of Margaret K. Brady in a reservation school near Window Rock and Fort Defiance, Arizona, in 1976; the initials include those of children listening to the story, while "I" is the interviewer. Both texts are abbreviated versions of the urban legend with a Native American reference incorporated. The Navajo version also uses the radio warning motif of "The Hook." Contemporary tellings of the story usually conclude with the police arriving to save the girl, warning her "Don't look back!" She does look, of course, since taboos in folklore are always broken. When the girl sees her boyfriend's body hanging or lying on top of the car, her hair immediately turns white from fright. "The Boyfriend's Death" has been a favorite scare story of American teenagers since the early 1960s; many versions include spooky visual and sound effects—scratching, bumping, ghostly shadows, sounds of dripping, etc. In Europe, where the legend is also popular, often the maniacal killer is seated on top of the car bumping the severed head of his victim on the roof. Brady's students recorded numerous stories for her, some of them in the form of personal experiences or of fictional stories—such as this one—and others being the older traditional legends of the "skinwalker," a fearsome shape-shifting witchlike character of the native mythology. This text includes modern references, such as the pickup truck, and exhibits some stylistic features of "spontaneous narrative creation" analyzed by Brady: for example, the group's confirming in chorus that the storyteller had a skinwalker in mind when she hesitated to identify the threatening figure. This story is in Brady's 1984 book "Some Kind of Power": Navajo Children's Skinwalker Narratives, *pp. 185–86.*

"The Slasher under the Car"

RUMORS OF SLASHERS AT MALL DISPUTED

Nobody can find victims of 'robbers' who 'hide' under cars.

Authorities have heard dozens of reports in recent weeks about robbers at Hanes Mall who hide under cars in the parking lot and slash shoppers' legs to get at their packages.

But nobody has found any victims.

People have called the *Winston-Salem Journal*, the police, and the mall to try to confirm rumors about the supposed robbers.

But police and hospital workers say they haven't seen any such cases.

The thin thieves supposedly hide under shoppers' cars until the shoppers approach. As a victim unlocks a car door, the thief slashes the victim's lower leg. Less vicious versions report that a softer-hearted crook pricks the ankle with a sharp object.

The slashed person falls, the story goes, and the thief wriggles from under the car, snatches purse and gifts and runs off, arms laden with Christmas booty.

Someone first called the *Journal* to ask about the reports about two weeks ago.

Sgt. Charlie Taylor of the Winston-Salem Police Department reported hearing the same rumor then and checked into it. There were no police reports about such crimes.

But the exploits of the thieves continued by word of mouth.

One caller to the *Journal* said that Hanes Mall was keeping victims from reporting the crimes by giving them $500 gift certificates.

Monday night, a radio dispatcher in the Forsyth County Sheriff's Department said that a deputy talked to a doctor who treated 18 slashed patients in the emergency room at Forsyth Memorial Hospital.

When reached, the deputy said he did not talk to the doctor, but a friend of his had. The friend was unavailable for comment.

Freda Springs, a spokesman at Forsyth Memorial, talked to emergency-room workers yesterday. They had heard the rumor, she said, they haven't treated any victims with slashed ankles.

She said that the head nurse in the emergency room heard that the patients were being treated at Baptist Hospital, even though Forsyth is just across the road from the mall.

A spokesman at Baptist said that emergency-room workers there have not treated slasher victims and were not even aware of the rumor.

Thomas E. Winstead, the general manager of the mall, said he has fielded questions about the non-existent crime wave. "I've heard it. I've had it mentioned to me at parties. Several store personnel have called me to ask about it," he said.

He said he heard similar rumors at other shopping centers he has managed.

"Unfortunately, I can't do anything to stop the rumor, but fortunately, there's no truth to it either," he said.

Capt. Roscoe Pouncey of the police department said that parking-lot crime at shopping centers actually seems to be lower this year than in previous years. He said last week that there had only been one robbery in the Hanes Mall parking lot during December. . . .

From an article by Christopher Quinn in the Winston-Salem (North Carolina) Journal *of December 16, 1992; the article concludes with advice from the aptly named Capt. Pouncey and others on strategies for avoiding assaults. In* The Baby Train *I summarized 18 reports of "The Slasher under the Car" from 1984 through 1992 that supposedly occurred in 16 cities in 14 different states. Two sources remembered hearing prototypes for the legend in 1978 and even as far back as 1950. Since then I have received nine more reports from 1992 and 1993, adding ten further cities and five more states to the list. The slashers usually were said to strike the ankle, sometimes aiming for the Achilles tendon, but some grabbed the ankle, or hit the ankles with a tire iron, or crawled out from under the car to slash at the victim's cheek or cut off a finger. The motive for the attack was usually robbery—often of Christmas gifts—but sometimes the attack led to rape. Occasionally an accomplice joined the attack from under a nearby car, and in one curious version the attackers wrapped the victim in Christmas paper. The idea of a police coverup of the crimes, or of the malls buying off victims to protect their business, is typical. In some communities, notably Tacoma, Washington, during the Christmas season of 1989, police actually set up field stations at the targeted mall, not to combat the fictional crimes, but simply to calm the fears of shoppers.*

"The Elephant That Sat on the VW"

WE POP THE ELEPHANT MYTH

It was a good story.

A reliable guy called the *Philadelphia Bulletin* and said a girl he works with knows a woman who took her kids to the Philadelphia Zoo.

When she came out, there was a big dent in her Volkswagen, and a zoo employee was waiting in the parking lot. He said an elephant being unloaded from a truck sat on the Volkswagen and the Zoo would pay the damages.

Doc Rowe

On her way home, the woman was mistakenly stopped for leaving the scene of an accident. She told the policeman she hadn't been in the accident she had just passed. The dent in her car was caused by an elephant sitting on it.

She was given a sobriety test at a police station. Finally the police called the Zoo and confirmed her story.

The reliable guy said he would get the name and address of the woman and call right back.

He never did.

That was no surprise. A call to the Zoo immediately established that no Volkswagen has ever been abused by one of its elephants and that Zoo officials have heard this one before.

Within two weeks, another reliable person from another part of the area called another *Bulletin* reporter and told him the same story. . . .

How these stories begin to circulate is a mystery. But anybody who has his Volkswagen dented by an elephant might as well keep quiet about it. No newspaperman will believe him.

From an article by James Smart in Small World: For Volkswagen Owners in the United States, *fall 1970, p. 7. This editor's note follows: "*Small World's *'elephant file' contains 27 accounts of the sat-upon-VW story dating from as early as 1962. Depending upon which version you believe, the elephant came from the St. Louis Zoo, Benson's Animal Farm in New Hampshire, California's Marine World, or a circus in upstate New York, New Martinsville, West Virginia, Anaheim, California, or Paris, France, to name just a few. We hope these discrepancies will debunk the elephant story forever, but that may be too much to ask. Mr. Smart's article appeared in the* Philadelphia Bulletin *last February. Shortly thereafter, elephants squashed two other Volkswagens in other sections of the country." My own "elephant file" contains about another two dozen reports, including ones from Canada, France, Germany, Sweden, England, and New Zealand. The 1985 Australian film* Bliss, *based on Peter Carey's 1981 novel of the same title, has a scene in which a circus elephant sits on an old red Fiat.*

"The Arrest"

Every profession has its legends, and police work is no exception. Here's the latest wild and wooly yarn to do the rounds in Fairfax County law enforcement circles:

Seems a local motorist was pulled over by a local police officer. The motorist had had a bit too much to drink. Correction: He had had a lot too much to drink. He flunked the Breathalyzer test, the walk-the-straight-line test and the get-out-of-the-car-without-falling-on-your-face test. So, as any cop would in this situation, the officer announced that the motorist was under arrest.

But at that very moment, on the other side of the road, a terrible accident took place. The police officer ran across the road to investigate. Because the accident was a messy one, the officer was busy with it for quite some time. So the inebriated motorist figured the cop had lost interest in him. He hopped behind the wheel and drove off.

However, the wheel the inebriated motorist hopped behind was the wheel of the police car. When the cops finally tracked the guy down a couple of hours later, they found the police car parked in his garage. The motor was still running and the dome lights were still spinning and flashing.

Ever since, according to the story, the police have been so embarrassed by what happened that they've tried to hush it up.

However, Fairfax County police spokesman Warren Carmichael says there's only one thing wrong with the story: It almost certainly isn't true.

"Certain stories develop and they seem to get a life of their own," Carmichael told researcher Karina Porcelli.

This one has had an especially long life. Carmichael said he first heard it about two years ago, and has been hearing it around Fairfax County ever since. Capt. Curt Durham of the Fairfax City police confirms the yarn's longevity. He says he first heard it about 18 months ago at a party, and has been hearing it steadily from then on. But neither policeman has been able to verify the story—and both say they'd know about it if the incident had really happened.

I can understand why people would want to spread this one. As legends go, it's top-rank. But since its truth is doubtful, let's give the tale early retirement, okay? The police have enough troubles without being accused of losing cars they almost certainly didn't lose.

From "Bob Levey's Washington" column in the Washington Post, *April 7, 1986. Paul Harvey broadcast a version of "The Arrest" from Raleigh, North Carolina, on January 15, 1986, and published it in his 1991 book,* For What It's Worth. *I've received reports of the story from New York, Connecticut, West Virginia, Florida, Canada, Australia, and England. A version was in the 1997 film* Good Will Hunting, *told by Will's friend about his uncle. In most versions the man is said to have driven "the car" home, without any mention that it's the* wrong *car. He convinces his wife to furnish an alibi if the police come looking for him, but her story falls flat when the cops find their cruiser in the garage. The flashing dome lights on the police car are evidence of just how drunk the man must have been. See the following for another legend about a drunken driver that became popular the same year.*

"The Body on the Car"

A man came home at 2:00 a.m., drunk as a skunk. But he had managed to drive his car all the way home and to get it parked in the driveway before he stumbled into the house and fell asleep on the living-room couch.

The next morning he was rudely awakened by his wife's screams. She had gone outside to pick up the newspaper and glanced over at his car. There, embedded on the front grill of the car, she saw the twisted body of an eight-year-old girl!

Reported to me several times in 1986 and 1987 as a cautionary story sometimes told by representatives of either SADD—Students Against Drunk Driving—or MADD—Mothers Against Drunk Driving. Ann Landers printed the story in her column on September 24, 1986, quoting a letter from Portland (Oregon, I presume). A horror comic-

book version of the story published in the 1950s was reprinted in a Marvel Comics anthology in 1975, and cartoonist Gary Larson has his own version among the examples published in his 1989 book Prehistory of "The Far Side," *but never used it in daily newspapers. An allusion to the legend also appeared in a "Bizarro" cartoon in 1991. Readers have pointed out to me several well-documented accounts in newspapers of similar accidents, some occurring as long ago as the 1930s, but none exactly matched the legend. I conclude that victims of hit-and-run accidents have indeed sometimes become stuck to vehicles and dragged or carried for some distance, but "The Body on the Car" story seems to have a life of its own separate from any specific real-life incident. Whether literally true or not, it is certainly an effective warning against mixing alcohol and gasoline. It's worth noting that a similar story circulates among seafaring folk: A large ship is said to have struck a small vessel in the dark without anyone aboard the ship noticing; the smaller boat is carried along, stuck to the bow, until the ship reaches port. This story has even been told on the* Queen Elizabeth II *and on U.S. Navy aircraft carriers and battleships.*

"The Wife Left Behind"

In 1986, a family from Oregon traveling in their RV through California stopped at a freeway-interchange restaurant. The wife went to the restroom, and her husband drove off without her, believing she had gone to the back of their vehicle for a nap. He drove 300 miles before discovering his error. They were reunited with the help of the highway patrol.

I know of six cases of this incident from 1986 to 1992, all reported in well-documented news stories; there's no doubt that each incident really happened. The reports mention several different states and a variety of vehicles and stopping places. I also have reliable newspaper articles about a truck driver in 1986 leaving his wife behind in a New York State motel, a Democratic state senator from Indiana in 1988 leaving his campaign director behind in a Tennessee rest stop, and a husband in 1992 leaving his wife behind in another Tennessee rest stop. Adding to the data on riders left behind, I have a first-person account of a California family in 1973 leaving their nine-year-old son behind in a California gas station. I'm sure, if I applied myself to further research, I could easily double the number of reports of similar incidents. So is it an urban legend? Calvin Trillin, in discussing the 1992 Tennessee occurrence, which he heard of directly from the participants, described it as "a palpably authentic example of the sort of experience you hear now and then in the sort of modern folk-tales that usually carry the sniff of the apocryphal and the embellished." I couldn't have said it better myself. Surely "The Wife [and others] Left Behind" incident did *happen—and several times at that—but in telling and retelling the story people tend to focus on the salient details, and the story probably becomes funnier and more pointed with each telling. At the same time, there's a certain whiff of true legendry in the story when you encounter the undeniably 100 percent fictional story of "The Nude in the RV," another left-behind-during-travel yarn containing further juicy details, which I've grouped with other slapstick humor in Chapter 19.*

"The Baby on the Roof"

Did you hear about this couple driving through Southern Utah? They were on their way to California, and they went to change drivers and the wife took the baby out of the car and put him on the roof of the car. Then they both switched sides and got back into the car. She just assumed that the husband had put the baby back in, but he hadn't even seen it.

They drove off, and the baby slid off, but he was OK because he was in a plastic infant seat. About two hours later they realized that they forgot the baby. So they drove back, and someone had stopped for the baby, and the baby was OK.

Collected from his mother in 1981 by M. Steven Marsden for his folklore project in one of my classes at the University of Utah. This is the generic, or "legendary," form of an incident that has happened more often than you might think. I have on file documented news stories or firsthand accounts dating from 1975 to 1993 of 14 such incidents occurring in several states, as well as one in Germany. Not surprisingly, some babies have been injured or traumatized in these adventures. Other items forgotten on car roofs are purses, wallets, books, groceries, lunch bags or boxes, ski gloves, fishing rods, cameras, miscellaneous packages, a bottle of whiskey, and even a rare violin. It certainly happens, but as such stories circulate in oral tradition, they become "folklorized" when narrators generalize the plot details, elaborate on favorite points, and focus on a happy ending. Sometimes the baby is forgotten while the mother is loading groceries into the car, or while a family is repacking the car after changing a tire. The 1987 film Raising Arizona *contained a hilarious scene based on this story, and I am told that a 1990 episode of the TV sitcom* Married with Children *referred to the story as well, but I'd rather ride clinging to the roof of a car than watch reruns of that program to verify this reference.*

"The Nut and the Tire Nuts"

Summarized:
Found both as a published "puzzle story" and an oral legend. A motorist changing a flat accidentally loses the four tire nuts from the wheel. A mentally retarded person (or perhaps an escapee from a nearby asylum) comes by and suggests a simple way to solve the problem. (What's the answer?)

How to tell this story:
To wring the most enjoyment from this incident, it is imperative that

the story embrace enough of the following detail for the listener to fully visualize the incident.

1. The scene was rural, at near dusk, with the point made that the flat tire was on the left rear wheel and occurred while the motorist was driving along a winding, two-lane, rural road.
2. The motorist drove off the road just a few feet from a fence surrounding the mental institution where an inmate was leaning idly against the fence.
3. After the driver [here a stuffed shirt, pompous type can be identified] confidently jacked up the left rear of the car, thinking he would demonstrate his efficiency to the inmate-observer, he took off the wheel cover [the "hub cap" back in the '50s] and placed it, concave side up, behind him on the edge of the paving.
4. The wheel had *five,* not four, lug nuts.
5. As the driver removed the nuts with his lug wrench, he carefully deposited each lug nut in the wheel cover for what he intended to be efficient retrieval.
6. The motorist then retreated to the trunk of his car to get the spare tire and wheel. Just as he lifted the wheel from the trunk, he noticed an automobile approaching on his side of the road.
7. Conscious of his own safety, the man discreetly stepped back until the car could go by, then watched in dismay as the passing car's right front wheel hit the edge of the wheel cover, launching the five lug nuts into space and scattering them over a wide area.
8. His hands-and-knees search along the shoulders of the road and in the wild ground cover along the roadside in the diminishing daylight produced only one lug nut.
9. Holding the single lug nut between a thumb and a forefinger, the driver was dejectedly contemplating his predicament when the inmate who had been watching the whole episode spoke up. He suggested that the driver take one lug nut from each of the other three wheels, which would give him four for the spare wheel and permit him to drive safely to a service station to replace the lost lug nuts.

10. The driver, in his grateful astonishment, said, "Thanks for the great idea. But what in the world is someone as intelligent and resourceful as you doing in a mental institution?"
11. The response: "I may be crazy, but I'm not stupid."

The summary is from my article "Urban Legends in the Making: Write Me if You've Heard This," in Whole Earth Review, *fall 1985. The instructions on how to tell the story properly came in a letter from M. B. Cox of Bountiful, Utah. Cox, who said he had been telling it for more than 40 years, was responding—as did dozens of other people—to my newspaper column ("Flat Joke Drives Folklorist Nutty") questioning what is so funny about this particular story. Numerous readers over the years have sent me "The Nut and the Tire Nuts," declaring it to be their favorite joke or legend, and the puzzle version of the story has been published several times. Yet I've always failed to see the humor of the situation or of the punch line, even when it was pointed out to me that the latter is a twist on the expression "I may be stupid but I'm not crazy," something one might say, for example, after taking an icy swim in the ocean on New Year's Day, but remaining in the water for only ten seconds. The tire-nut story was formerly told as a rural anecdote, illustrating the triumph of native wit over city sophistication; in that spirit, Winston Groom included it in his 1986 novel* Forrest Gump *with the punch line "Maybe I am an idiot, but at least I ain't* stupid.*" Lately the story has been given an urban setting, with the tire nuts disappearing down a street drain. I still don't find it very funny, but I'm sure that if I failed to include it with other automobile legends some people would think I am either crazy or stupid.*

"The Pig on the Road"

A friend of mine was driving along happily, minding his own business, when all of a sudden a woman driver came tearing round the corner in the opposite direction on the wrong side of the road. Passing him, she rolled down the window and shouted, "Pig." My friend, quite astonished by this insult, replied, "Silly old cow." On turning the corner, he drove straight into a herd of pigs.

From Robert Morley's 1983 book, "Pardon Me, But You're Eating My Doily!" *where it is credited to Serena Fass, travel agent. This version, from England, quotes the common British expression "silly old cow," but lacks the usual line "Bloody pig!" The story popped up on the* Benny Hill Show, *and it was formerly told about an English driver in France where a passing Frenchman shouts "cochon!" (pig). In American versions, such as the one broadcast by Paul Harvey in January 1988, the man is a police officer, so the word "pig" sounds like a specific crack about his profession. Harvey's story named names and identified places, but an Associated Press writer tracked down the presumed source and learned that it was merely a story the policeman had repeated, not an actual occurrence. Leo Buscaglia, the Southern California "professor of love," has used the story in his lectures, and published it in his 1982 book* Living, Loving, and Learning. *The humorist Bennett Cerf beat him to it, though, by publishing it in a 1970 collection, and several writers since then—as well as* Reader's Digest*—have used the story.*

"Let's Give Toll Takers a Hand"

I was in Johns Hopkins Medical School at the time. As a prank, somebody cut one of the fingers off the cadaver I was working on and kept it. When I went to turn in the cadaver, I couldn't account for the finger.

I knew who'd done it. So the next day, while he was doing a dissection on the leg, I took the arm off his cadaver and snuck it out. I put it in an ice chest and drove out to the Beltway around Baltimore. At a tollbooth, I stuck the frozen arm out of the window with some money in the hand and left the toll attendant with the arm.

This got back to the president of the school, who was Dwight Eisenhower's brother, Milton, a real fucking hawk. He told me to take a leave of absence to reconsider my commitment to medical school. I thought that was probably a good idea. I said, "Great." A week later I had my draft notice. They turned me right in to the board.

From Mark Baker's 1981 book Nam: The Vietnam War in the Words of the Men and Women Who Fought There. *This prank, much discussed among medi-*

cal students, is very seldom claimed as a first-person escapade, and has never, to my knowledge, been reported by toll takers as an actual incident in their professional experience. Still, the story is attached to numerous toll highways and bridges all over the United States and in several foreign countries. If we accept this Vietnam veteran's claim, we have a rare instance of a traditional prank story being acted out in real life. An illuminating study of such stories is Frederic W. Hafferty's 1988 article in the Journal of Health and Social Behavior, *"Cadaver Stories and the Emotional Socialization of Medical Students." Dr. Hafferty found that, although these accounts always include references to supposedly real people, places, and things, the incidents themselves are complete fabrications. With constant variations in details coming about as they circulate, cadaver stories are a major part of medical student folklore.*

"The Bargain Sports Car"

A friend of the guy who told me this story, sometime in the mid-1970s, needed to get another car, since his old one was falling apart and barely running any more. All he could afford was another used car, so he started reading the want ads looking for a bargain.

He saw an ad for a '65 Chevy for sale at $200, so he called the number. The woman who answered sounded elderly, and she said that the car was still for sale and the price was as advertised. So he got his old clunker started and went over to take a look at the old Chevy.

The old woman took him out to the garage, and when she opened the

$200...UH NO, THAT'S NOT TOO MUCH.

door and pulled off a tarp covering the car, he couldn't believe his eyes. It was a 1965 Corvette, bright red, up on blocks, mint condition, and not a scratch on it.

He held his breath as he got out his checkbook, poised his pen over it, and asked one more time, "Two hundred bucks?"

"Yes," the old woman said. She explained that her son had left the car with her when he was sent to Vietnam, but he was killed in action. She now just wanted to get rid of it and the memories that it inspired, so she called a car dealer and asked how much a 1965 Chevy might be worth, and he said maybe $200. "Is that too much?" she asked. "After all, it's ten years old, and it's pretty small; it only holds two people."

The friend of a friend assured her that this was not too high a price to ask for the car.

Much told in the post-Nam years, but never verified. This is a wishful-thinking story along the lines of "The $50 Porsche" legend in Chapter 3, but minus the revenge motif. In another version the would-be buyer cannot make it to the seller's home right away. When he gets there the next day, he sees his lost prize, the vintage Corvette, just rounding the corner with the lucky buyer at the wheel. Prices vary in these stories from $100 to $500, but the make and model of car is consistent. There are, of course, many other stories of people selling valuable items for a ridiculously low price, and some of these stories are even true.

5

Sexcapades

Movies, TV, advertising, and politics, among other areas of life, are saturated with sexual content and innuendo, so it's no surprise that urban legends exploit the sexual theme as well. There are many ULs concerning sex, and I've scattered most of them through this book according to their other themes, reserving the present chapter for just a few of the more saucy examples. Surprisingly, most legends that mention sex are fairly innocuous, in contrast to sex *jokes,* at least. But the sexcapade legends still shock us because they seem so lifelike and plausible. Take "The Husband Monitor," for example. The story itself might rate only a PG-13, but it suggests the strong possibility that such an embarrassing incident could easily have happened to anyone:

> In a home's upstairs nursery a couple of modern young husbands were changing their babies' diapers while their wives were downstairs getting dinner on the table. The nursery had a baby monitor installed; it's something like a little radio with the microphone in the baby's room and the receiver carried around as the parent works elsewhere in the house, so the parent can hear if the baby cries.
>
> The husbands were unaware that the monitor was turned on.
>
> The receiver was downstairs with the wives.
>
> The husbands began to discuss in somewhat graphic and personal terms what the presence of a newborn in their household had done to their sex lives. Every word they said was broadcast directly to their wives.

More deserving of an X rating is an urban legend that we might call "A Dog's Life"; this one has been going around for the past few years:

> Coworkers of a pretty, unmarried young woman decided to give her a surprise birthday party. They managed to get into her house and hide in the basement waiting for her to come home from work. One of them had previously dog-sat for her while the woman was away on vacation, so she had no difficulty keeping the woman's Great Dane quiet while they waited.

The young woman was heard to arrive home and go into the shower. Her friends waited patiently. Finally they heard her come out of the shower, and she came to the basement door calling her dog, "Rex, Rex. Come here, Rex. Mama's got a treat for you."

The dog bounded up the stairs, and the coworkers sneaked up quietly, then burst into the kitchen shouting "Surprise!"

The surprise was on them: the young woman was naked and had smeared peanut butter on her body. Rex was eagerly licking it off.

The theme of, shall we say, *indiscretion* revealed in both stories, and the variation on the familiar surprise-party plot in the second, clearly mark these two stories as urban legends, whatever grain of truth they may contain. Besides, you always hear about things like this at hairdressing salons and at parties, not on the evening news or in reputable newspapers. And if you've been paying attention so far in this book, you'll know that there are always some variations in details, as in the above example, the breed of dog, the hiding place, the fine points of the victim's peanut-butter application, and her response to the surprise.

An old sex legend that's been brought up-to-date is one I call "Dear Old Dad." In earlier times the story concerned a sheriff and deputy, or two cops—a veteran and a rookie. One version:

One Saturday night they were patrolling in their squad car, and in a dark area of a closed cemetery they saw a car parked with its lights off. The rookie cop went up to the car and found a teenage couple making love in the back seat. He told them to stay put and went back to ask his partner what to do.

The old cop chuckled and said, "Just tell that guy that you will arrest them both and turn them over to their parents unless he lets us both have sex with his girlfriend." The teens were terrified, and agreed.

After the rookie cop had his turn and went back to the squad car, the veteran policeman said, "Now it's my turn." He went up to the car, shined his flashlight into it, and recognized his own daughter crouched there, wide-eyed and trembling.

Some versions of the story describe a businessman on an out-of-town trip who visits a prostitute who turns out to be his runaway daughter. The spin on this one is that instead of repenting and coming back home, the girl blackmails her father.

In its latest form, "Dear Old Dad" concerns a couple who meet in cyberspace under assumed names. After months of exchanging highly erotic talk in an Internet sex-chat room, the couple decide to meet in a hotel room. There, after a naked embrace in the dark they turn on the lights, and . . . you guessed it—Dear Old Dad and Darling Daughter meet again.

"Gay Pride, No Ride"

An airline employee whose last name was "Gay" boarded a plane using his company pass. Finding his assigned seat occupied, Mr. Gay took another vacant seat nearby. But before the plane took off, another flight was canceled, and flight attendants were told that they had to pull nonpaying passengers off the plane to make room for ticketed passengers.

A flight attendant came down the aisle and asked the occupant of Mr. Gay's assigned seat, "Are you gay?" The man looked surprised, but he answered, "Well, yes I am."

"Then you'll have to get off the plane," the flight attendant said.

Overhearing this exchange, the employee named Gay spoke up, saying, "No, No, I'm *Gay, and I'm the one who will have to get off."*

Immediately two men sitting nearby jumped up and said, "Well we're gay too, and they can't make us all *get off!"*

"The Stuck Couple"

A friend of a friend was getting ready to go out one evening, when he noticed from his bedroom window that there was a car blocking the mouth of the drive. As he had some time to spare, he ignored it, expecting it to go away. However, nearly an hour later he found that it was still there, and as he could see no signs of life, he walked down to investigate. There, inside, was a couple, coupled. "Thank God you've come," shouted the man. "Something's gone in my back, and I can't move." So the FOAF went back and called the police, and they called an ambulance and the fire brigade. The upshot of it was that the firemen had to cut the top off the car to lift the man out. While they were waiting for the other stretcher, the officer-in-charge said to the woman: "I'm frightfully sorry that we've had to cut up your husband's car." She smiled wanly, and replied: "That's all right. It's not my husband."

From Rodney Dale's 1978 book The Tumour in the Whale. *Another English version—the more common one that describes the couple stuck while having sex in a Mini [tiny British car] in a public square—appears in Paul Smith's 1983* The Book of Nasty Legends. *In* The Choking Doberman *I discuss how medical authorities have debunked the idea that humans can actually become "stuck" during intercourse; one well-known supposed instance of* penis captivus *turned out to have been a hoax. Stuck-couple stories in ancient myths and legends were reborn in modern folklore as car/sex legends, sometimes taking other traditional forms, such as this limerick:*

There once was a fellow named Brett,
Loved a girl in his shiny Corvette;
We know it's absurd
But the last that we heard
They haven't untangled them yet.

"Stick-Shift Frenzy"

Oh, V——, something terrible happened to a girl at our school. She was at a party when some boys thought it would be a good joke to put a Spanish Fly in her drink. (You know what it is don't you?) If you don't, it's something that makes you want to go all the way! Well anyway after drinking her drink, she told her boyfriend to meet her out in the car.

When he went out there, she had f—— herself to <u>death</u> (No lie) on the gearshift. This is true. It was in the papers even.

*From a letter handwritten by one teenage girl to another in 1959 or 1960, sent to me in 1984 by an Oregon educator who had happened to save it among some miscellaneous school papers. This alleged incident, often set in a drive-in theater, was widely believed by teens in the 1950s. The writer here displays a charming mix of modesty and forthrightness as she tells the story. But obviously, she does not realize that "Spanish Fly" is a substance, not a thing. The supposed aphrodisiac effects of cantharis, as it's called, made from dried Spanish, or blister, beetles (*Lytta vesicatoria*) were believed in by many young people who had never actually seen the stuff nor had any idea what it was or how to obtain it. "The Girl on the Gearshift Lever" legend faded with the introduction of steering-post shift levers and automatic transmission; one wonders if we'll be hearing the story again as stick shift once more becomes a popular option. Frankly, I hope not.*

"The Bothered Bride" and "The Grumbling Groom"

Stunned wedding guests are still talking about a posh California ceremony that began as a happy event—but wound up with a shocking finale.

The bride and groom, an unidentified couple from Simi Valley, Calif., never went through with their marriage because the bride revealed a little secret just as they were tying the knot, according to Los Angeles society columnist Mary Louise Oates.

The young lady walked down the aisle in her gorgeous gown, joined the groom, the maid of honor, and the best man at the altar—then whispered to the minister that she wanted to make a little speech.

First she thanked her parents for their love and support, for all they had done for her throughout the years, for the love and planning they had lavished on her beautiful wedding. Guests were filled with emotion.

Then she thanked her friends for their devotion, for their kindness and affection, for the presents they had showered on her on the happy occasion.

Friends and relatives choked back their tears.

Finally, the bride turned her attentions to her maid of honor.

"And I would like to thank the maid of honor," she said sweetly.

"I would like to thank her for sleeping with my groom last night."

With that, the blushing bride left the church, amid gasps and whispers.

She did not look back—and she did not toss her bouquet to the guests.

The bride's father—shocked but chivalrous—invited the wedding guests to a reception, explaining that it would be a shame to waste the elaborate preparations.

Apparently, the bride did not attend—and neither did the groom or maid of honor.

[Caption, on a photograph of a blindfolded bride: "The identity of the bride was withheld to save her from any further embarrassment."]

Dearly Believed

The Bridegroom's Revenge: A Myth Too Good to Be Untrue

Some stories are just too good to spoil with the facts.

Here's one: A big wedding, very lavish and stylish. At the reception, the best man gets up to make the toast. The groom hops to his feet and says he'd like to say something first:

Thank you all for coming, and for your lovely gifts. But I am going to honeymoon in Hawaii and the bride is going to Aruba, and when we come back the marriage will be annulled. And if you want to know why, look under your plates. (In some versions, he says look under your chairs.)

In yet another version, he just holds up the under-your-plate or under-your-chair picture: the bride and the best man in what is called a "compromising position" in polite company. He leaves.

Gasps. Fainting. But the party continues.

In some versions he and the bride leave, after some breakage of glass.

As with other urban myths (alligators in the sewer, people being kidnapped for body parts, movie stars appearing in emergency rooms with gerbil troubles), many people swear this story is true. They have heard it on the radio. They know someone who knows someone who was there. In some cases *they were actually there themselves.*

But it didn't happen.

One source said a friend heard this story at a hotel in New Hampshire while checking in to attend another wedding.

"I've heard that," said Gene Bryant, director of sales at the Clarion-Somerset Hotel in Nashua. "Just when you think you've heard everything . . . I'll ask someone on the banquet staff and call you back."

He called back. "It did not happen here," said Bryant. "But it did happen in New Hampshire. Someone on our staff heard it on the radio. I think it was KISS 108."

That would be WXKS in Medford, Mass. Seems it has a morning show with a feature about weird weddings. Listeners call in to share.

A version of the tale was spread on the Internet, too, by someone who heard the best-man-and-bride story on a radio station in Chicago. In this version the groom had taped an 8-by-10 manilla folder (note the precision of the details) to the bottom of every chair, directed the guests to open their surprise and waited for them to see the picture. He then turned to the best man and said "[Expletive] you," and then to the bride, and said the same thing.

Then came a tip that this wedding took place at the Glen Sanders Mansion in Scotia, N.Y., near Schenectady. A colleague's sister's housemate's nephew's wife's colleague heard it and swore it was true.

The mansion is a premier spot for weddings in the Schenectady area. People there were also familiar with the story.

"It did not happen," said Kimberly Kaminski, who has been delegated to handle these inquiries. "We've had over 300 calls about this. Five to 10 calls a day. Some people even say they were there! It came out of a project in a marketing class at Schenectady County Community College. They were doing an experiment in how word of mouth travels. It sure does!"

Brrring. Brring. "Thank you for calling Schenectady County Community College. If you are calling from a touch-tone telephone, press 1 now . . ."

"We don't have any marketing classes this semester," said Carol Chiarella, chairman of the business and law department. "But there is one professor I can ask."

That was Toby Strianese, chairman of the hotel, culinary and tourism department. He had heard the story from his wife, who heard it on the radio. Then he heard it again from the dean's secretary, who heard it at a cocktail party. So he told the story in his class while his students were working on a marketing plan, to illustrate how rumors get started and can hurt a business. There were two students who work at the Glen Sanders Mansion, and he asked them if the story was true. They said it wasn't.

Another student said he had a cousin who was actually at the wedding. Strianese asked him to find out from the cousin what day the wedding was and the name of the groom, but the student never reported back.

"It's clearly an impossible story," said Strianese, who has worked in the restaurant business for 30 years. "Most people, if they think there will be a favor at the wedding, pick up the plate first thing to see if it's underneath. Also, who would have put the pictures under the plates? It would have to be the staff, because the groom would have been at the ceremony at the time the plates are being put out. And a staff person would not have been able to resist looking at the picture and talking about it."

The thread could perhaps be unraveled further, back to the person who actually dreamed it up. But that seems unlikely now that so many people—normal people—insist that it happened.

Strianese came across the story two more times. A student had a friend in Plattsburg who heard it on the radio. And a colleague heard it at a party of lawyers, where three of them were trying to figure out which principal was liable.

Now it has traveled to Washington. People love this story. They *want* to believe it. The Internet writer called it the Wedding Revenge story, emphasizing the retributive aspect of the groom going through with the ceremony, making the bride's parents pay for the huge reception for 300, and then wrecking the miscreants' reputations in front of all their nearest and dearest. Something so delicious just had to be true.

And Paul is dead.

"The Bothered Bride" story is from Weekly World News, *December 24, 1985. The tabloid had taken a tiny notice printed tongue-in-cheek in a gossip column and expanded it into a "news" article. The same story was widely told in the late 1980s, but the last*

"bride" version I've collected was in 1990. Two reports of the "groom" version of the story came to me from Scotland in 1991, but the legend did not really catch on again in the United States until 1995. "The Grumbling Groom" article above, by Megan Rosenfeld, was on page one in the Washington Post *on October 25, 1995. I reprint Rosenfeld's entire article because it illustrates so well the usual path of attempts to trace urban legends. Other reports continue right up to the present from cities across the country, always with some reference to the hidden compromising photographs. Evidently, it never occurred to the people who claim to have been present at the incident to have saved one of the photographs as proof that the story is true.*

"Filmed in the Act"

This is not an advice column, so readers don't usually ask me for my wisdom about their love lives. I was pleased, however, to receive the following letter:

"I think (I *hope!*) that I have an urban legend for you," a woman from a large city in the East wrote me early last spring. "Any reassurance would be welcome. My husband and I have taken a suite at one of those honeymoon resorts in the Poconos for a weekend. While I was showing the brochure to my brother-in-law, he said something about being careful of the mirrors.

"When I asked what he was talking about, he explained that some friends of a friend of his had spent their honeymoon at one of those places. Then, years later, watching an adult channel on TV in Las Vegas, what should come on for all the world to see but movies of their honeymoon! They had been made through two-way mirrors.

"Of course the suite we've booked is full of mirrors—over the bed, around the pool, etc. I really need to hear that this story isn't true, and that 'Betty does Bill' [made-up names] won't be playing in motel rooms across the country."

I wrote back to assure "Betty and Bill" that they can take their vacation without worrying that they will become porno stars. The story that couples in honeymoon hotels are "filmed in the act" for later screening as X-rated movies is widely told—but completely untrue.

I guess it's true that many honeymoon resorts feature mirrors, round beds, heart-shaped tubs and pools, "theme" rooms, etc. But research into such matters extends beyond my professional speciality in folklore.

As for what goes on behind those mirrors, the popular Pocono region in northeastern Pennsylvania seems to be the most common resort area where honeymooners are allegedly filmed by hidden cameras. But the same story is told about other resorts throughout the East and Midwest and in vacation centers in the Rockies and on the West Coast as well.

Often, as in Betty and Bill's version, the films are supposed to be made in one region for showing in another. This, one assumes, lessens the chance of a filmed couple or their friends later seeing the movies.

Some people believe that these films are made in low-cost motel chains for showing in such imagined sin-centers as Las Vegas or Atlantic City. Maybe this is supposed to indicate the "price you pay" for using cheap motels.

Sometimes it's said that the films are made to be shown to later occupants of the same suite. On these suites there is alleged to be a one-time-only rule to prevent people from seeing themselves on film. Another variation claims that the mirror room is rented very cheaply so as to provide a supply of "performers" for the films.

None of these ideas makes economic sense in the hotel business. Why would managers take the enormous risk of secretly filming guests, when X-rated videos are readily available?

The most common ending for the "filmed in the act" stories is that the couple sues the hotel for damages. Surely they would do so, if the story were true, but I haven't heard of any such suits.

Further evidence of the story's dubious origin: I heard from one resident of the Poconos who had worked as a waiter in a popular resort hotel. He told me he was asked so often by guests about the honeymoon-film story that he took the question to the president of the resort chain. The executive told him that every major vacation area in the country has similar stories, and none have ever been proved—nor would any resort owner be so stupid as to try such a thing.

In my opinion, the rumors may give business a boost. The honeymooners—or whoever they are—who patronize places with "fantasy" mirrored suites enjoy more than just the change of decor. They also gain the delicious thrill that other people may know or suspect what fun they've been having. I suppose we could call it a kind of imagined reverse voyeurism, which is certainly better and more legal than the real thing.

By the way, I recently got a picture postcard discreetly showing a couple in the private swimming pool of a "fantasy suite" in a Poconos resort hotel. The message written on the card was simply this: "Having a *wonderful* time! Thank you!!! Betty and Bill."

This was my newspaper column for release the week of August 24, 1987. In other versions the married couple find themselves watching a tape of the husband cavorting with another woman. Some people claim that certain resorts can offer bargain prices because they reap huge profits from selling homemade porn tapes. Many hotels and resorts are bedeviled by this story, and some managers, hoping to stop the rumors, have even called in the local police to search their premises thoroughly for any hidden cameras, bugs, or peepholes. A recent version of "Filmed in the Act" circulating on the Internet claims that the couple were so thrilled to see how well they performed ten years previously that they ordered a copy of the tape from the resort.

"Superhero Hijinks"

I would like to share a story with you that I heard in December of 1989 and accepted as true until I saw a similar story in Ann Landers' column in early 1990. This was told to me by my supervising teacher at East Haven High School, East Haven, Connecticut, when I was doing my student teaching.

My supervisor's sister had a friend of a friend who moved into a quiet neighborhood in Madison, Connecticut. One morning, in the fall of 1989, the woman was raking leaves on her front lawn when she heard someone calling, "Help me, somebody help me!" At first she thought she was just hearing things, and nobody seemed to be around on this Saturday morning. But the sound persisted, "Help me, somebody please help me." So the woman took her rake and started walking across the yards toward the faint cry. It led her to a house a few houses down from her own, and the woman went near the back door; she realized the cry was coming from inside the house.

The woman went to the back door and called out the name of the person who lived there. "Help me. In here! In here!" was what she heard next. So she opened the back door and went inside, following the cries to the bedroom.

The lady of the house was completely naked, and her hands and feet were tied to the bedposts. On the floor was her husband, naked except for a Superman cape. It seems that the man had stood on the bedroom dresser and made a flying leap to the bed, but he hit his head on the night table and was still out cold. The couple's children were at a religion class or something.

The neighbor called paramedics to come, and she covered both husband and wife with blankets, but she was unable to untie the wife. When the paramedics came in they couldn't stop laughing.

My supervisor said that this story spread throughout the neighborhood, and the husband and wife started leaving for work very early and returning very late so as not to face the neighbors. Eventually they put their house up for sale.

Told in a letter from Rosemary Lyons of New Haven, Connecticut, dated June 23, 1990. The laughing paramedics are a standard motif of legends about embarrassing situations. The Ann Landers column, quoting "A Minnesota Reader," and describing the husband dressed in a Batman costume, was published on January 30, 1990. The earliest published text of "Superhero Hijinks" I've found is in Paul Smith's 1986 The Book of Nastier Legends. *Although this version from England describes the man wearing a Superman costume, the accompanying illustration shows the couple dressed as Batman characters. Spiderman and Tarzan are also mentioned in the legend, which swept the United States from 1988 through early 1990, aided and abetted by Paul Harvey's reporting it from Dallas in 1989. The last time I saw the story in print was in the* Los Angeles Times *on October 7, 1994; the husband was dressed as Batman, and police were called "to revive the Conked Crusader."*

"Sex in Disguise"

Household Headquarters
Office of the Divorce Counselor

The American Home

Subject: A Halloween Party

To Whom it May Concern:

A couple was invited to a real swanky masked Halloween party, so the wife got costumes for both. On the night of the party she got such a terrible headache that she told her husband to go without her. He protested, but she said all she was going to do was take a couple of aspirins and go to bed; there was no need for his good time to be spoiled by not going; so he got into his costume and off he went.

The wife, after sleeping soundly for an hour, woke without a sign of pain. As it was just a little after nine, she decided to go to the party. In as much as her husband didn't know what kind of costume she was wearing, she thought it would be a good thing to slip into the party and observe how he acted when she wasn't around. So she joined the party and the first one she spied was her husband, cavorting around on the dance floor, dancing with one slick chick and then another, copping a little feel here and there, so the wife slipped up to him and, being a rather seductive babe herself, he left his partner standing high and dry and devoted his attention to the new stuff that had just arrived.

She let him go as far as he wished, (naturally) and finally when he whispered a little proposition, she agreed and they went out to one of the cars—etc.—etc.—etc. Just before unmasking at midnight, she slipped away, went home and got back into bed, wondering what kind of explanation her husband would make for his behavior. He came home and went right into the bedroom to see how she was. She was sitting up reading and asked what kind of time he had.

He said, "Oh, the same old thing. You know I never have a good time when you aren't there." Then she said, "Did you dance much?" He said, "Well, I'll tell you, I never danced a dance. When I got there, Bill Rivers, Les Brown and some other guys were stag too, so we just went back in the den, and played poker. But I'll tell you one thing; that fellow I loaned my costume to sure had a HELL-OF-A-TIME!!"

This piece of Xeroxlore has been around for many years, with or without the spurious memo-heading shown above. The terms "slick chick," "seductive babe," and "stag" echo dated slang, yet these words remain in most modern texts, as does the humorous dangling modifier in the second paragraph. Some texts are more graphic in rendering the sex scene, and various different personal names occur, including "Charlie" as the name of the man who borrowed the costume. I've always thought that this Halloween legend might be the basis for a successful ad campaign for aspirin. When Reader's Digest *ran a sanitized version in November 1988 the setting was a masked ball, but the borrower of the costume was still "Charlie." The story is also transmitted orally, as is another sexcapade story in which two husbands contrive to switch wives overnight on a camping trip, unaware that their wives had the same plan and had already switched positions in their tents.*

"AIDS Mary" and "AIDS Harry"

I'm scared to death," said Kristi, 23. She worked at a financial company in Denver with her 21-year-old girlfriend Elise; they were sitting on one of those carpeted seats high above the dance floor, watching the goings-on around them. . . .

"People are going to use AIDS to get back at other people," Kristi predicted. Then she told me this horrifying story. A guy she knows—the friend of someone she works with—met a girl at a club named Josephina's. He flirted with her, she responded; and before he knew it, they were at his place, having sex. He couldn't believe his good fortune. The next morning, he woke up alone, went to the bathroom and nearly fainted. There, written in lipstick on his mirror, was a note the girl had left him. It said, WELCOME TO THE AIDS FAMILY.

A woman meets a man in a bar. They hit it off right away, and the man asks her to join him on vacation at his beach house in the Bahamas. She accepts and goes with him. They make love, and the woman has never been happier.

On the day she has to leave, the man sees her off at the airport. He gives her a present, telling her not to open it until she gets home.

Back home, she finds a coffee maker inside. A note on it says, "This is for all the lonely nights you'll be facing. Welcome to the world of AIDS."

The legend of "AIDS Mary," as a Chicago journalist dubbed it, began sweeping the country, and eventually the world, in late 1986; the above version is from David Seeley's article "Night Life in the Age of AIDS," Playboy, *July 1987, p. 170. The handwriting-on-the-wall motif seems to be borrowed from "The Licked Hand" legend quoted in Chapter 2. Sometimes the punch line is "Welcome to the world of AIDS," or "Welcome to the AIDS club." The legend can be traced to much earlier stories about the deliberate spread of venereal diseases, combined with recent history and folklore about the origins of the AIDS epidemic. Some background to understanding the legend is provided in Michael Fumento's 1990 book* The Myth of Heterosexual AIDS, *Chapter 5, "The 'Perils' of Promiscuity." Occasionally in the story it was a man said to be deliberately infecting women, and by spring 1990 this "AIDS Harry" variation had taken over. The letter quoted above came from a 13-year-old in Millington, Maryland, in January 1992. The curious detail of a coffee maker as a gift derives from versions in which the warning note is presented inside a tiny gift-wrapped* coffin*—sometimes a black, purple velvet, or elaborately carved coffin. Then, probably through misunderstanding in oral tradition, this coffin became a can of* coffee*, and the recipient checked the can, fearing she had been set up to smuggle drugs home from the Caribbean. The above version has converted this detail to a coffee* maker*, with the explanation that it's for "all the lonely nights."*

6

Losing Face

I'm embarrassed to admit it, but when I started to recognize embarrassment as a major theme in urban legends I didn't know that there was already a considerable sociological and psychological literature on the subject. All *I* knew were a bunch of traditional stories concerning embarrassing situations. Like this one:

> A panicked woman who had just checked into a large and elegant New York City hotel called down to the front desk and pleaded, "Please help me! I'm trapped inside my room, and I don't know how to get out!"
>
> When the desk clerk asked her to explain how she was trapped, the woman answered, "Well, I can see only three doors here. The first one opens to a closet. The second one opens to the bathroom. And the third one has a 'Do Not Disturb' sign hanging on it."

To me—a folklorist—that story immediately calls to mind others that reveal a similar misreading of a situation with embarrassing results. Like the one about the person trying to look up something in the subject card-catalog of a library. (This story is precomputer!) At one point in the search, the library patron encounters a card that directs "Go to main entry," so he shuts the drawer and walks to the main entrance of the library building itself, expecting to find some kind of aid desk there. Or the one about the woman baking bread or cookies for the first time who follows the direction literally to put the dough in the pan, but "Leave room to rise." She arranges her dough, then leaves the kitchen, tiptoeing back and peeking in now and then to see if the dough has risen. (If you don't get these two stories, I hope you're not too embarrassed to ask a librarian or a cook to explain them.)

Two other things strike me about such stories. First, they seem to be a largely male narrative genre, since they're so often told about females who seem to be one French fry short of a Happy Meal; and second, the stories end abruptly without a second act in which the misunderstanding is explained and the dupe squirms.

What the experts on embarrassment itself have explained, as Edward

Gross and Gregory P. Stone did in a 1964 article published in the *American Journal of Sociology,* is that embarrassing situations and stories typically serve to undermine a person's identity, poise, and confidence. "Exposure," asserted Gross in a published interview, "is the key thing. . . . When you're embarrassed, you've committed some kind of public gaffe." The following story, unverifiable, but convincing nonetheless, offers a good example:

> A homeless person tried to get on a bus without sufficient fare, and he was kicked off by the driver. Going around to the back of the bus, the vagrant managed to slip in after someone had gotten off, and he hid behind a rear seat.
>
> A few stops along the bus line a woman got on the bus and made her way back to an available seat in the rear of the bus. Looking over the seat back, she noticed the stowaway crouched there, and said "Oh my God, there's a bum on the bus." Her remark was repeated and made its way to the front of the crowded vehicle where the driver misheard her statement as "There's a *bomb* on the bus."
>
> The bus driver immediately pulled over, opened both doors, shouted to the passengers to jump out, and started honking his horn to attract a policeman to summon the bomb squad.

(Who was more embarrassed here, the woman who inadvertently caused the alarm, or the driver who misunderstood? The legend doesn't tell us.)

People need strategies to deal with embarrassment in real life. The aforementioned Edward Gross, a University of Washington emeritus professor of sociology, has described the case of a four-year-old boy who fell off the toilet seat and became wedged between the toilet and the wall. "He looked up with rather plaintive eyes at his baby-sitter and said, 'That's my favorite thing to do.'" A well-known example of embarrassment-recovery from the world of opera is told about a famous Wagnerian tenor who, in a production of *Lohengrin,* missed the timing of his exit on a swan boat that went gliding empty across the stage. Supposedly, the tenor had the presence of mind to ask another person in the scene, "What time is the next swan?" In a similar vein, it is told that when a telephone on a stage set rang at the wrong time during the play, an actor answered it, and then handed the phone to another actor, saying "It's for you."

In my opinion, one of the world's best legends in the category of a horribly embarrassing situation defused by quick thinking is this one about a dropped turkey:

> The society guests in an elegant home were seated for dinner. The maid entered, carrying a large roast turkey on a platter. Just inside the dining room, however, the maid slipped, and the bird slid off the platter and onto the floor.
>
> After a moment of stunned silence, the lady of the house said in a calm, even voice, "That's all right, Lucy. Don't be embarrassed. Just take that one back to the kitchen and bring in the other turkey."
>
> Lucy picked up the fallen bird, left the room with it, and soon returned, bearing a roast turkey on a platter. She successfully delivered it to the table before the man of the house, who without comment carved and served it to the guests.

And now let me reveal to you a trade secret of male college professors. One of our worst fears is that someday we will unwittingly step in front of a class to lecture with the fly of our trousers unzipped. How embarrassing!

This may explain why so many men in my profession prefer to lecture from behind a podium. And those who do lecture standing before the class habitually hesitate in their offices just before class for a quick zipper check. The code term to warn of an open fly—something all American males learn in boyhood—is "XYZ," or "examine your zipper." And it's not just male college professors who suffer this fear; the problem of open zipper flies is common enough to have generated several urban legends.

At the simplest level, there's the story of the businessman seated at his desk who notices that his fly is open. He hastily closes the zipper, not realizing that the end of his necktie is now caught in it. When he stands to greet a visitor, he is nearly strangled.

Slightly more complicated are the unzipped-fly stories told about bus or subway passengers. In one such tale, a man is warned that his zipper is open; he hastily closes it, catching a piece of the skirt worn by a woman standing next to him. An embarrassing extrication follows, as it always does in these legends, with the driver, conductor, and other passengers all joining in the struggle to free the two strangers from the zipper's firm grip.

Another fly-on-the-bus story tells of a woman who accidentally drops her handkerchief, which lands in the lap of a seated man. She points at his lap, calling his attention to the hanky, and he glances down and thinks his shirttail is hanging out through his trouser fly.

The man eases the zipper down, stuffs the hanky inside, and rezips, leaving the woman speechless. One wonders how he explains the hanky in his pants when he gets home.

The first two urban legends following in this chapter (after the box) are open-zipper stories. Concerning the first story—an international classic of this genre—Robert Friedel in his wonderfully comprehensive book *Zipper: An Exploration in Novelty* (1994) wrote, "the ancient comic elements of mistaken identity, sex, and slapstick are all thrown together, with a readily available zipper in the middle." Read on.

"Two Painful Nose Jobs"

My cousin's husband told me that a friend of his was at a wedding once and saw this happen: The bride and groom took turns cutting the cake, and as playful newlyweds often do, the groom started to mash the cake into his bride's face instead of just gently feeding it to her.

As a reflex, the bride raised her hands to her face, and when she pulled them away they were covered with blood, and her white gown was stained with blood! The groom had pushed the cake so hard that he broke her nose.

One night this guy came into the ER with both hands cupped over his face. He wouldn't take his hands down until the paramedics promised not to laugh at him.

When he finally took one of his hands down, they saw that one of his fingers on one hand was stuck inside his nose.

He told them that he had been picking his nose while waiting in his car at a red light. Then somebody had rear-ended his car, which threw his head forward and into his steering wheel. His nose had swollen so fast that he couldn't get his finger out of it, and so he had come to the emergency room for help.

"The Unzipped Plumber (or Mechanic)"

Newspaper friend Tom Ungles of Satanta, Kansas, an occasional visitor to Woodland Park, has forwarded a copy of a lighter vein item appearing in a Kansas newspaper.

The item gave us a few chuckles, so we pass it along to *Courier* readers for hopefully the same purpose. . . . We give you this "believe it or not" from the *Arkansas Daily Traveler:*

This story, purported to be true by those who tell it, has its locale in Lawrence, Kansas.

It seems a young wife noticed that the trailer home occupied by her husband and herself had developed a plumbing problem. She informed her husband of this fact and left the mobile home for an errand.

Returning, she found a pair of legs extending from beneath the trailer and, feeling playful, giggled, lowered the zipper on the pants, and entered the door of the house.

Imagine her chagrin when she found her husband lolling on the sofa watching television! When she had recovered her composure enough to explain to her mate what she had done, he in turn explained to her that he called a plumber when he found the repair job beyond his abilities.

Gathering their courage, they ventured outside together to attempt to explain to the plumber below the home. They found the plumber in the same position as before, except that he appeared to be unconscious from a blow to the head he evidently suffered when he reacted to the playful prank of the young housewife by quickly raising his head to see what was happening.

Horrified, the young couple called an ambulance and soon the vehicle with two attendants arrived on the scene to aid the injured plumber.

When the circumstances surrounding the injury to the man were subsequently related to the two attendants, however, they became so overpowered with the humor of the situation that during a fit of convulsive laughter, they dumped the hapless plumber to the ground, breaking his arm.

Imagine, if you can, that plumber awakening in the hospital with a broken arm, and a knot on his head with the last positive memory being that of feeling his zipper being lowered.

We'll bet that young couple received a bill for $51.88 . . . at least.

From Australia's *Rockhampton Morning Bulletin:*

A central west couple drove their car into Rockhampton Kmart only to have their car break down in the car park. The husband told his wife to carry on with the shopping while he fixed the car.

The wife returned later to see a small group of people near the car. On closer inspection she saw a pair of male legs protruding from under the chassis. Although the man was in shorts, his lack of underpants turned private parts into glaringly public ones.

Unable to stand the embarrassment, she dutifully stepped forward and tucked everything back into place. On regaining her feet she looked across the bonnet and found herself staring at her husband standing idly by. The repairman had to have three stitches inserted in his head.

The first item is from the Ute Pass Courier *of Woodland Park, Colorado, April 15, 1971, sent to me by Charles Pheasant of Littleton, Colorado. The second is from the "Editorial Report" column of the* National Lampoon, *August 1988 "True Facts" issue. Though somewhat stilted in style, these items illustrate how newspapers borrow legendary material from one another and thus contribute to the spread of folk narratives. This story has had more versions than the victim had stitches on his clobbered head, but perhaps the most "standard" variation has the husband simply working on his car that is parked in his own driveway; unbeknownst to his wife, he enlists a neighbor or a professional mechanic to help him. This legend may reflect, on one level, the male fear of sexual exposure and, on another level, female uneasiness about initiating sex. The laughing paramedics are a typical motif of this and other urban legends about hilarious accidents.*

"The Unzipped Fly"

The version that I heard in Denmark from my father (in the late 1960s or early '70s) runs as follows:

A couple is at the Royal Theatre in Copenhagen. They have stalls and the theatre is packed. The drama has just begun when some latecomers appear, among them a young lady in a big chiffon dress. They have to get past a couple, and as everybody on their row gets up as well, the man notices that his fly is open. At the moment when the festively dressed lady is passing he pulls the zipper and, most unfortunately, the chiffon skirt gets caught. However much he tries, he can't get it open again, and the woman angrily turns on him as he stammers some explanation. Hushing and irritated whispering is already being heard behind them. Her surprised escort and his confused wife see them go out close together, as he nervously whispers, "We have to get out and fix it outside."

They had to have help from the attendant who cut them loose, and he had to pay for a new dress.

Reported by Carsten Bregenhøj in FOAFtale News *(newsletter of the International Society for Contemporary Legend Research), no. 24, December 1991. A similar version from Belgium was reported in a 1990 article in* Fabula, *(a journal of folktale studies). American versions of the legend usually involve an unzipped man on a bus—as in the May 10, 1991, Ann Landers column—or an unzipped man dining in an expensive restaurant. In the latter versions he snags the edge of the tablecloth in his fly and pulls the whole cloth and all the dishes to the floor when he rises from the table. In one of the few folkloristic studies of such stories, "The Most Embarrassing Thing that Ever Happened: Conversational Stories in a Theory of Enactment,"* Folklore Forum, *vol. 10, no. 3 (1977), Roger D. Abrahams relates a restaurant version of the legend as a personal experience. Later in the essay, however, he admits that it actually happened not to him but to "a couple of friends of mine exactly as recounted,* or so it was reported to me*" (my emphasis). Finally, there are some extremely elaborated versions of the story that include several further embarrassing incidents taking place in the restaurant; when the young man apologizes for the disturbance, the headwaiter invites him to "Come back anytime. You're worth it in entertainment value."*

"The Golf Bag"

A golfer was having a terrible round, hitting ball after ball far out into the woods or straight into sand traps or water hazards. Finally at the eighteenth hole, after plunking three more shots into a pond, the disgusted player flung his whole bag of clubs into the pond and strode out to the parking lot, vowing never to play this stupid game again.

Five minutes later, watched by the same group in the clubhouse bar who had seen the earlier scene, the golfer returned. He borrowed a rake from a groundskeeper and fished out his golf bag, then sheepishly got his car keys out of a zippered pocket, flung the golf bag back into the water, and walked back to the parking lot.

Told around numerous golf clubhouses as a true local occurrence, although—to my knowledge—it has never been verified by eyewitnesses. In a 1990 newspaper column the story was told about Indiana University's volatile basketball coach, Bobby Knight. The story resembles much fictional golf humor that circulates in the form of anecdotes and cartoons.

"The Unlucky Contacts"

Every spring Tom Dodds, a contributing editor of *Family Safety & Health* magazine, published by the National Safety Council, compiles a list of what he calls "Freak Squeaks"—accidents with a humorous twist.

Several readers of my column sent me Dodds's 1987 list, published in the spring issue. I enjoyed the collection, as I always do, but two "squeaks" described in the article seem to be urban legends.

One is a variation of "Cruise Control," included in Chapter 14. The other suspicious story deals with another fairly recent innovation—contact lenses. Dodds tells the story like this:

"When the DePaul University basketball team went on the road to play Dayton, forward Kevin Golden and guard Andy Laux were paired as roommates. Before Golden hit the sack, he put his contact lenses in a glass of water next to his bed. Laux woke up thirsty, grabbed the water, and guzzled down his roommate's contacts in one mighty gulp."

I have heard several versions of the swallowed-contacts story, generally attributed to some anonymous friend of a friend. And in a 1985 column attacking the vanity of contact wearers, columnist Mike Royko wrote, "We've all heard the stories about people who awake thirsty during the night and, in reaching for a glass of water on the nightstand, accidentally drink their contact lenses."

A common variation of the swallowed-contacts story has a clever and provocative angle. In this version, a prominent man or woman is engaged in an illicit affair. He swallows his mistress's contacts, and the accident leads to their misbehavior becoming known to the public.

In 1982, Diana McLellan reported such an accident in her *Washington Post* gossip column "Ear," saying that it happened to an unnamed Midwestern congressman and his secret lover.

The congressman, she wrote, "gratefully gulped the glass of water his charmer had thoughtfully placed beside the bed." The glass contained her contacts, which he swallowed unawares, and he only learned of it when she called him at the office the next day.

From my syndicated newspaper column for release the week of October 28, 1987. It seems to me that people who wear contacts do not usually park them overnight, like a set of false teeth, in a water glass on the nightstand, since usually the right and left lenses must be stored separately. Nor would most people, in my opinion, pick up a half-full glass of tepid water and drink it. Still, since this column was published, readers have continued to send me "true" accounts of swallowed contacts.

"The Wrong Teeth"

A husband and wife were taken to the Gold Coast [of Australia] for the day by friends. Relationships had been strained between them for some time, and the friends hoped that by taking them out for a carefree day together, they might salvage their relationship. However, the husband made many sour remarks about his wife.

The party went surfing. The wife was overtaken by a wave and dumped, and when she splutteringly broke surface she gasped and confessed that in her panic she had opened her mouth and lost her false teeth. Husband sneered, then, when her back was turned, slipped his false teeth from his jaw and pretended to retrieve them from the sand. His wife washed them hastily in the sea, and slipped them into her mouth. Then she took them out with an exclamation of disgust and hurled them seaward, remarking, "Those aren't mine. Somebody else must have lost them!"

Titled "The Teeth of the Evidence," in W. N. Scott's 1985 book, The Long & The Short & The Tall: A Collection of Australian Yarns, *pp. 235–36. A different version of the yarn is included in Scott's 1976* Complete Book of Australian Folklore. *A parallel story is found in the Netherlands, as documented in "The False Teeth in the Cod," a paper by Dutch folklorists Eric Venbrux and Theo Meder.*

"Bungling Brides"

For years our rabbi has used his own version of the story you call "The Bungling Bride" to make a point about the necessity of understanding the reasons behind the performance of religious rituals. Rabbi Robert Schreibman of Temple Jeremiah in Northfield, Illinois, tells the story like this:

A wife always prepared the roast for holiday meals by cutting it in two and roasting each half in a separate pan. When her husband asked why she did it this way, she said that her mother had always done it that way and she was just following her practice.

When they asked her mother why she cut the roast in half, she said it was because *her* mother had always done it that way.

So they asked grandmother, and she said it was because she never had a pan large enough to hold a roast that would feed the whole family at a holiday dinner, so she was forced to cut the roast in half.

Ours is a Reform Jewish congregation, and Rabbi Schreibman uses this story to point out the need to understand why a certain ritual is done, and to perform it because of knowledge and understanding rather than as mere rote repetition of a no-longer meaningful activity.

The rabbi and I thought you would enjoy learning how an urban legend is told for a special religious purpose.

Sent to me by Victoria S. Weisenberg, and quoted in my newspaper column for the week of May 20, 1991. This use of a legend parallels what I told students in folklore courses—to remember the message of the opening number in the musical Fiddler on the Roof. *In that song, Tevye explains why people in his village have done certain things for generations. "Tradition! Tradition!" he sings. Tradition is the essence of folklore, and teaching via storytelling is an essential part of Jewish, as well as most other religious, traditions. Another way I heard "The Bungling Bride," the woman was cutting a ham in two, but that version wouldn't be told by a rabbi. In yet another variation, the man sees his bride removing the drumsticks from a turkey before roasting it. She says that's how her mother told her to prepare a turkey. But her mother explains that she needed to do that simply because she never had an oven large enough to fit a whole turkey inside with its legs sticking up.*

I've also heard about a bride who fastened little cotton balls to the screen door with hairpins. Her husband was puzzled, and asked her why she did this. "That keeps flies out of the house," she answered, but she was unable to explain how this worked. She said her mother had taught her that little trick. So the husband asked his mother-in-law about the cotton balls, and she explained that she always used the cotton from pill and vitamin bottles to plug up holes in her screen door. She said it worked well to keep flies out of the house.

My favorite story about a meaningless ritual is one I call "The Holy Place." I heard it from a man in Indiana:

> *Members of a Catholic congregation always knelt and crossed themselves at a certain point in one of the church aisles. However, nobody knew why that particular spot was especially sacred, so someone asked one of the older members of the church to explain.*
>
> *After some thought, the member recalled the reason. There had once been something projecting from the wall at just that spot, and anybody walking by had to duck to get past. After the obstacle was removed, the people kept on ducking out of habit, and eventually, this evolved into the act of genuflecting at that point.*

"The Nude Bachelor"

In a 1987 release, Jim Davis, creator of the popular "Garfield" comic strip, retold a classic urban legend in seven graphic panels and a few well-chosen words. By such means urban legends sometimes gain an assist from the mass media and again pass by word of mouth with renewed vigor.

In the first panel of Davis's Sunday strip for March 15th, the feisty feline Garfield gives his owner Jon a sharp "SMACK" for using up all the hot water during his shower. The next five panels depict the cat's revenge: He waits until Jon has stepped out the front door, wrapped only in a towel, to pick up the morning paper, and then he gives the door a quick "SLAM!" stranding Jon outside. In the last panel two neighbors comment on the disgusting scene of the bachelor caught outside in the nude.

"The Nude Bachelor" has been told for years as one of the most popular "caught-with-your-pants-down" urban legends. It usually is said to have

happened to a friend of a friend. But the very widespread telling of this story is a virtual guarantee that it didn't really happen to anyone even remotely connected with the storytellers.

"I honestly had never heard the story before," said Davis, when asked about the origin of this particular strip. If he's right, it may be that the gag is such a good one that, inevitably, any number of people think it up independently. Or it is possible that Davis heard some version of the story, forgot about it, but then dredged it up in a new form during the creative process.

The newspaper is a key element in most versions of the story. Often the sound of the paper hitting the porch is what causes the nude man to peek outside. Then usually he gets stuck out there when the door accidentally slams shut, and so he has only the paper to cover his nudity.

"The Nude Bachelor" is popular in eastern Europe. Hungarian-American folklorist Linda Dégh reported hearing it in Budapest in 1960. A version of it also occurred in the 1961 Russian novel *Twelve Chairs.* This, in turn, was depicted in the 1970 Mel Brooks film based on the novel, so another media treatment of the legend may have aided its oral circulation here.

I heard the story told twice in Romania some years ago. Once it was supposed to have happened to a man staying in his girlfriend's apartment who woke up nude just as the mail arrived, and stepped out to reach the box. In the second Romanian version the nude man was reaching across the hall to drop some trash down the building's garbage chute when his apartment door closed behind him.

Sometimes the victim of the misadventure may attempt to climb a tree and re-enter through a bathroom window, but he drops his towel as he climbs, and he is apprehended by the police, who were called by nervous neighbors who had looked out and seen a nude man in a tree looking into the bathroom window of the house next door.

Part of my newspaper column for release the week of April 20, 1987. In a later column I reported on several people who had written me describing similar experiences of their own when they were stranded outside in the nude or nearly so. In the entry for December 16, 1960, in John Kenneth Galbraith's 1969 book, Ambassador's Journal, *the then "aspiring diplomat" suffered a similar nude escapade. Attempting to return an item left in his room by a visitor who was still waiting for the elevator to arrive, Galbraith, who had undressed for a shower, suddenly found himself "inelegantly and utterly naked in the hall of a sizable hotel." He borrowed the visitor's coat to wear as he went in search of a pass key.*

"Come and Get It!"

My mother used to tell a story about two or three young, recently married couples who were sharing a cottage. One of the wives, having prepared dinner, found that a man she thought was her husband was still in the shower. So she reached through the curtain, gave his penis a yank, and said "Ding-dong, supper's ready." Later she discovered that her own husband was not in the shower.

My mother, unfortunately, has died, and her sister does not remember the story. My brother does, however—and although neither of us can remember the names she gave the couples, we do agree that they *were* named as she told the story. My guess is that the story—legend or not—was current in Grand Rapids, Michigan, in the late '30s or very early '40s, when (and where) my mother was in high school.

I kept practising it [a difficult phrase in a Mozart opera duet] to myself over and over again until my room-mate, the tenor Murray Dickie, who was singing Pedrillo in *Die Entführung aus dem Serail,* eventually screamed at me: "If you sing that damned thing once more you'll drive me mad." And for years afterwards he would greet me with that phrase whenever we met, while I in my turn would call out to him: "Ding-Dong! Time for tea." This stemmed from an incident at his London home when friends were visiting for a performance of *The Marriage of Figaro* at Covent Garden in which Murray and I were singing. Going to call her husband from his bath, Anne Dickie saw him stooping over, as she thought, to retrieve something from the floor, still naked. Reaching one hand between his legs she called gaily, "Ding-dong! Time for tea!" and went into their bedroom. There she was confronted by her husband dressing and realised what an embarrassing surprise their visitor must have had.

The first version was sent to me in 1989 by Professor Jonathan Wylie of the Massachusetts Institute of Technology. The second is from the 1984 autobiography of singer Sir Geraint Evans, titled Sir Geraint Evans: A Knight at the Opera, *pp. 70–71. Evans and Dickie had appeared together in* The Marriage of Figaro *at Covent Garden the year before, when the "Ding-dong" incident presumably occurred. The English folklorist Paul Smith, in his 1986* The Book of Nastier Legends, *gives a version in which a sergeant invites a fellow NCO home for the weekend. The punch line is "Ding-dong. Tea's ready darling," and a cartoon illustration is captioned "They're not my Sergeant's privates!" Gershon Legman, the great chronicler of sexual folklore, reported "The "The Stranger in the Shower" told as a true story in 1940, and I heard variations with a "Come and get it!" punch line from the 1970s and later. Although the story is similar to "The Unzipped Plumber (or Mechanic)," the two legends seem to have different histories and distributions.*

"A License to Practice"

A couple from, say, Minneapolis (or another American city) were touring France. They were staying in an expensive hotel in Paris, and one morning shortly before their return home, they decided to go their separate ways for half a day.

The husband wanted to go sightseeing, while the wife had a bit more shopping to finish. They agreed to meet again around noon in front of the hotel.

The wife arrived back first, and while waiting for her husband she paced back and forth in front of the hotel or in the lobby.

Some passing *gendarmes* noticed the woman and said something to her that she did not understand. They were just writing her out a ticket when her husband arrived and added his voice to her strong protests that she had done nothing amiss.

The Americans were both taken to the police station, where the wife was booked for soliciting sex in a public place. Although the couple explained what was going on, the police insisted that to correct the mistake would take more time than the Americans had left in Paris, so it would be simpler if the woman would just buy a license to practice prostitution.

They did so, and now have the license framed in their home in Minneapolis.

There are countless other versions of this story, some set in Mexico, where the woman is wearing a red, white, and blue outfit and is arrested as a prostitute because, supposedly, only prostitutes wear red shoes there. Sometimes the travelers in Mexico are two women who go into a small cantina *but are soon asked to leave. It turns out that there is a $100 fine for a woman to be there unless she has a yellow card identifying her as a licensed prostitute. The card costs only $2, so the women each buy one and now, of course, they proudly display their professional cards at home. I've heard that some French and Mexican shops sell such documents to tourists as souvenirs, although I've never seen one. In Utah the innocent American ladies are sometimes said to be a Mormon Relief Society president and her two counselors, who live near the Mexican border and cross it one day to attend* *a bazaar. They part for a while and agree to meet later at a certain corner. Taken in by the police and told they are being arrested for prostitution without a license, the Mormon women call their stake president for advice. He tells them to buy a license, since it's cheaper than the fine, then to get out of Mexico and stay out. How far back does this legend go? One reader told me he had heard this story in the early 1960s, but Henry D. Spalding, compiler of several collections of ethnic humor, wrote me in 1987 saying that he had heard the story in the late 1920s.*

"The Witness's Note"

In the locker room of the Los Angeles Athletic Club recently two young deputy city attorneys, sweat-stained from the handball court, were discussing current trials.

"Did you hear," the winner of the game asked, "about that rape case in Van Nuys? I dropped in to see how a friend of mine was handling the prosecution.

"The victim was testifying. My friend asked her what the defendant had said when he broke into her apartment. She said 'I want to . . . I want . . .' and then said she just couldn't repeat it out loud. So the judge had her write it down on a slip of paper.

"The attorneys and the judge looked at it, and the bailiff passed it to the jury. Each juror read it and passed it along. It was after lunch, and kind of warm, and the last guy in the back row was dozing.

"The woman juror sitting next to him nudged him and handed him the note. He woke up and read it, looked at the note again, broke into a big smile, and tucked it into his coat pocket."

The second attorney, loser at handball, showed no mercy. "Then how come," he asked, "I heard about the same thing happening in Long Beach Superior Court three years ago?"

"Really?" the first man said. "Could it have happened twice?"

From an early article on the UL genre, Dial Torgerson's "Twice Told. The American Legends—They Refuse to Die" in the Los Angeles Times, *January 6, 1974. A read-*

er from Berkeley wrote me saying that he heard the same story from a coworker in San Francisco in 1973. Stephen Pile included "The Witness's Note" as a British occurrence among his "Stories We Failed to Pin Down" in his 1979 The Incomplete Book of Failures, *while W. N. Scott included an Australian version dated 1980 in his 1985 book* The Long & The Short & The Tall. *In 1988 the story was used in an episode of the TV series* L.A. Law. *Beyond these published versions, the story is frequently told, both as a joke and a legend. Often the awakened juror comments, "Judge, this note is a private matter between this lady and myself."*

"The Blind Date"

May 1, 1994

Dear Ann Landers: I met a young woman at college who has it all—looks, brains and personality. I finally got up enough nerve to ask her out, and she accepted.

After we had been dating for a few months, it became apparent that she was beginning to feel as strongly about me as I felt about her, so we made plans to go on our first out-of-town (overnight) trip together—a drive to San Diego for a three-day weekend.

Although I didn't know for sure that anything was going to happen, I thought I'd better be prepared, so I stopped by a drugstore on the way home from school to buy some condoms. I had never bought condoms before (I usually got them from friends), so I was a little ill at ease. I tried to make small talk with the pharmacist as he rang up my purchase and foolishly blurted out that I might "get lucky" over the weekend.

When I went to pick up my girlfriend the next morning, imagine my shock when that pharmacist answered the door. He was her father. I was so embarrassed I couldn't speak. Fortunately, my girlfriend was ready on time, and we managed to leave after a brief introduction.

We had a lovely weekend, but I didn't tell her that I had bought the condoms from her father. I now am feeling guilty and uneasy. Should I say something and get it over with or keep quiet?

—Van Nuys, Calif.

Dear V.N.: Keep quiet. It's enough that YOU are embarrassed. Why make your girlfriend uncomfortable too?

There are times when the less said, the better, and this happens to be one of those times.

May 1, 1994
Dear Ann Landers: The story in today's column about the guy buying condoms from a pharmacist who turns out to be his date's father is an old urban legend. . . . Many readers have written me about this story, several of them pointing out that it also appeared in a 1972 underground comic book as one of the adventures of the "Fabulous Furry Freak Brothers." I think the reader from Van Nuys, California, who sent it to you either read it in my book, saw the comic book, or simply heard the story in oral tradition. . . .

Best wishes from a faithful reader,

—Jan Harold Brunvand

May 16, 1994
Dear Jan H. Brunvand: Sorry to be so late in responding to your letter of May 1, but I just returned from a cruise and am catching up with the mail that accumulated in my absence.

I am really embarrassed by the fact that I've been had. Dozens of readers have written to tell me the condom letter was a gag. I am amazed that no one in my Chicago office or my California syndicate caught it.

I'm signing myself,

Red-Faced in Chicago,
Ann Landers

This story made more sense when told decades ago, before condoms were openly displayed in grocery stores, drugstores, convenience stores, and the like. More recent versions describe a young woman either being fitted for a diaphragm or buying a pregnancy-test kit from a doctor or a pharmacist who turns out to be her boyfriend's mother or father. Along a similar line, Joe and Teresa Graedon in their syndicated "People's Pharmacy" column for

January 29, 1995, tell the story of a young man who returned to the drugstore where he had purchased his high-tech metal Wham-O slingshot to buy a new rubber sling. When he told a young girl at the pharmacy counter that he needed "a rubber for his Wham-O," she "turned bright red and suddenly turned to some urgent business in the back of the store, leaving him standing there."

"Buying Tampax"

I have heard this one so many times that I've stopped counting. I've heard it from actual grocery store clerks, both in Arizona and Florida, who swear they've heard it live!

A beautiful woman went shopping in a grocery store. After reaching the check-out counter, the clerk, also female, asked her, "Will there be anything else, Ma'am?"

"Well, yes, there is," the shopper replied. "I looked for a box of Tampax on the shelves, but I couldn't find it."

"No problem," the clerk said, grabbing the store microphone. "Stock boy," her voice boomed over the loudspeaker. "We need a box of Tampax at Register Three."

The woman grew embarrassed, waiting, as all the other shoppers were looking at her, smiling.

In the back room, two stock boys were working, listening to the announcement.

"What do they want?" the first stock boy inquired.

"Thumbtacks," the stock boy who had just entered said.

The first stock boy grabbed his own microphone and boomed his own message over the loudspeaker: "Do you want the kind you push in with your finger, or the kind you pound in with a hammer?"

The shopper fled the store without waiting for an explanation.

Sent to me in 1987 by Kevin Fellman of Phoenix; I earlier got the same story from readers in Texas and Connecticut, and a student of mine told me that she had heard it told dur-

ing a training session for grocery-store cashiers. In some versions the stock boy inquires over the loudspeaker, "What happened to that price check you wanted on a box of thumbtacks?" In 1996 David Altom of St. Louis, Missouri, reported to me that his fiancée and a friend actually heard the Tampax/thumbtacks dialogue broadcast over a loudspeaker at a local Target store. I suspect that this was a deliberate prank carried out by someone who had heard the old story.

7

Accidents Will Happen

Modern urban legends are full of warnings against the imaginary hazards of everyday life—hook-handed killers, lethal tanning rays, exploding toilets, spider-infested cacti, and the like. When you hear horror stories told repeatedly about these supposed dangers, with many a variation and never a verifiable detail, you know you're in legend land.

But what about plausible, simpler, and less structured warning stories that you hear or read about? Many of them concern occupational health and safety, a genuine concern of workers and employers. Other such stories deal with common aspects of daily life. These accident stories sound suspiciously legendary, since they often describe incidents that seem to be pretty darn unlikely, if not impossible.

To illustrate: here's a story that I got in 1991 from Dan Shaffer of Bloomington, Indiana, a carpenter who had heard, as he wrote, "many stories of unlikely work-related disasters." These are stories like "The Lethal Sanding Machine" that Shaffer was told by a coworker who did floor sanding:

> Supposedly, this man was sanding a floor with one of those big drum sanders, and the machine blew the circuit breaker. So he went to the basement of the house to flip the breaker back on. But he forgot that he had locked the sander switch in the "on" position, and as he walked back through the basement to the stairs, the sander ground through the floor, fell into the basement on the man's head, and killed him.

To me this sounds like an apocryphal warning story intended to drill into a workman's head, so to speak, the importance of using the equipment properly. But what are the odds that the man would be directly below the sander when it fell through the floor? I checked this out with the company that refinished some floors in my house, and learned two things—these workmen had heard the same story with several variations, and they insisted that it couldn't happen, given the safety features on sanding machines.

A British reader clipped an item describing a rumored auto hazard from a 1991 issue of the *Evening Standard* (London). It was headlined "Beware: Garfield can set your car on fire." The gist of the story was that "the plastic suckers which secure Garfield cats to windscreens can cause fires." Supposedly, if the "suckers" (suction cups) are transparent, they focus the sun's rays like lenses and may start a fire inside your car.

The news story concluded with the information that "Two manufacturers of transparent suckers were alerted and had responded helpfully."

I wonder if these company reps said something similar to what my reader did in her letter forwarding the clipping: "Garfield's a glutton, YES; but a pyromaniac? NO!"

I agree, since other automobile gadgets—including many radar detectors—are also held to windshields with suction cups, commonly transparent ones, and I've never heard of any of these cups starting fires. In fact, I even tried to focus sunlight with one of these suction cups and got nowhere, since they tend to disperse light, not concentrate it. Another thing: I don't think the sun ever shone brightly enough or often enough in Merry England to constitute a genuine danger of this kind. But it's the story that counts, isn't it?

A woman from Minnesota sent me a doubtful accident story she'd heard several years ago from, as she wrote, "science-minded kids in southern California." Supposedly a woman disregarded the warning labels on some household products she was using and mixed together several floor-cleaning and -waxing products, with tragic results. She put the mixture on the floor, and once it dried it became a contact explosive. When she stepped into her clean room, BANG!

I suspect that this unlikely story was invented by someone who was plain sick and tired of cleaning and waxing floors. On the other hand, as several chemists have since informed me, a mixture of something called "aqueous ammonia" and solid iodine creates something called "nitrogen triiodide ammoniate" (NI_3NH_3), which is a stable compound when wet but an extremely sensitive contact explosive when dry. So perhaps a day-dreaming Chem 101 student dreamed up the legend.

Describing another accident hazard on the home front, here are the opening sentences from a 1990 article in the *Chicago Sun-Times*:

> If all the stories of mothers, aunts, grandmothers and friends who had pressure cookers explode were true, there wouldn't be a ceiling left in America.

> The pressure cooker is prey to more apocryphal tales than those poor alligators said to roam New York's sewer system.

Thus began *Sun-Times* food editor Bev Bennett's interview with Lorna Sass, author of a book called *Cooking under Pressure.*

My own mother, aunts, grandmothers, etc., never used pressure cookers, so I'm not familiar with this genre of accident stories. But my mother-in-law does cook under pressure, and she assures me that her cooker blew up once. Frankly, I can't see much potential for interesting legends here. What's there to say, besides who was there and what was inside when the pot exploded?

I prefer more detailed accident legends; so, back to the Chem lab. Here's one a New York reader heard from her eighth-grade general science teacher when he was demonstrating the properties of liquid nitrogen:

> You must be very careful with this stuff, because terrible things have happened to careless students and teachers. For example, one teacher was holding an object in his left hand while pouring liquid nitrogen onto it with his right.
>
> Some of the liquid splashed onto his left thumb, freezing it instantly.
>
> Instinctively, he shook his hand in pain, and his thumb flew off and slid across the table like an ice cube.

When I repeated that story to students in one of my folklore classes, three of them recited variations: The thumb had shattered. The teacher lost a whole hand. The flying frozen digit struck a student, causing frostbite.

Steve Seidman of Ithaca, New York, in 1990 sent me some further Chem lab "sodium stories" that fit in nicely here. Pure metallic sodium is highly active chemically and must be handled with care and stored submerged in oil. In high school, Seidman heard of a student who, despite the teacher's warning, secretly cut a small chunk from the sodium block in the chemistry lab and stuck it in his pocket. Later, moisture from the student's perspiration ignited the sodium and set his pants on fire. Another story claimed that a janitor accidentally disposed of some sodium by putting it down a drain. When it hit the water in the pipes, sparks flew from the drain in another classroom, temporarily blinding several students.

Most such accident stories, though grounded in fact, seem to drift slightly beyond the plausible. The following tale, sent in 1990 by Nick Wolf of Columbus, Ohio, drifts further than most:

> A coworker was told by a friend that employees of a chemical plant in Charleston, West Virginia, are equipped with long knives.
>
> The reason is that in the event another worker exposes an arm or a leg to the nerve gas manufactured there, a fellow employee can chop off the exposed limb before death occurs.

What a lot to expect from a factory worker—to perform neat surgery under pressure, while risking infection from the same gas!

Finally, here's another accident story about reacting to pressure, but with a happier result. I got this one in a letter from Robert M. Ryan, who said the story was going around among undergraduates at the Massachusetts Institute of Technology in the 1950s. It concerns final examinations at MIT, which Ryan described as being "three-hour, red hot, hellers." The fourth-floor room in which the exam was being held on a June afternoon was also super hot. As the instructor went down the rows passing out exam papers, there was much muttering, moaning, and groaning from the students. Then one student walked to a window and started to open it to let more air in the room.

Misunderstanding the student's intent, the instructor ran towards him shouting, "No! Don't Jump! Don't Jump!" With that, the whole class collapsed in laughter, and the tension was relieved.

That's something like the top blowing off a pressure cooker, or like steam escaping from a safety valve. And, as Robert Ryan concluded his story, "If this didn't happen, it should have."

Accidents *do* happen, as the proverb states, and people are bound to talk about accidents they have suffered, witnessed, or even just heard or read about. What converts the accounts of plausible, if unverified, accidents into genuine urban legends is the process of repeated transmission. By this means the stories become pointed and more ironic, sometimes laughable but with a tinge of horror, and—above all—they become irresistible to repeat and repeat and repeat. . . .

Murphy's Laws

If anything can go wrong, it will.
Nothing is as simple as it seems.
Everything always costs more money than you have.
Everything takes longer than you expect.
If you fool around with something long enough, it will eventually break.
If you try to please everybody, somebody is not going to like it.
It is a fundamental law of nature that nothing ever quite works out.
Whatever you want to do, you have to do something else first.
It's easier to get into a thing than to get out of it.
If you explain something so clearly that no one can misunderstand, someone will.

O'Toole's Commentary on Murphy's Laws

Murphy was an optimist.

"Give Me a High Three"

I heard my father tell this story when I was a little girl, and I believed it until last summer when I told it at a party and a man told me that it had been floating around for years. Have you heard it?

A man is working at a factory. His job is to feed something into a machine that has a big part that stamps down on it. (I know that this sounds fuzzy, but I first heard it when I was about five and the technical details were lost on me.)

He is careless, and he gets his thumb caught in the machine; it stamps down and smashes his thumb off. He goes into shock and just stands there, dazed. The foreman comes over to see what's wrong, and when he sees that the man is bleeding, and his thumb is gone, says, "My God! How did that happen?!"

The man says, "Just like this!" and he shoves his other hand into the machinery and loses the other thumb.

In a letter from Karen Urbanowski of Rossford, Ohio, sent to me in March 1989. This story has been told since at least the turn of the century, usually with reference to pieces of farm machinery or to sawmills. Sometimes it was toes that were lost. Often the older story involved an ethnic stereotype, with the Norwegian or Swedish or Italian or Irish victim exclaiming, as he loses a second digit, something like "Voops! Dere goes anudder vun!" Later the legend migrated to assembly plants and other factories, where it continues to be told as a "true" story. In modern versions, often the workman is asked by an attractive woman touring the plant how he lost a finger; he demonstrates with a gesture . . . and loses another one.

"The Lawn Mower Accident"

Several years ago, when I took a lawn mower in for repairs, just to make conversation I asked the shopkeeper what was the worst mower accident he had run into. Well, he said, this didn't happen to anyone he knew personally, but he had heard of a mower accident in which sixteen fingers were cut off the hands of two men who were holding a power mower over a hedge to trim the top of the hedge. It didn't get their thumbs because they were outside the blade area. Let's hope all those fingers were put back on the right owners!

From a 1982 letter sent to folklorist Ernest Baughman, professor emeritus at the University of New Mexico. Baughman, a specialist in Anglo-American folk narratives, published some of the pioneering work on urban legends in the 1940s and '50s; he died in 1990. Usually just one man lifts the mower and loses the tips of four fingers; then he makes an insurance claim against the manufacturer for failing to warn users of the potential harm when lifting the mower. In September 1977 several insurance-company ads running in national publications claimed that "The Lawn Mower Accident" was true and that the suit had actually been filed. But an article in the October 31, 1977, issue of the trade journal Advertising Age *called it instead, "The case of the missing case." The article traced the story to an insurance executive who said he read a newspaper account of the accident in either late 1975 or early '76. He repeated the story to business and political acquaintances, and they in turn repeated it to others, varying the details as they did so. Neither the original news story nor records of any such court case were found. In a 1986 article in* Consumer Reports *titled "The Manufactured Crisis," the story of the lawn mower used to trim fingers as well as hedges was called one of the "favorite horror stories" among insurers. The article concluded, "The tale has been repeated dozens of times in support of the notion that consumers injure themselves foolishly and then seek out greedy lawyers to bring groundless lawsuits. But the story was purely apocryphal." An editorial in the November 1989 issue of the trade journal* Machine Design *repeated "The Lawn Mower Accident" once again, but a letter to the editor published in the January 11, 1990, issue stated, "A friend contacted all U.S. manufacturers of lawn mowers and many insurance companies. They had all heard of the case, but none had been involved." Legal scholar Anita Johnson had debunked the same story back in 1978, in the journal* Forum, *in an article titled "Behind the Hype on Product Liability."*

"The Ski Accident"

March 11, 1987
The Grapevine

Grapevine hears it all, as evidenced by this story about a few couples from DeKalb who were skiing recently in Colorado. While on the slopes, one of the ladies had to use the facilities. There weren't any close by, so she tried the woods. Unfortunately for her, she had her skis on and, as a result, began to slide down the hill with her pants down. Even more unfortunately, she crashed and was slightly injured. At the ski patrol station where she was getting medical attention for bruised ribs, she began to talk to a male skier who had just been brought in on a stretcher with a leg injury. When she inquired about his mishap, he told her that he had fallen out of a chair lift while watching some crazy woman skiing down the mountain with no pants on. Fortunately, he did not recognize our heroine with her clothes in place. She swore her friends to utmost secrecy about this embarrassing incident, and of course, they honored her request. Right!

April 8, 1987
The Grapevine

In the "grape on our face" department, *The MidWeek* joins the ranks of the *Akron (Ohio) Beacon Journal*, the *Atlantic [sic] Constitution*, the *Montreal Gazette* and the Swedish newspaper *Sundsvalls Tidning* in being duped by the ski accident story. Like our notable counterparts, we were convinced our story in last month's Grapevine was true. We heard it from several unrelated sources, and although names were never attached, it seemed too

Olle Johanssen

funny to ignore. But thanks to an astute and obviously well-read reader, we discovered that the story is part of urban America's folklore as detailed in the book *The Mexican Pet* by Jan Brunvand (W. W. Norton & Co., 1986), which is available at the DeKalb Public Library. Brunvand said he first heard "this hilarious accident legend" in 1979–80 in connection with a Utah ski resort and later uncovered similar versions retold in newspapers and by word-of-mouth world-wide. The book jacket says Brunvand is one of America's leading folklorists who has written four books on the subject. We'll make sure he knows the legend made it to DeKalb too, so he can include our name in his next book.

Sent to me by Sharon Emanuelson, editor of the MidWeek *of DeKalb, Iowa. "The Ski Accident" first got into print in 1982 and has been revived annually during the ski season. It's a favorite story used to introduce speakers or warm up audiences at banquets, especially those held at or near ski resorts. Kent Ward, columnist for the* Bangor (Maine) Daily News, *was one of the first to publish the story—on February 13, 1982—and, after numerous requests, he yielded to "droves of discriminating readers" and reprinted it in his column of February 8, 1992. Often the male victim is a ski instructor or patroller, and sometimes the two skiers meet in the bar, both hobbling on crutches or swathed in bandages. The story was told in New Zealand ski resorts as long ago as 1985, and on July 4, 1992, it was reported in the English journal the* Spectator *as the adventure of a British skier in Switzerland, but on August 29 the letters column identified it as an urban legend and "too good to be true."*

"The Barrel of Bricks"

I am writing in response to your request for additional information. In block number 3 of the accident reporting form, I put "Trying to do the job alone," as the cause of my accident. You said in your letter that I should explain more fully, and I trust that the following details will be sufficient.

I am a brick layer by trade. On the date of the accident, I was working alone on the roof of a new six story building. When I completed my work,

I discovered that I had about 500 pounds of brick left over. Rather than carry the bricks down by hand, I decided to lower them in a barrel by using a pulley which fortunately was attached to the side of the building, at the sixth floor.

Securing the rope at ground level, I went up to the roof, swung the barrel out, and loaded the brick into it. Then I went back to the ground and untied the rope, holding it tightly to insure the slow descent of the 500 pounds of brick. You will note in block number eleven of the accident report form that I weigh 135 pounds.

Due to my surprise to being jerked off the ground so suddenly I lost my pressence of mind and forgot to let go of the rope. Needless to say, I proceeded at a rather rapid rate up the side of the building.

In the vicinity of the third floor, I met the barrel coming down. This explains the fractured skull and broken collarbone.

Slowed only slightly, I continued my rapid ascent, not stopping until the fingers of my right hand were two-knuckles deep into the pulley.

Fortunately, by this time I had regained my pressence of mind and was able to hold tightly to the rope in spite of my pain.

At approximately the same time, however, the barrel of bricks hit the ground and the bottom fell out of the barrel. Devoid of the weight of the bricks, the barrel now weighs approximately fifty pounds.

I refer you again to my weight in block eleven. As you might imagine, I began a rapid descent down the side of the building.

In the vicinity of the third floor, I met the barrel coming up. This accounts for the two fractured ankles and the lacerations of my legs and lower body. The encounter with the barrel slowed me enough to lesson my injuries when I fell onto the pile of bricks and fortunately, only three vertebrae were cracked. I am sorry to report, however, that as I lay there on the bricks—in pain—unable to stand, and watching the empty barrel swinging six stories above me—I again lost pressence of mind—and—let go of the rope. The empty barrel weighted more than the rope so it came back down on me and broke my legs. I hope I have furnished this information you require as how the accident occurred.

Quoted verbatim from a faded, undated sheet produced on a dot-matrix printer and distributed in a San Antonio, Texas, insurance company. "The Barrel of Bricks"—one of the most-often reproduced pieces of typescript lore—has also been presented as a stage monologue and an oral announcement, in song and poetic form, as a cartoon, and in countless handwritten and printed copies distributed in person, on bulletin boards, via fax, and as E-mail. Some versions are organized with numbered points as a formal memo or report and may conclude, "I respectively request sick leave." Besides insurance companies, this item has circulated in the military and in such trades as building construction, oil drilling, manufacturing plants, radio-tower erection, and even among collectors of old glass insulators for telephone poles. The American comedian Fred Allen turned it into a radio skit popular in the 1930s and '40s, while the British humorist Gerard Hoffnung delivered his version from the stage and in recordings during the 1950s. The Down East humorists "Bert and I" recorded it in 1961. In 1966 a version purporting to be from a native workman employed by the U.S. Army in Vietnam was widely published, both in newspapers and in such periodicals as Playboy, Games, *and* National Lampoon. *The song renditions of "The Barrel of Bricks"—titled either "Dear Boss" or "Why Paddy's Not at Work Today"—have been performed and recorded by numerous "folk" and popular singers. A short version of the story in Irish dialect appeared in a 1918 joke book published in Pittsburgh, and some later treatments have preserved the ethnic stereotype; for example, a fake memo from Bethlehem Steel in 1984 gave two participant's names as "Vito Luciano" and "Geovani Spagattini." Cowboy poet Waddie Mitchell's versified version, involving a whiskey barrel full of horseshoes, was published in* Mother Earth News, *January/February 1990. In* Curses! Broiled Again! *I furnish a detailed debunking of a version alleged to have been written by a Jewish Revolutionary War corporal to General Washington in 1776. Perhaps the ancestor of all of these stories is a traditional European folktale in which a wolf and two animals descend or arise from a well in two buckets strung at either end of a long rope hung over a pulley.*

"Up a Tree"

Faustin in waggish mood early in the morning was transformed into Faustin the somber by the evening. He had heard news from the Côte d'Azur, which he told to us with a terrible relish. There had been a forest fire near Grasse, and the Canadair planes had been called out. These operated like pelicans, flying out to sea and scooping up a cargo of water to drop on the flames inland. According to Faustin, one of the planes had scooped up a swimmer and dropped him into the fire, where he had been *carbonisé.*

Curiously, there was no mention of the tragedy in *Le Provençal,* and we asked a friend if he had heard anything about it. He looked at us and shook his head. "It's the old August story," he said. "Every time there's a fire someone starts a rumor like that. Last year they said a water-skier had been picked up. Next year it could be a doorman at the Negresco in Nice. Faustin was pulling your leg."

Reprinted with special permission of King Features Syndicate

From Peter Mayle's popular book A Year in Provence, *published in 1989. A version involving a scuba diver's charred body found in a fire-blackened tree circulated in 1987 and '88 with the locale specified as either the United States or Australia. The legend was suddenly revived in 1996 and discussed in newspapers and on the Internet as an incident that had supposedly occurred recently in Alaska, Oregon, California, or Mexico. An official from Canadair, the company that makes fire-fighting tanker planes, told Don Bishoff, a newspaper columnist in Eugene, Oregon, that this story is "very prevalent in France, Spain, Italy, Greece, even Yugoslavia," all places where Canadair fire-fighting planes have been dispatched. He also assured Bishoff that the water intakes on these planes, as well as on fire-fighting helicopters, are far too small to scoop up a person.*

"The Last Kiss"

This story was told to me when I worked for the Santa Fe railroad in Los Angeles back in the early '70s.

Being "coupled-up" means being caught between the couplers of two freight cars as they come together. This supposedly happened to a young brakeman on the night shift, and he lived for a time after the accident, so his supervisor called his wife, and she came and kissed him one last time as he stood between the two cars.

Then, as the train crew was about to pull the cars apart, the man said, "Wait!" He requested a lantern, and he himself gave the signal to the locomotive engineer to reverse. So the cars separated, and the man toppled over dead. The idea was that, although the couplers had crushed his vital organs, they also held him together long enough for the man to see his wife one last time.

The bit about the lantern is a touch of bravado showing how tough and enduring railroad men can be. It is almost certainly a fictional story since the accident described would be almost instantly fatal. Also, the width of a freight car is such that a person so trapped would have a great deal of difficulty in making his signal visible to an engineer on straight track. (A flat car without a load would be an exception.) But the story was related to me as fact.

Told to me in 1990 by a retired railroad worker. Several other American railroaders sent me the same story, always set on a different line and in another state. In some versions a priest is sent for to administer last rites, and sometimes the dying man dictates his last will and testament to a lawyer. "The Last Kiss" is also told in the military services, usually involving an accident with a heavy vehicle, such as an armored personnel carrier, which overturns; the man stays alive until they turn the vehicle back over again, and sometimes he smokes one last cigarette before dying. As told to U.S. Army troops in Germany in the mid-1980s, a general had a field telephone patched to the civilian telephone system so the man could speak to his wife back in the States one last time. I heard "The Last Kiss" told in New Zealand concerning an accident in a large rock-crushing machine, and in Utah about an accident in a steel-rolling mill. Richard M. Dorson in his 1981 book, Land of the Millrats, *quotes a harrowing account of "The Man Who Was Coupled" from the northern Indiana steel-making district. In this version a telephone is hooked to a radio so the man can call his wife, but the conversation gets picked up by the plant's loudspeakers, and all of the other workers stop work to listen to the tragedy unfold. In his 1991 book,* The Soul of a Cop, *Paul Ragonese, "the most highly decorated police officer in New York City history," gives a firsthand account of an actual "Last Kiss" accident. In September 1982, Ragonese responded to an accident call at the Grand Army Plaza subway station in Park Slope, Brooklyn; a man was squeezed at waist level in the two-inch space between a train car and the platform. While waiting for equipment to extricate him, the police ran a telephone line to the victim, a Vietnam veteran, so he could talk to his wife. He told her that he loved her, did not reveal his predicament, and ended the conversation with "a kissing sound into the phone." Then he smoked a last cigarette. Seconds after the train car was moved, the man died. Another policeman held a body bag below him to catch the lower half of the man's body as it fell.*

"The Death of Little Mikey"

1. Have you ever heard any rumors or stories about the cute little kid named "Mikey" who appeared on the LIFE Cereal commercial?

Yeah, poor kid. I heard he OD'd on them. You see, he was working terribly long hours on those cute little LIFE Cereal commercials. He drank lots of pop to keep awake. He was also snacking on Pop Rocks candy. When the two got together inside his body, they exploded. I hear it killed him.

2. When, where, and from whom did you hear this?

In 1979, I think, at school, from friends. The year may be wrong. The introduction of Pop Rocks to our society was not exactly a major event in my life.

Response of an 18-year-old female student from Michigan in 1982 to a survey about "Little Mikey" and Pop Rocks stories made by student Randall Jacobs of Goshen College, Indiana, for a folklore class taught by Professor Ervin Beck. Pop Rocks, a General Foods fruit-flavored "Action Candy" that effervesced in the mouth with what the company described as "a carbonated fizz," sold in phenomenal quantities after being introduced in

1974. However, rumors that the candies, eaten along with soda pop, had exploded in a child's stomach led the company to take direct action in 1979 to counter the stories. General Foods ran full-page ads in many American newspapers and eventually withdrew the product. The long-running "Little Mikey" television commercials for the Quaker Oats Company's LIFE Cereal first aired in 1971, when actor John Gilchrist, who played Mikey, was just 3 1/2 years old. Gilchrist did not speak in the commercial, but his two brothers—parts played in the commercial by his actual older brothers—offered the cereal to the youngster, saying, "He won't eat it. He hates everything." The key line in the commercial, after Mikey enthusiastically started eating the cereal, was, "Hey Mikey! He likes it!" The Pop Rocks rumor quickly attached itself to the "Mikey" character, although neither company ever mentioned the other in its advertising or press releases. Pop Rocks candy was reintroduced in 1989, but so far no further rumors or legends have sprung from that product.

8

Creepy Contaminations

You've just enjoyed dinner with a friend in a nice restaurant and, after paying the bill, you reach toward the bowl of mints standing on the counter next to the cash register. "Don't eat one of those!" your dining companion gasps. "Don't you know that one of the main ingredients in those mints is *urine?*"

That's certainly enough to stop you in mid-reach; outside the restaurant your friend explains: "They did a study on this and found that 80 percent of men who use the toilet in restaurants don't wash their hands afterwards. So when these men pick up mints, they leave traces of urine on the other mints, and it really adds up after a while." Who's the "they" who studied male hand-washing and mint-grabbing behavior? It's not explained, but the rumor puts you off restaurant mints forever.

This may remind you of the Great Corona Beer Scare of 1987. That was the year that the bright yellow Mexican-import brew sold in the clear bottle was rumored to be contaminated with urine by disgruntled, underpaid brewery workers. It was also the year that Corona was peaking as a fashionable brew. Bummer. But again, who was the "they" who had discovered this terrible trade secret, and where was the scientific report to back the rumors of anything from 2 to 22 percent urine per batch?

Helping to debunk the story was Fredrick Koenig, a professor of social psychology at Tulane University, who while attending an August 1987 convention in Chicago was cornered by reporters. Koenig, author of the 1985 book *Rumor in the Marketplace,* had his picture taken by the *Chicago Sun-Times* while sipping a Corona beer and explaining the genesis and growth of such unsavory canards as this. In essence, his advice to companies plagued by rumors was first to try waiting them out, since few people believe such stories anyway, and rumors typically are short-lived. But if a story persists, and a company wants to go public, Koenig advised never to repeat the specific terms of the rumor, but instead to stress the positive facts that oppose it. In this instance, it was the documented health and cleanliness standards of Corona breweries that combatted the rumor. In truth, as another newspaper reported the story, these rumors were completely unfounded; thus, if you are a beer drinker, "urine no danger." (That was the newspaper's pun, not mine.)

The Corona rumor behaved just like the textbooks said it should: the story was dead by the end of the year, and it developed just a few variable details, such as that the company had been unmasked on TV's *60 Minutes* (or 20/20), and that the label contained a confession of the pee-factor, but written in Spanish. Not true, as numerous published reports in 1987 asserted. You heard it here last.

The biggest companies are often the specific targets of contamination rumors and legends, and, although their business may slump for a time, they can usually withstand the whispered assault. McDonald's, for example, lived through the false stories during the late 1970s of worms, kangaroo meat, or cancerous cows supposedly being ground up for Big Macs. Smaller companies, like the makers of various soda drinks, including Mistic, Tropical Fantasy, A-Treat, and Top Pop, suffered a much higher percentage of loss, and some were even forced out of business. These particular victims of 1990s rumors were said to have included a secret ingredient that rendered black males sterile, a story that also fastened itself onto Church's Chicken.

Speaking of chicken tales, here's a particularly vivid creepy contamination story from the letters column of the September/October issue of *Spy* magazine:

> I decided never again to dine on poultry after I heard a strange story in Chicago last weekend.
>
> A young woman ordered a broiled chicken sandwich from a fast-food joint, sans the mayo. Driving along in her car she took a bite out of the sandwich, only to discover that they had included the mayo after all. A dedicated dieter, she immediately threw the sandwich back in the bag and continued to drive.
>
> Later that evening, she checked herself into a local hospital, violently ill with food poisoning. Examination of the broiler found that the chicken contained a tumor and that the substance she mistook for mayonnaise was actually pus from the tumor.

I love that story! Not only does it echo features of "The Kentucky Fried Rat" (see below), but it manages to revive a detail of the famous "Tumor in the Whale" legends of wartime Britain. And *Spy* got it just right in its reply:

> First of all, congratulations on the most disgusting letter of the month. But, come on! That's an urban legend if we ever heard one. Isn't it?

I found a suspicious contamination story in another published letter, this time written to the Lands' End company by a reader from Palos Hills, Illinois, and printed in the 1988 Christmas catalog:

> Last summer I was visiting some relatives when I accepted an invitation to ride on a combine which was harvesting wheat. Somewhere in the field I lost my Lands' End mesh knit shirt. (Unknown to me at the time, it had been picked by the combine.)
>
> Six months later, I purchased a loaf of bread at a Chicago area supermarket. Imagine my surprise when I found my undamaged shirt in the loaf of bread! The rugged mesh knit had survived the searing heat of the oven and the razor-sharp blades of the automatic slicer.
>
> I am convinced your knit shirts are perfect for a weekend trip to the farm or for loafing around Chicago.

Although this story sounds like a tall tale, complete with a punning punch line, it actually borrows from a contamination legend. The item usually found inside a loaf of bread in legends is a rodent. Folklorists call this story "The Rat in the Rye Bread."

Of course, mice and other vermin *do* get into food, even in the best-regulated kitchens. It's the reality of the situation that makes the folklorized legends so believable. (Ironically, I interrupted the writing of this very chapter to set traps to catch a persistent mouse in our kitchen. Turned out to be *mice,* and we got several!) Nebraska folklorist Roger Welsch, writing about pioneer foodways, described the strategy used by one Plains housewife who found a mouse in her butter churn. Wishing to serve her family "unmoused" butter, she offered to trade her own butter at a local grocery store for someone else's. "The grocer agreed," Welsch wrote, then he "took her butter to the back room, trimmed it, stamped it with his mark, took it back out to the counter, and gave it back to the woman as her trade."

"Moused" food also shows up as a traditional prank. A review in the June 30, 1986, issue of *Time* of a biography of George Herriman (1881–1944), creator of the "Krazy Kat" comic strip that ran from 1913 to 1944, contains this detail:

> [Herriman] had two early loves: language and practical jokes. The verbal agility could be practiced alone; the gags needed victims. After George had salted the doughnuts in his father's Los Angeles bakery and then buried a dead mouse in a loaf of bread, he was informed that if he sought a career away from home, no one would stand in his way.

Not all contaminants are rodents, nor are all contaminees food items. The stories in this chapter provide a nice tasty selection of all kinds of creepy contamination legends. *Bon appétit!*

"Fingered by a Dry Cleaner"

A man eating in a Chinese restaurant bit into something too hard to chew or swallow. Rather than causing a scene, he held a napkin to his mouth, removed the offending morsel, wrapped it in the napkin, and put it into his jacket pocket.

After dinner the tough morsel was forgotten, until one afternoon when the man heard a knock at his front door. It was his friendly neighborhood cleaner, accompanied by two police officers. "That's him," declared the cleaner.

The policemen produced the jacket and asked the man to identify it. He easily did so, and asked, "What's wrong, officer?"

One of the police officers showed him an evidence bag in which was the shriveled first two joints of a forefinger. It had been found wrapped in a napkin in the man's pocket.

"Where's the rest of the body?" demanded the police, and the man told them where to look.

The good news was that a cook at the restaurant had lost only a finger. The bad news was that a pathologist's report had already found the finger to be leprous.

"The Kentucky Fried Rat"

Is there any truth to this story? I heard it in California in 1970 from a friend's mother, who claims she knew the people it happened to.

A couple went to the drive-in movies and took a bucket of Kentucky Fried Chicken with them. During the movie, they ate the chicken and the girl complained that it tasted funny. Finally, her boyfriend turned on the light in the car and saw that she was eating a fried rat which apparently had gotten into the chicken and was cooked along with it.

There was a wife who didn't have anything ready for supper for her husband. So she quick got a basket of chicken and tried to make her dinner look fancy with the preprepared chicken. Thus, she fixed a candlelight dinner, etc. When her and her husband started eating the chicken, they thought it tasted funny. Soon to find out it was a fried rat.

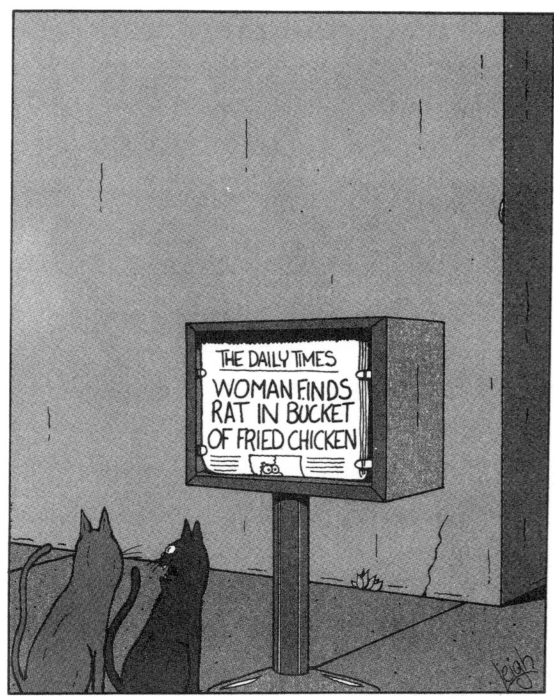

"Why is it that some people have all the luck?"

By permission of Leigh Rubin and Creators Syndicate

My sister told me that her friend told her that a lady went to Kentucky Fried Chicken. She was out in the car eating it and noticed that one of the pieces tasted funny. She looked and it had a tail. Then she looked again and saw it had eyes and was a rat. She threw up and went crazy and is in the State [Mental] Hospital in Kalamazoo. She won't eat any food.

The first story comes from a reader's query. The second and third are from Gary Alan Fine's chapter "The Kentucky Fried Rat: Legends and Modern Society" in his 1992 book, Manufacturing Tales. *Fine's first version came from a Central Michigan University female, age 24, in 1976; his second from a University of Minnesota female, age 19, in 1977. These variants illustrate the flexible nature of the* legend, *as opposed to the many* lawsuits *based on actual rodents or rodent parts served in food. The legends are anonymous—though sometimes specific as to locale—attributed to a FOAF, short, pointed, and ironic; they often suggest an obvious message like "Always check before you bite," or "Serves her right for not making supper herself!" It's also notable that the woman in the legends most often gets the batter-fried rat, and that low light is a prerequisite of her dreadful error. The lawsuits, in contrast, as reported in official court proceedings, contain lengthy detailed accounts of specific incidents that are documented by eyewitnesses or even with a sample of the contaminated food. Rodent/food lawsuits have been brought against a great variety of eating establishments, but seldom, if ever, are the tellers of the legends drawing from any personal experience, or even from direct knowledge of a lawsuit. In recent years, when Kentucky Fried Chicken outlets were opened in Australia and New Zealand, a local variation of the story developed. A man came into a takeout franchise and slung a dead possum onto the counter. In front of a group of horrified customers, he announced, "That's the last one I'm going to bring you until you pay me for all the others I brought in!"*

"The Mouse in the Coke"

Waiter, there's a mouse in my Coke!

Have you heard about the guy who found the dead mouse in his Coke? It's time to set the record straight about this piece of Cokelore.

Many people have read or heard presumably reliable accounts of a mouse that was inadvertently sealed in a bottle of you-know-what. And they wonder: Did a cola-loving customer really tip back a frosty bottle only to discover the little rodent on the bottom—after he'd drained the bottle? And did the victim—sick from the shock, and haunted for life by a fear of cola—really sue the bottler and win hundreds of thousands of dollars in damages?

R. H. of Milwaukee wrote to me recently demanding an explanation for the account of the legend in one of my books. "One of your so-called urban legends isn't," R. H. said, in the debunking spirit of a true folklore aficionado. "It's an actual event or really several—as shown even in courts of law."

"Your column has too light a tone," Mr. H. went on, "leading the reader to believe that you don't take any story seriously."

I plead guilty to taking most of the wild stories I hear with a grain of salt, R. H. I'm in the wild story business, so it's my job to doubt. Beyond that, though, I plead innocent to all charges. First of all, yes, I do know about the lawsuits involving mice in Cokes. There are cases and cases of this stuff—and I don't mean cases of Coke bottles full of mice, but cases brought before courts of law.

In fact, much of my mail asking about bottled mice comes from lawyers or law students who remember studying the suit brought by Ella Reid Creech of Shelbyville, Kentucky, against a Coca-Cola bottler (1931), or Patargias vs. Coca-Cola Bottling Co. of Chicago (1943), or the 1971 case in which 76-year-old George Petalas was awarded $20,000 in a suit against an Alexandria, Virginia, bottler.

Petalas, the *Washington Post* reported, found the legs and tail of a mouse in a bottle of Coke he bought from a vending machine outside a Safeway store. He was hospitalized for three days, and afterward, no longer liking meat, lived on a diet of "grilled cheese, toast and noodles."

A search of published appeals-court records made in 1976 turned up forty-five such cases, the first in 1914. One can only guess how many similar cases were never appealed or were settled out of court.

Most of the people who tell the mouse-in-Coke legend don't know the legal history, though. What they do know is a good story, whether it's told by a friend, neighbor or coworker. The tellers assume that somewhere, sometime, an actual lawsuit was brought against a soft-drink bottling company.

So while the lawsuits are real, the oral stories are not, because they are so far separated from the original facts that they've turned into folklore. In this way, a story can be both an actual event and a legend. And the mouse-in-Coke legends, like most urban legends, have lives of their own completely separate from the facts.

What has occurred, I believe, is something like this: The theme of foreign matter contaminating food is a popular one in urban legends. And "Coke" has become virtually a generic way to refer to soft drinks. So the legends get started, and gain credibility from lawsuits that people vaguely remember in which mice were said to be found in soda bottles. And naturally, it is usually Coke that is mentioned in the legend—whether or not the original suits were against Coke.

As the legend spreads by word of mouth, the trauma is exaggerated, the drama heightened, and the size of the settlement grows. The end result is that indignation against the giant corporation that is selling contaminated food is pumped up to a full measure of outrage.

Adapted from my newspaper column for release the week of April 11, 1988. Since then numerous further lawsuits involving mice (or other foreign matter) found in soft-drink bottles (or other food containers) have been reported. Some of the incidents proved to be hoaxes, suggesting that some people are either acting out a story they've heard, or trying to repeat the success of a lawsuit they've read about. The problem of mice contaminating food is universal and age-old. In William R. Cook and Ronald B. Herzman's book The Medieval World View *(1983), an Irish monastery's rules for dealing with the situation are quoted: "He who gives to anyone a liquor in which a mouse or a weasel is found dead shall do penance with three special fasts. . . . He who afterwards knows that he has tasted such a drink shall keep a special fast." The Irish monks also received specific advice about how to handle "moused" food: "If those little beasts are found in the flour or in any dry food or in porridge or in curdled milk, whatever is around their bodies shall be cast out, and all the rest shall be taken in good faith." In other words, "Just eat around it, brothers."*

"Alligators in the Sewers"

FLUSHING A PIPE DREAM

GATORS IN NEW YORK SEWERS? IT'S A CROC

New York—like Capt. Hook in "Peter Pan," John T. Flaherty is dogged by crocodiles and, in addition, alligators. Flaherty is chief of design in the New York City Bureau of Sewers, but he is also the resident expert on the most durable urban myth in the history of cities, of reptiles, or of waste disposal.

"Dear Sirs," writes a correspondent from Stockholm, where sewers are called cloaks, "I take the liberty to write to you, since I from many sources have been informed that, for many years, a substantial number of krokodiles have found themselves a suitable athmosphere of living in the cloak tunnels of New York."

"Dear persons," begins a letter from a high school student in Wilkesboro, N.C. "Recently I have become very interested in a very uncommon subject, 'Alligator population in the New York City water system.' "

And a man from Celoron, N.Y., writes: "I disagree with a co-worker whom insists that an alligator which had lived in a sewer system over a long period of time does not change color. I said I believe the pigmentation of the alligator would become much lighter and in some cases turn almost white."

Flaherty, a good-humored man with an alligator cigarette lighter on his desk, must reply to all these, "No, Virginia, there are no alligators in the New York City sewer system."

In the "sewer game," as Flaherty calls it, which is not a glamor business, this has made John T. Flaherty something of a celebrity. There is even a makeshift star on his door and a mock-up of a *Variety* headline that reads, "Flaherty says new alligator in sewer movie is a flimflam and is nothing but a croc."

Alligators are a small part of Flaherty's business. His office is filled with blueprints, and his mind is filled with budget estimates for capital expenditures or expenses. There are 6,500 miles of sewer lines in New York City, ranging from 6-inch pipes to monster sewers as big as a small band shell, from brick sewers circa 1840 to concrete structures under construction; these are Flaherty's daily concern.

"Like so many New Yorkers, I've lived here all my life and never been to the top of the Empire State Building."

He has worked as an engineer in this business for almost 30 years, and he has no disdain for it. Touring an underground chamber of brick and concrete in Brooklyn, damp and noisy with running water, he said, "A well-functioning sewer is a rather pleasant atmosphere—nice and cool in summertime, warm in the wintertime." It seems just the place for an alligator, but it is not.

Alligators have become Flaherty's sideline, and he handles them with flair. The myth is that travelers to Florida adopted the baby reptiles, tired of them and flushed them down the toilet and into the city sewer system, where they grew to immense size.

Perhaps a half-dozen people write to the city every year asking for particulars; once they got a very formal reply, but now they get Flaherty, who uses this opportunity to give vent to his creative impulses.

To a woman from Denver, who asked if it were true that sewer workers carried guns in case of alligator attack: "As the resident expert on all matters relative to subterranean saurians, I can state with authority that there ain't no such animal. Rumors! How do they start? It is ironic for instance, that you should write of sewer maintenance personnel here in New York carrying .38s to protect themselves from the ravages of rapacious reptiles. Did you know that there are many New Yorkers who believe that all residents of Denver carry .38s at all times?"

To the man from Stockholm, confirming that alligators have been adopted as pets: "I myself was bitten on the little finger of my right hand by one some 25 years ago in the stacks of the New York Public Library building. Please be reassured that the injury I suffered was quite minor, as the alligator in question was quite a little chap whose dentition was of the puniest."

And to the man from Celoron, who thought alligators would pale below ground: "I could cite you many cogent logical reasons why the sewer system is not a fit habitat for an alligator, but suffice it to say that, in the 28 years I have been in the sewer game, neither I nor any of the thousands of men who have worked to build, maintain or repair the sewer system have ever seen one, and a 10-foot, 800-pound alligator would be hard to miss. Of course, following the thought that you advance in your letter to its ultimate conclusion, perhaps the pigmentation effect has been so radical that they have been rendered invisible."

Flaherty says there are things living in the sewers, most of them rats. There are also insects and some stray fish; there once was a duck that got stuck in a pipe and flapped about wildly until it found a way out. There have been some bodies and a few gangs that have set up subterranean sewer clubhouses.

There are, however, no alligators because, Flaherty says, there is not enough space, there is not enough food—"the vast majority of it has been, to put it as delicately as possible, pre-digested"—and the torrents of water that run through the sewers during a heavy rain would drown even an alligator.

Article by Anna Quindlen, New York Times, *May 19, 1982; except for the misnomer "urban myth," this is an excellent account of the spread of and the response to what is probably the best-known American urban legend. There are, oddly enough, numerous verified published reports of alligators found in unlikely habitats, including some sewers, and even including a story in the* New York Times *of February 10, 1935, describing an alligator pulled from a sewer on East 123rd Street. None of these reports, however, men-*

tions the folk idea of baby pet alligators flushed down toilets. Robert Daley's 1959 book The World Beneath the City *includes an interview with one Teddy May, said to have been a New York City sewer commissioner during the 1930s. May claimed that alligators up to two feet long inhabited the sewers until 1937, when he had them eradicated. When I queried John T. Flaherty about this, he replied in his trademark cheerful style, "Yes, Professor, there really was a Teddy May . . . almost as much of a legend as the New York City Sewer Alligator [*Alligator cloaca novum eboracum*] itself. . . . [He] was a sewer worker who, in the fullness of time, rose to become a Foreman or, perhaps, a District Foreman. . . . From what I can gather, Teddy was a very outgoing, ebullient man with a wide circle of friends and an even wider circle of admiring acquaintances. Part of his charm was his undoubted abilities as a raconteur and a spinner of yarns." The "Alligators in the Sewers" legend has been celebrated in cartoons, comic books, children's books, art, literature, and films—including* Alligator, *the 1980 movie alluded to in Quindlen's article. The New York City Department of Environmental Protection, under which the Bureau of Sewers operates, markets T-shirts and sweatshirts picturing an alligator sporting a pair of fancy sunglasses crawling out from under a manhole cover marked "NYC Sewers" and with the caption "The Legend Lives." In 1993 sculptor Anne Veraldi installed 15 gators made of tiles in a subway station as part of the Metropolitan Transportation Authority's Creative Stations program. A possible nineteenth-century English prototype for the legend is reported in Thomas Boyle's 1989 book* Black Swine in the Sewers of Hampstead. *The title says it all.*

"The Snake in the Store"

March 31, 1987

RUG SHOPPER AMBUSHED BY DEADLY COBRA

Unsuspecting Louise Park was rummaging through a pile of expensive rugs at a ritzy furniture store when she was attacked—by a deadly cobra.

Louise, 24, was rushed to a London, England, hospital after the enraged reptile sank its fangs into her arm. She was released after several days of painful treatment.

Store manager David Ross said the critter must have stowed away in the rugs when they were shipped from India and Pakistan.

November 17, 1989
The rumor is rampant in Springfield [Illinois] and goes like this.

A woman slips into a coat in a local department store and feels a jab in one arm. She assumes she was stuck by a pin.

Later in the day pain sets in, she detects a redness in her arm and goes to a hospital emergency ward for treatment.

Medics find she was bitten by a snake. Police are sent to the store. A search of the coat inventory turns up a snake in a sleeve lining.

Turns out the coat is a foreign product and it's an exotic snake that slipped into, or was slipped into, the shipment before it left the Orient.

The snakebite victim, depending on which version of the story you've heard, was either released after treatment or remains in the hospital in a coma.

No such snake, says the manager of the department store in question. Hospital spokesmen say they have had no such patients. They've all heard the story, too, and say it's a hoax.

April 7, 1991
An Omaha woman trying on a fur coat at a local store is supposedly bitten by a poisonous snake. It seems, the tale goes, that the coat had been imported after a snake had laid eggs in the fur. The eggs hatched, and the coat became infested with young snakes. . . . The story is bunk, bosh, hot air, hooey and baloney.

September 17, 1994
Brick Township [New Jersey]: Police and the management at a local clothing store say a rumor making the rounds about a female customer being bitten by a snake is unfounded.

"We've been getting calls about this every day, but it's nonsense," Georgine Wilson, assistant manager of the Burlington Coat Factory store on Brick Boulevard, said yesterday. "I have no idea how this got started."

According to the rumor, an elderly woman shopping at the store shortly before Labor Day reached into a coat and was bitten. When workers examined the coat, which purportedly came from Mexico, they found a snake in the lining.

A spokesman for the township police department said they had checked out the report and determined it to be unfounded.

"If that had happened, one of my managers would have told me about it, and I haven't heard anything. Maybe it was a competitor jealous about how well we're doing here, I don't know," Wilson said. "But you know a lawyer would have contacted us by now if it were true."

From, respectively, Weekly World News, *the* Springfield State Journal-Register, *the* Omaha Herald, *and the* Asbury Park Press. *Typically, the tabloid press furnishes the characters in the traditional legend with names and ages, making the item sound more like legitimate news. I was dead wrong in my 1981 book* The Vanishing Hitchhiker *in suggesting that this extremely popular legend of the late 1960s had mostly faded away by 1970; in fact, it has never stopped circulating, right up to the present. Often the alleged incident is said to have happened in a discount store: the Kmart chain was mentioned so often in the 1980s that the company maintained at its Troy, Michigan, headquarters a "snake file" containing hundreds of inquiries. Often the contaminated item is a blanket, sometimes an electric blanket; in these versions, the woman feels a prick and assumes it is a loose wire. She plugs in the blanket anyway, and the warmth causes snake eggs to hatch. Invariably, if an origin is mentioned, the snake is said to have come in on imported goods. This suggested to some during the late 1960s that perhaps the snakebite symbolized an unconscious national guilt complex about the U.S. involvement in Southeast Asia. Certainly some distrust of foreign and bargain goods, as well as fear of snakes, is reflected in the legend. Other urban legends about snakes are included in Chapter 17.*

"A Bug in the Ear"

EARWIG ALERT

The Department of Health has brought to our attention the growing infestation of earwigs in Northern Illinois. The earwig is a small insect with forceps-like antennae, short forewings, many-jointed feelers, and pincer-like "beaks" at the end of the tail. Because of the mild days in January, the reproductive instincts of these insidious carnivores were triggered. Unfortunately, many of our children who were out in that relatively warm January weather, playing on the grass, may presently be host to this ravenous parasite.

These insects attach themselves to hair, clothes, and/or skin, and under the cover of darkness wend their way to the ear canal, burrowing then through the middle and inner ear and on into the brain. Upon reaching the brain, the earwig first severs the cranial nerves, which serves as both a blessing and a curse to the victim. Whereas the victim suffers no pain hereafter, neither is he or she immediately aware of the progressive degeneration of cerebral tissue, although it is often suspected by acquaintances. Both female and male earwigs require a human host in order to reproduce the species.

During the course of several days, the female earwig carves a catacomb-like network of tunnels through the temporal and frontal lobes of the brain, implanting numerous eggs in the soft, moist recesses of brain tissue. The female emerges in the sinus cavity, where, having deposited her eggs, she expires. She often is passed out of the body as a dark mass when the victim unexpectedly sneezes. The eggs of the female earwig begin to hatch after three or four days of incubation. These hatchlings, which are sometimes called "wiglets" or "letties" for short, or "lettes" for shorter, will hereafter be referred to as larvalettes. Immediately after emerging from their pupal sacs, each larvalette burrows backwards, using its pincer-like tail to shred brain tissue, passing the torn flesh to the mouth with its many-jointed feelers, whereupon it is ingested. This ability to both burrow and feed simultaneously makes it, pound for pound, an eating machine superior to even the Great White Shark.

If a male earwig enters the brain, mental debilitation will also result, but to a lesser degree. The male earwig enters the temporal lobe and moves directly to the posterior scleral membrane (the back of the eye), penetrating the sclera, choroid, and retina, finally entering the vitreous body of the eye. From there the earwig works its way to the aqueous humor between the lens and the corneal membrane. Thereafter, the male earwig leaves the body through the opposite ear; hence the phrase characterizing one who cannot process verbal information: "It goes in one ear and out the other!" Although mental debilitation and sometimes myopia result from the pres-

earwig
WHAT DO YOU THINK THE PROBLEM IS, Doc? WHY DOES MY EAR AND HEAD HURT SO BAD?
HAVE YOU EVER HEARD THE EXPRESSION "TO PUT A BUG IN YOUR EAR"?
NO.
WHAT ARE YOU TRYING TO SAY?
IT'S A SUPERSTITION.
IT COMES FROM THE OLD IDEA THAT EARWIGS CRAWL INTO THE EARS OF SLEEPING PEOPLE TO LISTEN TO THEIR THOUGHTS AND DREAMS.
A LITTLE SUGAR WATER AND TWEEZERS IS ALL YOU NEED.
OW-OOH-OW-OW!
GOT IT.
THIS WAS YOUR PROBLEM RIGHT HERE.
YOU'RE LUCKY YOU CAME TO ME WHEN YOU DID.
THERE'S A SILLY NOTION THAT THE EARWIG LIKES TO MAKE ITS WAY THROUGH THE EAR CANAL TO FEED OFF THE BRAIN AND EVEN LAY EGGS.
CHOMP CHOMP
IS SOMETHING WRONG?
YOU PULLED THE BUG OUT OF MY LEFT EAR.
NOW I HAVE AN EARACHE... IN MY... RIGHT EAR...

ence of the male earwig, the greatest danger has been found to be the trauma resulting in shock, should the victim awaken while the earwig is present in the aqueous humor. In this case, if the victim should open his or her eyes, an image of this hideous, pulsating parasite, magnified one hundred times, will appear. Treatment is usually effective only on larvalettes as once the adult earwig is beyond the middle ear, removal is usually impossible without a frontal lobotomy, which in almost 50% of the cases causes some personality changes. Larvalettes, which pose the greatest threat anyway, can be removed through a technical process in which the suspected victim is administered heavy doses of vitamins with iron. Immediately upon hatching, larvalettes begin eating. As the larvalettes ingest brain tissue, laden with vitamin-induced iron, they are susceptible to removal through the entry point created by the mother, by the application of a strong electromagnetic force (usually a forty pound pull magnet is sufficient, although a ten pound pull magnet applied four times should also be effective). If the victim is wearing braces or has a steel plate in his/her head, an orthodontist or neurosurgeon should be contacted for particulars on the safe removal of the larvalettes.

The most effective preventative measure yet developed requires the careful positioning of a small ball of cotton, which has been soaked for several minutes in blackstrap molasses, in the middle ear whenever one might be exposed to an infested area. In a household where a member has already been stricken by this dread carnivore, all other family members should follow the preventative measures described above before going to bed at night.

NOTE: Nurses checking for earwigs should wear rubber gloves and be sure not to inhale deeply near the ear canal as these insects could be transmitted nasally!!

An anonymous, undated, photocopied sheet sent to me in 1990 by Joyce deVries Kehoe of Seattle. This elaborate joke-memo—which I have shortened in quoting it—must have been composed by someone familiar with earwig folklore, plus having a wild sense of humor and some medical knowledge. The vague references to "Department of Health" and to an actual location are typical of photocopied bogus warnings (see Chapter 20). Earwigs get their names, as any good dictionary will tell you, from the mistaken idea that they particularly attempt to invade the human ear. Earwigs do occasionally get into ears, as numerous readers—some in the medical professions—have informed me after I published accounts of earwig lore. But these creatures, which are neither carnivores nor parasites, despite their name, are no more likely to enter a person's ear than are ants, bees, cockroaches, centipedes, spiders, or any other small creepy crawly bugs. The typical earwig horror tales are that earwigs burrow into the brain and hollow out the head, or that earwigs can eat their way into one ear and come out the other, or that female earwigs lay their eggs in the brain while burrowing through. This memo expands on such themes, and caps them with ludicrous suggestions for treatment and prevention. Ironically, just as the very name "earwig" is derived from the notion that they frequently enter people's ears, the folk beliefs probably continue to circulate largely because of the insect's suggestive name.

"Spiders in the Hairdo"

When I was in high school, the big thing was for girls to tease their hair. Now this looked nice on a lot of kids, but some girls carried it to extremes. They had these huge, bouffant hairdos, and they sprayed them really stiff with as much hair spray as they could get on. We used to wonder if some of these girls ever bothered to wash their hair so they could get all that sticky stuff out. One day we heard about this girl who went to a high school in Evansville who had just died because of teased hair. I think some of the teachers were trying to scare us into not teasing our hair anymore. Anyway, this Evansville girl had had one of these bushy teased hairstyles, and she'd kept lots of spray on it. They said she hadn't washed her hair for three months. One day while she was sitting in class, she just keeled over, and when the teacher went to check on her, she saw blood trickling down her face. When they got her to the hospital, they found that a nest of black widow spiders had made a home in her hair and had finally eaten into her scalp.

Text number 289 in Ronald L. Baker's 1982 book Hoosier Folk Legends, *as told in 1969 by a young woman from Princeton, Indiana. The next three legends in the same source, all from 1968 or '69, describe hairdos similarly infested with cockroaches, ants, or maggots. This legend dates at least from the 1950s, when beehive hairdos became popular; the story lingers on now both in the memories of people who were students in those days or in legends about ethnic minorities, foreigners, or eccentrics of some kind. For example, one hears of "hippies" with insects in their long hair, or that the "dreadlocks" of reggae fans and musicians become infested with maggots. A possible prototype for the modern legend is an account in a thirteenth-century English collection of moral fables in which the Devil in the form of a spider attaches himself to the hair of a woman who is habitually late for Mass because she spends too much time arranging her coiffure.*

"The Spider Bite"

A twenty-year-old woman goes to Florida on vacation. She had a small sore on her face when she left and when she returned it kept getting bigger. When it became the size of a quarter, she went to a doctor who told her it was a boil and she would have to wait it out. Time passes, the bump grows, and is becoming very painful. She goes back to doctor who tells her that he will have to lance it but that he doesn't have time in his schedule that day and that she should return the next day. During the night the pain becomes so intense that the woman wakes up screaming. The facial contortions from the scream make the boil break and out come all these spiders and pus. When the woman realizes what has been on her face, she has a heart attack.

I was told this tale in 1980. The victim was a female relative (I believe an aunt) of a female colleague of my then girlfriend. The unfortunate woman was bitten by an insect while on holiday in Spain. The resulting lump failed to clear up with medical treatment on her return. Eventually it spawned a brood of small spiders and the woman needed psychiatric treatment to recover from the shock.

My daughter came home and related a story her friend had told her. I don't believe it, but she does, because she says her friend wouldn't lie. Here it is.

The friend's sister-in-law noticed a very deep pimple developing on her cheek. After two weeks it finally came to a head, and when she popped it, tiny spiders ran out onto her face. She screamed and fainted. It seems a spider had laid its eggs under her skin two weeks earlier while she had been camping and had been sleeping out on the ground.

Please tell me it's not true.

The first example is from a letter from Donna Schleicher of Madison, Wisconsin, responding to my article in Psychology Today *(June 1980). The second is from a 1983 letter from Philip Tanner of Reading, England. The third version was sent by Christine Ackerson of West Valley City, Utah, in 1992. "The Spider Bite" was first noted in northern Europe—England, Scandinavia, Germany, etc.—in 1980, with the bite always occurring on or near the face during a time when the victim is vacationing in the south—Spain, Italy, or Africa. In many versions, on both sides of the Atlantic, the boil bursts and the spiders emerge while the victim—always a woman—is showering or taking a tub bath. Similar horror legends describe ants, cockroaches, maggots, etc., infesting a person's sinus cavities or the flesh underneath a plaster cast. In most instances, the sufferer is said to have scratched the infested part of her body open with fingernails, a knife, fork, or rock, until the skin is broken and some of the critters come running out. See also the earwig alert above.*

"Spider Eggs in Bubble Yum"

Bubble Yum, the first *soft* bubble gum to come on the market, contains spider eggs; that's the ingredient that makes the gum so soft and easy to chew. A kid one time fell asleep chewing Bubble Yum, and he woke up with his mouth full of spider eggs. Some people also say the gum causes cancer.

This short-lived rumor appeared and faded away in 1977, just at the time when the Life Savers, Inc., product had become a best-selling new gum. In his 1992 book Manufacturing Tales, *Gary Alan Fine quotes a variant from Minnesota that claimed the contaminant was spider* legs. *Beyond this, the claim had few variations and almost no narrative development as a true legend. An article in the* Wall Street Journal *on*

March 24, 1977, detailed the company's problems with the rumor. In response to the stories, Life Savers placed full-page advertisements in the New York Times *and other major newspapers, headlining them "Someone is telling your kids very bad lies about a very good gum." In 1984 satirist Paul Krassner claimed to have invented the Bubble Yum story, as well as the one about worms in McDonald's hamburgers.*

"The Spider in the Cactus"

July 18, 1991
Dear Dr. Brunvand:

I have come across a story that has all the earmarks of an urban legend and thought you might be interested in learning about it.

Last weekend, while visiting my parents in Detroit, my sister, who was also in town from New York, related the following story about her assistant's friend. . . . My sister swears this story is true.

My sister's assistant told her about a female friend who bought a saguaro cactus from an Ikea store in New Jersey. The friend brought the cactus home to her apartment and was very happy with it until one day it started pulsating. She thought this was bizarre behavior for a cactus, so she called several different places to see if "experts" could tell her what was wrong with it. After the public library and a couple of nurseries were unable to help her, she called a botanist at the natural history museum. He told her to immediately take her cactus outside, douse it in gasoline, and set it on fire. My sister's assistant's friend did as she was told, and, much to her horror, after she set the saguaro alight, dozens of burning tarantulas crawled out of the charred wreckage of her cactus.

Somehow, this story seems rather farfetched to me. I was wondering if you had heard anything about lethal cacti in the past.

Sincerely,
Sarah P. Beiting
Kalamazoo, MI

Week of September 23, 1991
Dear Sarah:

Farfetched? How can you say that? A home-size saguaro cactus, a supply of gasoline in the apartment, and a stampede of burning tarantulas . . . It sounds just like a typical day in New York to me. And, of course, the cactus technically wasn't lethal, except to the spiders.

But seriously, folks, we all know this is an urban legend, do we not? In fact, some readers may remember that Kalamazoo is where it all began, at least as far back as my own information on "The Spider in the Cactus" goes.

I'm sure if you ask around in your hometown, Sarah, you'll find someone who remembers the Kalamazoo version of your cactus story. You see, back in 1989 I received my first American report of the story from a man in Kalamazoo who heard that the plant had been purchased locally at an outlet of Frank's Nursery and Crafts.

During the next couple of years many other versions surfaced throughout the United States, some mentioning Frank's, others claiming the cactus had been dug up illegally in the deserts of Mexico or the southwestern United States. Wherever it came from, the wiggling, vibrating, trembling, humming, squeaking, buzzing cactus was usually torched and thus found to be a home for a horde of deadly spiders or scorpions. . . .

Letter from a reader as incorporated into my newspaper column. The prototype for this legend circulated in Europe starting in the early 1970s; a 1990 German collection of urban

legends is titled The Spider in the Yucca Palm. *I give a detailed history of this legend in my 1993 book* The Baby Train, *pp. 278–87, concluding with a brief reference to Ms. Beiting's letter. During the seven years that the story was popular in this country, I received 65 letters, clippings, or other queries about it. The release of the horror film* Arachnophobia *in 1990 may partly explain the interest in "The Spider in the Cactus" that year. The problems that Ikea, the home-furnishings chain, suffered from the legend were mentioned in* Business Week *for February 11, 1991, with the headline "So, Let's Go Hunt Alligators in the Sewers."*

"The Poison Dress"

My cousin's cousin who works in Fine Women's Wear at Neiman Marcus in Beverly Hills told me this "true" story last Thanksgiving. He told me that since Neiman's has a very lenient return policy, many wealthy women put $10,000 dresses on their charge accounts, wear them once, have them dry cleaned, and then return them to the store for a refund.

Someone at the store told him what happened one time because of this practice before he started working there. After a woman returned a very expensive designer dress, another woman bought the same dress, and she later broke out in a horrible rash while wearing it.

She went to a dermatologist who said he had to treat her skin for exposure to formaldehyde, and so she sued Neiman's for the doctor's charge. The store traced the dress to the first woman, who admitted that her mother had wanted to be buried in that dress. But the daughter didn't want to bury such an expensive dress, so she got it back from the mortician after the funeral service and returned it to the store.

The second woman had been exposed to formaldehyde that soaked into the fabric from the corpse.

I thought this was true until my girlfriend told me just the other day that her grandmother wouldn't let her buy dresses from thrift shops because of a woman who had died from formaldehyde in a second-hand dress. So this hot new story turned out to be at least 60 years old!

Sent to me in 1991 by a reader in Los Angeles. "The Poison Dress"—also called "Embalmed Alive" and "Dressed to Kill"—was one of the first American urban legends to come to the attention of folklorists. In the 1940s and '50s several folklore journals described a rash of reports, so to speak, of the story, and some informants remembered hearing it in the 1930s. Often, the woman who "borrows" the dress for a funeral is from an ethnic or racial minority, and she is usually poorer than the woman who sickens and/or dies from wearing the dress the second time. Formaldehyde, which many people encounter only in high school biology classes, is not used for embalming. As for the threat of real embalming fluid, often mentioned in the story, I heard from a Chicago journalist who had asked a mortician about this point in the story. The mortician opened a bottle of the fluid and splashed some over his own face, saying, "Does this answer your question?" The modern legend may derive from older stories about disease-infected blankets or clothing given to native peoples in order to eliminate them. These stories, in turn, may derive from various ancient Greek stories about poisoned or "burning" garments given to someone as an act of revenge. Classical folklorist Adrienne Mayor discusses these background traditions in one article in the Journal of American Folklore *(winter 1995) and another in* Archaeology *(March/April 1997). Bennett Cerf included an embellished version of this legend in his 1944 book* Famous Ghost Stories, *saying that it was a favorite among New York literary circles of the time.*

"The Corpse in the Cask"

Some years ago, the father of a friend of mine bought a fairly enormous house in the middle of Bodmin Moor, a sort of Georgian/Regency house built on the site of an older farmhouse.

In the capacious cellars they found half a dozen very large barrels. "Oh, good!" said the mother. "We can cut them in half and plant orange trees in them."

So they set to work to cut the barrels in half, but they found that one of them was not empty, so they set it up and borrowed the necessary equipment from the local pub. The cellar filled with a rich, heady Jamaican odour.

"Rum, by God!" said the father. It was indeed, so they decided to take advantage of some fifty gallons of the stuff before cutting the barrel in half.

About a year later, after gallons of rum punch, flip and butter had been consumed, it was getting hard to get any more rum out of the barrel, even by tipping it up with wedges. So they cut it in half, and in it found the well-preserved body of a man.

People who died in the colonies and had expressed a wish to be buried at home were shipped back in spirits, which was much more effective than brine.

From Rodney Dale's 1978 book The Tumour in the Whale, *pp. 64–65. Dale characterizes this story as a "Whale Tumour Story," his term for urban legend, despite its being told to him as true by an individual whom he names. Probably it is an English legend derived from the reality that corpses were sometimes shipped home from abroad preserved in barrels of spirits. After Admiral Horatio Nelson fell at the Battle of Trafalgar in 1805, for example, his body was preserved in a barrel of brandy and sent back to England, with the brandy replaced at Gibraltar with wine. According to legend, some of the wine serving as Lord Nelson's impromptu embalming fluid was tapped off by thirsty sailors. A similar legend is told in France regarding a corpse found inside a tank of cheap bulk wine shipped from Algeria to France. Supposedly the body of a man either has a knife in its back or a hangman's noose around its neck. The American equivalent to these stories describes a decomposed body found in a town's water tank when it is opened for cleaning or to clear an obstruction in the outlet pipe.*

"The Accidental Cannibals"

I can't vouch for the authenticity of this story. But Ellis Darley of Cashmere [Washington], retired plant pathologist, says it happened to one of his former colleagues in California.

The colleague, another scientist, grew up in Yugoslavia. During World War II, his Yugoslavian friend experienced severe food shortages, which were alleviated by CARE packages from relatives living in the United States.

The food came in tins. It seems that one package arrived without a label. It was a powder, and the Yugoslavian family assumed it to be a food supplement, which was welcomed at that time.

They tried it out on their meal, found it added some zest to the food, and polished off the whole tin.

It was many weeks later that a letter arrived describing the sending of the package.

The letter said that the Yugoslav's grandmother had died, and that they sent her cremated remains back to her home country in that tin!

Well, she got back home all right.

From the "Talking It Over with Wildred R. Woods" column in the Wenatchee (Washington) World, *August 27, 1987. Variations of this story are known all over Europe, with the "cremains" being mistaken for an instant powdered drink, soup mix, flour, cake mix, or condiment. In 1990 a BBC radio program included a letter from a listener who claimed his family had mistakenly stirred into their Christmas pudding the cremains of a relative shipped back from Australia, eating half of it before receiving a letter of explanation. A story found in Renaissance sources tells of pieces of the pickled or cured body of a Jew being returned home for burial being mistakenly snacked upon by other shipboard passengers. In modern times, in countries with serious food shortages, there are persistent rumors of human flesh being sold as beef.*

"Hold the Mayo! Hold the Mozzarella!"

I overheard this in line at a grocery store in Tampa, Florida, in November 1988. One teenager said to another, "You know why Burger King is putting out all those free Whopper coupons? The company is going bankrupt. There is a big lawsuit filed against the company in New England. Some employee had AIDS and decided to get back at people by jacking off in the mayonnaise. You can get AIDS eating Whoppers. That's why they're giving them away."

I am Publicity Director of the local hospital. In June 1993 I received a call from one of the local radio reporters asking that I help him confirm a story. As he told it the story went like this:

A couple in a neighboring city ordered a pizza from the local Domino's. It was duly delivered and eaten. After their meal the couple received a phone call from a man identifying himself as the delivery person. He said he was doing a follow-up quality check and asked if they had enjoyed their pizza. They told him yes, at which point he said, "Good. Because I ejaculated on it and I have AIDS." The couple panicked and—out of embarrassment—came to the hospital in our city for examination. Once there they had their stomachs pumped and it was discovered that there were traces of semen in the stomach content.

I checked our ER and lab records and no such incident was reported.

The Burger King story came in a letter from Robert Pomeroy of Tampa, Florida, in 1989. The Domino's story is from Tim L. Cornett of Pineville, Kentucky, writing in 1993. Folklorist Janet Langlois discussed this cycle of contamination legends in an article published in Contemporary Legend, *vol. 1 (1991). Other foods sometimes mentioned are coleslaw, beans, and tacos; other contaminants include sweat, saliva, and urine, and other specific fast-food chains include Hardees, Taco Bell, and Pizza Hut. But the majority of the "Hold the M . . . !" legends have concerned Burger King and Domino's Pizza, both of which have been targeted since at least 1987. When the unfounded rumors became rampant, I wrote a short piece for the Domino's Pizza in-house publication,* The Pepperoni Press *(April 13, 1990), outlining the usual careers of such negative stories and suggesting how to cope with them. Evidently, I did not help the company much, as the stories broke out again all across the nation in 1993, usually in the version quoted above, in which the pizza defiler telephones his victims to reveal his guilt. Recalling that the Corona Beer Scare mentioned in the introduction to this chapter also began in 1987, we must judge it a bad year for food products, but a good year for contamination legends.*

9

Sick Humor

Medical horror legends come in two forms: highly technical stories, bizarre but supposedly true, and widespread accounts of horrendous supposed incidents in the process of "health care delivery" that are in layman's language. Typical themes are weird injuries and accidents, hellish ERs, inaccurate diagnoses, and treatments that are worse than the original ailments. Often the screw-ups are said to have resulted from human failings like faulty recordkeeping, flopped X rays, overworked hospital personnel, and officious hospital or clinic administrators. Clearly, in these legends there's the feeling that doctors might sometimes do more harm than good, despite their Hippocratic oath.

Sometimes the apocryphal stories stem from simple ignorance about how things work. For example, a reader wrote me, "When my sister was about to undergo amniocentesis, a friend advised against it because someone she knew had the procedure, and the energy generated by the machine had caused the amniotic fluid to boil, severely injuring the developing infant." (What about the mother?!) Another medical legend uses a simple plot to deliver the message that babies, even unborn ones, can be real fighters. It's the story that babies are sometimes born with an intrauterine birth-control device clutched tightly in their tiny fists. Gynecologists assure me that it cannot happen, since an IUD is always outside the bag of waters containing the baby.

Another hospital story, sent to me by an Ohio reader, cautions volunteers to keep patient information confidential. Supposedly two candy stripers (young female hospital volunteers who traditionally wear striped uniforms) were speaking indiscreetly on an elevator about the patients with whom they were working. One of the girls mentioned an old man in the ward that everyone liked, and the other girl said very sadly that she had just heard a doctor say that the man was expected to die soon. Suddenly another passenger on the elevator fainted. It turned out that she was the old man's daughter (or wife) who was coming for a visit, and the doctor had not yet explained his condition to her.

One of the classic medical horror legends involves an accidental patient death caused by a hospital visitor or worker. Merium Malik of San Antonio, Texas, sent me this one in 1991:

> A priest made weekly rounds at a hospital, and one day he was visiting a parishioner in the intensive care unit. The man was connected to many tubes and wires, but he greeted the priest cheerfully.
>
> However, as the priest stood at his bedside, the man grew visibly worse and seemed to be fighting to breathe. Still, he could gesture for a pencil and paper from the table next to the bed, and he scribbled something and pressed the note into the priest's hand.
>
> The priest stuffed the note into his pocket and rang for help, but the man died before anyone arrived to render aid.
>
> That night as the deeply shaken priest prayed for the man, he remembered the note and pulled it out of his pocket. He uncrumpled it and read, "Please, father! You're standing on my air hose!"

A recent variation on this lost-patient story started circulating on the Internet in July 1996. It was credited to a South African newspaper's report of an incident in a hospital there. Here's the verbatim wording of one such version:

> "For several months, our nurses have been baffled to find a dead patient in the same bed every Friday morning" a spokeswoman for the Pelonomi Hospital (Free State, South Africa) told reporters. "There was no apparent cause for any of the deaths, and extensive checks on the air conditioning system, and a search for possible bacterial infection, failed to reveal any clues.
>
> "However, further inquiries have now revealed the cause of these deaths. It seems that every Friday morning a cleaner would enter the ward, remove the plug that powered the patient's life support system, plug her floor polisher into the vacant socket, then go about her business. When she had finished her chores, she would plug the life support machine back in and leave, unaware that the patient was now dead. She could not, after all, hear the screams and eventual death rattle over the whirring of her polisher.
>
> "We are sorry, and have sent a strong letter to the cleaner in question.

> Further, the Free State Health and Welfare Department is arranging for an electrician to fit an extra socket, so there should be no repetition of this incident. The enquiry is now closed."
>
> From (*Cape Times*, 6/13/96)
>
> BTW [by the way], the headline of the newspaper story was "Cleaner Polishes Off Patients."

There *was* such a story in the *Cape Times*, but the version that got on the Net failed to include a sentence that mentioned that the incident had not been confirmed. Also, it ignored the fact that the Cape Town story was datelined from another city, Bloemfontein, and the Net text punctuated as actual quotations some of the general information from the newspaper's account. Arthur Goldstuck, Johannesburg journalist and author of three books on urban legends, tracked down the source of this story and posted his findings on the Net. The *Cape Times* got its information from an article in Cape Town's Afrikaans-language newspaper, *Die Burger*, which had clearly stated that this lost-patients story had been a mere rumor for the past two years and characterized the event as an "alleged incident." This example illustrates how the Internet may virtually "create" an urban legend by circulating in doctored form, so to speak, an already doubtful news item. There's more to the story, which you can look up for yourself at http://www.urbanlegends.com/medical/hospital_cleaning_lady.html.

Finally, from reader Paul Teeples of Richmond, Virginia, a medical horror story with a different twist. He heard it on a job site during his days as a sheetrock installer:

> Another sheetrocker started out, "Did you hear about the local high-school player who fractured his leg so severely that when they took him to MCV [Medical College of Virginia] they had to amputate? But the doctor accidentally amputated the good leg!"
>
> Everybody stared in disbelief, until somebody chimed in with, "They must have sued the hell outta that place."
>
> "Nope, they couldn't sue," the first guy said.
>
> "Why not?" we all asked.
>
> "He didn't have a leg to stand on."

A story like that (technically, a "catch tale," not a legend) gives the term "sick humor" a whole new connotation.

"Two Sad ER Stories"

This guy was brought into the Emergency Room of another hospital here in town late one Saturday afternoon with really bad burns on both his ears. At first, all he would say was that he had been watching football on TV and drinking beer all day. Finally, when they had to fill out an accident report, the man confessed.

What was there to confess?

He explained that his wife was ironing at the same time that he was watching the big game, and when she left the room for a minute, the telephone rang. The phone was on the table next to his chair and she had left the hot iron nearby. Without taking his eyes off the screen, the man reached for the phone. "I put it up to my ear" he explained, "thinking it was the telephone."

"So how did your other ear get burned?" the medic asked.

"Well, I hadn't any more than hung up when the person called back."

I heard something similar to that. A woman was brought in to an ER with a really bad gunshot wound in her face. She was lucky to survive, and they said she would probably be disfigured for the rest of her life.

Was it a murder attempt or suicide or what?

No, it was an accident. She lived in a bad neighborhood, and she had bought a pistol to protect herself with. She kept it under her pillow. But she had asthma, and she also kept her inhaler under the pillow.

Oh, no!

Yes! She woke up late one night, reached for the inhaler, and got the gun instead and put a shot right through one side of her nose and out her cheek.

"The Kafkaesque Hospital Visit"

A man came to the general clinic of a university hospital complaining that the frames of his eyeglasses were crooked and wouldn't sit straight on his face. To have anything done about the glasses, he had to be seen in the Ophthalmology Clinic. Hospital rules required that no one could be referred from the general clinic to a specialty clinic until a complete physical examination was done.

When the intern did a rectal exam as part of the required physical, a mass was found. Since this took priority over the problem with the glasses, the patient was referred to General Surgery Clinic for a proctoscopy. During this examination, a benign polyp was found and removed, but the intern performing the examination accidentally perforated the man's colon with the proctoscope without realizing it.

The patient was finally given his appointment for the Ophthalmology Clinic and left, but he returned to the Emergency Room in the middle of the night very sick indeed. He had emergency surgery for his perforated colon. In spite of this, and despite massive antibiotic treatment, he developed peritonitis and a host of other complications and had to spend several weeks in the intensive care unit.

He finally recovered in time to be discharged from the hospital by the same intern who had originally seen him in the general clinic many weeks earlier and who had now rotated into the General Surgery service. On his first day there the intern immediately recognized the patient by the crooked way his glasses sat on his nose.

Sent to me by Dr. Charles Gauntt of Phoenix, Arizona, in 1986. A related story lists in detail the escalating costs of a hospital stay as the patient stays on and on while trying to complete required hospital paperwork before discharge, all the while being billed for a seemingly endless array of supplies, equipment, and services. Problems with the proctoscope (a much-dreaded diagnostic tool), according to legend, usually involve a spark generated by a loose wire that ignites intestinal gases and causes an explosion in the patient's lower abdomen. Explosions have actually occurred, though rarely, during inspection or treatment of colon polyps. If you want the details, just run to your nearest medical school library, get volume 77 (1979) of the journal Gastroenterology, *and check out pages 1307–10 for a fascinating and illustrated article titled "Fatal Colonic Explosion during Colonoscopic Polypectomy." The case described there happened in France, which is about as close as I want to get to the subject. Evidently, this is a famous case, since four different doctors, including my own, have forwarded me copies of this article.*

"Dental Death"

My elderly dentist told me that it was a standard joke in his dental school that if a patient should die in your chair, you should carry the corpse out to the restroom and leave him there to be discovered.

But how could someone die just from having dental work?

Well, another person told me about a dentist who had twin treatment rooms in his suite, and one time he decided to work on two patients at the same time, since both of them would be under anesthesia. But after he had both of them out, one patient started to react badly, and while the dentist was trying to help him, the other patient died. Then when he turned to the dead patient, the other one died too.

A reader wrote me about a dental death-and-rebirth story he had heard. A dentist who had a patient die in his chair late in the day when few other people were in the building did actually hoist the corpse onto his shoulder and head out for the bathroom. The men's room was one flight down in the building, but the dentist managed to get there unseen and to leave the body on a toilet. He returned to his suite to tidy up and calm himself before going home, but a few minutes later he heard the door open, and he turned to see the "dead" man walk in, dazed but very much alive. Apparently the repeated bumps of being carried down the stairs had provided a sort of accidental CPR and jolted the man back to consciousness.

This is a summary of all the dental death stories I have heard during two decades of collecting urban legends. Considering the fear and loathing that most people harbor for dentistry, it's surprising there are not more such legends. At least I hope they're legends.

"The Relative's Cadaver"

I overheard this in a conversation between two students. One student told the other that last semester he heard that there was a girl taking an anatomy class, and when the professor unveiled the cadaver, the girl realized it was her aunt, whose funeral she had just attended two months earlier. The girl was unable to cope with the thought that she would be studying the body of a relative, and she dropped the class.

When I was in high school a friend who was a pre-med student enlightened me to the fact that first year med students are required to dissect a real human body. "Furthermore," she said, "there was one busy young med student halfway through his first semester when his mother called to tell him that his grandfather had just passed on. He flew home to attend the funeral, then hurried back to school. Shortly thereafter, the students were led into a room filled with sheet-draped corpses all ready for dissection. When the young man lifted up his assigned sheet, he was horrified to see Grandpa! No one had told him that the old man was leaving his body to science.

"That," explained my friend, "is why all cadavers given to med students have bags put over their heads."

Every medical school has stories like these two which were sent to me, respectively, from the Midwest and from New England. In variations of the legend, the body is said to be that of the student's mother, father, uncle, or some other relative with whom the student had suffered a falling-out and had failed to keep in touch. The bag-over-the-head strategy would seem to make it very difficult for future brain surgeons and ear, nose, and throat specialists to learn anatomy. In 1982, an actual instance of the cadaver of a student's relative—a great-aunt—showing up in a gross anatomy laboratory of the University of Alabama, Birmingham, School of Medicine was reported in a letter to the Journal of the American Medical Association, *vol. 247, no. 15, p. 2096. Although it was not the same cadaver that the student was working on, according to the letter, "further trauma to the student was obviated by the immediate substitution of another cadaver by the state anatomical board." "The Relative's Cadaver" legend became attached to the eighteenth-century English novelist Laurence Sterne. Shortly after Sterne's death in 1768, a story began to circulate saying that Sterne's body had been stolen by grave robbers and sold to Cambridge University's medical school, where it was recognized by one of his friends. Early biographers of Sterne included and embellished the story, but more recent scholars failed to find any evidence for the incident and have rejected it as folklore.*

"Gerbilling"

A colleague at work related a gruesome tale about homosexuals. It seems that certain elements in the gay community have taken to deriving sexual stimulation from the insertion of a live rodent into their anus. (This is not a joke!) Gerbils appear to be the animal of choice. The stimulation evidently arises from the motion of the animal after insertion, and therein lies the problem: Some devotees of this practice have been badly injured when the gerbil became overly frisky and began clawing at the person's insides. My colleague claimed to have reliable information about this because he had a friend who was a doctor. His friend, while working in the emergency room, had actually seen X rays of the insides of a homosexual who had been injured by practicing this ritual.

When I told my colleague that this story sounded extremely hokey and implausible, he became adamant in vowing for the story's authenticity. When I pressed him for the name of his doctor friend, he backed off somewhat, saying that he thought he remembered that it was not actually his friend who saw the X rays, but his friend's brother (also a doctor). It was not clear whether the doctor who saw the X rays was the same one who supposedly treated the patient.

A friend of mine knows a nurse at Cedars-Sinai Hospital in Los Angeles. She told him that [insert name of a handsome male actor here] visited the emergency room the other night. The actor confessed that he had been engaged in a kinky gay sexual game that involves sticking a live gerbil up your rectum. Only this time, the gerbil got stuck. The nurse actually saw the X ray. It's absolutely true.

. . . There was one problem. The story wasn't true.

The generic version of the story is from a 1987 letter from a reader in Illinois. The Hollywood version is from Stephen Randall's "Media" column in Playboy, *December 1990. References to gerbilling, also known as "filching," "felching," and "tunneling," have circulated since the late 1960s, and the malicious homophobic legend suddenly erupted in 1984 and has been rampant ever since. The lives and careers of several male media personalities—news anchors, weathercasters, and film stars—have been plagued and sometimes even ruined by the attachment of gerbilling stories and rumors to their names. Usually the stories claim that a FOAF has seen actual X rays of sufferers, as is the case in Dr. Richard T. Caleel's 1986 book* Surgeon! A Year in the Life of an Inner City Doctor, *but here, as in the oral tradition, the supposed source is a friend of a friend working in a different hospital. For a definitive discussion of the extensive folklore of gerbilling see Norine Dresser's "The Case of the Missing Gerbil" in* Western Folklore, *vol. 58 (July 1994), pp. 229–42. Dresser concludes, "There is nothing or no one to verify the practice of gerbilling. A computer search of all the medical/scientific literature reports zero entries testifying to that act. Furthermore, it has been impossible to find a first-hand witness or a self-professed practitioner." One published source seemingly disagrees with this widely held view—the 1989 book* News of the Weird, *compiled by Chuck Shepherd,*

John J. Kohut, and Roland Sweet, which claimed that "Medical researchers, tabulating cases in which items were recovered from the rectums of patients, reported . . . a live, shaved, declawed gerbil. . . ." However, the source cited, a 1986 article on "rectal foreign bodies" published in the medical journal Surgery, *contained no references to gerbils or other small animals. Confronted with this anomaly by Cecil Adams, author of the popular "Straight Dope" column, Shepherd explained that he had "made a transcribing error." An account of gerbilling combined with a colonic explosion circulated on the Internet in 1996 and '97, attributing the incident to "the Severe Burns Unit of Salt Lake City Hospital." There is no such-named hospital in Salt Lake City, and, believe me, if any such thing had happened in* any *local hospital, I would have heard about it.*

"Scrotum Self-Repair"

A man comes into the hospital emergency room and asks to see a doctor. When the attending physician comes into the examining room the man removes his pants, and the doctor sees that the man's scrotum is wrapped in yards of soiled linen and has swollen to huge size. The man won't tell the doctor what happened to him, so the doctor takes X rays. He finds that there are staples in the man's scrotum. When confronted with this information the man finally tells his story.

He is a wood-worker, and since one day he had a little spare time on his hands, he decided to use his stationary belt sander as a means of sexual gratification. He had done this many times before without any undue incident. This time, however, he slipped and fell onto the belt sander as it was running at full speed. The man was thrown eight or nine feet forward into the wall. When he picked himself up he discovered that he had torn open his scrotum. In spite of the awful pain, the man just couldn't face a doctor with such a story, so he stapled his scrotum together. Unfortunately, the staples were neither sterile nor proof against rust, so his scrotum became horribly infected, forcing him to eventually go to the doctor after all. Well, the doctor cleaned the wound and fixed the poor guy up the best he could, but then he had to break the horrible news: when the accident had happened the man's testicles had been ripped free from his scrotum and had been lost.

With all the blood and pain the man had never noticed, and now it was too late to go looking for them. He had been castrated by a belt sander.

From Hans P. Broedel's note "On the Dangers of Close Proximity to Power Tools," in Northwest Folklore, *vol. 10 (fall 1991), pp. 47–48. The teller of this story said that he had heard it "on good authority from a friend who works in the emergency room of a large local hospital." Broedel, a graduate student in history at the University of Washington at the time, wrote that "this story looks very much like an urban legend," and confirmed his hunch by noting that "recently an acquaintance told me that he had seen the same story floating around in a local computer net." In another report of the same story told orally, the scrotum is said to have swollen to the size of a basketball after being repaired with drywall staples. The doctor put the patient under full anesthesia for treatment, and the patient explained how he was injured after regaining consciousness. Incredibly enough, this horrific story actually derives from an incident reported in a medical journal; copies of the single-page article, often showing signs of being repeatedly photocopied, have circulated since shortly after it appeared. In the July 1991 issue of* Medical Aspects of Human Sexuality, *p. 15, William A. Morton, Jr., M.D., reported this instance of "Scrotum Self-Repair." He told essentially the same story, although with full clinical and anatomical detail couched in precise medical terminology. However, details were changed somewhat in person-to-person transmission. For example, the actual victim worked in a machine shop and was involved with "the canvas drive-belt of a large floor-based piece of running machinery." His injury was wrapped in "two or three yards of foul-smelling stained gauze wrapper" and his scrotum was swollen to "twice the size of a grapefruit." In the accident the man was thrown "a few feet," and he lost only his left testis. Is this journal article, perhaps, a hoax? David Herzog, then a writer for the* Allentown (Pennsylvania) Morning Call, *spoke to Dr. Morton in 1992 and was told that the case happened 20 years ago.*

"Superglue Revenge"

I heard this story from a woman I worked with who used to work at the court house in Wheaton, Illinois; she heard it from the girl in "records" who claimed to have read it as a legal action complaint.

The story goes that a woman married to a cheating husband was so sick and tired of it that she decided to get even. So one night when he was sleeping she stripped off his underwear and Superglued his area of anatomy with which he was cheating to his tummy. Supposedly he had to have surgery to undo this deed, and he sued the wife for malicious assault and won. Have you heard this?

Nurses in a provincial [English] hospital recently took charge of a man who had been bizarrely punished by his wife for infidelity. She had returned unexpectedly to the family home, and could hear him misbehaving. He was engaged in sexual congress that was both noisy and enthusiastic, characteristics which had been missing for some time from his dealings with his wife. She herself made no noise, let herself out of the flat, and returned at her usual time. She cooked a fine dinner, taking care to grind up some sleeping-pills and include them in the mashed potatoes. Her husband retired early to bed, pleading tiredness, and a little later on she stripped him as he slept, and stuck his hand to his penis with Super Glue.

The doctors and nurses faced the problem of separating manual and genital flesh from their tangle, and they had moreover to improvise an arrangement to enable the patient to urinate; plastic surgery was eventually required to restore the appearance of the parts.

The decorously worded query ("area of anatomy" indeed!) came in 1988 from a reader in Illinois whose signature was illegible. In other versions of the story the aggrieved wife sometimes substitutes Superglue for the husband's lubricating jelly. The second version quoted is from a story titled "Structural Anthropology" by Adam Mars-Jones, in The Penguin Book of Modern British Short Stories *(1987). The rest of the short story consists of Mars-Jones's mock dissection of the legend using "the techniques of structural anthropology pioneered by Lévi-Strauss." The numerous reports of "Superglue Revenge" in my files are often credited to people who claim to know personally one of the principals involved. Invariably, upon checking back with their sources, my informants failed to validate the incident. A correspondent from Texas actually asked the ex-wife of the promiscuous husband point-blank if she had done the deed attributed to her in local gossip. She replied, "There was absolutely nothing to that story, and I don't have any idea how it got started. If I had thought of it, I would have done it!"*

"The Runaway Patient"

My next-door neighbor, he's a physician," Morgan said. "He told me that at the VA hospital he worked in there was a man in bed on the sixth floor who'd had a stroke and was completely paralyzed and couldn't speak. This man was getting therapy down in the basement. They made an appointment for him one day to have some therapy at a certain hour and the people on the sixth floor put him in the elevator and he went down to the basement. But there'd been a screw-up. They weren't aware down there that he was coming. No one was there to take him off the elevator. So he was on this elevator and he couldn't speak and people on the sixth floor assumed he was being kept in therapy. And he rode up and down the elevator for three days."

Actor Harry Morgan—Colonel Potter of TV's popular M*A*S*H*—quoted by Steve Gelman in "Operation Transplant," an article on a proposed sequel to be titled* AfterMASH, *in* TV Guide, *November 5, 1983, pp. 19–23. Anne Phipps, a faculty member of the Indiana University School of Nursing in Indianapolis, recorded her own and four colleagues' variations of the same story in 1980, presenting them in an article in* Indiana Folklore, *vol. 13, pp. 102–11, as "The Runaway Patient: A Legend in Oral Circulation and the Media." The media sources were nine newspaper accounts of an actual incident that occurred in a Chicago-area Veterans Administration hospital in May 1975. A detailed summary of the incident appeared in Gary L. Kreps's 1986 book* Organizational Communication Theory and Practice, *pp. 18–19, quoting it from a 1976 source.*

10

Bringing Up Baby

There are so many genuine dangers threatening children that you wonder why we need horror legends. Real life already gives us plenty to worry about: child abductions and seductions, dangerous toys, faulty car seats and unsafe airbags, heavy traffic, threatening pets or wild animals, contaminated baby foods, drugs, toxic household products, environmental hazards, sex and violence in the media, and on and on and on. You can't even put your baby to sleep without being concerned whether side, stomach, or back is supposed to be the safest position. All of these threats and more are constantly covered in the news, so what's left for urban legends to shock us with? Mostly it's accounts of disastrous failures in the simple, common, everyday acts that we tend to take for granted, chief among them being the routine daily care of children. Who's doing the care, the legends ask, and how reliable are the caregivers?

While hard news about the genuine dangers to children reaches the public through the media, in lawsuits, or via government bulletins, the legendary accounts circulate by word of mouth and in occasional unverified published reports. Take, for example, the old story of "The Harried Baby-Sitter," as Jerome Beatty summarized it in a piece in the November 1970 issue of *Esquire*:

> The basic plot is that a lady on a bus hears two young girls chatting in the seat behind her. They are talking about their problems handling kids when baby-sitting. One of the girls tells the other a method she uses of quieting any little kid who cries too much: She lays him down with head in the oven, and opens the gas vent for a while. When he is drowsy, she puts him in the crib and never has a bit of trouble. If he gets too lively again, back into the oven he goes.

Beatty first heard the story around 1950 from his wife, who got it from a woman friend, a practical nurse in New Rochelle, New York, who claimed that she herself had been the woman on the bus. But—true to the rules of legend development—the story showed up twice again in Beatty's experience from different places, with different details, and with no verification.

Several people have written to me saying they remember hearing "The Harried Baby-Sitter" in the 1940s or '50s. The legend commonly centered on a conversation between two young girls on a bus or a subway. But "The Harried Baby-Sitter" was told even earlier than that, in the 1920s and '30s—when gas ovens had to be lit manually. Back then, two nursemaids who worked for wealthy families were said to have been overheard while chatting on a trolley car. A variation of this older story from England is quoted in Jonathan Gathorne-Hardy's 1972 book *The Unnatural History of the Nanny.* A man sitting in Hyde Park by the Albert Memorial overhears two nannies chatting about the children they are caring for. One nanny, "a large, red-faced Somerset girl," described her method of putting the baby in her charge to sleep: "If mine won't go to sleep, I just hold the gas ring over her dear little face and give her a whiff."

"The Harried Baby-Sitter" continues to resonate in modern folklore, and is still quoted as a horrible example of the hazards of absentee parenthood. In Rosanna Hertz's book *More Equal Than Others: Women and Men in Dual-Career Marriages,* published in 1986, the legend pops up in the chapter "Childcare Arrangements." Hertz contrasts the child care practices of the past, when "the nanny or governess employed by the wealthy family had on-the-job supervision," to the situation with "today's dual-career couples," who must leave their children with strangers for hours at a time, and who may express their concerns by telling the same old horror story, like this:

> I have a friend who had a baby, and one day she forgot something at home. So she went home, and her childcare person had her baby's head in the oven. And she said, "What are you doing to my baby?" and the childcare person said, "Well, I always do this. He seems to sleep better."

"Forgetful Dad"

A woman in a two-job one-child household had to get to work early one day, so she asked her husband to drop their infant daughter off at day care on his way to work. It was a very busy time for the man at his job, and he had a major business meeting coming up that day. He was on his cell phone double-checking the details of the meeting most of the way to his office. The baby was sound asleep in her car seat in the back of the car, and her daddy completely forgot about her and drove right past the day care to his usual parking spot at the office. Around noon the mother received a call from the day care service asking why their child was out that day. She called her husband, who then remembered that he had left the baby in the car. He rushed to the parking lot to find the baby dead from heat exhaustion.

"The Hippie Baby-Sitter"

There was this couple who were going out one night, and they couldn't get their regular baby-sitter, so they called someone they knew and arranged to get a new girl to come and sit their baby. When she showed up they were a little surprised, because she was dressed like a hippie and had a kind of spaced-out look in her eyes. But they gave her instructions about caring for the baby and went out anyway.

Later in the evening the mother called home to see how things were going, and this hippie girl said, "Oh just fine. I just put the turkey in the oven." Well, they didn't have a turkey, and they didn't know what she was talking about, so they decided to go back home right away.

By Ivan Brunetti

When they went into their house they smelled something cooking, and rushed to the kitchen and looked in the oven. The baby-sitter had put the baby in the oven and roasted it! She had been taking LSD and was completely freaked out.

Lyons, Indiana
April 16, 1990

Dear Professor: Here's a new story that I think must surely be an urban legend. A high-school student of mine, a senior, says that he heard from a friend who heard it during a state policeman's talk on drugs. He insists it is true, otherwise why would a policeman be telling it?

On Thanksgiving, a man returned home expecting to find his wife, his infant daughter and a wonderful turkey dinner with all the trimmings. Instead, his wife was in the living room acting strangely. She was evidently under the influence of drugs.

When the man went to look for his daughter, he found a turkey in the crib. After a frantic search, he found the baby in the oven where the turkey should have been.

This must be a legend that has arisen since the advent of widespread drug use.

The first version is typical of how this legend emerged in the United States in the late 1960s. Sometimes the mother asks the baby-sitter to put the baby to bed and put the turkey in the oven; the drug-dazed hippie reverses these instructions. The 1990 letter is from teacher Jack Johnson; he was right about the legend having its roots in the culture of American illegal drug use, but that was some 20-plus years earlier. Versions of the story in which the mother, rather than a baby-sitter, cooks the baby are known worldwide, and one version was told on June 19, 1989, on PBS's MacNeil/Lehrer NewsHour *by an antidrug lecturer. I discussed the cooked-baby and cooked-pet urban legends in considerable historical and comparative detail in an essay appended to the third edition of my textbook* The Study of American Folklore. *This essay, revised and updated, appears in my 2000 book* The Truth Never Stands in the Way of a Good Story.

"The Baby-Sitter and the Man Upstairs"

This is a story about a baby-sitter and a terrifying experience that she had. There was a young girl about high school age who went to baby-sit one evening. She arrived at the house early in the evening so that she had to cook dinner for the children, play with them a little bit, and then later on, about 7:30, she put them to bed. So she went downstairs and was just sitting around reading and watching television and the telephone rang. And she went to answer it and there was this male voice on the other end saying "At 10:30 I'm going to kill the children and then I'm going to come after you." And the girl thought it was a crank call and she was a little scared but she just put it off as a joke that someone was playing on her and she hung up. About half an hour later the phone rang again. And the same male voice said, "At 10:30 I'm going to come in and I'm going to kill the children and then I'm coming after you."

At this point the girl was getting a little more scared because she thought the man might be, you know, a maniac and might actually come and do something. But she decided that she would still go on and just sit around and wait. And she thought about going upstairs and looking in on the children because she hadn't been up there for awhile but she decided against it, just . . . she didn't think anything was wrong. And the third time, about half an hour later, the telephone rang. And this male voice said, "It's getting closer to the time and I'm going to come after the children and I'm going to get you too."

And at this point the girl got very upset and she decided that she would call the police. And she called the operator and told her the story of what had happened and the operator said, "All right, you know, we'll take care of it if he calls back again just keep him on the line and we'll put a tracer on it."

And the girl sat around; she was very nervous but decided that it was the best thing that she could do. Pretty soon the phone rang again. She ran to answer it. And it was the man. She tried to talk to him a little bit more and tried to get some information out of him but all that he would

By permission of Dave Coverly and Creators Syndicate

say was, "I'm going to come in at 10:30 and I'm going to kill the children and then I'm coming after you." And the girl hung up the phone and was just terrified but could do nothing but just sit and wait. And the phone rang again. And she answered it and the operator was on the other end and she said, "Get out of the house immediately; don't go upstairs; don't do anything; just you leave the house. When you get out there, there will be policemen outside and they'll take care of it."

The girl was just really petrified and she thought she should check the children or something but decided that if the operator told her to get out she should get out. So she went outside and when she got out there she was talking to the policemen and they told her that when they traced the call it was made on the extension from the upstairs line and that the whole time the man was talking to her he had been in the house and that he had already murdered both the children who were found torn to bits in the bedroom. Had she waited any longer she would have gotten it too.

Told in 1973 at Indiana University by a female student who had repeated the story many times previously; it was published in Sylvia Grider's article "Dormitory Legend-Telling in

Progress: Fall 1971–Winter 1973," Indiana Folklore, *vol. 6 (1973), pp. 1–32. This telling is unusually polished and detailed, but it lacks the refrain usually repeated by the killer, "Have you checked the children?" Another version was published in a verbatim transcript of a tape recording made in 1984 at Leicester University, England, in which three students took part. See Gillian Bennett, "Playful Chaos: Anatomy of a Storytelling Session," in* The Questing Beast: Perspectives on Contemporary Legend, *vol. 4 (1989), pp. 193–212. "The Baby-Sitter and the Man Upstairs," in common with "The Killer in the Back Seat" and "The Choking Doberman," tells of a dangerous intruder hiding right on the premises, and with the latter story it shares the "telephone warning" motif. The 1979 horror film* When a Stranger Calls *opened with a chilling dramatization of this legend.*

"Baby's Stuck at Home Alone"

A Norwegian couple, who had not had a proper holiday for years, decided to treat themselves to a long winter holiday in the sun. At last the great day dawned; everything was packed and loaded into the car—as soon as Nanny arrived they could away. But today of all days, Nanny was late. At the last minute she phoned and told them that her car had broken down. The man said that if they came to collect her now they would miss their flight; was it too far to walk? Nanny said it wasn't, they could leave and she'd be there in a quarter of an hour. So the wife strapped their young son into his highchair, told him Nanny wouldn't be long, and set off for their island in the sun. During the long, hot weeks away they missed the news that the girl had been hit by a lorry and killed on her way to their house. When at last they returned, sun-bronzed and rejuvenated, they found their starved son still strapped into his chair where they had left him.

From Rodney Dale's 1984 book It's True . . . It Happened to a Friend, *p. 89. Dale is probably retelling a press account of a story circulating in Norway and Sweden in the early 1970s. As a newspaper in Bergen, Norway, reported the rumors in 1972, in several different Nordic cities, the couple had left without waiting for their baby-sitter or grandmother to arrive, and the caregiver became terminally ill or was hit by a car. Unfortunately, none of these missing caregivers had mentioned the long-term job to anyone else, so the baby was abandoned and helpless. Three American readers from California, Texas, and Mississippi have sent me variations of this legend. Also in 1990 a woman from Elkhart, Indiana, wrote to report a version in which a dog slipped into the house, bumping the door, which closed and locked. The letter concluded, "The rest of the gruesome story involves the dog eating the baby . . . and so on."*

"The Inept Mother"

In Leicester a favourite was the account of how a mother had told her young daughter that her younger brother was going in to hospital to "have his end snipped off" (circumcised), so the daughter, to be helpful castrated him with a pair of scissors. The mother, trying to take the boy to hospital, backed out of the garage in such a hurry as to run over the daughter and kill her. This was recounted to Jekyll as fact, with a wealth of supporting detail, in 1964.

I heard this in the mid-1950s; that's as close as I can remember. I was a grammar school kid living just north of Philadelphia.

Some little four-year-old girl's mother had come home from the hospital with a new baby brother for her. Shortly afterward, when the mother was changing the baby's diaper, the little girl asked what that thing was that the baby had and she didn't.

The mother put her off with the fateful remark, "Oh, that's just something that the doctor forgot to cut off."

Later, hearing the infant's screams, the woman ran into the nursery to find her daughter with the best scissors, all bloody. She, of course, had cut off the baby's penis. The mother swept up the baby, raced to the car, hit the ignition and jammed it into gear. The tragedy doubled because the poor mother had forgotten all about the little girl, who was trailing along hurt and confused. She happened to be right behind the back wheel of the car when her frantic mother jammed it into reverse. The daughter was crushed—killed outright. The baby died on the way to the hospital.

The English version is from the "Doctor Jekyll" column in World Medicine, *July 10, 1982, under the subheading "Medical Myths." I am indebted to Dr. T. Healey of Barnsley, South Yorkshire, for sending me this and many other items of English medical rumor and legend. The American version was sent to me in 1985 by Jerome Shea of Albuquerque, New Mexico. Often the tragedy is tripled when the mother has a baby in the tub while two toddlers play; after the daughter severs the son's penis, the mother backs the car over the girl, loses her injured son en route to the hospital, and returns home to find the forgotten baby drowned in the tub. In yet another English variant of the story, a harried mum crossing to Ireland via ferry with a baby and a toddler threatens to put the baby out the porthole if he continues to cry. When the mother leaves the cabin briefly, the baby resumes crying and his older sister enacts the mother's threat. These stories teach an age-old lesson, as evidenced by the Aesop fable that begins "'Be quiet now,' said an old Nurse to a child sitting on her lap. 'If you make that noise again I will throw you to the wolf.'" The fable has a happy ending, which is more than you can say for one of the grimmest of the original Grimm fairy tales, one that has been seldom printed since the first edition of 1812. It's called "How Children Played Butcher with Each Other." The story describes the accidental sudden deaths by stabbing and drowning of three children, followed by the deaths of both parents. Janet L. Langlois analyzed this whole complex of horror legends in the chapter titled "Mother's Doubletalk" in the 1993 book* Feminist Messages, *edited by Joan Newlon Radnor. Yet another variation on this dismal theme is the story told during both world wars of a mother bathing her babies who runs to answer the doorbell, where a government messenger waits to inform her that her husband has been killed in action. The mother trips on the stairs, breaks her neck, and dies instantly; her two children drown in the bathtub before the messenger manages to enter the home to check on its occupants.*

"The Stuffed Baby"

The most memorable legend I recall is one that my mother told me about 15 years ago [around 1971]. It seems that a friend of hers was on a flight—I believe the departure point was in the States and the destination in Canada. One young couple of "hippies" boarded with a baby wrapped in a blanket. The woman kept the baby wrapped in the blanket and held it tightly. More than once the stewardess asked if she would like a bottle or some food heated, but the woman refused.

Over the course of several hours the stewardess became suspicious since the baby did not eat or cry. She notified the authorities, who detained the couple at the airport. The baby, of course, was dead, and had been gutted and stuffed with marijuana.

This past Christmas [1989] I heard a story of a Georgia State Patrolman stopping a northbound motorist on I-75 between Tifton and Valdosta for speeding. Next to the driver was a baby strapped in a car seat. The patrolman noticed that the baby was not moving, and when he inquired about this, he was told that the baby was sick and the motorist was trying to get the baby home quickly.

The patrolman let the man go, but he began to have second thoughts about the baby's well being, so he radioed ahead to another patrolman to pull the motorist over again and see if he could be of any assistance to the sick baby. When the second patrolman stopped the car he discovered that the baby was dead and had been disemboweled, filled with cocaine, and sewn back up.

These stories were sent to me in 1986 and 1990 from readers in Canada and Georgia, respectively. This is the domesticated version of a legend that usually describes the smuggling of drugs into North America from South America or elsewhere. In 1985 the incident, said to have happened on a Miami-bound flight, was reported in Life, New Republic, *and the* Washington Post; *the latter publication quickly retracted the story, quoting customs officials who traced it as far back as 1973 but said that they were unable to confirm it and believed it to be mere rumor. In a* National Geographic *article on emeralds, published in the July 1990 issue, a story is told about a Senegalese family smuggling these precious gems abroad in the body of a dead child being sent home for burial; supposedly, these criminals were caught on the folklorically appropriate* third *commission of the crime.*

11

Strange Things Happen

Very few modern urban legends that are collected and studied by today's folklorists concern the supernatural; instead, most such stories are plausible accounts of fairly ordinary experiences that have a bizarre or ironic twist. "The Runaway Grandmother," "The Hook," or "The Crushed Dog," for example, are weird legends, but their weirdness does not stem from the presence of ghosts, ghouls, or gremlins—it was plain old theft, crime, or bad luck that caused the problems.

In part, this shortage of the supernatural in ULs is a matter of definition, since folklorists tend to assign the supernatural stories people tell to other categories like "scary stories" or "ghost stories," implying that these tales are told merely to scare someone and not with any real sense of belief. Belief, of course, is an individual matter, so that one person's fictional scary story may be another person's trusted true incident. Also, in a typical storytelling context—say, a slumber party or a campfire circle—a story like "The Baby-Sitter and the Man Upstairs" may be told either as a believed legend or as a spooky joke. But in either case, the tellers never introduce a witch or ghost as the threat to the baby-sitter; it's always some guy hiding upstairs calling on the telephone extension.

Another distinction folklorists make is between standard urban legends that are widely told among a diverse population and other, equally bizarre stories that circulate mostly among fringe groups, often in the first person. In this category would go the stories of Bigfoot, lake monsters, UFOs, alien abductions, cattle mutilations, Satanic cults, conspiracies, the Bermuda Triangle, Elvis sightings, and so forth. There's plenty of supernaturalism involved in such stories, rich material for folklorists to investigate, but the style, content, and function are clearly different from the typical urban legend. Furthermore, such topics are exploited in the media, so that it's difficult to say where oral tradition and mass media treatments diverge.

Tabloids, science fiction, and film and television treatments of supposed paranormal topics—all aided nowadays by freewheeling Internet communication—have taken over many of the supernatural themes formerly reserved for folk tradition; one might even speculate that the genre of genuine supernatural legend is a dead issue, so to speak. Well, not quite, although certainly some individual stories have died out in the oral tradition.

The legend called "The Dream Warning" is a good example of what may happen to a specific supernatural legend. In the 1940s and '50s this story was a living legend in the United States. One version, published in the journal *Arkansas Folklore* in 1953, was heard "from the mouths of friends" some years earlier in a big city, as the collector Albert Howard Carter explained. Carter was told it by more than one person with different details, and all of the storytellers regarded their tales "as true accounts of actual happenings," except that they supposedly had happened "to a friend of a friend." Clearly, Carter had defined an urban legend here, and he attributed it to a FOAF years before these terms came into use. Here is his story:

> This girl—she was a friend of [another friend]—was at a house party, and late one night after everyone had gone to bed, she was awakened by the brightness of the moon shining into her room. So she rose to pull the shade further down, but while at the window she looked out to see a coach, of all things, coming up the drive, with a coachman with the most haunting kind of face. She was extremely puzzled, and the more she thought about it the more mysterious it seemed to her, especially the fact that the coach had made no sound whatsoever. The next day, she looked on the gravel drive for horses' hoof prints and wheel tracks, but there were none. At first she thought it was part of the entertainment, a surprise, and so she didn't mention it to her hostess. As a matter of fact she dismissed it as part of a dream. But some time later, she was in Marshall Field's [department store] waiting for an elevator. One came, and the operator called out, "Going down?" She gave one look at him and saw that he had the face of the coachman she had seen at the house party. She was so taken aback that she walked away from the elevator and didn't get on. The doors closed, and the elevator crashed to the basement, killing all the occupants.

Although there were varying renditions of "The Dream Warning" circulating orally, it had been published earlier as a sort of literary ghost story; the tale was Bennett Cerf's contribution to a 1944 anthology titled *Famous Ghost Stories.* Cerf couldn't resist souping up the style as he retold the legend:

> . . . a familiar voice rang in her ear. "There is room for one more!" it said. The operator was the coachman who had pointed at her! She saw his chalk-white face, the livid scar, the beaked nose! She drew back and screamed, and the elevator door banged shut in her face. . . .

As Cerf explained in his introduction, he had heard the stories told "more than once" over a period of years, and although details of the tellings varied, he wrote, "the essentials were always the same."

However "The Dream Warning" has not been reported by folklorists since the 1950s, probably for several reasons. For one thing, some details of the story—house party, coachman, and elevator operator—have become outdated. Secondly, the notion of prophetic dreams is less compelling than it may have been some 50 years ago, and the chances nowadays of a fatal accident in an elevator are minuscule. Another powerful reason for the demise of this legend, I believe, is its own success in another medium, television.

On February 10, 1961, Rod Serling's famous TV series *The Twilight Zone* first aired an episode that was a dramatic version of "The Phantom Coachman" variation of "The Dream Warning" legend. Titled "Twenty-Two," the episode featured a dancer named Liz Powell (played by Barbara Nichols), who was hospitalized for fatigue. She suffered recurring visions of following a nurse to Room 22—the hospital morgue. And the nurse always said, "Room for one more, honey."

Her doctor and her agent dismissed her fears as merely bad dreams. But when she was discharged from the hospital, Powell was about to board Flight 22 to Miami when the flight attendant—a woman identical to the nurse in her visions—said, "Room for one more, honey." Powell ran screaming back to the airport lounge, and the plane exploded in midair just after takeoff.

According to *The Twilight Zone Companion,* Serling based his plot on Bennett Cerf's version of the legend in *Famous Ghost Stories.* And according to my readers when I wrote a newspaper column in 1989 about the old "Dream Warning" legends, *The Twilight Zone* version was the only one most of them knew. After numerous reruns, the TV episode had virtually replaced the folk legend in the popular mind. Every reader who wrote me following my column mentioned this episode, with one exception, and this person mentioned that he saw the plot enacted in a mid-1940s film called *Dead of Night.* I'll bet my legend-hunting license that this film, too, borrowed from the Cerf version.

And yet, and yet . . . as pop singer Dickey Lee sang in his mournful vanishing-hitchhiker ballad "Laurie" in 1965, "Strange things happen in this . . . [pause] worrrrrld!" Yes, Bennett, Rod, Liz, and Laurie, there still *are* a few modern urban legends that at least skirt the edge of the supernatural. Strange things *do* happen in this world.

"The Devil in the Ham"

Late one night a mother was fixing lunch for her child for school the next day. She decided to use Underwood Deviled Ham, but as she was opening the can she cut her finger, and she swore, saying "Oh hell!" or "Damn it!" At the same time a drop of her blood fell into the meat. Suddenly a bunch of little devils just like those pictured on the label popped out of the can and began stabbing her with their tridents. The woman was found dead the next morning with tiny little scratches all over her body. (In other versions the mother grabs a Bible and chases the little devils back into the can, then puts the Bible on top of the opened can until the devils are all dead.)

"The Vanishing Hitchhiker"

Last night I visited on the telephone with a friend who is a retired school librarian. She had a story for me. The woman who lives next door to her has a friend who knows some people to whom this happened. They are a couple who have a business in Sioux Falls, South Dakota, as well as Sioux

City, Iowa. (The two towns are about 90 miles apart on Interstate 29.) These people travel the route often and are very familiar with the highway.

One day not long ago they were driving along I-29 toward Sioux Falls when they happened to notice a hitchhiker. They do not normally pick up hitchhikers, but they did stop to pick up this one. They visited with him as they rode along, and then he suddenly announced, "The world is going to end tomorrow!" They looked around, but there was no one in the back seat. They thought he might have opened the door and jumped out, although they had been going 65 miles per hour. So they stopped and reported the incident to a highway patrolman. His comment was, "You know, this is the sixth time that this has been reported to me this month."

Another friend of mine who is a policewoman in Sioux City reports that she has heard the story nine or ten times from the police community, her church group, and others. The highway patrolman supposedly has heard it 15 or 16 times. Sometimes the message is "The Lord is coming for the second time, and you should prepare yourself."

BIZARRE TALES OF A MYSTERIOUS HITCHHIKER

Frackville [Pennsylvania]—If someone walked up to you and told you a story about an experience they had or about which they heard concerning a hitchhiker who foretold, "The end is near" and disappeared from "inside" a vehicle, what would you think?

Like most people, you would probably doubt the report or maybe turn the TV set to the popular *Unsolved Mysteries* show and try to summon its host, Robert Stack, to unravel the bizarre event.

Such a story was brought to the attention of the *Evening Herald* recently and the reactions of editorial department personnel were predictable: "Yeah, right."

A check with state police, however, revealed troopers had received several calls relating to the hitchhiker incident.

Sgt. Barry Reed, station commander at Frackville, confirmed receiving three or four calls about the mysterious vanishing hitchhiker, from reliable and credible individuals who all shared the same experience.

The hitchhiker was described as a tall, thin man with long dark hair and wearing a long dark coat. He was picked up on Route 61 near Frackville's southern end on Monday, Jan. 31, between 6 and 7 a.m.

However, contrary to the "unofficial" reports, state troopers said they received no reports about the "hitchhiker" in conversation about the weather, the turbulence of society or the Angel Gabriel "tooting his horn for the second time."

However, troopers did say the reports made to them concerned the hitchhiker having said, "I am here to tell you the end is near," before vanishing into thin air.

Some of the reports relayed to the *Evening Herald* alleged the mysterious hitchhiker warned, "Jesus is coming! Jesus is coming!" and then disappeared.

Sgt. Reed recalled that while he was stationed in Lancaster County about 10 years ago, a similar "hitchhiker" tale was circulated.

My neighbor who lives across the street from me told me that her boyfriend's boss's aunt was driving down I-10, going east toward Baton Rouge about two months ago when she spotted a young man with long hair hitchhiking right around the Breaux Bridge area. Not one to pick up hitchhikers, she surprised herself by pulling over and offering the man a ride. He got into the car. The man stayed quiet throughout the drive, even when the woman questioned him about where he was from, his family, etc.

Suddenly the man looked at her and said, "Gabriel will soon blow his horn." Then the man vanished into thin air. The woman became hysterical, driving faster and faster, until a Louisiana State Trooper pulled her over. After telling the State Trooper what happened, he told her that hers was the seventh report of the same vanishing hitchhiker that day.

The Iowa story is from Thelma Johnson of Sioux City, in a letter sent in September 1990; the Pennsylvania story is from the Shenandoah Evening Herald *for February 4, 1994; and the Louisiana story is from Keigh Granger of Scott, Louisiana, in a letter sent in March 1994. These examples typify the most common recent form of the legend with the FOAF attribution, the precise highway details, the mysterious statement and "vanishing" of the hitchhiker, and the police affirming that several such reports were received. "The Vanishing Hitchhiker" has international distribution as one of the oldest and most widely told of all urban legends; as such, it has long attracted the attention of folklore scholars. In the earliest book that I know of devoted entirely to urban rumors and legends, Maria Bonaparte's 1947* Myths of War, *is a study of "The Corpse in the Car" variation of "The Vanishing Hitchhiker" legend. ("Proof" of the hitchhiker's prophecy is the truth of a second prediction—that the driver will have a corpse in his car by the end of the day.) My 1981 book bearing the same title as the legend contained 20 pages of discussion and notes on the legend and merely scratched the surface. A published bibliography of contemporary legend studies listed 133 publications concerning "The Vanishing Hitchhiker" up to 1991. Many American versions describe a teenage girl in a light party dress who hitches a ride home; she vanishes and is identified—often from a portrait—as the ghost of a girl who died on the same date many years earlier. A sweater she borrowed from the driver is found draped over her tombstone. This is the version that Dickey Lee turned into a song, as did various other pop singers and groups in their own times and styles. The legend has also inspired films, radio and television dramatizations, short stories, and an unending series of tabloid "reports." In 1987, after recording a discussion of this and other urban legends for a Salt Lake City radio station, I tuned in to hear the broadcast of my interview a few days later. I was amused that the song aired immediately after it was Dickey Lee's 1965 "Laurie,"* so *I sent a note to the interviewer complimenting him on digging out this appropriate golden oldie. But it turned out that the selection was not intended; the announcer on duty had just picked this song as the next one up in the regular rotation of new and old favorites, without knowing what had preceded it in the recorded interview. As I said, strange things* do *happen in this world!*

"The Lost Wreck"

Jasper [Alberta, Canada]—The mystery of the Miette Hot Springs Road, along with the four human skeletons who made the tale so intriguing, can finally be laid to rest.

Like many a tantalizing story which gains credibility with repeated tellings, this rumor seems to have sprung from a fertile imagination fed by the clean mountain air.

A story doesn't have to be true to be told again and again.

According to one resident, who preferred to remain nameless, a friend of a friend heard about a gruesome discovery made by a work crew widening the road to Miette Hot Springs over the summer.

"They were killing time over lunch by pushing boulders over the edge when they heard one of the rocks hitting metal.

"That got them interested. When they went down to look, they found this car with 1950s license plates and four skeletons inside."

As the story goes, for reasons never explained, authorities wanted to keep the discovery a secret. Of course the hint of a cover-up simply added zest to the tale.

Don Dumpleton, Jasper's chief warden, chuckled when asked about the mystery before he explained there is no truth to the story.

"I've heard the story. The only thing is the place keeps changing," he said.

Part of an article headlined "Miette skeleton mystery as real as mountain mist," by Paul Cashman, in the Edmonton Journal, *December 15, 1985. As mentioned in my discussion of this story in* Curses! Broiled Again!, *the discovery motif in this modern legend seems to have been borrowed from a Norwegian legend about the discovery of a medieval village that was decimated by the Black Death, or bubonic plague. In a version of this story collected in 1835, a hunter found the long-forgotten village when an arrow he shot into the woods struck the bell of the village church; when he pushed through the undergrowth to find the source of the strange clang, he found the village, peopled only by skeletons. An even stranger aspect of "lost wreck" lore was the discovery in a canal near Boca Raton, Florida, on February 22, 1997, of a wrecked van containing the skeletal remains of five teenagers missing since July 14, 1979. Copies of news articles from the* Tampa

Tribune (March 2nd), the Palm Beach Post (March 3rd), the St. Petersburg Times (March 10th), and the Fort Lauderdale Sun-Sentinel (April 29th) contain full details about this tragedy and its aftermath. The van was spotted in the 20-foot-deep murky waters of the canal next to a busy highway by a man wearing polarized glasses to search for fish. Now if he had been casting for catfish with a heavily weighted line, and if his lead sinker had struck metal, then I would wonder about the total accuracy of these reports.

"The Death Car"

I heard this story in about 1968; it was very popular in this area at the time. Supposedly, the car was a new dark blue Thunderbird with a black vinyl roof. The owner had shot himself in the head while parked on a lightly traveled prairie road outside Steinbach, Manitoba [Canada], and his body was not found for about two weeks. It happened during the summer, when temperatures sometimes reach 115 degrees, and his remains had more-or-less liquefied in the vehicle.

According to the story, after the Steinbach police discovered the car, it was towed into a nearby Ford dealership. Eventually, the Thunderbird's interior was ripped out and the car interior was completely sandblasted, re-painted, re-carpeted, and re-upholstered. But the smell had embedded itself directly into the molecules of the metal frame.

Though the car was priced at only $500, nobody would buy the used Thunderbird. The smell was still too strong. But then, nobody could find that car on a sales lot anyway.

Based on notes from my conversation on March 16, 1989, with Paul E. Pirie of the Fort Frances, Ontario, police force. Fort Frances is in far western Ontario, just across the river from International Falls, Minnesota. Folklorists traced "The Death Car" legend back to the mid-1940s before losing the scent. Its prototype seems to be a traditional legend about ineradicable bloodstains left at a murder site. Presumably, as the story was told and retold, the stains became a stench, and a car became the death scene. The low price for the flawed *classic car is a detail that entered just after World War II, when new cars were in short supply. When I was in high school, the deal was $50 for a befouled Buick; the story has evolved to mention many different makes of cars on sale for various bargain prices. Frequently, the car is a Corvette that has the smell embedded in its fiberglass body. In my 2000 book* The Truth Never Stands in the Way of a Good Story, *I dispute the claim of folklorist Richard M. Dorson to having found the origin of the legend in an actual incident in a Michigan small town. However, in July 1990,* Automobile Magazine *reported on a 1959 Cadillac Eldorado Seville, with only 2,216 miles on the odometer, that was garaged as evidence for a murder case after its owner had been executed in the front seat. After 22 years in storage, the Cadillac was sold to car collector John Pfanstiehl, who drove it just 16 more miles before placing it in the Car Palace Museum in Somerset, Massachusetts. Pfanstiehl wrote to me in 1986, "I am sure all the previous reports of the death cars were false, so sure that I almost dismissed the one true legendary car when I was told about it."* Automobile Magazine *commented, correctly, "not all of the legend is intact. The seats don't smell."*

"The Missing Day in Time"

THE SUN DID STAND STILL

Did you know that the space program is busy proving that what has been called "myth" in the Bible is true? Mr. Harold Hill, President of the Curtis Engine Co. in Baltimore, Maryland, and a consultant in the space program, relates the following development:

I think one of the most amazing things that God has for us today happened recently to our astronauts and space scientists at Green Belt [*sic*], Maryland. They were checking the position of the sun, moon, and planets out in space where they would be 100 years and 1,000 years from now. We have to know this so we don't send a satellite up and have it bump into something later on in its orbits. We have to lay out the orbits in terms of the life of the satellite, and where the planets will be so the whole thing will not bog down! They ran the computer measurement back and forth over the centuries and it came to a halt. The computer stopped and put up a red signal, which meant that there was something wrong either with the information fed into it or with the results as compared to the standards. They called in the service department to check it out and they said, "It's perfect." The head of operations said, "What's wrong?" "Well, they have found there is a day missing in space in elapsed time." They scratched their heads and tore their hair. There was no answer!

One religious fellow on the team said, "You know, one time I was in Sunday School and they talked about the sun standing still." They didn't believe him; but they didn't have any other answer so they said, "Show us." He got a Bible and went back to the Book of Joshua where they found a pretty ridiculous statement for anybody who has "common sense." There they found the Lord saying to Joshua, "Fear them not; for I have delivered them into thine hand; there shall not a man of them stand before thee." Joshua was concerned because he was surrounded by the enemy and if darkness fell they would overpower them. So Joshua asked the Lord to make the sun stand still! That's right—"The sun stood still, and the moon stayed . . . and hasted not to go down about a whole day." Joshua 10:8,12,13. The space men said, "There is the missing day!" They checked the computers going back into the time it was written and found it was close but not close enough. The elapsed time that was missing back in Joshua's day was 23 hours and 20 minutes—not a whole day. They read the Bible and there it was—"about (approximately) a day."

These little words in the Bible are important. But they were still in trouble because if you cannot account for 40 minutes you'll be in trouble 1,000 years from now. Forty minutes had to be found because it can be multiplied many times over in orbits. This religious fellow also remembered somwhere [*sic*] in the Bible where it said the sun went BACKWARDS. The space men told him he was out of his mind. But they got the Book and read these words in II Kings: Hezekiah, on his death-bed, was visited by the Prophet Isaiah who told him that he was not going to die. Hezekiah asked for a sign as proof. Isaiah said, "Do you want the sun to go ahead ten degrees?" Hezekiah said, "It's nothing for the sun to go ahead ten degrees, but let the shadow return backward ten degrees." II Kings 20: 9–11. Isaiah spoke to the Lord and the Lord brought the shadow ten degrees BACKWARDS! Ten degrees is exactly 40 minutes! Twenty-three hours and 20 minutes in

Joshua, plus 40 minutes in II Kings make the missing 24 hours the space travelers had to log in the logbook as being the missing day in the universe! Isn't that amazing? Our God is rubbing their noses in His Truth!

From an anonymous, single-spaced, typewritten, and photocopied sheet telling a spurious story that has circulated with variations in details for at least two decades, especially in fundamentalist Christian circles. Essentially the same story has been repeated in periodicals, religious tracts, letters to editors, and in sermons or lectures. A press release from the Goddard Space Flight Center of Greenbelt, Maryland, flatly denies the story and explains that Harold Hill worked only briefly there in the 1960s "as a plant engineer, a position which would not place him in direct contact with our computer facilities or teams engaged in orbital computations." The "Missing Day" story—precomputer version—can be traced to C. A. Totten, a lieutenant and instructor who taught military science and tactics at Yale from 1889–92 and also preached anti-Semitism and predicted an imminent apocalypse—several times. For a detailed discussion of this story and its history see my 2000 book The Truth Never Stands in the Way of a Good Story.

"The Ghost in Search of Help"

Most of the incidents in this book have taken place in Nova Scotia, but we need an occasional one from outside to confirm experiences here. I have a story from England . . . [which] is both strange and beautiful and came to me in a surprising way. I had spoken to the School of Community Arts at Tatamagouche one evening and dropped in to see some friends there the next day. In the hall I met Rev. Mr. Minton from Lockeport . . . an Anglican rector, and so is the man of whom he spoke. Knowing of my interest in ghosts, he asked if I would like to hear a story from England. He had heard it from the sister of the man to whom it happened, and she has been a friend of many years' standing. . . .

"Rev. Mr. Gray belonged to a large family and had been recently ordained. This was in the early Edwardian period. He had taken a parish in the East End of London. His housekeeper had gone to bed and he was

sitting in his study smoking his pipe and thinking out his sermon for Sunday. Presently the door bell rang—a spring bell—and he went to answer it. Standing under the gas light in the fog stood a little old lady in poke bonnet and shawl and a once black skirt now green with age. She pleaded with him to go to an address in the West End of London. She said he must go because he was urgently needed. The young clergyman tried to put her off as it was very late, but she pleaded so earnestly that he finally promised to go that same night.

"He took a cab and at length arrived at the address. It turned out to be one of the large mansions in the West End and it was lit up and obviously there was a party going on. After he had rung the bell and waited, the butler came and the clergyman said, 'I believe I'm wanted here. My name is Gray.'

"The butler said, 'Have you an invitation?'

"'No, but I've been asked to come. Some one needs me.'

"The butler asked him to wait in the little anteroom and presently brought back the master of the house. He was a well-known titled gentleman. Mr. Gray then told him what had happened and the man looked very odd and asked if he could describe his visitor. As he did so, the man looked terrified. He then confessed to having led a wicked life of crime which included white slavery, whereupon the clergyman tried to help him. He urged him to stop this life and make his peace with God, and the man finally made what appeared to be a serious confession. The clergyman then gave him absolution and said in leaving,

"'Just to show that you're in earnest, I'll be celebrating holy communion at eight-thirty in the morning and I want you to be there.' Then he went away.

"The next morning as the priest turned to administer the sacrament it was obvious that the man was not there and he wondered what he should do about it. After breakfast he decided he should see him again. He arrived at the mansion house, now still and quiet, and at his ring, the butler came. When he asked to see his master the butler told him he was dead. Mr. Gray said,

"'It can't be true. I was talking to him last night.'

"'Yes, I know. I recognize you,' the butler said. 'He died shortly after you left.'

"Mr. Gray asked if he could see the body which he knew must still be in the house, and the butler took him up to a very spacious room. There, lying on the bed, was the dead body of the man he'd been talking to the night before. He stood for a moment thinking, trying to puzzle it out and, as he did so, he glanced around the room. His eye caught an oil painting above the bed. It was of a little old lady in a poke bonnet and shawl—the same little old lady who had come to him and had sent him to this house. He said to the butler,

"'Who is the little old lady?'

"'That is the master's mother. She died many years ago.'"

From Helen Creighton's 1957 book Bluenose Ghosts, *pp. 185–87. This text shares the "portrait identification" motif with many versions of "The Vanishing Hitchhiker." A variation of the "Ghost in Search of Help" legend in which the messenger is the spirit of a young girl seeking medical attention for her gravely ill mother has long been associated with Dr. Silas Weir Mitchell (1829–1914), a prominent Philadelphia physician; in fact, the evidence is convincing to suggest that Dr. Mitchell himself had told the story as a personal experience, although whether intended as a hoax or to be taken seriously is not perfectly clear. The Mitchell version has been frequently embellished and often reprinted, including in the Reverend Billy Graham's 1975 bestseller* Angels: God's Secret

Agents. *In my 2000 book* The Truth Never Stands in the Way of a Good Story, *I devote a chapter to "The Folklorists' Search for the Ghost in Search of Help for a Dying Person."*

"The Well to Hell"

Scientists are afraid that they have opened the gates to hell. A geological group who drilled a hole about 14.4 kilometers deep (about 9 miles) in the crust of the earth, are saying that they heard human screams. Screams have been heard from the condemned souls from earth's deepest hole. Terrified scientists are afraid they have let loose the evil powers of hell up to the earth's surface.

"The information we are gathering is so surprising, that we are sincerely afraid of what we might find down there," stated Mr. Azzacov, the manager of the project to drill a 14.4 kilometer hole in remote Siberia.

The geologists were dumbfounded. After they had drilled several kilometers through the earth's crust, the drill bit suddenly began to rotate wildly. "There is only one explanation—that the deep center of the earth is hollow," the surprised Azzacov explained. The second surprise was the high temperature they discovered in the earth's center. "The calculations indicate the given temperature was about 1,100 degrees Celsius, or over 2,000 degrees Fahrenheit," Dr. Azzacov points out. "This is far more than we expected. It seems almost like an inferno of fire is brutally going on in the center of the earth."

"The last discovery was nevertheless the most shocking to our ears, so much so that the scientists are afraid to continue the project. We tried to listen to the earth's movements at certain intervals with super-sensitive microphones, which were let down through the hole. What we heard, turned those logically thinking scientists into a trembling ruins. It was sometimes a weak, but high pitched sound which we thought to be coming from our own equipment," explained Dr. Azzacov. "But after some adjustments we comprehended that indeed the sound came from the earth's interior. We could hardly believe our own ears. We heard a human voice, screaming in pain. Even though one voice was discernible, we could hear thousands, perhaps millions, in the background, of suffering souls screaming. After this ghastly discovery, about half of the scientists quit because of fear. Hopefully, that which is down there will stay there," Dr. Azzacov added.

Translated from *Ammenusastia*, a newspaper published in Finland.

This article was published in the February 1990 issue of Praise the Lord, *a publication of Trinity Broadcasting Network; the odd style and punctuation of this report may in part stem from its translation from Finnish. Variations of this story were widely repeated among evangelical Christians in sermons, broadcasts, and publications. When a caller to his daily talk-radio program based in Los Angeles asked about "The Well to Hell," host Rich Buhler tried to track it down. His search, reported in the July 16, 1990, issue of* Christianity Today, *revealed that the "respected Finnish scientific journal" mentioned in some versions was merely a newsletter published by a group of Finnish missionaries. A trail of oral and printed sources eventually led Buhler to a Norwegian schoolteacher who claimed to have fabricated the whole story. An article by Soviet geologist Y. A. Kozlovsky on "The World's Deepest Well" in the December 1984 issue of* Scientific American *may have inspired both the idea of an ultradeep drilling operation in Siberia and possibly the name "Azzacov." A story in the tabloid* Weekly World News *for April 7, 1992, claims that a similar incident happened in Alaska two years later, killing three oil workers and releasing a huge cloud shaped like the head of Satan. This article includes a photograph of the cloud and of "Dr. Dmitri Azzacov," who appears remarkably cheery for a man who has had to face such terrors*—twice!

"The Ghostly Videotape"

C.G.K. [folklorist]: Tell me what you heard about *Three Men and a Baby.*
Virginia: We saw it!
Kim: Oh yeah, the ghost.
Virginia: There's a young boy standing behind the drapes.
Kim: Yeah, Ginny's got the tape. We can show it to you.

Virginia: They say that the apartment where they filmed the movie, that that boy lived there.

Kim: The lady that rented the building out to them to make the movie, her son shot himself there.

C.G.K: Shot himself?

Virginia: They say in another part of the movie you can see the rifle that they didn't know was there, the gun he used.

C.G.K: Did you see the gun?

Virginia: We haven't looked yet.

Kim: The only reason I saw the boy is because somebody told me exactly where it was. I never saw it. I watched like three times before that, and I never noticed. You can see him real clear. I don't see how I missed it.

C.G.K.: What does he look like?

Virginia: He looks like about a thirteen-year-old, fourteen-year-old boy.

Kim: He was about thirteen, and he had dark hair, and he was standing there was like a window, and he was standing in the curtains—like standing in between the curtains. They interviewed Ted Danson, and

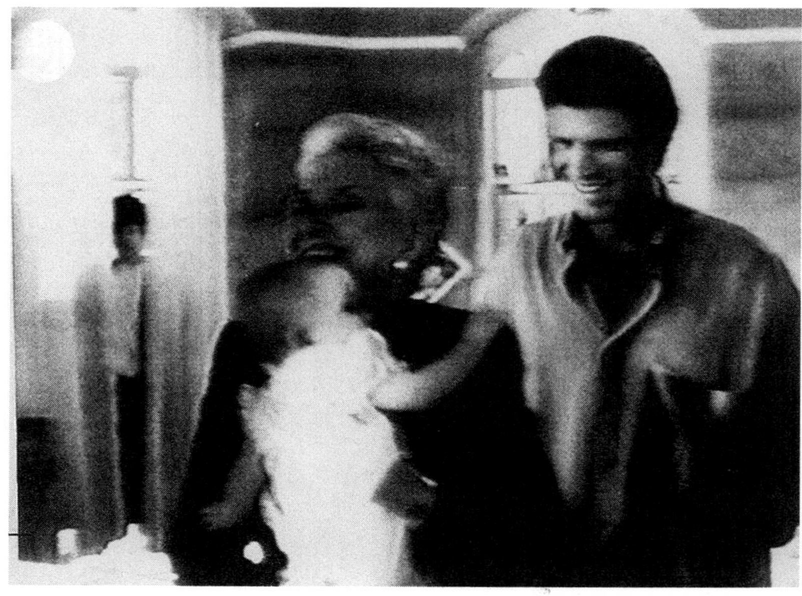

AP/Wide World Photos

they asked him what he thought about it. He said it scared the shit out of him. He said that he didn't notice it. He didn't see it there until they were watching the movie.

C.G.K.: How did it get past the editors?

Virginia: That's what was weird about it. They didn't see it when they edited it.

Kim: The mother of the little boy saw it, and she said that's him.

Virginia: Do you think it's a plant?

Kim: It can't, well it might be.

Virginia: What I don't understand is, though, why the people at the movies didn't catch it. First run, nobody ever caught it. Nobody ever noticed it.

Kim: I didn't catch it. I watched it a bunch of times, and I didn't see it until somebody told me it was there. It's just like in the background. I can see how they missed it. But he's just staring at them. I mean I turned the movie off. I turned it off, and I came downstairs with everybody else because I was watching it up there [laughter].

C.G.K.: You can see his face?

Kim: Yeah. Clearly.

From Charles Greg Kelley, "Three Men, A Baby, and a Boy Behind the Curtain: A Tradition in the Making," Midwestern Folklore, *vol. 17, pp. 6–13; this is text "L" on pages 12–13, "Collected from Virginia Jamison, an art supply store manager, and her daughter Kim, a high school senior. Birmingham, Alabama. November 17, 1990." This transcription of an interview is a fine example of the "discussion" mode of transmitting urban rumors and legends; nobody actually "tells" the story, but instead they talk it over. In the summer of 1990, shortly after the 1987 film* Three Men and a Baby *was released on videotape, people noticed a shadowy figure looking like a young boy that appears briefly in the background of one scene. Videotape allowed viewers to search for and freeze the frame with the image, options not available in a movie theater. The rumor quickly spread that it was the image of a boy who was killed or committed suicide in the apartment in which the scene was filmed. The film's producers, the Touchstone Pictures division of the Walt Disney studios, explained that the image was a cardboard stand-up cutout of actor Ted Danson and that the New York City "apartment" was actually a sound stage in Toronto. In further versions of the story, new details emerged, including the suspicion that the "ghost" may have been planted as a publicity ploy by the film's distributors. Some people also claimed to have seen the boy's mother interviewed by Barbara Walters on* 20/20. *Another factor to consider is that spectral images in photographs have been described in traditional legends almost since the invention of photography. In some strange way this old motif was recycled to fit a new situation.*

"A Dirt-Cheap Way to Sell Real Estate"

He outsells his closest competitor, the Blessed Virgin, five to one at the downtown Tonini Church Supply Co. He is sought by people who can't tell a scapular from a rosary.

He is St. Joseph, the patron saint of family and household needs—and underground real estate agent.

More and more Louisville-area home sellers and agents are burying statues of St. Joseph in yards and asking for his intercession to bring buyers. The practice—which is popular in Chicago and on the East and West coasts—is spreading locally by word of mouth.

"It's gone crazy. We can hardly keep the statues in stock," said Bill Tonini, vice president of the firm that calls itself the largest religious-goods supplier in the South. "A lot of real estate agents swear by it."

Tonini said that each week he sells 250 to 300 statues of St. Joseph, who was a carpenter by trade. Tonini carries the statues in several sizes and materials, ranging in price from $1 to $8.

The saint's popularity has even spawned a mail-order firm in Modesto, California, that sells a 3 1/2 inch plastic statue and burial instructions for $8. Karin Reenstierna, co-owner of the firm, Inner Circle Marketing, said her company has sold more than 4,000 of the statues since December.

According to Reenstierna, the practice of burying the saint's image began centuries ago in Europe, where nuns buried their St. Joseph medals and prayed for more land for their convents. . . .

The Roman Catholic Church has no official stance on the practice of burying saints for commerce, according to Rosemary Bisig Smith, director of communications for the Archdiocese of Louisville.

But after consulting with several priests, Smith said, "We certainly don't mind having this personal devotion to St. Joseph, we are concerned about people using this practice for personal profit."

Reenstierna instructs her customers to bury St. Joseph head first with his feet toward heaven and his face toward the street. He should be wrapped in plastic and placed near the "for sale" sign.

To prod St. Joseph into action, sellers are instructed to say the following words over the saint before shoveling in the dirt:

"O St. Joseph, guardian of household needs, we know you don't like to be upside down in the ground, but the sooner escrow closes the sooner we will dig you up and put you in a place of honor in our new home. Please bring us an acceptable offer (or any offer!) and help sustain our faith in the real estate market."

From an article by Kyung M. Song in the Courier-Journal *of Louisville, Kentucky, April 12, 1991. The burying of St. Joseph to stimulate a real estate sale is known even more widely across the United States than this article suggests, and starting in 1990 it was written about by publications ranging from the* Wall Street Journal *and the* Washington Post *to supermarket tabloids. I have found no evidence for the supposed centuries-old European origin of the practice mentioned above, but I have found other mail-order catalogs offering inexpensive statues suitable for burying. While the planting of statues can be accepted as a genuine folk custom that was spread via example and word-of-mouth and varied in execution, the prayer to St. Joseph quoted above has not been collected elsewhere and sounds like the invention of a realtor or a seller of statues intending to make a better "ritual" out of the practice.*

"The Devil in the Disco"

My brother was involved in a car accident and was taken to the hospital. My mother went to see him that day, that is when she overheard some nurses speaking of a girl that was being treated there for mental disturbance and burns claimed to have been given to her by the devil.

That afternoon my mother told me about the saying [rumors] but she didn't know exactly what had happened. So I called a few friends and got more or less a complete story.

According to the information I obtained, this girl had told her mother that she was going dancing at Boccaccios 2000 [a discotheque]. Her mother objected and the girl very determined, said she was going. So right before the girl walked out of the door, her mother yelled out, "Well if you go I hope you meet with the devil."

After the girl had arrived at Boccaccios she was sitting down when all the girls started a commotion about a young man who had walked in the door. Everyone claims he was so handsome, it was unreal. It is also said that he was dressed extremely well.

After a while the young man came and asked the girl to dance, she was thrilled at the thought that she was the one he had chosen. So while they were dancing the girl noticed that everyone on the dance floor was walking away and staring at them. When she turned to look at her partner she noticed he was not dancing on the floor [i.e., he was floating in the air].

She was puzzled, so she looked again and then she noticed he had animal feet. So she began to scream and tried to run away from him, but the young man began to laugh very loud and mysterious, and he grabbed her. When he grabbed her he burned her shoulders. Another man tried to help the girl and he was also burned. So much commotion was made that the young man, by then known as the devil, had disappeared. No one knows how or when. The only thing was that he had left an odor of sulfur. And a laughter of horror was heard. But no one knows how he left.

SOMETHING EVIL IS ON THE PROWL IN OUR CASINOS

HARRISON FLETCHER

This story comes from my wife, who heard it from my sister, who has a friend, who knows this lady, who says she saw the whole thing.

A while ago—it could have been Good Friday—an elderly woman and her best friend were playing the slots at Isleta Gaming Palace. They had been there all day long and had been winning off and on.

Toward the end of the day, one of the women put all her money in a machine and lost. Just as she was getting ready to leave, a handsome old man, who had sat behind her the entire time, tapped her on the shoulder.

"Here's $3," he said. "I have a feeling you might win."

"No thanks," the old woman said. "I'm getting ready to leave. But you go ahead and play."

The man smiled a handsome smile. "Please," he said. "I insist."

So the woman took the $3 and began to play. No sooner had she punched the first button than the winning words flashed on her screen: Jackpot: $3,000!

The woman was amazed.

Stunned.

What luck!

She turned to thank the man and share her winnings—as is the casino custom—but he was gone. She searched the entire casino, but he had vanished. Just like that.

The woman cashed her winnings and headed to the parking lot, when suddenly, she saw the old man sitting in his car and rummaging through his glove compartment. She walked up and tapped gently on the window. The man slowly turned to face her.

"He had these burning red eyes and pointy horns!" the woman recalled later. "It was . . . the devil!"

The woman is resting at a local hospital now. The collection box at her church is $3,000 richer.

But wait.

There's more.

That same day—and it could have been Good Friday—another woman was playing blackjack at Isleta Gaming Palace. She too had been gambling all day and losing her money. Just as she stood to leave, a tall, dark and handsome man in a black coat tapped her shoulder.

"Why don't you play the slots?" he said. "The one in the corner will win."

At first, the woman refused, but she too relented. Two minutes later, a $5,000 jackpot! She wheeled around to thank the man, but he had begun walking away into a crowd. Just before he disappeared, she noticed something peculiar poking from the back of his coat: a pointed tail!

"Give me a break," says Conrad Granito, the general manager of Isleta Gaming Palace. "I've heard about 16 different versions of that story."

The disco story was collected from a Mexican-American male, age 21, in Edinburg, Texas, fall 1978, and published in 1984 by Mark Glazer in "Continuity and Change in Legendry: Two Mexican-American Examples," Perspectives on Contemporary Legend: Proceedings of the Conference on Contemporary Legend, Sheffield (England), July 1982, *pp. 123–27. Other disco versions of the story appear in the third* Perspectives *collection, published in 1988, in an article by Maria Herrera-Sobek, "The Devil in the Discotheque: A Semiotic Analysis of a Contemporary Legend," pp. 147–57. Fletcher's column on the devil in an Indian casino appeared in the* Albuquerque Tribune *on May 9, 1996. Both stories are modernizations of old traditional devil legends; they recycle such motifs as the mother's curse, the diabolical well-dressed stranger, floating in air, physical characteristics (flashing eyes, horns, animal's feet and tail), burning, a smell of sulfur, and dancing being forbidden on Good Friday. Although these themes are consistent with Mexican-American culture in the Southwest, I have heard of the devil visiting a tavern in a small town near Yakima, Washington, and there are several published stories about the devil coming to a Cajun party in Louisiana or to a French-Canadian dance in Quebec. The devil is described in many older European legends as playing cards with gamblers; there he is recognized by his cloven hoof when a player drops a card and reaches under the table to pick it up. I won't be surprised if the dark, mysterious, and dangerous stranger shows up eventually in sushi bars, espresso shops, and aerobics classes.*

12

Funny Business

Judging from the topics of urban rumors and legends concerning the business world, Americans don't trust big business either to behave honorably or to avoid doing things that are just plain silly. Chapter 8 illustrated how contamination stories have plagued some companies, but modern folklore goes beyond these claims to levy charges that businesses have supposedly mistreated, misled, and misinformed their employees and clients on a regular basis. There are also turnabout stories—equally unverified—about how people have fought back against big business. A letter from a company executive published in *Time* (May 11, 1992) demonstrates how one such story leapt from anonymous tradition to the pages of a major publication:

> I was very disappointed in your article [on April 20, concerning Wal-Mart stores]. What Hugh Sidey referred to as a Wal-Mart employee chant—"Stack it deep, sell it cheap, stack it high and watch it fly! Hear those downtown merchants cry!"—is a figment of someone's imagination. It was erroneously reported some time ago; it was simply not chanted then and never has been. You have done your readers a disservice.
>
> Don E. Shinkle
> Vice President for Corporate Affairs
> Wal-Mart
> Bentonville, Ark.

Very likely what we have here is a piece of anti-Wal-Mart folklore—a story passed among the teeming millions who both shop at Wal-Mart (or similar huge chain stores) and, yet, at the same time regret the decline of downtown business districts and small, locally owned companies. The apocryphal chant, parodying an athletic cheer, sums up the buyers' dilemma: whether to support the downtown locals or to save money at the place where they "stack it deep/sell it cheap." The solution is to save the money, but also to chant the chant. Did a Wal-Mart employee ever actually chant this cheer? It's hard to know for sure, but my rule is "Never say never."

The bigger a company is, the more likely there will eventually be some derogatory stories circulating about it. You can't sell all those Big Macs or Whoppers or Domino's Pizzas without someone sooner or later starting rumors about things like worms or worse getting into the ingredients. And whenever a big company changes something, like its name, logo, or product line, watch out! Example: Why did Kentucky Fried Chicken alter its name to just KFC? Ask around, and you'll hear:

- They developed a mutant four-legged chicken, and now the government won't allow them to use the word "chicken" for the creature.
- Colonel Sanders had a rule that as long as the company kept the word "Kentucky" in its name, they could never refuse service to someone who lacked money, and too many homeless people were taking advantage of the free food.
- A psychic advised the company that the old name had bad vibes.

Or is it just because the word "fried" carries negative health connotations? Yes, probably, but that isn't nearly as interesting as the rumors.

Sometimes there's such perfect logic to a business rumor that you yearn to believe it, whether or not there's proof—or even the possibility of proof. Is it true that the Apple computer company uses a Cray supercomputer to design its hardware systems and, conversely, that the Cray company uses an Apple? The Internet newsgroup alt.folklore.urban marks this one as "true," and, as a devoted Macintosh user, I really want to believe it.

Speaking of the Internet, this marvelous electronic data conduit and grapevine for gossip is simply crawling with folklore. Cartoonist Scott Adams, that leading satirist of business foibles, alluded to the Internet's lore-sharing potential in his book *The Dilbert Future* (1997):

> About three times a day, different people forward the same e-mail to me about an alleged incident involving Neiman-Marcus and their secret cookie recipe. This is a famous urban legend. . . . I want my Bozo Filter to look for the words "Neiman Marcus" and "cookies" and reject those messages. And I want a mild electric shock sent back through the Internet to whoever thought I needed to see that.

(If you don't know what Adams is referring to, the answer is just three stories down in this chapter.)

Even when the company is not named in a legend, the *type* of business involved, and its supposed chicanery, may be made perfectly clear. Consider the role of the insurance company (not to overlook the actions of the cigar smoker and the legal authorities) in the story related in this piece of E-mail I received recently:

> A Charlotte, North Carolina, man, having purchased a case of rare, very expensive cigars, insured them against . . . get this . . . fire. Within a month, having smoked his entire stockpile of fabulous cigars, and having yet to make a single premium payment on the policy, the man filed a claim against the insurance company. In his claim the man stated that he had lost the cigars in "a series of small fires."
>
> The insurance company refused to pay, citing the obvious reason that the man had consumed the cigars in a normal fashion. The man sued and won!
>
> In delivering his ruling, the judge stated that since the man held a policy from the company in which it had warranted that the cigars were insurable, and also guaranteed that it would insure the cigars against fire, without defining what it considered to be "unacceptable fire," it was obligated to compensate the insured for his loss.
>
> Rather than endure a lengthy and costly appeal process, the insurance company accepted the judge's ruling and paid the man $15,000 for the rare cigars lost in "the fires." After the man cashed his check, however, the insurance company had him arrested . . . on 24 counts of arson! With his own insurance claim and testimony from the previous case being used as evidence against him, the man was convicted of intentionally burning the rare cigars and sentenced to 24 consecutive one year terms.

Most people would grasp the flaws in law and logic involved in this story of what one commentator has called "cigarson"; nevertheless, the tale does satisfy our notions of what it takes to fight the system, plus how the system fights back and wins most of the time.

Published reports of legitimate settlements of class-action suits against big companies sometimes spill over into legend land, where the facts are merrily mixed with fantasy, and a whole new set of specifics may emerge. A case in point is a 1996 settlement involving the pricing of infant formulas. On January 1, 1997, at just about the time the deadline for filing claims expired, a new twist in the story was faxed, E-mailed, phoned, and posted all across the country. Supposedly, Gerber Products Company, which had absolutely no involvement in the formula suit, had been ordered to give every child under twelve years of age a savings bond or cash in amounts ranging from $500 to $1,500. All the parents had to do was forward a copy of the child's birth certificate and Social Security card to a post office box in Minneapolis. Take a look at the "Gerber in the News" page on the Gerber Products World Wide Web page to see their blunt denial. Business folklore may often be funny, but it's no fun fighting back.

"Lego 'homeless' rumor false"

Chicago Tribune *[distributed to news sources in January 1992]*

The rumor was persistent: In an effort to be more relevant, Lego, maker of those colorful interlocking blocks, had added a plastic, homeless person to some of its kits.

FAO Schwarz heard it. So did Marshall Field's. A salesperson at Toys R Us even said it was "to teach kids sensitivity and compassion."

But a spokesman for Lego was confident that such gritty realities of urban life never would be packed into each box, which stretches children's imaginations from medieval England to the outer reaches of the galaxy.

"Oh, there must be some mistake," said the spokesman. "You see, only smiling, happy people live in Legoland."

"The Bedbug Letter"

My recent essay on "duck letters" has brought forth the classic of that species. Thanks to Ernest R. Kaswell, of Reston [Virginia], for passing it along.

In case you've never had the pleasure of receiving one, "duck letters" appear to offer up great compassion and hasty action in response to whatever you've requested. In fact, they are designed to hug your request to death in an avalanche of words. They duck, even as they appear to help. Of course, Capitol Hill offices and government agencies are past masters of the art.

Anyway, Ernest says the classic (and perhaps original) duck letter is "The Bedbug Letter."

Before airplane travel became routine, Ernest recalls, business executives traveled by train. They slept in berths in Pullman cars.

What would happen, Ernest says, is that Mr. Jones would have dinner and a drink in the dining car, then retire to his bedroom for the evening. "A couple of hours later, he feels itchy, starts to scratch, sits up, turns on the light and finds that the bed is infested with bedbugs," Ernest writes.

"He calls the porter and conductor. They apologize, but say they can't give him another bunk because the train is sold out. So he sits up all night in the club car, gets off the train in Chicago, is mad as hell and fires off a letter to the president of the Pullman Company in New York.

What comes back is a letter that fairly drips with abject caring and regret.

"We are very sorry about your experience," it says. "Be assured that we do everything possible to keep our beds and facilities absolutely immaculate, and we do apologize for this unusual situation. We hope this does not cause you to stop traveling by Pullman. Try us again, and we know you will have a more pleasant experience."

There's only one trouble. A note is attached to the letter with a paper clip. Obviously, it's an interoffice memo that should have been removed but wasn't. It reads:

"Bill, send this SOB the bedbug letter."

From "Bob Levey's Washington," the Washington Post, *May 6, 1993. The term "duck letters" is new to me. I replaced Levey's string of symbols representing profanity with the more common term, "SOB." Usually the quoted letter is more detailed, reporting actions like these: "[The car] has been stripped of all furnishings. The bedding, upholstery, curtains, carpet, and all other combustible materials have been burned. The toilets and their fixtures have been scrubbed down and sterilized with carbolic acid. By the time you receive this letter, the car will have been fumigated and steam cleaned from end to end . . . the responsible personnel have been reprimanded, docked two weeks' wages, and assigned to refresher training. . . ." Sometimes the original letter of complaint is accidentally sent back with the reply, and it bears a rubber stamp reading "Send the bug letter." In other versions the routing memo refers to the passenger as "this jerk" or "this dame." The story has been reported from the 1940s and was probably popular even earlier. A tongue-in-cheek letter to the editor in the* Princeton Alumni Weekly *for February 5, 1992, even claims that "The Bedbug Letter" dates to 1889 and attributes it directly to George M. Pullman, the president of the sleeping-car company.*

"Red Velvet Cake"

Red Velvet Cake and Its Story

The story behind this cake is both interesting and expensive. It seems that a woman from Seattle was dining at the Waldorf-Austoria Hotel in New York and was deeply impressed with the cake served to her one evening. It looked like red velvet with a beautiful white frosting. She asked them if they would send her the recipe. They did, but it arrived C.O.D. with a charge of $300! She paid the cost and then consulted her lawyer who told her she could do nothing to get her money back. Since the price of the recipe had been costly to her, she decided all her friends should enjoy baking and eating this luscious and extravagant Red Velvet Cake.

Red Velvet Cake

1/2 cup shortening
1 1/2 cups sugar
2 eggs
2 ozs. red coloring
2 Tbsp. cocoa
1 tsp. salt
1 tsp vanilla
1 cup buttermilk
2 1/4 cups sifted cake flour
1 Tbsp. vinegar
1 level tsp. soda

Cream shortening, sugar, eggs. Make a paste of cocoa and food coloring and add to the cream mixture. Mix salt and vanilla with buttermilk and add alternately with flour to the cream mixture. Then mix soda and vinegar and fold into the mixture. Do not beat. Bake in two 9-inch pans, greased and floured. Bake 20 min. at 350 degrees.

Frosting

5 Tbsp. flour
1 cup milk
1 cup granulated sugar
1 cup butter
1 tsp. vanilla

Cook flour and milk until thick, stirring constantly. Let cool until cold. Cream together sugar, butter, vanilla. Add to cold flour mixture. Beat until the consistency to spread. When finished it looks like whipped cream, but until then is curdy.

NOTE: the 2 ozs. of food coloring is the correct amount, and this is the reason for the color and texture of red velvet.

Copied verbatim from a mimeographed sheet handed out by a Home Economics teacher at the University of Idaho in 1961. This story bedeviled the Waldorf-Astoria until the early 1980s, when the expensive-recipe legend shifted to the Mrs. Fields company and eventually to Neiman Marcus as a story about a cookie recipe. In some versions of the legend the woman's lawyer charges her an outrageous fee for his advice, thus adding insult to injury. Prototypes for the legend in the 1930s and '40s featured recipes for various kinds of candy, fudge, ice cream, and cake supposedly sold for an outlandishly high price. The earliest published high-priced cake recipe found so far was for "$25 Fudge Cake" as made by a railroad chef and included in a Boston women's-club cookbook in 1948. Although red cakes have been known to American cooks since the early twentieth century, a ripoff-priced red *cake recipe is not found in legends until the 1950s, about the same time that the story attached itself to the Waldorf-Astoria. Even while disavowing the legend, the hotel has given out copies of the "authentic" recipe at no cost. Often served at Christmas, Valentine's Day, or the Fourth of July by those who enjoy it, Red Velvet Cake represents a strictly* *"fun food" aspect of American cuisine, similar in that respect to creations like "Mock Apple Pie" (made with Ritz crackers) and "Tomato Soup Cake."*

"Neiman Marcus Cookies"

THIS IS TRUE—PLEASE TAKE THE TIME TO READ IT AND PLEASE SEND THIS TO EVERY SINGLE PERSON YOU KNOW WHO HAS AN E-MAIL ADDRESS.....THIS IS REALLY TERRIFIC.

My daughter & I had just finished a salad at Neiman-Marcus Cafe in Dallas & decided to have a small dessert. Because both of us are such cookie lovers, we decided to try the "Neiman-Marcus Cookie."

It was so excellent that I asked if they would give me the recipe and the waitress said with a small frown, "I'm afraid not." Well, I said, would you let me buy the recipe? With a cute smile, she said "Yes." I asked how much, and she responded, "only two fifty, it's a great deal!" I said with approval, just add it to my tab.

Thirty days later, I received my VISA statement from Neiman-Marcus and it was $285.00. I looked again and I remembered I had only spent $9.95 for two salads and about $20.00 for a scarf. As I glanced at the bottom of the statement, it said, "Cookie Recipe - $250.00."

That's outrageous!

I called Neiman's Accounting Dept. and told them the waitress said "two-fifty," which clearly does not mean "two hundred and fifty dollars" by any *POSSIBLE* interpretation of the phrase. Neiman-Marcus refused to budge. They would not refund my money, because according to them, "What the waitress told you is not our problem. You have already seen the recipe - we absolutely will not refund your money at this point."

I said, "Okay, you folks got my $250, and now I'm going to

have $250.00 worth of fun." I told her tht I was going to see to it that every cookie lover in the United States with an e-mail account has a $250.00 cookie recipe from Neiman-Marcus . . . for free. She replied, "I wish you wouldn't do this." I said, "Well, you should have thought of that before."

So, here it is!!!

Please, please, please pass it on to everyone you can possibly think of. I paid $250 dollars for this recipe . . .

"Neiman-Marcus Cookie"
(Recipe may be halved)

2 cups butter
4 cups flour
2 tsp. soda (club soda)
2 cups sugar
5 cups blended oatmeal**
24 oz. chocolate chips
3 cups chopped nuts (your choice)
2 cups brown sugar
1 tsp. salt
1 8 oz Hershey Bar (grated)
4 eggs
2 tsp baking powder
2 tsp. vanilla

**Measure oatmeal and blend in a blender to a fine powder.

Cream the butter and both sugars. Add eggs and vanilla, mix together with flour, oatmeal, salt, baking powder, and soda. Add chocolate chips, Hershey Bar and nuts. Roll into balls and place two inches apart on a cookie sheet. Bake for 10 minutes at 375 degrees. Makes 112 cookies.

Have fun!!! This is *not* a joke - - - this is a true story!

Verbatim from the Internet, one of literally hundreds of copies of this that I have received since 1989. In the early 1980s the story was told about the Mrs. Fields company with the typical detail that the "two-fifty" misunderstanding took place during a telephoned request for the recipe made to the company headquarters in Park City, Utah. The blenderized oatmeal and Hershey bar are direct quotations from the Mrs. Fields version, which mutated briefly to "Marshall Fields," the Chicago department store, before settling on Neiman Marcus and the chain-letter format. Numerous Internet newsgroups and mailing lists have circulated these recipes, with participants gravely discussing such weighty matters as possible copyright restrictions, whether one could not simply cancel the credit card charge, and how best to grate the chocolate bar. Nobody, as far as I know, has commented on the minimal effect of one candy bar spread among 112 cookies, nor the confusion of club soda and baking soda in some versions. Frankly, I have not tested the recipes, and there may be some logic to these ingredients. Mrs. Fields fought the legend with a disclaimer that was printed on cookie bags and on a poster displayed in her outlets. Neiman Marcus debunked the story on the store's Web page and offered a cookie recipe there for free. As an update of "Red Velvet Cake," the expensive-recipe legend may be said to have had a life of about fifty years—so far.

In July 1998 a parody of "Neiman Marcus Cookies" reached me via the Internet. In this version a man has his car's oil changed at the "Neiman Marcus All Tune and Lube" and asks the mechanic if he can have the chemical formula for their best oil. The rest of the story follows the cookie plot closely, and the man ends up paying $250 for the "recipe." The parody ends by quoting the complex chemical formula for a hydrocarbon compound (which may be motor oil, for all I know). Yet another Neiman Marcus parody is included in the epilogue to this book.

"Find the Hat"

I work in Chicago for McKinsey and Company, an international management consulting firm; two weeks ago I heard this story from a colleague during a discussion on the difficulty of wearing hats in the "windy city."

Back in the days when McKinsey consultants had to wear hats, one of the consultants was walking down a street in Chicago when the wind picked his hat off his head and blew it down the street. Since the consultant was rushing to a client meeting, he did not have time to chase it. The next time the consultant filed an expense report with Accounting, he listed this lost hat as a business expense and claimed a reimbursement.

About a week later, he received back the expense report with a note attached which said he could not claim a reimbursement for personal items such as a hat. He immediately called Accounting, and there followed a rather vociferous conversation regarding whether his hat was lost in the line of duty. As is true with most discussions with Accounting, they prevailed and he did not get the claim.

About a month later, the consultant filed his next expense report. It was perfectly documented with hotel and restaurant receipts for all the previous month's travel. But he attached to the report a note to Accounting: "Here's my expense report. Find the hat."

I first heard this story in 1984 when I worked for Morgan Guaranty Trust Company in New York. The only differences were that it was a Morgan banker's hat which was blown off while he was on a sales call in Chicago, and that the Morgan version placed the story in the recent past.

Sent to me in 1988 by James E. Hyman, who commented, "These stories seem to represent the business sub-species of urban legends used to socialize business people to the ever-present game of pulling the wool over the bean-counter's eyes." After I published a summary of Hyman's story I heard from five more businesspeople. A man in Columbus, Ohio, had heard the story told in New York in 1942 concerning a Bell Laboratories employee whose hat was cut in two by a streetcar. A man in Huntington, New York, had heard the story from his "trusted Sales Manager" who said it was a lost umbrella belonging to another salesman that had been buried in the expense account. A woman in Annandale, Virginia, knew a version in which a Unisys employee in Flemington, New Jersey, had tried to claim the cost of a raincoat he had to buy during a business trip to Seattle; she also phrased the story's lesson as, "If you have questionable expenses, pad the legitimate expenses." A man from Danbury, Connecticut, also knew a coat version of the story, which he had heard his father tell in the 1930s. Finally, a man from Wilmette, Illinois, wrote in 1995 to say that during an ad agency lunch a few years before he had been told the "Find the Hat" story by someone who claimed personal acquaintance with the instigator of the padded claim. This correspondent asked, "Is he the truth behind the myth, or just a man of mythic achievement?" I guessed the latter, and did not try to contact his source. Surely this is just a legend whose moral lives on.

"The Wife on the Flight"

Remember that campaign a long time ago when businessmen were first beginning to use airplanes?"

...Remember you are
my wife...
I'm his
wife

Deseret News

"You mean the one where the airplane company allowed a man's wife to accompany him free, just to prove there was no danger in airplane travel?"

"Yes, that's the one! Did you ever hear the payoff on that?"

Everyone was interested.

"Well, it seems the company kept a record of the names of the wives who made the trip. And about six months later they wrote to all of them asking how they had enjoyed their airplane trip. And ninety per cent of the letters came back with the question, 'What airplane trip?'"

From Marguerite Lyon, And So to Bedlam (1943), *pp. 280–81. This story has been published several times in sources ranging from newspaper columns to books concerning business practices, airlines, and even extramarital affairs. Variations on the theme include a story in which a hotel chain sent follow-up letters to the spouses of travelers who had never actually stayed there, and a story in which a university sent inquiries to married people who had stopped attending evening classes. For straying spouses, the moral of the stories is "Maintain your cover story." For businesses, the moral might be "Don't ask, don't tell."*

"Redemption Rumors"

Spokane—An old rumor and a cruel hoax has just taken a new turn, Mrs. Marie M. Ferrell, manager of Better Business Bureau of Spokane said Tuesday.

"Thousands of people have been duped into saving useless items in the futile hope of supplying a seeing-eye dog to a blind person," she said.

First, she said, it was empty match folders, then cellophane strips from cigarette packages.

"More recently it has been tabs off tea bags and empty cigarette packages," she said. "Now there is a false report going the rounds which started people saving beer can tabs."

These rumors persist, she said, despite the fact that seeing-eye dogs cannot be obtained through collection of any type of items.

False rumors have plagued the aluminum industry and the national Kidney Foundation for years concerning beverage can pull tabs and kidney dialysis. Across the nation, at various times, word has spread that aluminum can pull tabs could be recycled in exchange for time on a kidney dialysis machine for someone with kidney disease. Many well-intentioned yet misinformed groups and indivuals collected pull tabs only to find that there was no pull tab/kidney dialysis donation program. It never existed. Anywhere.

PULL-TOP PRICE RUMORS DON'T HAVE A RING OF TRUTH

Fort Worth—A gallon jug full of pull tops from aluminum cans is worth:

A) $90 cash?

B) A pint of blood at a blood bank?

C) Free time on a kidney dialysis machine?

D) 46 cents, the going rate at local recycling centers for roughly 2 pounds of aluminum?

The correct answer, of course, is 46 cents.

As odd as the other answers sound, however, dozens of people a day have been calling Texas recycling centers in recent months, saying that they have heard that the pull tops are somehow valuable or special.

"I've gotten calls from all kinds of people who have heard these rumors: kids, schoolteachers, individuals old and young alike," said Susan Dequeant, marketing specialist for Alcoa Recycling Co. in Grand Prairie.

Dequeant said the most common variation of the rumor is that the pull tops are a purer type of aluminum and that a gallon jug filled with them is worth between $80 and $100.

She said the rumor that one can receive medical services for the pull tops might be related to rumors that the tops are made into hypodermic needles. Neither is true. . . .

TEEN'S EFFORT HITS SOUR NOTE

Fort Walton Beach [Florida]—Kerra Hensley was on the verge of tears.

"It's gotta be true," the 14-year-old said.

Thursday afternoon, she learned a month's worth of work would not end as she hoped.

Her goal was to help her 5-year-old neighbor, a blond, blue-eyed little girl who loves to jump on trampolines. The child needs kidney dialysis to stay alive.

Kerra collected 50,000 soda can tabs to exchange for 50,000 free minutes of kidney dialysis at a Gainesville hospital.

But the Daily News, while pursuing a story about Kerra's good deed, discovered no such program was available.

A hospital spokesman knew nothing of an exchange of tabs for dialysis minutes. . . .

First, a May 19, 1965, story in the Spokane, (Washington) Spokesman-Review*; second, "Keep Tabs on Your Cans," a brochure issued by Reynolds Aluminum and the National Kidney Foundation in 1988; third, an October 30, 1992, article by Thomas Korosec from the* Fort Worth Star-Telegram*; fourth, a January 3, 1997, article by Teresa Wood from the* Fort Walton Beach (Florida) Daily News. *Rumors that huge numbers of otherwise useless things can be redeemed for direct health ben-*

efits for needy patients have circulated for at least forty years. The companies and hospitals named in the rumors are often perceived as heroes until the falsity of the stories is revealed; then they become the villains. The first article above anticipates the eventual focusing of all such rumors on the opening tabs on aluminum drink cans; as kidney dialysis machines became available in the 1970s, pull-tabs-for-dialysis became the standard version. Despite the development of opening tabs designed to remain attached to cans, and despite the fact that costs of dialysis are largely borne by government programs and health insurance, the rumors persist. Year after year newspapers report individuals and groups that have amassed enormous quantities of pull tabs, believing that they can be exchanged directly for time on dialysis machines. Often these efforts are combined with an elementary-school teacher's desire to illustrate for a class how a million of something would look. The unintended lesson that all of these collectors learn is that aluminum is worth its weight in . . . aluminum. It would make more sense to recycle the entire can, or in states with a can deposit, to redeem the cans at collection centers. Complicating this whole picture is the establishment of several genuine pull-tab collection campaigns since 1989 to raise money for various health concerns; but all *of these efforts conclude by simply selling the aluminum to recycling centers. Since most of these programs ask people to mail in their pull tabs, it is considered impractical and unsanitary to collect the whole cans. Nobody seems to be bothered by the cost of postage versus the very low value of pull tabs, and nobody seems interested in a program in which donors would recycle their aluminum in their home communities and then simply mail a check to the sponsors. Somehow, pull tabs by the millions and millions seem to have captured people's imaginations, and many people are willing to believe that doctors will not turn on dialysis machines to save the lives of poor little children until enough pull tabs arrive at the hospital. Question: what do people think the hospitals want with the pull tabs?*

"The Body in the Bed"

My aunt told me this story. She said that it really happened to her nephew's friend. It seems that the friend and her husband were staying in the Excalibur Hotel in Las Vegas. There was a slight but unpleasant odor in the room. They checked the room for rotting food, unflushed toi-

lets and the like, but found nothing. Being that it was in the wee hours of the morning, and they were exhausted, they decided to retire for the night and tell the management in the morning. When they woke up, the stench had become unbearable. They complained to the management. It was then discovered that in the box springs lay the corpse of a prostitute. They had literally slept with a prostitute!

From Curtis Minato of Los Angeles, writing me in August 1991. This was a very popular story in 1991 and '92; sometimes the body was said to be that of a Mafia hit victim. Most versions ended with the hotel management—at either the Excalibur or the Mirage—cancelling all charges on the room, or even promising the victims a free room for life if they will keep their experience quiet. Both the lingering smell of death and the freebies are reminiscent of the much older "Death Car" urban legend. In 1988 the decomposed body of a murder victim was found under a bed in an Oceanside, New Jersey, motel room, but, except for the report of a bad smell, this case was different from the Las Vegas legend. Instead of being a luxury hotel, the New Jersey business was described in news stories as one that "attracts a 'transient type' of clientele who often stay only a few hours at a time." According to newspaper reports, in March 1994, after German tourists complained of a bad smell in a motel room near the Miami International Airport, the decomposed body of a woman was found under the bed. Five months later, according to further news stories, another decomposed body was found in a Fort Lauderdale, Florida, motel room by—would you believe?—another group of German tourists. As unlikely as these last two cases seem, I read it in the newspaper, which is better than hearing it on the grapevine. No further body-in-bed urban legends seem to have emerged since 1992.

"The Cabbage Patch Tragedy"

In the Christmas seasons of 1983 and 1984, Cabbage Patch Kids, those moon-faced soft dolls, were the hottest toys of the season. You did not merely buy a Cabbage Patch Kid, you adopted one, and you got the papers to prove it.

Eventually some of the dolls got broken, or run through the wash, or chewed on by the dog. When the doll's "parent" sent the damaged "kid" back to the factory, she got in return . . .

- A letter of condolence?
- A death certificate?
- A bill for the funeral?
- The "kid's" remains in a tiny coffin, ready for burial?
- A citation for child abuse?

Answer: None of the above. The doll's manufacturer, Coleco Industries (sometimes misunderstood to be "Conoco"), provided repair services at set fees for their dolls, but no funerals, coffins, death certificates, etc. A spokeswoman in the Cabbage Patch public relations department in Georgia, when contacted by a reporter in November 1984 about the stories, sighed and said, "Has that story surfaced again? I thought we buried it. No pun intended."

13

The World of Work

There's a wonderful continuity in certain legends of the workplace. Over and over again through the years—according to the stories—the working stiffs have found ways to one-up and frustrate the bosses. In his 1981 book *Land of the Millrats,* folklorist Richard M. Dorson collected this classic example in a steel mill of northwestern Indiana in the mid-1970s, calling it "the classic folk legend of mill thievery":

> John was an immigrant laborer from eastern Europe who worked in the mills. And every afternoon when leaving work he trundled out a wheelbarrow with his work tools, covered with straw. The gate guards were suspicious of John, and they always examined the wheelbarrow carefully, poked under the straw, but never found anything except the tools, which clearly belonged to him. So they had to let him go through.
>
> So this went on day after day, year after year. Finally the day came for John's retirement. He had worked thirty years in the mill. So, as he is leaving on his last day, trundling out his wheelbarrow, the gate guard said to him: "All right, John, we know you have been stealing something. This is your last day; we can't do anything to you now. Tell us what you have been stealing?"
>
> John said: "Wheelbarrows."

Forty years earlier, during the Great Depression, a similar story was told about another eastern European worker, this one a Jewish salesman of "pazamentry" named Sam Cohen. (Pazamentry, the storyteller explained, "is the decoration that's added to a garment"—lace trim, embroidery, ribbons, fancy buttons.) Again the worker is a trickster who gains the last laugh on management just as he's about to retire. This beautifully elaborated version of the payback story was told by Jack Tepper of Brooklyn to folklorist Steve Zeitlin and appears in Zeitlin's book *Because God Loves Stories* (1997).

> Well after forty years Sam is going to retire, and he's talking to another salesman, and he says, "What I really want to do is, there's a Mr. O'Connell who owns a dress house, and he would never buy anything

from me 'cause he hates Jews. And to me, the high-light of my career, is before I retire I could sell him an order."

So he goes to Mr. O'Connell to sell him an order. Mr. O'Connell looks at him and says very sardonically, "I hear you're retiring, Cohen. You've been bothering me for years, and you know I don't deal with Hebes. But, okay, you want an order, I'll give you an order—token order." He says, "You have any red ribbon?"

Cohen says, "Sure we got red ribbon. What width?"

He says, "Half inch."

"We got half-inch ribbon."

"You got it."

"How much you need?"

"All you need is an order, right? Just to show you sold me. I want a ribbon that will reach from your belly button to the tip of your penis. That's as big a piece of ribbon as I want." And Mr. O'Connell throws him out of his factory.

Six weeks later, Mr. O'Connell goes to open up his factory, and in front of his door are five trailer trucks. And they are unloading thousands and thousands and thousands and thousands of yards of ribbon. He runs upstairs, gets on the phone, and says, "Cohen, you miserable animal, what the hell did you send me?"

He says, "Look Mr. O'Connell. Exactly what you asked me is what I sent you. My belly button, everybody knows where it is. You said till it reaches the tip of my penis. Fifty-five years ago I was circumcised in a little town outside of Warsaw, Poland. . . ."

Legends like these portray the bad old days in the world of work, and sets of strict rules purporting to prove the bad side of the "good old days" are also passed around as anonymous photocopied folklore. These rule lists, like urban legends, have many variations. Usually the lists are claimed to date from the 1860s or '70s; however, every copy I have seen of "The Good Old Days" is printed or typed in a modern format and never reported directly from an authentic century-old source. Most of them are claimed to be guidelines for the office workers in a "carriage shop." Some of the lists have as many as a dozen entries, but here is a typical example with six items from Robert Ellis Smith's 1983 book *Workrights*:

> Working hours shall be 7:00 A.M. to 8:00 P.M. every evening but the Sabbath. On the Sabbath, everyone is expected to be in the Lord's House.
>
> It is expected that each employee shall participate in the activities of the church and contribute liberally to the Lord's work.
>
> All employees must show themselves worthy of their hire.
>
> All employees are expected to be in bed by 10:00 P.M. Except:
>
> Each male employee may be given one evening a week for courting purposes and two evenings a week in the Lord's House.
>
> It is the bounden duty of each employee to put away at least 10% of his wages for his declining years, so that he will not become a burden upon the charity of his betters.

Smith credited the *New York Times* for these rules, which sounded impressive, so I looked up the referenced November 17, 1974, issue. All I found was the list itself, appended to a *Times* article about privacy; the list was credited to "a New York Carriage Shop, 1878." The *Times* was probably merely reprinting as a sidebar a piece of contemporary photocopy lore, just as the *Boston Globe* once did with a similar list credited to "a carriage works in Boston" from 1872. I have further versions of "The Good Old Days" on file that modify the rules slightly to fit the jobs of warehouse workers, furniture-store employees, nurses, and teachers. Every one of them requires workers to save part of their wages so as not to be a burden to society and/or to their "betters." And, curiously, most lists, whatever the occupation involved, make some reference to employees having to "whittle nibs" for their pens and bring some coal for the office stove. Is it possible that so many different businesses a century ago in scattered locations had parallel sets of strict rules? If so, then where are the specimens of actual dated documents listing these rules?

Not surprisingly, stories about the modern-day workplace are no easier to verify than are the stories claimed to be from the past. Take the story told to me a few years ago in Portland, Oregon. This time the venue is a jet airliner:

> Supposedly, George Shearing, the blind jazz pianist, was flying from Los Angeles to Seattle. The flight made a brief stop in San Francisco. The pilot, a big jazz fan, went back to meet Shearing during the stopover. When the pilot offered to provide any service or assistance that the pianist might require, Shearing said that he'd appreciate it if someone would take his Seeing Eye dog out for a brief walk.
>
> The captain himself was happy to oblige. He took Shearing's guide dog out for a stroll on the tarmac next to the parked jet. When the other passengers saw their pilot walking to and fro with a guide dog, most of them deserted the flight. The plane was nearly empty on the hop to Seattle.

Or take this workers' story from the contemporary world of computer manufacturing. It's told among industrial engineers and quality-control specialists:

> An American company needed some computer memory chips, so they placed an order with a Japanese company. The Americans specified an acceptance criterion of 0.2 percent defective, and they ordered 1,000 chips.
>
> The order arrived in two packages. The larger package contained 998 perfectly good memory chips. The smaller package contained two defective chips with a note saying that they didn't know why the company wanted two defective chips, but it was their policy always to meet customer requirements.

Work at any level has its characteristic folklore, usually including a few legends. When a former pizza delivery man told me about the time he delivered a hot pizza to a nude woman on a warm summer night in southern Michigan, I asked him how he knew she was nude, since he mentioned that he had not actually seen her. For two reasons, he replied. First, she had kept the door hooked on the locking chain and made him slip the pizza in vertically through the crack. Second, he had heard many stories from other delivery men about nude customers who had greeted delivery persons working for that company. Indeed, I myself subsequently heard several other accounts of pizza delivery to nude customers, and I was reminded of people in other legends who were said to have been caught at home in the buff by other service personnel—plumbers, meter readers, and carpet layers.

I don't want to identify any particular company as the most frequent target of these tales, but I do think that something we folklorists call "The Goliath Effect" is operating. What this means is that the dominant company in any business tends to become the magnet for all legends told about particular products and services. That being true, and because such stories also spill over to smaller competitors, I would identify the pizza-delivery legends as exhibiting "The Domino Effect."

I got another twist on pizza delivery in a letter from a reader in Australia. The writer had heard that the Goliath of the industry there (Guess who?) had an agreement with the city's drug squad. Whenever a delivery person suspected that the people who had ordered pizza might be under the influence of drugs ("and especially if they ordered double anchovies"), then the driver would immediately notify local police to stage a raid.

Supposedly, in return for this reporting service, the pizza company's drivers never received speeding tickets. Personally, I wouldn't trust anyone who would order even a regular-size dose of anchovies on their pizza.

"Wheeling and Dealing"

A seaman who was steering the ocean liner Queen Mary *across the Atlantic got bored one day and carved his initials on the wooden steering wheel. When the captain saw this, he ordered the seaman to pay for a new wheel.*

The seaman did as he was ordered, but after he paid for the wheel he stated that now it was his, and he disconnected it and took it to his cabin. The ship was helpless in the middle of the Atlantic Ocean, and they had to beg the seaman for the wheel so they could bring the ship into port.

"The Rattle in the Cadillac"

Let me tell you the moving saga of an almost perfect luxury car—a dream machine, but for a single irritating flaw due to sabotage on the assembly line. The car, so the story usually goes, is a sparkling new Cadillac, outfitted with every available option. But soon after purchasing it, the car's wealthy owner discovers one feature that nobody wants—a persistent, unexplained rattle coming from somewhere in the car.

The owner returns the new car to the dealership again and again. Mechanics tune and retune the engine, tighten every nut and bolt, and lubricate everything that moves. But each time the owner pilots the big car back out onto the street, the rattle is still there, as loud as ever.

Finally, in desperation, the owner instructs the mechanics to dismantle the car completely, piece by piece, until they find the elusive rattle. When they remove the left-hand door panel they spot the problem. Inside the hollow door, a soda bottle is suspended by a string. As the car moves, of course, the bottle swings to and fro, bumping the inside of the door. The bottle contains a collection of nuts, bolts, and pebbles—and a note: "So you finally found it, you rich SOB!"

Some Caddy owners, it is claimed, have had the bottle and its contents

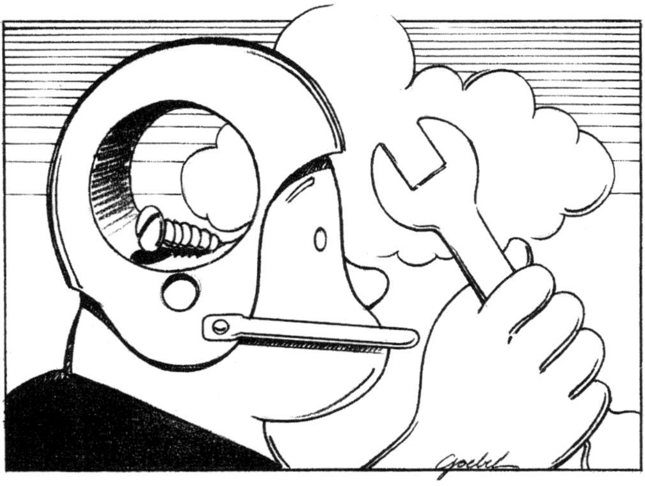

Illustration by Joe Goebel, copyright 1987, 1998

framed as souvenirs of the odd incident. But, oddly enough, I've never seen such a display, or one of the alleged notes, although I've heard about them from many friends of friends of friends of the supposed car owners.

I retold this old story in a newspaper column released the week of August 8, 1988. In response to the column, W. K. Petticrew of New Castle, Delaware, wrote, "I have grown weary of hearing the soda-bottle-in-the-door-panel story; I've heard it so often since 1969 when I started 'twisting wrenches' for a living. The story has more holes in it than a hobo's teeth." Those holes, of course, are what make "The Rattle in the Cadillac" a bona fide urban legend that suggests how blue-collar autoworkers seek to gain revenge against the people who can afford the luxury cars they build. Sometimes the story is told about employees at an auto plant that is about to be moved or closed down; the workers played the prank to protest the loss of their jobs. This legend was given national prominence in 1986 by Brian "Boz" Bosworth, then a star linebacker at the University of Oklahoma, who claimed, in Sports Illustrated's *preseason football issue, to have encountered the prank while working at a General Motors plant in Oklahoma City during the summer of 1985. Boz's anecdote raised the roof in Oklahoma City, and in Detroit, where GM executives denied that any such incidents of sabotage had occurred. Eventually Boz apologized, and a fellow plant employee added, "He heard a lot of auto war stories [but] we don't even have any nuts or bolts in the part of the plant where Brian worked."*

"The Roughneck's Revenge"

I heard this story several times while working in the East Texas oil fields in the early 1960s:

The crew of a drilling rig had just finished pulling several thousand feet of drill pipe from a drill hole, in preparation to replace the work-out drill bit. While working on the new drill bit, a roughneck [an oil-drilling crew member] accidentally dropped his wrench into the open hole. Drilling had to be halted, and several days and a great deal of money was expended to "fish" the tool out of the hole.

When the wrench was finally brought to the surface, the drilling superintendent grabbed it and pushed it at the offending roughneck. "You and this wrench cost us thousands of dollars, you dumb S.O.B," he said. "Take it and get off the rig. You're fired!"

"Well, if that's the way you want to be about an accident," the roughneck said, and he dropped the wrench back into the open hole, turned and walked away.

Sent to me in 1982 by Colin Neal of Salt Lake City. Mary C. Fields includes the same story in her article on offshore oilfield lore published in the winter 1974 issue of the journal Mid-South Folklore. *Similar "revenge" actions are frequently described in connection with numerous other occupations, and probably such things do occur from time to time: "You're fired!" "Oh yeah, then take* that." *In the worst cases, disgruntled employees go beyond folk stories and pranks to committing serious crimes. Clearly, the safety valve of storytelling and prank-playing is better for all concerned.*

"Fixing the Flue"

Bert Willey, the painter, heard this story at his father's knee: A mason builds a new fireplace for a wealthy man. When the mason finishes the job, he asks for his money, but the wealthy client says he can't pay just now. He doesn't have the right change. That's all right, the mason says. But if he has to wait, then the client does, too. The wealthy man agrees. He won't build a fire in his new chimney until he's paid the mason. The mason goes home. Just an hour or so later, his wealthy client appears at the door. "My house is full of smoke, goddammit!"

"I told you not to use that chimney until you paid me," says the mason. "When you pay me, I'll fix it."

So the client gets out his wallet, which is full of change after all, and the mason returns to the rich man's house. The mason brings a brick with him. He carries the brick up a ladder to the roof and drops it down the chimney, smashing out the pane of glass he had mortared across the flue.

Bert says his father told that story as if it had actually happened, but

others tell the same story. It must lie mainly among the wishful thoughts of the building trades, like the retort you think of only after the argument.

From Tracy Kidder's 1985 book House, *p. 319. I heard the same story in 1988 from a builder who called in to a radio talk show out of Youngstown, Ohio, on which I was a guest. Two other people have sent me the story, one from Alabama who had heard it "a long time ago," and one from Massachusetts who thought he remembered reading it in* Popular Science *magazine in the late 1930s or early '40s.*

"The Locked-Out Pilot"

Civil air transport was not without its operational problems. For example, when the 737 was first used by what will be, for the purposes of this next true story, an unnamed airline, it endured an interesting initial experience. On the inaugural flight, the well-qualified crew was flying an FL 310 in the clear blue sky. The pilot and copilot were on schedule at altitude—all was right with the world.

The pilot, in accordance with company policy, told the copilot to take control while the pilot went aft to talk with the passengers. He left the cockpit area. The copilot diligently attended to his duties until he became aware that he needed to relieve himself. He waited for the pilot—and waited.

Finally, discretion being the better part of valor, he checked position, the surrounding sky for traffic—there was none and they were cruising at a hard altitude. The auto pilot was functioning perfectly—the airplane was performing beautifully. He took a last look and quickly got up from the right seat, ducked out of the cockpit area, and into the forward lavatory. Completing what he had set out to do, he hurriedly left the lavatory and placed his hand on the cockpit door. It was locked. He reached for his key only to remember that the key was in his jacket in the cockpit.

Not wanting to stand on ceremony he walked back into the cabin area where he saw the Captain talking earnestly with a passenger. He tapped the Captain on the shoulder and asked him for his cockpit key. Without looking up, the Captain said it was in his jacket pocket in the cockpit and, at the same time, came to full alert and gave the copilot an incredulous "What are you doing here" look. Both pilots ran forward.

One fire axe, one smashed door, and two bruised ego's later, the airplane was under manned flight again. Needless to say, the airline changed procedures.

From Aviation, Space, and Environmental Medicine, *May 1986, pp. 478–79. On December 30, 1987, Rick Anderson, a columnist for the* Seattle Times, *repeated a version of this story credited to "a Boeing representative, based on a first-hand account from one of Boeing's Far East agents." In February 1991, Mabel M. Shaw of Lillington, North Carolina, sent me a version of the story she had read in a guide book to China; it supposedly happened on a Chinese airline. The first person to tell me "The Locked-Out Pilot" legend was David L. Webster IV, a United Airlines pilot who had heard that it was a DC-9 flown by another airline that was said to have suffered the incident. Webster also explained that the crash axe is kept in the cockpit, not in the cabin, and that "a swift kick will open the door in any Boeing aircraft; the door is designed to open in either direction in case it gets jammed in a crash."*

"Language Boners: The Folklore of Paperwork"

Every office where letters and applications from the general public are processed has its own "funny file" of mistakes in language that were supposedly written by semiliterate patrons or non-native speakers of English. Other mistakes allegedly come from the professionals themselves who commit unwitting slips of the tongue or pen. Lists of these boners are often duplicated and passed around, posted on bulletin boards, or published in company newsletters. Some of the examples undoubtedly come from actual written material submitted to the same office, but most of them are reprints of similar lists that have been circulating for decades. Evidence for the traditional nature of boner lists is that certain phrases and sentences appear again and again through the years, no matter where or when the lists are said to have originated. While these language boners are not, strictly speaking, *legends*—lacking a narrative element—they do exhibit the anonymity, variation, and typical functions of modern folklore. Here are just a few examples from some of the most common categories of boners, a complete set of which would require a book in itself. All are quoted from anonymous photocopied sheets collected from office workers, teachers, nurses, and others.

From "The Welfare Letter"

Unless I get my husband's money soon, I will be forced to live an immortal life.

My husband got his project cut off two weeks ago, and I haven't had any relief yet.

I want my money as quick as I can get it. I have been in bed with the doctor for two weeks and he doesn't do me any good.

In accordance to your instructions, I have given birth to twins in the enclosed envelope.

Please send my wife's form to fill out.

From "Drivers Say the Darnedest Things" [accident reports]

An invisible car came out of nowhere, struck my vehicle and vanished.

The guy was all over the road. I had to swerve a number of times before I hit him.

Coming home I drove into the wrong house and collided with a tree I don't have.

In my attempt to kill a fly, I drove into a telephone pole.

From "Actual Letters Received by the Army, Draft Boards, etc."

I have already wrote to the President, and if I don't hear from you I will write Uncle Sam and tell him about you both.

I am glad to say that my husband who was reported missing is now dead.

I am a poor widow and all I have is at the front.

Please send me a letter and tell me if my husband made application for a wife and baby.

Unless I get my husband's money soon, I will be forced to lead an immoral life.

From "Excuses for Students from Parents"

My son is under the doctor's care and should not take P.E. Please execute him.

Please excuse Dianna from being absent yesterday. She was in bed with gramps.

Please excuse Gloria. She has been sick and under the doctor.

Dear School: Please ectuse John for been absent January 28, 29, 30, 32, and 33.

From "That's What You Dictated, Doctor!"

The patient has no past history of suicides.

The patient has been depressed ever since she began seeing me in 1983.

Between you and me, we ought to be able to get this lady pregnant.

She is numb from her toes down.

The patient refused an autopsy.

From "Lawyer's Questions from Actual Court Records"

Was it you or your brother that was killed in the war?

Was that the same nose you broke as a child?

So you were gone until you returned?

Have you lived in this town all your life? [The reply, "Not yet," surely marks this as folklore!]

How long have you been a French Canadian?

From "Signs Posted in Foreign Hotels, Restaurants, etc."

Tokyo: Is forbidden to steal hotel towels please. If you are not a person to do such thing is please not to read notis.

Leipzig: Do not enter the lift backwards, and only when lit up.

Yugoslavia: The flattening of underwear with pleasure is the job of the chambermaid.

Austria: Not to perambulate the corridors in the hours of repose in the boots of ascension [i.e., while wearing ski boots].

Switzerland: Special today—no ice cream.

From "Authentic Announcements from Various Church Bulletins"

This afternoon there will be meetings in the South and North ends of the church. Children will be baptized at both ends.

This being Easter Sunday we will ask Mrs. Brown to come forward and lay an egg on the Altar.

The ladies of the church have cast off clothing of every kind and they can be seen in the church basement on Friday afternoon.

From "Actual Excerpts from Student Exams"

History calls people Romans because they never stayed in one place too long.

The Greeks had three types of columns—Corinthian, Doric, and Ironic.

Magellan circumcised the globe with a giant clipper.

Bach practiced on an old spinster in the attic.

The pistol of a flower is its only protection against insects.

Three kinds of blood vessels are arteries, vanes, and caterpillers.

Egyptians lived in the desert and traveled by Camelot.

Many actual errors in language are so obvious that they may well have occurred repeatedly and independently; I am thinking here of mistakes like "pubic" for "public," or "pros-

trate" for "prostate," or "cavalry" for "calvary." But the series of more complex errors above are surely invented and have become traditional. "The Welfare Letter" seems to be the oldest of these lists; published examples come from the 1930s and '40s, and I have one such list made by a woman who copied them down when she worked for the "Bureau of War Risk" in 1919–20. Among the published collections of language blunders are a 1931 book called simply Boners, *with illustrations by Dr. Seuss, and chapters in Richard Lederer's popular books* Anguished English *(1987) and* Crazy English *(1989). Many teachers have saved examples of language slipups made by their own students; my own personal examples gleaned from 35 years of college teaching include "conspicuous conception" (for Thorstein Veblen's socio-economic theory of "conspicuous consumption"); the misnomer "Fringed Genital" for William Cullen Bryant's poetic subject, "The Fringed Gentian"; and a reference to "The Pullet Surprise" for the annual award "The Pulitzer Prize." Topping these, though, is advice columnist Abigail Van Buren's report of a letter typed from dictation in which a new secretary wrote, "These figures were calculated with a sly drool," that is "a slide rule." When collecting and studying boners, it is well to remember, as mentioned in* Boners, *that "an antidote is a funny story that you have heard before."*

"The Wordy Government Memo"

Undue length of statement is always dangerous, especially where the person addressed is not compelled to read; and there is no law compelling judges to read the briefs that are filed. . . .

Lincoln needed fewer than 300 words for his Gettysburg address; to compose the Ten Commandments required some 290 words; but it is said that a Federal agency found it necessary to employ 29,711 words to set forth the regulations governing the prices that may be charged for fresh fruits.

Just open Utne Reader to any page. Overturned truisms. Shattered shibboleths. Debunked bromides. Truth! . . .

UTNE READER saves you time and money. The New York Times notes that the Lord's Prayer contains 56 words, the 23rd. Psalm 118 words, the Gettysburg Address 226 words, and the Ten Commandments 297 words, while the U. S. Department of Agriculture directive on pricing cabbage weighs in at 15,626 words.

First, from Frank E. Cooper's 1953 textbook Writing in Law Practice, *p. 60; second, a 1990 sales pitch from* Utne Reader. *This bogus criticism of supposed bureaucratic verbosity has been around for at least 50 years. Sometimes the directive is said to refer to the pricing of foghorns or of duck eggs. Two further legends about supposed government ineptness are included with "Bogus Warnings" in Chapter 20.*

14

Baffled by Technology

Technology, as pundits like to say, is both a blessing and a curse. The blessing part is not very prominent in urban legends; the curse part is definitely where the action is. Take computers, for example. For all the wondrous tasks that computers perform nowadays, there are no interesting folk stories about their successes. But since computers are only as reliable as their operators, there are lots of legends about computers disabling the inept. Most often the stories hinge on a telephone call for technical support made to a manufacturer of hardware or software.

According to one story, a caller to tech support was unable to print a document, and the telephone consultant at the software manufacturer spent 20 minutes suggesting solutions to the problem. Nothing worked. Finally the frustrated operator asked the caller whether the printer was turned on. The caller exclaimed, "That couldn't be the problem, because that was it the last time I called [pause] . . . Uh oh. . . . I'm soooooo embarrassed."

Another classic: An office worker called for a repair person because his computer's display failed to light up when he turned the unit on. The technician walked in, turned up the brightness knob, and departed. Lesson: the simplest solution is often the right one. But people expect their computers to have complex problems, so they overlook simple and easily solvable ones.

Yet another classic: A user called tech support about an accounting program that contained the instruction "Press any key to continue." The caller complained that his program always crashed at that point:

> "What were you doing right then, when it failed?" the operator asked.
>
> The caller replied, "I pressed the ANY key, just like the manual said, but then the screen went blank."
>
> "The ANY key? What's that?"
>
> "Well, I couldn't find it on the keyboard," said the user, "so I figured it must be the one on the back that's not marked."
>
> The programmer explained the obvious fact that "any key" in the instructions meant literally any key on the keyboard, and that the unmarked but-

ton he had pressed was the restart button. Pressing it would wipe out all previous work not saved to a disk.

The computer story I've heard most often lately is about the guy who called the manufacturer of his machine to see if they could replace or repair a broken cup holder:

"Cup holder?" asks the operator.

"Yes," said the caller. "I accidentally pushed it too hard, and I bent it so that it won't retract any more the way it used to."

"Where is this cup holder?" asks the operator.

"Right on the front of the computer—left side—you know, that handy little shelf that is supposed to slide out to hold a coffee cup while I'm working."

"You're resting your coffee cup on the CD-ROM drive??"

Maybe someday there will be an urban legend about every gadget in the Sharper Image catalog, but for now most of the doubtful stories about technology seem to be about computers, ATMs, a few household appliances, and—of course—cars. Where are the stories about, say, talking bathroom scales, nail-polish driers, exercise machines, answering machines, VCRs, satellite dishes, shredders, crepe cookers, pasta makers, food processors, and deep fryers? Oops, I just heard one about a deep fryer:

There was this guy who did a lot of drugs, and one night he came home from work, got stoned, and then decided to fix some dinner. He turned on his deep fryer to make some French fries (no health-food nut this!). And when he thought the oil was hot enough for cooking, he checked it out by sticking his hand in the fryer, which immediately deep-fried his hand.

A legend focusing on the other end of the social scale is the one about the nice middle-class woman who found someone's bank card lying in the street one night, and thought of the easiest way to turn it in via an ATM:

> She inserted the card into the slot of the next ATM she saw and punched in some numbers at random. She knew that without the proper Personal Identification Number [PIN] the machine would keep the card and a bank official would find it in the morning. But, against all odds, she hit the right PIN number, and the screen obligingly flashed the message, "How much do you wish to withdraw?"

The story does not explain what the woman did next, but it does sometimes mention that her image was caught by the bank's surveillance camera.

Often a new technological gadget will spawn a new legend. The stories in this chapter about microwave ovens, tanning beds, and cruise control illustrate the process. Another example concerns those little microchip music boxes used to make musical greeting cards. When you open the card, an appropriate tune plays; when you close the card, it stops. Shortly after the musical cards came on the market, a story about them followed:

> Someone got a musical birthday card, and family members fooled around opening and closing the card until they all got tired of hearing "Happy Birthday." Unfortunately, at that point the card—stuck in the open position—somehow got lost under the flooring, behind a wall panel, or in some other hard-to-reach place and "Happy Birthday" kept on playing and playing and playing. Supposedly, the family called the manufacturer (there's *that* theme again!) and learned that the card should only play for X number of hours. But evidently the device was over-engineered; according to the story, "It's still going strong, and they can't stop it without ripping out the floor."

Could such things happen? Of course they could, and probably they have happened. I assume that the next report is genuine, because I've heard many first-person accounts of roughly the same occurrence. The following is from *Ask Anne and Nan*, a 1989 book of reprinted columns of household hints:

> Q: We have lived in our house for many years and have never had this problem. We are bothered by a loud chirping, and although we can't see

> them, we suspect that they are crickets. They have chirped night and day for two months. Our house is insulated. Have you any solution? Would sonar waves help?
>
> Annoyed, Springfield
>
> A: It sounds like crickets to us. They come into the house when it begins to turn cold outside; they could have gained access through the cellar, on wood you brought in, or just through the door. We suggest you follow the chirping to its source. Crickets like dark, warm places: around hearths, under cabinets in the bathroom or clothes closets are good places to start.
>
> Reader Feedback: Ferris Harris, of Proctorsville, wrote: "The question of chirping noises brought to mind the experience of a family member. She also heard chirping and found the source was a smoke detector in a drawer. It had been there some time, and when the battery got weak, it chirped, as described in Annoyed's letter."
>
> Annoyed Replied: "Thank you so much for your help in solving our cricket problem. We put a new battery in our smoke detector and it did the job! No more chirping!"

Way to go, Ferris Harris! In variations on this story—or is it variations on the actual problem?—the chirping sound comes from the basement, which the family seals off with duct tape around the access door until the exterminator arrives. The conclusion is much like the others about mechanical problems, in that the workman shows up, applies the simple obvious solution, and departs, while red-faced techno-innocents remain.

"Unlocking the Modern Car"

A woman came out of a department store at a large shopping mall to the parking lot carrying a big stack of packages. As she approached her car, she fumbled with her battery-powered remote door-opener, but the car doors did not click open. She rested the packages on the hood of the car and tried again and again, no luck.

"Oh, darn," she said aloud to herself. "The batteries in this opener are dead, and now I'll have to schlepp these packages all the way back into the mall when I go in to buy new ones."

A man who had just parked in the space next to hers heard her and asked if he could try the opener; perhaps he could get it to work. "It's no use," the woman said, "I should have changed the batteries long ago." But she handed over the opener.

The man took a look at the device, then selected a key from the attached key-chain and opened the car with its own key.

"The Microwaved Pet"

Windhoek, South Africa—A distraught elderly woman here is cursing modern technology because her beloved cat died in a microwave oven.

Auctioneer Mr. Gerry Heij related the story of a call from the shocked woman, who said she wanted to sell the oven.

She explained that her cat got soaking wet in the rain and she thought the quickest way to dry him out would be to put him in the microwave oven.

She put the cat in, set the timer to "defrost" and switched on.

The cat's hair immediately stood on end and 10 seconds later it exploded, the woman told Mr. Heij.

The auctioneer cleaned up the hairs and sold the oven for 150 rands.

From the Argus *of Cape Town, South Africa, May 6, 1988. Although I have collected several published accounts of actual microwaved pets, with names, dates, and sometimes photographs, snippets like this one in the media are clearly just reports of legends. The auctioneer in this instance retells a well-known story as part of his sales pitch, and a local paper reports it as news. When microwave ovens first became available for home use, the story was told that a woman had always used her conventional oven to dry her pet after washing it, and then her son gave her a microwave oven for Christmas. Sometimes it is a child who has zapped the pet. A cooked-poodle version of the story was illustrated beautifully on the cover of* Whole Earth Review *(fall 1985) in an issue featuring my arti-*

cle on urban legends. Entertainer Arsenio Hall, in the persona of his character Chunky A, alludes to "The Microwaved Pet" in his rap song "Sorry," included on his CD Large and In Charge. *For a horrendous variation on this theme, see "The Hippie Baby-Sitter" legend in Chapter 10.*

"The Technology Contest"

Waterbury [Connecticut] used to be called the Brass City. It was the Silicon Valley of its day, when clocks and locks and metal instruments carried the day. A friend of mine, Al Bell, owned a factory here. He told me a story that might help you understand what's going on: Once upon a time, early in World War Two, engineers from Rensselaer Polytechnic Institute sent their latest engineering breakthrough to a Waterbury wire factory. It was a length of wire so thin they delivered it with a microscope. Top that! The Waterbury boys drilled a hole through it.

I first heard this story about 15 years ago, only then it was set in a Texas trade show. It was related as from a friend of a friend who was an engineer in the firm. They had produced an exceedingly thin glass rod which they were displaying on a specially built stand. A day or two into the show, a group of Japanese engineers from one of the adjoining booths stopped by and asked to borrow the rod for two hours so they could examine it more carefully. The engineers, flattered by the attention from the Japanese and unduly proud of their accomplishment, agreed. Two hours later the rod was returned with bows of thanks. Some days later, when the Texas engineers were back in their labs, there was reason to examine their prized rod. They were startled to find that a hole had been drilled through it lengthwise.

The first is from Justin Scott's 1995 novel StoneDust*; in 1996, Daniel Cruson, town historian of Newtown, Connecticut, sent me the relevant pages as well as the second exam-*

ple in his accompanying letter. There are several variations of this story involving different rival nations and other products. Prototypes for "The Technology Contest," in which artists compete to produce realistic paintings, exist from the ancient world through the Renaissance. Bowls of fruit, insects, curtains, and the like were painted with such exquisite realism and detail that they were mistaken for the real thing. A modern counterpart describes an art student who, on the envelope containing his application for a scholarship, draws a postage stamp that fools the post office. A 1994 printed advertisement for Lexus automobiles showed a photograph of fingers stretching out a "wispy wire" with the caption, "We told our engineers to make tolerances thinner than the human hair. They replied, 'Blonde or brunette?'" Now all we need is for the Infiniti car company to produce an ad in which the Lexus hair is drilled lengthwise by Infiniti engineers.

"Curses! Broiled Again!"

Recently my secretary told me this story. It was told to her by a girlfriend who heard it from a coworker who said she heard it from a friend who was in the same wedding party as the victim.

A young woman was going to be in a wedding party, but she was unhappy at her pale un-tanned body. Since there are 30-minute-per-day limits set at tanning salons, she visited several salons each day, thus increasing the speed of tanning in the shortest time possible.

After several weeks of this regime, she noticed that she was not feeling at all well, and she had a foul odor about her body, even after bathing.

So she made an appointment with her doctor, and after examining her he pronounced that she had managed to cook her internal organs by overexposure to the tanning rays. The odor was actually the rotting of these organs, and further, this foolish girl had just two weeks to live.

Sent to me in January 1988 by Bill Kestell of New Holstein, Wisconsin. This story mistakenly assumes that microwaves are generated by tanning lamps; it was told nationwide in the summer of 1987 and got massive media publicity in "Dear Abby" columns of September 22 and November 6, both of which firmly debunked the tale. Sometimes the vic-

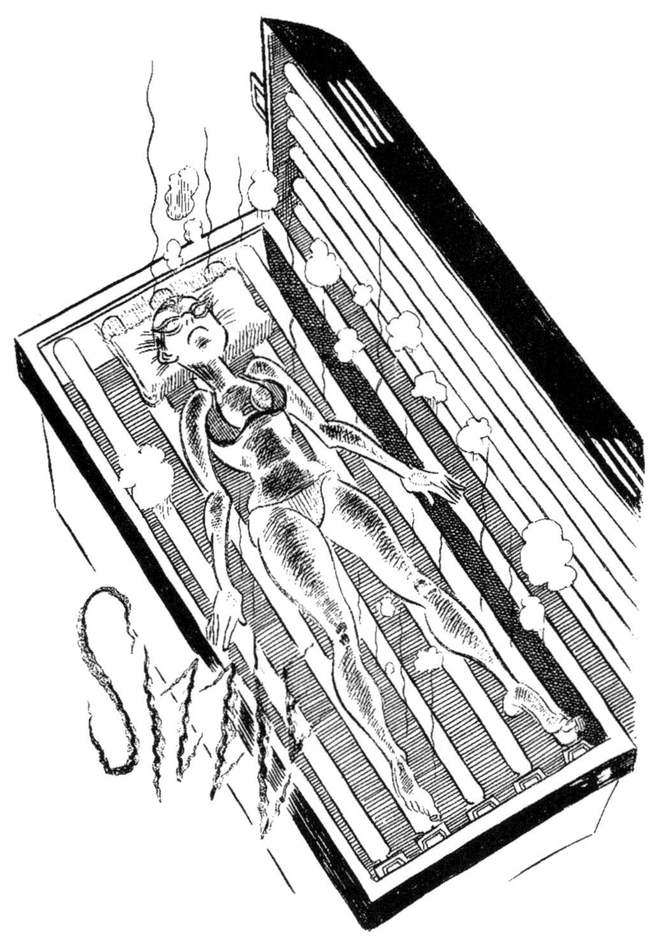

tim is a cheerleader preparing herself for a training camp, or a bride-to-be anticipating her honeymoon in Hawaii. The legend continued to annoy tanning-salon owners to such a degree that the June/July 1989 issue of the industry magazine Tanning Trends *had to debunk it once again. But telling continued. In October 1994, a student at West Liberty (West Virginia) State College reported to me that her instructor in a health class included the story as an example of everyday causes of skin cancer; this victim was getting tanned so she would look nice at her homecoming dance. There are, of course, real dangers inherent in overexposing oneself to ultraviolet rays, whether from the sun or from tanning lamps, but the "broiled again!" legend derives from fantasy, not science.*

"Push-Starting the Car"

A motorist from Cranston, Rhode Island, sheepishly swears this story is true—but even if it isn't true it has to be told. He was driving on the Merritt Parkway when his battery died. He flagged down a woman driver, and she agreed to give him a push to start his car. Because his car had an automatic transmission, he explained to her, "You'll have to get up to 30 or 35 miles an hour to get me started."

The lady nodded wisely. The stalled driver climbed into his car and waited for her to line up behind him. He waited and waited. Then he turned around to see where the woman was. She was there all right—coming at him at 35 miles an hour.

Damage to his car: $300.

Later the *[Providence] Bulletin* checked with state police, and had to announce that the story was not true. It appeared as a joke in a Boston paper, and was phoned into the Providence paper as straight news by a prankster.

From what the *[Reader's] Digest* editors have been able to discover, this is another of those "true" stories that sweep the country. Before the AP item appeared we had already received more than 100 accounts of the incident. The earliest came from California, but it was followed in a few days by a version from Massachusetts. The story also came from Texas, Illinois, Michigan, Pennsylvania, Connecticut—even from the Canal Zone, where the car was on the Trans-Isthmian Highway. In each case the writer insisted that the driver was his mother, a neighbor, a close friend or a coworker. One writer was the mechanic who repaired the cars, another was the insurance adjuster. One version had a wife pushing her husband—and she landed in the hospital with a fractured skull.

After the AP carried the story, hundreds of clippings poured into the *Digest*—and they're still coming—including one from a woman in Tennessee who vowed that the Cranston motorist was her brother.

From Reader's Digest, *July 1954, p. 90, based on an Associated Press story picked up from the* Providence Bulletin. *The AP story and its aftermath were also summarized in* The Unicorn Book of 1954. *This is an instance when the media were ahead of the folklorists in recognizing, collecting, and comparing versions of an urban legend. The push-starting legend actually pre-dated automatic transmission when it was applied to various car models of the late 1930s and early '40s, which were equipped with "Hydro-matic," "Fluid Drive," or "Dynaflow." It was necessary to push a car so equipped fast enough to develop sufficient torque in the drive-shaft fan blades to rotate the motor set of blades and start the engine. The legend continues to be told, with updated damage figures, and nowadays invariably mentioning automatic transmission. The blame for the misunderstanding always goes to a woman driver. Readers still send me versions of this story purporting to be firsthand experiences. Another legend describing a different misunderstanding of automatic transmission describes a young man taking a stolen car out for a drag race on the highway. He starts out with the shift lever in "D for drag," and when another car starts to pass he shifts into "R for race" and tears out the transmission.*

"Cruise Control"

I heard this story about five years ago while I was living in Omaha, Nebraska, and I believe the source was supposed to be a Paul Harvey newscast.

There was this wealthy student from the Middle East attending either the University of Kansas or Kansas State. He goes downtown and buys this fully equipped van; it has everything—fancy paint, sun roof, carpet,

From *Billy and the Boingers Bootleg* by Berke Breathed. Copyright © 1986 by the *Washington Post*. By permission of Little, Brown and Company.

power everything, and a bar complete with a refrigerator. Picks up the whole works and pays cash. Hops in and drives off.

A little while later motorists on the Interstate see this van veer off the highway and go into the ditch where it overturns. They stop and rush over to see if the driver is hurt, and it turns out that he is only badly shaken up. Asked how he could lose control of his van on a flat stretch of Kansas Interstate, he replies, "Well, I put the van on cruise control, and went in back to fix myself a drink. . . ."

Sent to me by Tom R. Roper of Waterloo, Iowa, in October 1982. I first heard this updated version of the latest-option car legend in 1977, and it has been popular ever since, often told about a foreign driver in the United States or Canada, usually one from a Middle Eastern country or from Pakistan. In the July 9, 1986, issue of the Wall Street Journal *an article on strange insurance claims attributed the incident to a woman driving a new van on a highway near Washington, D.C., who left the wheel to tend to her crying baby in the back. When I queried the Allstate Insurance official mentioned in the news story, he said that he had heard about the case from a claims manager eight or nine years previously and had no other knowledge of it. Another Allstate spokesman swore that it "really happened," but his attempts to track down a record of the case were unsuccessful. A reader who assured me in a 1987 letter that the incident had occurred in St. Louis in 1985 to an Arab student whose insurance claim was handled by the reader's own sister never responded to my fervent plea for more information about the case. A "Bloom County" comic strip released on April 8, 1987, pictured all the members of the "Boingers World Tour" in the back of their van having a conference when somebody asked, "Who's driving?!" The reply, from Opus the penguin, was, "Keep yer pants on. I pushed Cruise Control."*

"The Ice-Cream Car"

After the engine is shut off the underhood temperature begins to rise. When the engine has been shut off for 20 minutes, referred to as a "hot soak" period, the temperature will usually reach it's peak. This condition will occur particularly in the summertime or when the car is stored in a heated or attached garage.

Fuel will frequently drip from the ends of the throttle shaft or can be observed dripping out of the main discharge nozzle or pump nozzle into the manifold. . . . Hard hot starting occurs if the driver attempts to start the car after it has stood for 20 minutes.

This condition is PERCOLATION, not flooding. . . .

A classic example of percolation was recorded recently. A lady driver stopped frequently at an ice cream store to buy ice cream. When she bought a quart of Vanilla and returned to her car the car started instantly. When she purchased Butterpeacan and returned to her car it wouldn't start.

An alert service Representative made two trips to the store with the driver. The first trip she bought Vanilla. It was pre-packed and she returned to the car in 5 minutes and the vehicle started perfectly. When she returned to buy the Butterpecan she waited 20 minutes for it to be hand packed and pay her bill. When she returned to the car she pumped the accelerator 2 or 3 times; adding additional fuel to the already over rich mixture in the manifold. The car wouldn't start. It was necessary for the Representative to explain the correct procedure to start a hot engine.

Verbatim, with a few deletions as indicated, from the Holley Carburetor Co. Service Guide #2, *Part #36-71, p. 5. Frank W. King, national technical director of the Mercedes-Benz Club of America, who sent me a photocopy of this page in February 1990, did not know the date of the guide. But references on the page to "since 1968," plus the part number, suggest 1971. Percolation and flooding are real enough mishaps, but the "classic example" cited is a legend. Several readers have written me to say that they remember the same finicky-car problem discussed in the "Model Garage" section of* Popular Science *sometime in the 1940s or '50s. The June 1978 issue of* Traffic Safety *magazine repeated the story from* Automotive Engineering, *saying it was hand-packed pistachio ice cream that caused the problem, and that it occurred in Texas. A reader in Milwaukee wrote to say that she also heard the story about Texas, and that the problem was traced to "any flavor but vanilla." The February 6, 1992, issue of* Bits & Pieces *magazine, "A monthly mixture of horse sense and common sense about working with people," included a detailed account of "The Ice-Cream Car," saying that it had happened to a Pontiac owner whose family voted each night after dinner which flavor of ice cream to have for dessert. Any time vanilla was chosen, the car would not start on the return trip. The problem was traced to the layout of the ice-cream store, which kept all the vanilla in a separate case at the front of the store for quick pickup. According to this source, the story was "a favorite at General Motors."*

15

The Criminal Mind

What makes the urban legends about crime interesting is not so much the depictions of actual crimes themselves. The daily news gives you enough of that—muggings, assaults, thefts, burglary, murders, bombings, graft, scams, etc.—the whole gamut of criminal activity in rich detail. What the legends give us instead is some insight into the minds of the "perps," as law-enforcement officers like to call crooks. We gain these insights from allegedly true reports of the ongoing battle of wits between criminals and their victims.

Take, for example, the story of a minor crime that Ann Landers published back in 1989 from a reader's letter:

> When I attended high school in Minneapolis, a student bought a piece of pie in the cafeteria and carried it to his table. He decided to go back for a carton of milk and wrote a note saying, "Don't eat this pie. I spit on it." When he returned someone had added, "So did I."

Although that episode may have been true, it echoes a much older theme in rural legendry. Likely the pie-protection gambit-that-failed—whether actual or mere hearsay—was based on someone's memory of a story like this:

> A farmer was losing way too many watermelons due to nightly raids on his fields, so he posted a sign that said "Warning! There is a poisoned watermelon in this patch." The day after he posted the sign he found not a single melon missing, but the sign had been altered to read, "There are TWO poisoned Watermelons in this patch."

For an update on the theme of supposedly "foolproof" schemes to avoid theft see "The Unstealable Car" legend in this chapter.

Lists of tips to avoid theft often seem to echo legends. A *New York Times* article of May 19, 1992, had these examples, along with advice about home alarm systems, deadbolt locks, and the like:

> From a distance, look under your car. Check the back seat up close. . . .
>
> Place large dirty dog dishes outside [your home], even if you're petless.

The *Times* article opened with a capsule summary of "The Attempted Abduction" legend found below in this chapter, plus two other unverified "nightmare" scenarios, then added "Some of these stories may be true. It doesn't really matter." (The article did not mention another piece of anticrime advice: "If you want to drive off a would-be mugger, just start picking your nose." I do hope I'll never have to try this one, though!)

Legends illustrating the workings of the criminal mind are usually based on the relatively minor bad guys. Notice in this chapter that except for one reference to an organized crime family the rest of the stories deal with people scheming to steal a few groceries, some car parts, a Christmas tree, luggage, or the like. Typically, too, in the legends the baddies are nearly always caught, often nabbed in the very act of stealing. These details, of course, are what make the legends believable as well as gratifying to the law-abiding folk who want justice to prevail.

Another theme in crime legends is that even the most innocent-seeming act by a trusted person may be an actual scam. Herrick Jeffers of Melbourne Village, Florida, sent me an example of this kind of story a few years ago:

> A certain parishioner came to the back room of a church after Sunday services, seeking to cash a check, because, he explained, "all the banks were closed, and he was a little short of money." He wanted to write a check for the amount of loose change in the collection plates—the bills and coins that were not in envelopes. The ushers accommodated him, and this happened several times. Since there are usually different ushers each week, it took a while before anyone realized that this same person was writing a check to the church each week for from $10 to $40. It finally dawned on them that he was establishing an iron-clad tax deduction without paying a cent for it.

You have to wonder why none of the ushers ever suggested that the man just stop at an ATM on the way home from church.

"Is nothing sacred to the scam artist?" I wondered when I read an article a few years ago in one of my hometown newspapers, the *Salt Lake Tribune*. The headline was "LDS Scriptures Are Hot Items for Shoplifters." The term "LDS," for you outsiders, refers to members of the Church of Jesus Christ of Latter-day Saints—the Mormons—and the scriptures alluded to are four volumes collectively referred to as "The Quads," consisting of the Bible, the Book of Mormon, the Doctrine and Covenants, and the Pearl of Great Price, "all standard scriptures for Mormons—in a single uncondensed volume."

According to the *Tribune* article, people were shoplifting these $100 leather-bound Quads, sometimes justifying their actions by saying that they were teaching religion courses and could not afford to purchase the set. Some thieves even had the nerve to return the book to a different LDS bookstore and ask to get it engraved for someone's birthday. The article included this revealing passage:

> Linda Brummett, manager of Brigham Young University's campus bookstore for 19 years, recounts the story of a Mormon missionary at the Missionary Training Center in Provo caught stealing scriptures. The judge hearing the case gave the young man money to buy a set.
>
> "But this could well be an urban legend," she said. "I've heard this one many times in the last 18 years, and the story often changes."

Indeed! The way I heard it, the girlfriend of an LDS missionary had shoplifted the Quad as a consolation gift to accompany her "Dear John" letter to the absent lad. (Note to my friends at BYU: I *know* this is only a legend, except for the part about "Dear John" letters, which are a well-known fact of missionary life. At least so I've been told. . . .)

"Police Secrets"

(From the Vancouver [BC] Sun, *May 13, 1995)*

At a journalism conference in California last year, a reporter told a story about how he had been net surfing in the state on-line system and found a police map with certain addresses highlighted.

He thought it was a map of murder scenes, so he started visiting the places pinpointed on the map. Guess what? It was a map of all the donut shops in the county!

"The Colander Copier Caper"

We don't know if this qualifies to be included in our dumb crook series, but you would think by now that anyone over 12 would know the difference between a Xerox machine and a lie detector.

This is the scenario as it unfolded recently in the courtroom of Bucks County Court Judge Isaac Garb.

A small police department in the county took a man into custody on suspicion of a crime, and police asked the suspect if he was willing to take a lie detector test. The suspect agreed, and the police led him to a Xerox machine in which the police had already inserted a typewritten card that read, "He's lying." After seating the man next to the machine, the police placed a metal colander on his head and attached some wires to it. Then he was interrogated. Whenever the suspect gave an answer the police didn't like, they pushed the copy button on the Xerox and (cunkaching) out would come the message, "He's lying."

Finally, the police got a full confession from the suspect, who obviously believed that he couldn't beat the machine.

Judge Garb, of course, suppressed the confession because of the manner in which it was obtained, but he did get a good laugh out of it. "It's the sort of comic relief you need around here once in awhile," he says.

That police department will no doubt abandon its practice of using a Xerox machine to extract confessions. However, there's always the Mr. Coffee machine.

May 10, 1993
Dear Mr. Brunvand: I am pleased to report that I am alive and

extant in continuing to strive to be a legend in my own time.

I can confirm the veracity of the colander polygraph (lie detector). It occurred in Warminster Township, Bucks County, Pennsylvania, where the police had arrested an individual suspected of a crime. When he denied his culpability, he was offered the opportunity of a polygraph examination. He accepted, but they did not have a lie detector machine. Not lacking in ingenuity, they then caused the legend "you lied" on a piece of Xerox paper and put it into the Xerox machine, unbeknownst to the accused. They then placed a colander on his head and attached it to the Xerox machine by cable and alligator clamps. They then asked him an incriminating question to which he responded in such a way as to exculpate himself. They then activated the machine and the paper came out with the legend "you lied." When confronted with that, the accused confessed all.

The matter came before me in court on a motion to suppress the confession.

I hope the foregoing satisfies your curiosity and quiets the skeptics among us.

Very truly yours,
Isaac S. Garb

First is the earliest published account of this incident that I have found; it comes from a column by Clark DeLeon of the Philadelphia Inquirer, *July 27, 1977. Judge Garb's letter was sent from the Court of Common Pleas of Bucks County, Seventh Judicial District, Doylestown, Pennsylvania. Well might the good judge feel like a legend in his own time, since this is one of the most-often-repeated stories from the world of law enforcement. In my 1993 book* The Baby Train, *I quote or summarize versions of "The Colander Copier Caper" from four individuals and from seven published sources dated from 1977 to 1992. Most accounts do not name Judge Garb specifically, and many of them claim that the incident happened in the town of Radnor in Delaware County, Pennsylvania. The Chief of Police in Radnor Township denied the incident in a 1990 letter quoted in my earlier book. I regard this "caper" as a prank, well known to American policemen, which has made its way to a court of law at least once. For those wishing to pursue the story, here are five further references I have found to it: Chic magazine, June 1978; "A cop's-eye view of 'Barney Miller,'"* TV Guide, *March 21, 1981;* Glimpse: A brief look at things for members of the International Society for

General Semantics, *no. 38 (1986); Paul Levine,* Night Vision, *1992; and* Michigan Law Review, *March 1995, p. 857, n. 59. In his 1983 book* Sez Who? Sez Me, *Mike Royko reprinted a column of 1978 in which he described a "bowl-like gadget they had taken off a lamp" used by police in Chicago as part of a faked electrocution of a disorderly prisoner. I have also heard of police wrapping the spiral cord of the squad car microphone around a suspect's arm while questioning him; then they randomly key in the microphone, causing a red light to blink on the console, telling the suspect that these flashes indicate when he is lying. Most of the police officers who sent me these stories insisted that some of the people they have had to arrest were actually dumb enough to fall for such tricks; none of the writers claimed that they themselves had ever used them.*

"A Friend of the Family"

An upwardly-mobile couple moved into an expensive suburb of a big eastern city next door to a quiet family who were rumored to have ties to the Mafia. One Sunday night, returning from a weekend away from home, the couple were shocked to find that their home had been burglarized. After assessing the damage, the couple told their neighbors what had happened, asking if they had observed anything suspicious over the weekend.

The neighbors, puzzlingly, told them just to go to bed for now and not to notify the police right away. They would make a few phone calls and see what could be done.

The couple woke up the next morning to find all of their missing property piled neatly on the front porch.

There is an international physics institute in Erice, Sicily, which holds regular summer schools for graduate students and young researchers. I was told this story by a fellow graduate student before attending a session this past summer.

A few years ago, according to the story, a student at the institute had his car stolen while attending. He told the director about it, and the director asked him to wait a day before calling the police. The next morning the car was parked outside the school, intact and freshly washed.

I mentioned this story to a few other students when I arrived at Erice, and three or four others had heard variations, one involving a purse instead of a car.

I heard the first version in Washington, D.C., in 1984 and subsequently received it from several other locations. The second is from Steven Carlip of Austin, Texas, who sent it to me in September 1986. The stolen-car version is also told in the United States, as well as various stories about Mafia members offering someone a free hit job in return for a favor. I referred to this story as "The Helpful Mafia Neighbor" in my book The Mexican Pet; *in the Italian translation of the book the title was "I favori del vicino mafioso," which seems to have an authentic gangland accent. However, the background of the story may be American gangster folklore rather than traditions about the Mafia. An older story tells of a distinguished foreign scholar visiting MIT many years ago who had some valuable equipment and an expensive overcoat stolen from his rental car. Since his host was on familiar terms with Al Capone, the stolen goods were promptly returned. A similar incident is reported in* The Autobiography of Lincoln Steffens *(1931); Steffens, a muckraking journalist, supposedly had his pocket picked in New York City and mentioned it to his acquaintance, the head of the police detective bureau. Two days later, everything stolen was returned.*

"The Two Hitchhikers"

A traveling salesman was driving from Seattle to Spokane late in the day and found himself getting sleepy. He decided to pick up a hitchhiker to keep himself awake. Just past Vantage, he saw a man with his thumb out.

The man was no sooner in the car than the salesman feared he had made a serious error. In his 40s, the man was unshaven and roughly attired, had little to say, and began looking around the car as if to see if there was anything worth stealing.

The salesman decided to pick up another hitchhiker, hoping for safety in numbers. Before he got to the town of George, he saw another man hoping for a ride and picked him up.

The new passenger was a clean-cut young man who looked as if he were headed to college. The rider got in the back seat, behind the first hitchhiker in the front. The salesman's relief was short-lived, however, for the car was no sooner back on the highway when the young man pulled a gun and ordered the driver to stop.

When the car was on the shoulder, the holdup man ordered the pair out of the car with a gesture of the pistol.

The gesture pointed the gun away from the front-seat occupants, and the first hitchhiker promptly dived into the back seat and knocked the young thief cold with a solid right in the jaw. The older man pocketed the pistol and relieved the would-be robber of his wallet.

"Forty dollars," he reported to the salesman, "20 for you and 20 for me."

"No, thanks," the salesman replied, happy merely to have escaped. The older man shrugged; he was now expansive and talkative.

"He's new in the business," he said of the robber. "He'll have to learn that a gun ain't a pointer. I've been in the business 20 years. I don't make dumb mistakes anymore."

At the salesman's horrified look, the man laughed. "Oh, I ain't working today. Just going to Spokane on a visit."

This is the full text of the story I summarized in my 1989 book Curses! Broiled Again!, *as told by* Seattle Times *columnist Erik Lacitis in a feature published on February 10, 1983. The story was sent to Lacitis by a reader; subsequently I received another version remembered from the 1930s by one of my readers from Tooelle, Utah. Jasper Maskelyne, descendant of the famous English magician John Nevil Maskelyne (1839–1917), tells a similar story that was a personal experience in his 1938 book* White Magic: The Story of Maskelynes. *Mr. Maskelyne was driving a fast new car when he picked up a scruffy-looking hitchhiker who spoke in "a rather impudent Cockney voice." When a policeman stopped Maskelyne for speeding, the passenger backed Maskelyne's false claim that he was not exceeding the speed limit. The policeman took detailed notes, and let them proceed. When they arrived at the hitchhiker's destination, the man thanked him, "Then he pushed two fat wallets into my hands, and disappeared. One was the policeman's note-book and the other my own pocket-book full of pound notes!" Maskelyne claims that he removed the incriminating pages of the notebook and mailed the rest back to the police anonymously. Thus, in this instance, both the crook and the layman were schemers.*

"The Double Theft"

This "true" story was told to me back in 1970 in Silver Spring, Maryland. This woman, a friend of my friend who told the story, goes shopping downtown (in Washington, D.C.) at Lord & Taylor's department store. While there, she has occasion to use the restroom. She hangs her handbag on the hook provided in the stall and no sooner has she sat down, then a hand reaches over the door, grabs her purse, and the person runs out the door. By the time she pulls everything up or down, buckles or snaps, etc., the person is long gone!

So she goes into the store offices and reports the theft. Usually the person will take the money and throw the bag into a trash can, leaving all those pain-in-the@#&/-to-duplicate cards and keys in the bag. Sure enough, a couple of days later she gets a phone call from the store manager informing her that the handbag has been recovered. Such a nice man!

"How soon can you get here?" ("I only live 30 minutes away.") "Do you need a sitter for your children?" ("Oh no, they're all in school.") "I hope my phone call didn't wake your husband." ("Oh no, he works a regular 9-to-5 job.")

Anyway, she gets downtown and, you guessed it, nobody knows a thing about her purse! She drives home in confusion and upon arriving discovers that in her absence a moving van has backed up to the door (as her neighbors later testify) and cleaned out the house.

One of my coworkers swears this happened to her husband's coworker's sister's friends . . . which was what tipped me off immediately (clue #1). It apparently happened in Rouyn, a small town in northern Quebec.

A couple went out to dinner and when they returned, their barbecue was missing. They did not file a police report immediately (clue #2). The next day, after work, they returned home to find their barbecue back in its place, with a note—something to the effect that "We're sorry we borrowed your barbecue without permission; we had company over and our tank ran out of gas, so we borrowed yours. To make up for the inconvenience, here are two tickets to a show" (clue #3—who would bother doing that?).

The couple went to the show (clue #4—are people that stupid?) and when they came back their house had been robbed (clue #5—much too convenient).

The purse story was sent to me in October 1988 by Christine Turner in response to a column of mine on "The Double Theft." She confessed that until reading the column she had believed the story. The barbecue grill story was sent to me in September 1995 by Katrina Spencer of Ottawa, Canada, who represents the skeptical approach to urban legends. "The Double Theft" was reported by folklorists as early as 1972 from England and is a favorite international urban legend. English and Spanish versions claim that theater tickets were left by the thieves, Italian versions mention a dinner at a good restaurant, while a Norwegian version says the tickets are for a popular music hall revue in Oslo. I have Australian versions of the story in which tickets for either a ballet or an opera are sent to the victims. In the United States, the object stolen is usually a car, a car battery, or a barbecue grill; the tickets are most often to a sports event, but sometimes to a concert or a Broadway show. In the May 28, 1985, issue of the Wall Street Journal *an article reported on the "true" car-theft stories submitted in a Chicago contest. One of the entrants claimed that his car had been stolen, then returned, along with two tickets for a Rolling Stones concert. You can guess the conclusion. Lucky for him, his story did not win one of the $400 prizes.*

"The Robber Who Was Hurt"

Here is a story that I haven't seen in print anywhere. It always is set in new housing estates.

During the day when her husband is at work, a housewife is boiling

some milk for coffee when she sees a hand coming through the open window in the hall, about to unlock the door from the inside. She snatches the pan of boiling milk, runs up the hall, and pours it over the intruding hand.

Very shaken, she waits a few minutes then goes next door to her neighbour for comfort. At her neighbour's house, the neighbour's husband is in the act of bandaging his badly burned hand.

Sent to me in June 1983 by Roger Millington of Kingston, Surrey, England. This is a well-known legend in Great Britain with the intended victim sometimes burning the attempted intruder with a hot poker or an iron. This modern urban legend is an updating of older traditional stories, such as the fairy tale called "The Clever Maid at Home Kills the Robbers" and the legend "The Witch Who Was Hurt." In the latter, a witch is able to take the form of an animal—usually a black dog or a cat—when attacking a victim. After the animal is wounded in its paw, the witch is unmasked the next day when she shows up in the village with a bandaged hand. Only a few versions of "The Robber Who Was Hurt" have been collected in the United States, including the following example, which effectively combines two distinct legend types.

"A Double-Whammy Theft Legend"

As told by Jack Paar

Another story that goes on and on is the one about the couple who received two free tickets to the theater anonymously through the mail. On the evening they planned to use the tickets the husband had to work late so they had to give up their plan to go to the theater. The wife was home alone, doing some ironing, when to her consternation she saw a hand reaching through the mail slot on the door to open it.

Horrified, she realized they had been sent the tickets to get them out of their apartment so it could be burglarized in their absence. Grabbing a hot poker she struck at the hand reaching in to open the door. Then she dashed to the phone to call her friend down the hall and ask for help.

"I can't come," her friend said in a distraught voice. "My husband just came in with his hand horribly burned."

Where do such stories come from? Who makes them up in the first place? No one seems to know. Yet every once in a while someone tells one on our show—as having happened to them or someone they know.

From Chapter 16, "Stories in Their Anecdotage," in Jack Paar's 1961 book My Saber Is Bent. *This legend combines "The Double Theft" with "The Robber Who Was Hurt." Even though Jack Paar seems to have an ear for modern legends, he somewhat confuses the above example by having the woman grab a hot poker to stop the intruder rather than using the hot iron already in her hand. Possibly Johnny Carson inherited Jack Paar's* Tonight Show *story files, for in 1984 Carson told the same combined version of the two legends as quoted above, except that he* did *have the woman burn the intruder with her hot iron.*

"The Grocery Scam"

A girl walked into a supermarket and bought some groceries—a couple of things like bread and a carton of milk. At the checkout the woman in front of her turned around and said, "Oh, my God, it's my daughter back from the dead. You're my daughter, aren't you?"

"No, I'm not your daughter," the girl replied.

"You look so much like my daughter who died a couple of years ago. Would you do me a favour? When I leave and say 'Goodbye,' would you say 'Goodbye, Mum,' just for old time's sake?"

The girl agreed and did as she was asked when the woman left the store. Then, as the girl prepared to pay for her groceries, the checkout woman asked for $160.

"But I only bought a loaf of bread and some milk!" she said.

"But your Mum said you were going to pay for it."

"No, that's not my Mum," said the girl.

"Yes it is. You said 'Goodbye, Mum'."

"Caught at the Checkout" from Graham Seal's 1995 book Great Australian Urban Myths, *p. 100. This story is also known in the United States, where sometimes the scam artist approaches a young man, saying he looks exactly like a son who was killed in Vietnam. It's possible that this story represents an actual scam, with the con person and the "victim" working together to cheat the store or restaurant. In his 1991 autobiography* Take My Life, Please, *comedian Henny Youngman described using the same technique to get a free meal at a New York restaurant. He would leave the table first, and tell the cashier that "The person who waves will be paying my check." Then he would wave at the table of friends with whom he had dined, and "Someone would always wave back, and you'd be on your way." Several readers have reported to me that Jack Benny enacted the same trick either in one of his films or on his television series.*

"The Shoplifter's Hat"

I heard this one while working for a local grocery chain. While the store was full of local retirees, an older gentleman was seen slowly exiting the store with a drop of blood coming from under his hat. The manager rushed over inquiring about the blood, wondering if the man fell, etc. The

Lane Yerkes. From *Smithsonian*, vol. 23, no. 8.

man nervously explained that he just wanted to leave. The store manager, while trying to help the man out, lifted the hat to find an unpackaged steak sitting on the man's bald head. The man was promptly arrested for shoplifting.

What a meathead!

When she first saw blood dribbling from the customer's head, a California grocery clerk wanted to call an ambulance. But a closer look revealed that the man was trying to smuggle a steak out of the store by hiding it under his hat. Unfortunately for him, the package began to leak while he was waiting in the checkout line. You know, that sort of thing just wouldn't happen with broccoli.

The first version, sent to me in March 1997 by Rich Wickliffe of Coconut Creek, Florida, is a well-known story in communities with a large retired or homeless population. The second version is from Vegetarian Times *for July 1990. This story has been well known in Europe since the early 1970s, especially in England and in Scandinavia, and usually concerning a woman trying to steal a frozen chicken concealed in her hat. Older prototypes for the story describe another variety of meat or butter concealed under someone's hat in an attempt to steal the food. A version in which the chicken is concealed in the shoplifter's bra became popular in the United States and Canada in the early 1990s.*

"Indecent Exposure"

I heard a funny story the other day. It's true, though. My roommate heard it from a friend of his who lives in Boston. This couple he knows got married last year and decided to go to Jamaica for their honeymoon.

In the first couple of days they were down there, their hotel room was broken into. But nothing was taken. No money, nothing. So they forgot all about it. They just figured that the burglar must have been interrupted right after he got in. They had a great time the rest of their honeymoon. Hanging around on the beach, swimming, sailing around in the ocean. Everything was perfect.

And then they went home. About a week later they went and picked up the pictures from their trip. And as they flipped through them, through all the shots of the beach and the sunset and the waves, in among them was a shot of this native Rastafarian guy in the bathroom of their hotel room. And he's got his pants down with his back to the camera and when the couple looks closer, they can see that the guy's got the wife's toothbrush stuck in the one place in Jamaica where the sun doesn't shine.

This the earliest published example of this popular story I have found; it appeared in Jay Forstner's article "Local Legends" in the Ann Arbor (Michigan) Observer *for March 1991, p. 35. The earliest oral versions of this legend I have are dated in the autumn of 1990, and I have received some 60 further reports, half of them in 1991, and the latest in*

1996. Most versions claim that the incident happened to a couple vacationing in a tropical paradise, but the story is also told about various European capitals. In Australian versions the perpetrators are sometimes identified as Aborigines. Alan Dumas of the Rocky Mountain News *in Denver, Colorado, sent me a version in March 1991 in which the victims load their vacation slides into a tray without first viewing them; they discover the outrageous toothbrush picture when showing their slides to friends and family members. Issue number 30 of* FOAFtale News *(June 1993) included discussions of this story that had circulated on the Internet, plus reports of it being told in the Netherlands and in New Zealand. The Kiwi version claims that the thieves filmed their outrageous action on the victims' video camera. In the summer of 1991 a Chicago theater group called the Neo-Futurists included a short skit in their revue that involved several actors brushing their teeth in the background while a narrator told the "Indecent Exposure" story.*

"The Attempted Abduction"

A woman I work with at the Sierra Nevada Museum of Art in Reno came back yesterday from a vacation in Los Angeles with a horrible tale of an occurrence at Disneyland. Her brother told her that a friend of his reported that they turned around for a moment during the Parade of Lights one night at Disneyland, and their very young child disappeared. They searched all over and didn't find a trace of the child. They notified employees and positioned themselves near the exit gate in order to try and discover the child leaving. The child had been wearing very distinctive plaid tennis shoes. The Disneyland employees were helping them look, and suddenly someone saw one of the shoes and hurried into a nearby restroom where the child was found in new clothes and newly dyed hair. Just in time.

A few years ago as the editor of another newspaper I started getting angry calls from readers wondering why we were "covering up" a news story.

At the big local suburban mall, so the story went, two women were thwarted while trying to kidnap a little girl. Supposedly the women had cut the toddler's hair and changed her into little boys' clothes, planning to smuggle her out of the mall. A security guard caught them at it. So the story went.

Why, our callers asked, didn't the newspaper carry an article about it? Protecting our advertiser?

No! The reason is that there wasn't a shred of truth to the story. None. Zero. It didn't happen.

The same story had cropped up all over the nation, including in Muskegon, I'm told.

It was an "urban myth," one of those rumors that makes its way around the country, person-to-person, often over years' time. Urban myths are ridiculous, but have just enough plausibility to raise questions—and fears. They "could happen." That's what makes them so insidious, and so hard to kill.

After getting several of these calls, I decided to try to track down the rumor.

I asked a woman caller if she had seen the alleged kidnapping attempt take place. No, she said, but her sister had been there. I got her sister's name and number.

No, the sister said when I called her. She hadn't seen it happen, but her father-in-law had been at the mall at the time of the crime.

No, the father-in-law said, his daughter-in-law was mistaken. He hadn't been at the mall, but his neighbor was good friends with the security guard who caught the kidnappers.

No, the neighbor said, it was his buddy who was friends with the security guard.

No, the neighbor's buddy said. He'd heard the story from a mechanic who worked near the mall in question . . .

. . . who heard it from a salesperson . . .

. . . who heard it from her hairdresser . . .

. . . whose boyfriend was a police officer, etc., etc.

In each case the person passing along the rumor was sure it had come from a credible source. Some were absolutely positive the incident had happened; others were skeptical but passed the rumor along anyway.

The first story was sent to me in August 1986 by Nancy Peppin of Reno, Nevada. The second example is from a column written by Gunnar Carlson, editor of the Muskegon (Michigan) Chronicle, *for the April 28, 1991, edition; it was sent to me by Cornell "Corky" Beukema, who worked years ago with my father in the Michigan State Highway Department. My files bulge with further versions of "The Attempted Abduction," one of the oldest and possibly the most enduring of all urban legends concerning crime. I discussed this story's background and its history up to 1985 in considerable detail in* The Choking Doberman *and* The Mexican Pet. *It seems as if every time a new shopping mall or amusement park opens, "The Attempted Abduction" will pop up again on the local level; then, often, citizens become outraged that the newspapers and police are not "doing something" about the problem. Carlson's editorial is typical of most journalists' approach to the story: they have heard it so many times without ever finding evidence that it happened in their communities that they can quickly debunk it. The older and much more tragic variation of this story is "The Mutilated Boy," a legend that goes back to the Middle Ages and beyond; its prototypes were transmitted in ballad, story, and literature. Chaucer's "Prioress's Tale" is one anti-Semitic variation on the theme.*

"The Unstealable Car"

Detroit (AP)—A Florida motorist concerned about thieves used to keep his sports car chained to two palm trees in his yard each night.

One morning he noticed the rear bumper was chained where the front bumper had been. And there was a note on the windshield: "When we want it, we'll come back and get it."

A true story, swears David Manly of LoJack Corp. in Needham, Massachusetts.

Between my junior and senior years in high school—the summer of 1980—I attended a summer program at Wichita State University (WSU) in Wichita, Kansas. One of the RAs in the dorm where I lived told

me this story, saying it had happened to a friend of a friend the previous year.

It seems that this guy owned a large new motorcycle. He parked it in the courtyard of the dorm every night. He chained it to a light post with a heavy chain, using a massive padlock. One morning he found his motorcycle chained to a different light post, and there was a note attached that read "If we want it, we'll take it."

The Associated Press story on the "LoJack" device, named as a takeoff on "hijack," was distributed to newspapers in mid-September 1991. Variations of the foiled protection ploy devised for an expensive car are told all over the country. Sometimes the car is chained to huge steel staples embedded into the cement floor of a garage; or, the car is tightly surrounded by other vehicles and locked securely. Nothing works: the car is eventually found turned around or moved across the street with the taunting note attached. The motorcycle variation on the theme came to me from Joel W. Ekis of Lee's Summit, Missouri, in August 1990.

"Stripping the Car"

My husband, a surgeon at the Hospital of the University of Pennsylvania, came home with this story, not quite first hand, but the guy who told him the story knew the guy it happened to and "He could get more details." OK. There was a guy who was a surgeon up at Yale; big guy, athletic type, black. He's driving a BMW down the highway when the engine starts acting up. So he pulls over and lifts the hood to investigate.

Another guy—black too, or Puerto Rican, not sure—stops and taps him on the shoulder. "Hey, man," says the second guy, "I ain't gonna hassle you. You can have the engine, I'm just wantin' the wheels."

Sounds like an urban legend to me!

From a letter, whose signature is illegible, mailed from Philadelphia on May 15, 1993. Other versions of this story, often with a similar racist slant, specify that the car is a Mercedes or another expensive model stalled or with a flat tire on the Long Island Expressway or the Bronx River Parkway. The oldest report of "Stripping the Car" I have received dates from 1977. This is a story that G. Gordon Liddy also tells; in a 1991 article in Forbes, *Liddy claimed that the incident had happened "Recently, in New York City."*

"Get Out of Here!"

I heard this told on Long Island in the mid-1970s:

A man decided to get a free live Christmas tree by digging up one of the small pine trees recently planted along the Southern State parkway. He got as far as wrapping the root ball with burlap when a State Trooper pulled up and asked him what he was doing.

The man said, "My wife is Jewish, and she won't let me have a Christmas tree in the house. So every year, to celebrate Christmas, I plant a pine tree where the public can enjoy it."

The trooper replied, "You can't do that! Take your damn tree and get out of here."

Sent to me in March 1994 by Tricia Scarnati of Portland, Oregon. In July of the same year Mary A. Hochberg of Eugene, Oregon, wrote to me describing a story she heard as a child in New York City in the 1960s, in which a man using a similar ploy steals some bricks from a pile left near a building site. He tells the policeman that he is leaving some bricks left over from a home-improvement project. Both these writers were responding to a story from Belgium that I included in The Baby Train, *in which a man following the identical scheme steals cobblestones from a pile left by street-repair workers.*

16

Human Nature

It's just human nature to jump to conclusions (see Chapter 1)—also to seize at opportunities, miss the point, fudge the data, complain, criticize, rationalize, sympathize, brag, gloat, miss the boat, jump ship, blindly follow tradition (yet yearn to be different), and in general to act like the kids and grown-up kids that we are. At least, so the legends tell us. Urban legends reveal our self-image as being just semirational beings, and we tell and retell these legends in order to illustrate our candid view of our nature.

Here is the Chinese-American t'ai chi master Al Chung-liang Huang explaining an ancient principle of Asian wisdom about life, using a modern urban legend heard from one of his disciples:

> Living is a continuous rebirth process. If you learn something today, tomorrow morning you have to start all over again. If you accept that, then there's no need for a binding structure. A good structure should have the flexibility to change and adapt. It will emerge when you practice, but it will look and feel different every day.
>
> Yesterday I asked why can't we do the whole t'ai chi ch'uan in the reverse of the way it is handed down? Why does the first movement always have to turn to the right? Barry was telling us the story about the woman who always cut off the end of the ham and somebody asked why she did it. She said, "Well, I don't know, my mother always did it that way." And they asked her mother and she said, "I don't know, my mother always did it." And they asked grandma, and she said, "Well, I did it because otherwise it wouldn't fit in my biggest pot."

(From *Embrace Tiger, Return to Mountain.*) If that story seems familiar, check back in Chapter 6, where the same "Bungling Bride" legend is quoted from a rabbi who used it to encourage his congregation to learn the backgrounds of religious rituals. Whether told in a Zen, Jewish, or secular context, this traditional story illustrates a point about human nature, that sometimes we blindly follow tradition.

Here is another example, also revealing the wisdom of youth in the ways of human nature. This story was quoted in a Salt Lake City newspaper article that was part of a series on family relationships and counseling:

> One grandpa, after Grandma died, came to live at his son's home. He had a slight hand tremor and, as he sat at the dining room table, would occasionally spill soup on the tablecloth. The tremor got worse and finally the son thought the best thing would be for Grandpa to eat in the kitchen.
>
> This was arranged. But the tremor got still worse and Grandpa occasionally dropped and broke a piece of china. Then the son got him some wooden plates and a wooden cup to use at mealtimes.
>
> One day the son came home and found his own little boy, age 7, working at the tool bench in the basement. The boy was chiseling at a chunk of wood.
>
> "What are you making, Son?" he asked.
>
> "I'm making a wooden plate and a wooden cup," the little boy replied. "They're for you, Dad, so when you're old you can eat in my kitchen."

Years later, in the same newspaper, a letter to the editor concerning Social Security recounted a variation of the same legend, calling it "an Asian fable." This time the father made a basket in which to place grandfather so he could throw him in the river and end the drain on the family finances. One of the children commented, "When you dispose of grandfather, bring back the basket, because we will need to use it for you someday."

Characteristic of both the ancient stories and the modern legends of this type is that they reveal how people supposedly behave, but generally end abruptly without describing the reaction of the character whose inhumane human nature is exposed. Incidentally, these wooden-utensil/basket-casket stories are, in fact, both ancient fables and modern legends, since their plots can be traced widely in time and space and (as my examples demonstrate) they continue to be told.

Another aspect of human nature that is revealed in legends is our tendency to want to have a more glorious past. Many families tell stories of this kind to account for their average economic status when, of course, they would prefer to be—and feel they *deserve* to be—filthy rich:

"If Grandpa had held on to that piece of property, we'd be millionaires today."

"Uncle Ed invented an improved widget, but he let a big company develop it, and he lost the profits that should have been his."

"Our ancestors were English nobles, but they gave it all up to immigrate to the States."

Although these "family misfortune stories" may contain some grains of truth, they become exaggerated and stylized as they're retold through the generations. In short, they become wishful-thinking legends. Eventually that parcel of downtown Chicago property that Grandpa once owned becomes in the story "the exact piece of land where the Marshall Field's department store stands today." Uncle Ed's widget is said to be the key ingredient in the success of General Electric, General Motors, or another giant corporation, though the details of the device are always sketchy.

The family nobility, it is explained, was forsaken many generations ago, so that by now nobody is quite sure how it happened. Perhaps some ancestor ran off with a commoner, or lost the family fortune for love, or differed with the king, forfeiting wealth in order to uphold some moral principle. According to other stories, the land became worthless, the business went bust, or the railroad went elsewhere, leaving Grandpa and his descendants stuck in the middle class.

People tell such stories because they really believe that hard work and persistence—not just blind luck—*should* pay off. If we're not rich (industrious people that we are), then an ancestor *must* have done something wrong. That's just human nature, no matter how you look at it.

"THE COPIER IS OUT OF ORDER"

YES—We have called the serviceman
YES—He will be in today
NO—We cannot fix it
NO—We do not know how long it will take
NO—We do not know what caused it
NO—We do not know who broke it

YES—We are keeping it
NO—We do not know what you are going to do now
Thank You

"The Baby Train"

The first thing you hear mornings in Manitou is the early Q train to Chicago. It's too early to get up and too late to go to sleep again. They have a legend out there that the morning yells of that rattler do a good deal to keep up the birth-rate.

Dear Ann Landers: If you think this is as funny as I do, go ahead and print it.

—Longtime Reader in Bentonville, Ark.

Dear Ark: I do, and I will. Here it is:

"I asked my Uncle Jeb why he and Aunt Tessie had so many kids. He replied 'We lived down by the tracks. The train woke me up at 6 a.m., and I didn't have to be anywhere 'til 7.' "

The first is from Christopher Morley's novel Kitty Foyle, *published in 1939; the second is from Ann Landers's column of July 9, 1996. In my book of the same title I print longer versions of "The Baby Train" from the United States, England, South Africa, and Australia. This story, illustrating how people will presumably seize any opportunity for sex, goes back at least to the early Industrial Revolution, when train travel was just developing. Some Canadian versions describe a French-Canadian train engineer who deliberately blows his whistle long and loud early in the mornings, waking people up and leading them to do what comes naturally. The punch line in Canada is often something like "Gawdam that Jean-Pierre!" The baby-train legend has long been a favorite on college campuses, told to explain the supposedly high birth rate in certain married-student apartment units. In coastal locations the same story is told, with a fog horn waking up the couples. The English term "whistle babies" is sometimes used to refer to the results of these early morning incidents; it has a counterpart in the German* Jagd kinder *or "hunt children," referring to conceptions occurring during the hunting season. Contradicting the legends, demographers generally deny that events such as blackouts, earthquakes, and major snowstorms often spur a huge increase in births nine months later. However, following Hurricane Andrew in 1993 news stories claimed that hundreds of people in southern Florida had conceived unexpected babies during the storm. A Knight-Ridder article circulated in May of that year quoted a Florida obstetrician saying, "Major snowstorms, blackouts, anything that shuts business down . . . if you're stuck at home and there's nothing else to do, these kind of things do happen."*

"The Trained Professor"

There is an ancient legend that has been showing up in college classrooms for at least 20 years. According to the story, a group of psychology students was being lectured on the principle of positive reinforcement. The lecturer was boring, so to relieve the tedium, the students concocted a scheme whereby they would all look up and smile whenever the instructor spoke from the left-hand side of the room. According to another version, by the end of the semester they had trained him to lecture with one hand stuck into his coat à la Napoleon Bonaparte, speaking in terse, clipped sentences.

I heard the "Trained Professor" story from our psychology teacher in Psych 101 at Princeton sometime between 1963 and 1967. He said it was true. The behavior induced was lecturing from one side of the platform. Several of us in his class decided to test his hypothesis, and we succeeded in inducing the same behavior from him within about two weeks.

In 1978 while I was a teaching assistant in the English Department at California State University, Sacramento, a group of us decided to condition our seminar instructor. We used rapt attention as a reward when he stood in the most remote and darkest corner of the classroom to lecture. It wasn't long before he headed to that spot to begin each class. . . . I know that our idea was not original, but I've forgotten where it came from or who first suggested it.

The first report is from Jeffrey Swain of San Diego, California, writing in 1988. The second came from James C. Thompson, librarian at the University of California, Riverside, in 1989. The third came from Meredith A. Wilson of Solano Community College in Suisun, California, in 1990. Although I quote these examples of "The Trained Professor" from California sources, the story—and the prank itself—are well known all across the United States and in Great Britain, if not beyond. A report on an actual experiment of this kind published in Teaching of Psychology, *vol. 15, no. 3 (October 1988), commented "Anecdotes about groups of students conditioning their professors as a practical joke are legion." The induced behavior, according to the stories, may include lecturing while standing on a desk or on an overturned wastebasket. The legend is based on a technique that B. F. Skinner, the father of behavioralism, called "operant behavior." The underlying principle, often demonstrated in animal experiments (particularly using pigeons), is that any behavior followed by reinforcing stimuli, such as food or praise, is more likely to occur again. Skinner, who died in 1990, not only developed techniques for animal behavior modification, he also claimed to have applied the system to a human subject, specifically to a rival psychologist who was conducting a seminar. Skinner's story, often repeated or paraphrased in lectures and in published sources, is the likely basis of the campus pranks and legends. Two reviews of "Trained Professor" legends and the psychology underlying them appeared in* FOAFtale News *(Nos. 21 and 24; March and December 1991, respectively). In her 1975 book on animal behavior,* Lads Before the Wind, *Karen Pryor recounts Skinner's version of the rival-training episode and quotes the following story* about *Skinner, as told in 1966 by his daughter Deborah: "Two of his students decided to shape a piece of behavior in their roommate by giving or withholding smiling and approval. They succeeded so well that they could elicit the behavior of standing on a chair and doing a little dance, at will. Excited by success, they invited Skinner to coffee in their room one night and showed him the poor roommate, climbing in all innocence onto a chair and shuffling about. 'Very interesting,' says Skinner, 'but what does it tell us about pigeons?' "*

"Cussing and Clowns"

I grew up near Chicago and always watched Bozo, who was based in Chicago. I vividly recall talking with my friends in the late 1950s or 1960s about that cussing incident on TV. It was always a "friend" who had seen it. In our version, the kid was playing a game that involved tossing a ping pong ball into six buckets. The first was closest to him, and the 6th was farthest out. Each day, before the game started, the host of the show would place a silver dollar in Bucket Number 6, and each kid who was able to toss the ball into that bucket won all the silver dollars that had accumulated. Of course, for each other bucket he made, he won a prize too, and the prizes grew in value the farther he went down the line of buckets.

Supposedly, this kid had made five buckets, and was on the all-important Bucket Number Six. He blew it and said, "Shit!" So Bozo admonished him, saying "That was a Bozo no-no." And the kid replied, "Ram it, clown!" or something even worse.

The ringmaster of Bozo's Circus was called "Mr. Ned" on the show, and I heard too that he had once said something about "keeping the little bastards quiet" on the show.

Narrator: One lesson an announcer learns is to make sure he is off the air before he makes any private comments. But even the greatest sometimes slip. A legend is Uncle Don's remark after he had closed his famous children's program. Let's turn back the clock

Uncle Don: [Sung] "Good night little friends good night."

[Spoken] "Tune in again tomorrow at this same time and I'll be back with all my little friends. We're off? I guess that'll hold the little bastards for tonight."

The Bozo report came in a 1986 letter from Jack Bales, reference librarian at Mary Washington College in Fredericksburg, Virginia. The Uncle Don report is from the LP record Pardon My Blooper *(Jubilee PMB-1, undated), one of a series issued by Kermit Schafer. There are countless variations of the Bozo story with the offending child saying, "Cram it!" "Shove it!" "Climb it!" and the like to the clown, or to "Bozo," "Clownie," etc. Sometimes the child is said to have made obscene gestures, asked a sexual riddle, or played a game involving carrying an egg in a spoon. Although many people claim to have been eyewitnesses to this incident, every Bozo the Clown spokesperson and every published source on the program and its offshoots denies the story, and nobody has ever produced a recording of any such incident. The "little bastards" story, although long associated with "Uncle Don," actually circulated among broadcasters concerning various other radio characters before Howard Rice (who changed his name to Don Carney) had assumed the "Uncle Don" persona for his popular radio show that ran from the mid-1920s until the late 1940s. Carney consistently denied the story, as do all serious histories of American broadcasting. In an essay included in my book* The Truth Never Stands in the Way of a Good Story *I analyzed four examples of alleged actual recorded or transcribed reports of the Uncle Don incident issued by the "Blooper" industry. These reports differ in several details, and none can be accepted as original or authentic. The sound quality of the recordings is superior to that of early radio broadcasts, very few of which were recorded anyway. The phrase "A legend is . . ." used in introducing these blooper reports suggests that the producers regarded the story as doubtful. Some have claimed that Schafer was merely "re-creating" an actual incident, but it is hard to see how one may re-create something that most likely never happened. Nevertheless, the story in all its variations does nicely illustrate how human nature will presumably cause someone to respond in frustration with an inappropriate off-color remark.*

"Take My Tickets, Please!"

We've had a lousy football team here at . . . for the last few years. How bad? This story has been circulating:

This guy had tickets to the next game, but the team had been so terrible that he didn't really want to go. So on a Saturday he went over to the mall to go shopping instead.

Then he got to thinking that he didn't want the tickets to go to waste, so he came up with the clever idea to just put the tickets on the dashboard and leave the window down, inviting someone to steal them.

When he came back to his car he discovered that someone had put four more tickets to the game on his dash.

Sent to me in 1989 by a reader in the Midwest; I withhold further information to protect the feelings of the inept athletes alluded to. After I mentioned this story in a newspaper column, I heard from readers in other parts of the country who said that the same story was told there.

"The Dishonest Note"

I heard this story in Pittsburgh around 1983, and I believed it was true until last February when my father-in-law told me the same story, swearing it had been witnessed by a buddy of his in Buffalo a few months ago.

There were a lot of cars in a small parking lot in Shadyside, a Pittsburgh suburb. A college-age guy came out of a store and jumped into his car, and as he backed out of the parking space, the bumper of his car caught the passenger side of the next car. He scraped the entire length of the other car.

He got out of his car to survey the damage. His car seemed fine, but the other one was a mess. Several passers-by witnessed the whole scene, as the college student pulled a piece of paper and a pencil from his car. They watched him write a note, stick it under the windshield wiper of the damaged car, and drive away.

When the owner of the damaged car arrived, he freaked out at the state of his new car. Then he grabbed the note on the windshield, and found that it read, "Everyone watching me thinks I'm leaving you my name and insurance information—but I'm not. Ha ha!"

Sent to me in April 1990 by Aurlie McCrea of Redondo Beach, California. Herb Caen, columnist for the San Francisco Chronicle, *published a version of this legend in 1963, mentioning another from the* London Daily Mirror; *Caen published it once again in a 1971 column. A variation appears in an "Andy Capp" cartoon from 1973. "The Dishonest Note" is not only a* story *that reveals human nature, but the prank has actually been enacted by guilty motorists. A number of people have written to me confessing that they themselves wrote such a note, or knew someone personally who did. Others wrote to say that they found such a note on their damaged car.*

"Pass It On"

In a high school class back in the '60s, a narcotics officer from the local police department was brought in to lecture the students on the dangers of drugs. As part of his presentation, the officer brought along two joints from the evidence room which he placed on a tray to show the students.

"These," he said, "are marijuana cigarettes, and I'm going to pass them around the room so you can see and smell them and know what they are like. When this tray comes back, there better still be two joints on it!"

The officer started the tray passing around the room, and when it came back to him there were *three* joints on it.

A widely told story that some tellers claim to have witnessed firsthand. Certainly any officer who tried such a ploy would be asking for it, considering the wit and nerve of some students and the ready availability of marijuana in many schools. Other versions describe a teacher discussing birth control and passing around a couple of condoms. This legend, like several others in this category, deals with a minor infraction; it depicts more of a prank than a crime. The next story is an obvious variation of "Pass It On," but it involves higher stakes.

"The Lottery Ticket"

So this guy is a Colorado lottery winner—several thousand dollars—and he's bragging about it to a bunch of people crowded around a table in a bar and grill. Someone doubts his windfall and says "Let's see the ticket." He pulls it out, and it is passed from hand to hand, finally returning to him. Except that the ticket he gets back has a different number than the one he handed out.

© 1998 Hilary Barta

From Jack Kisling's column "Urban Legends Never Die" in the Denver Post, *May 31, 1988. Kisling commented, "Whether an urban legend is literally true isn't as important as whether it is true to life." This update of the "Pass It On" legend quoted above has emerged in just about every state that has established its own lottery in the past few years, although both are probably just variations of an even older legend about a winning racetrack tick-*

et being passed around a bar. Another lottery legend reported from diverse places describes a winner rushing out to his car (or to buy a new sports car) in which he will race to the state capital to collect his winnings; but he is killed in a car crash en route. In a recent popular story a man is fooled by his friends into thinking he has won a huge lottery payoff; after the man has kicked out his wife, moved in with his girlfriend, and charged expensive gifts on his credit cards, he learns of the hoax. Typically for urban legends, this last story has no follow-up saying what the man did next. A local lottery legend from Utah concerns the Mormon bishop who warned his flock not to participate in any form of gambling, including the lotteries run by surrounding states. Then the bishop has the good (or bad?) luck to win big on a lottery ticket he had impulsively bought in Idaho. When the Idaho lottery officials announced the winners, his name and picture were shown by all the newspapers and newscasts in the area.

"Dial 911 for Help"

People also talk about the time that Mitchell expressed doubt about the 911 emergency phone system. Why? Because there is no 11 on the phone.

"It was a joke," Mitchell says. But many delight in the notion that he wasn't joking. Such is Mitchell's reputation.

Dear Heloise:

Thank you, thank you, thank you for telling parents that the emergency number is 911 and not 9-eleven. You wouldn't believe how many people have said, "There is no 11 on my phone."

Jokes by and about the short-term acting mayor of San Diego, California, Bill Mitchell, were included in a Los Angeles Times *story sent to me about 1985 but without a specific date attached. The second example, from the "Hints from Heloise" column, was published on June 15, 1993; Abigail Van Buren had a longer version of the story in her "Dear Abby" column of March 3, 1990, and I have collected many other such accounts, the old-*

est in 1982. Some versions of the legend form of the story describe in detail horrible tragedies caused by people unable to find 11 on their telephones, but the worst such problem that any actual emergency service that I know of has been able to document was a momentary delay until the caller realized that the numbers to use were "one one" not "eleven." Still, several local telephone emergency services have circulated memos reminding people to think of the series as nine-one-one, not nine-eleven. The ancestor of this story is a "Little Moron" joke from the 1940s, as summarized in a folktale index: "Fool answers phone late at night; caller asks, 'Is this one-one-one-one?'—'No this is eleven-eleven.' Caller: 'Sorry I got you up.' 'That's all right; I had to get up to answer the phone anyway.'" I've also heard this legend transformed into an ethnic riddle-joke: "Did you hear why they had to get rid of 911 in Warsaw (Stockholm, Oslo, etc.)?"

17

Strays from the Wild Kingdom

Most urbanites seldom see wildlife except in zoos or, occasionally, when traveling through the boondocks. Thus, the possibility of an occasional contact with a wild creature *anywhere* deserves commemoration with a legend; for examples, see "The Elephant That Sat on the VW" in Chapter 4, "Alligators in the Sewers" in Chapter 8, and "The Stunned Deer—or Deer Stunt" in Chapter 19. In each of these legends, as well as in others, an animal has somehow wandered to a site or into a situation where it does not belong, and the result for human beings is a certain amount of discomfort and a whole lot of storytelling. Whenever wildlife strays from its home turf, or whenever people invade the wilds, the legends tell us that some contact is possible, often with bizarre results.

Of course you don't need *real* contacts with the Wild Kingdom to have legends. To the contrary, the more mythical the beast the better, legendwise. What are the chances of someone spotting an actual alien black panther, or even a native cougar, roaming free anywhere in the United States? Realistically, about nil, except for the very remote possibility of an escaped zoo animal or exotic pet. Despite the odds, local newspapers regularly report sightings like the following, quoted from the *Flint (Michigan) Journal* of February 3, 1995:

> Something's on the prowl in the township and it's got folks scared.
>
> A mysterious animal that some say is a cougar has been seen twice this week in the same neighborhood after first being spotted about two weeks ago near the busy Corunna and Linden roads intersection.
>
> But four witnesses, three sightings, and dozens of paw-prints still have township police no closer to solving the mystery.
>
> The Department of Natural Resources thinks cougar theorists are barking up the wrong tree.
>
> "As far as the DNR is concerned, it is, has been, and always was a dog. It never was a cougar," said Jon Royer, a DNR habitat biologist.

It turns out that reported sightings of big cats are not so unusual in eastern Michigan. As I wrote in *The Baby Train*, "Phantom panthers were reported in Manchester, Michigan, in 1984, in Milford in 1986, and in Imlay City in 1989." All of these communities are just 30 or 40 miles outside of Detroit, home of teams named the Tigers and the Lions. Could there be a connection?

The Motown-area panthers, like all these legendary stray monster felines, are hard to track and impossible to verify. As the Michigan DNR official was quoted saying in the Flint Township case, "I've been out on these things over the years and I don't think I've ever seen one where an exotic animal was found." (If only he had omitted "I don't think" from his statement; surely if he *had* found an exotic animal he would have remembered it!)

What accounts for the repeated claims of cougar-sightings in the same general area? Some people have suggested that there must be *something* out there or such reports would not recur. Another popular theory holds that since several people always say they've seen the big cats, these witnesses couldn't all be lying. Wildlife officials generally agree that people have indeed seen something—movements, shadows, unidentified animals, paw prints—and sometimes have heard strange cries in the night. But the authorities interpret these incidents to be mistaken identifications of large dogs, house cats, or possibly smaller local wildcats, bobcats, or the like. Not cougars, and certainly not black panthers. My own folkloric insight would add that such reports are not confined to one region, but occur widely in the United States and also in Europe, notably in England and Italy in recent years. Also, similar motifs recur in all of these stories, suggesting the transmission of folk rumors, hoaxes, and legends rather than the straying of actual panthers or cougars. People are not lying, but they are circulating unverified folklore.

There is also a folk style and structure to the news stories that report these alleged big-cat sightings. Here are just two more examples quoted from clippings in my files:

A COUGAR STALKING BETHESDA [MARYLAND]?

Some people claim to have seen one. Others think they have heard one wailing in the night.

But naturalists say it probably isn't so. . . .

The Department of Natural Resources, which deals with area

> wildlife, gets reports of cougarlike animals about five or six times each year, [Clif] Horton [district wildlife manager of the DNR] said.
>
> "None of them are ever substantiated," Horton said.
>
> (the *Montgomery [Maryland] Journal,* June 3, 1994.)

> The cougar remained a fugitive.
>
> The big cat eluded a roving circus of police, bloodhounds, news helicopters, reporters and gawkers yesterday, not once showing itself during an intensive four-hour search along West Cobbs Creek Parkway in Yeadon, Darby and Southwest Philadelphia. . . .
>
> Police still did not have a clue to the animal's owner, despite calls from tipsters throughout the day. One woman apparently called both the Philadelphia Zoo and Yeadon police to say she had lost her 4-year-old pet cougar, but that lead turned out to be fraudulent. . . .
>
> No exotic animal permits have been issued in the Philadelphia area by the Pennsylvania Game Commission.
>
> (the *Philadelphia Inquirer,* January 13, 1995.)

In another kind of Wild Kingdom legend an old rural story is repeated in a modern urban setting. I got this account of a storytelling session that took place in an Austin, Texas, bar in a 1990 letter from Brenda Sommer, then a bartender and one of my best correspondents. I quote only one of Ms. Sommer's beautifully told stories from her letter:

> I have to write to you before the bar napkin that my notes are written upon disappears into the mess that is my desk.
>
> To set the mood: it was a slow Wednesday night at the bar, muggy outside but just right inside for Margaritas. Two good-old boys who wouldn't allow me to ignore them had reached the end of their list of current jokes, when one of the Bubbas was reminded of a story his uncle had heard about a fellow in Beeville, Texas.
>
> It seems that one afternoon, this fellow had killed a big rattlesnake out by his woodpile, chopping its head off with a hoe. Later that night, he happened to recall that his grandson was collecting rattles for a school project, so this bright guy went out in the dark and over to the

woodpile. He felt around until he found the rattle end of the snake, chopped it off, and went back inside to bed.

The next day he went past the woodpile and noticed that the decapitated snake was still there with the rattle intact. After he awoke from his dead faint, he realized that in the dark he must have removed the rattle of this snake's live mate!

"Well, now, just a minute," said the other Bubba. "I heard that one in Louisiana."

Indeed, this "out of the mouths of Bubbas" yarn is an old southwestern favorite. Folklorist Linda Kinsey Adams, who researched folklore of the rattlesnake, found this to be the most common rattlesnake story told in north-central Texas. Since this thriller tale was usually told as the experience of a FOAF, the story was able to make an easy transition to the style and context of a modern legend told in an urban bar. I call it "The Wrong Rattler."

"Foiling Foxes"

From the Daily Mail, *an English newspaper, 1997*

Q. We are plagued by urban foxes whose antics keep us awake at night. How can we get rid of them?

Mrs. P. McGuire, Croydon

A. Place plastic bottles half-filled with cold water around the garden, especially at night. The wind will blow into the bottles, making a low whining sound that foxes hate.

Mrs. K. Bednall, Tonbridge, Kent

"The Kangaroo Thief"

The most traveled story about Australian kangaroos came during the America's Cup. There are at least three versions.

• First one we heard involved the fashionable Gucci people who came over to support the Italian cup entries. Between races, a group decided to drive into the country to look for *roos*.

As it turned out, their Land Rover ran into a kangaroo but only stunned it. As the animal lay in the road, trying to recover, one of the Italians decided it would be clever to take a picture of it in a Gucci jacket. The driver offered his.

So, the kangaroo was fitted with a jacket, but before the picture could be taken, the animal recovered and bounded into the bush, resplendent in its new attire.

There was one hitch. The keys to the Land Rover were in one of the jacket's pockets.

• A San Francisco writer uses crew members of the *Canada II* 12-meter. They drive into the outback and run into a kangaroo, which is temporarily knocked out. The Canadians dress the animal with crew jacket and baseball cap.

The kangaroo leaps up and heads for the hinterland, dressed in the sailor's jacket which contains money, and most important, a passport.

• This time it's the noted sailmaker and sailing star, Lowell North, who gets out of a car, puts a blazer from the *Eagle* 12-meter syndicate on the kangaroo.

Before he can take a picture, the kangaroo leaps into a thicket never to be seen again except, possibly, by two other kangaroos—one with a Gucci label, another with *Canada II* on it and a Canadian passport.

From his column "Some tall tales from the outback" by Red Marston in the St. Petersburg (Florida) Times, *August 12, 1987. All three versions of the story were rampant at the time, and were repeated by many print and broadcast media. Graham Seal mentions the story being told about visiting English cricket teams in the 1950s in his 1995 book* Great Australian Urban Myths, *and Amanda Bishop titled her 1988 compila-*

tion of similar stories from Down Under The Gucci Kangaroo. *Bishop mentioned prototypes for the modern versions told as a "bush yarn" in the 1930s; however, Australian folklorist Bill Scott told me that he had found an earlier record in a 1902 book called* Aboriginalities. *In the 1960s in the United States "The Kangaroo Thief" became associated with "The Kingston Trio" because Dave Guard of that popular folk-singing group told it as an experience the group had while touring in Australia. The story continues to circulate: it was in* Canadian Forum *in April 1992 and in the English periodical the* Guardian *on February 27, 1993, and I spotted it posted to an Internet message board in October 1997. The following legend is a variation on the theme.*

"The Deer Departed"

A HUNTER WITHOUT A GUN

George and his friend Peter were fond of deer-hunting, and whenever they had a free day during the deer-hunting season, they took their guns and went off into the forest.

One Saturday they were sitting on a log eating their sandwiches and drinking their coffee when they saw a man walking through the snow towards them. He was dressed in deer-hunting clothes, but he had no gun with him. When he got nearer, the two friends saw that he was following a deer's track in the snow. They were both very surprised to see a man tracking a deer without a gun. So when he reached them, they stopped him and asked him whether anything was wrong and whether they could help him. The man sat down beside them, accepted a cup of coffee and told them his story.

Like them, he had gone out deer-hunting that morning with a friend. They had seen a deer with very big horns, and had followed it for some time. Then he had fired at it, and it had fallen just where it stood. He and his friend had run over to examine it, and he had said to his friend, "This deer's horns will make a wonderful rack for my guns when I get it home." He had then arranged his gun in the deer's horns and stepped back a few yards to see exactly how they would look as a gun rack on the wall of his study. He had been admiring the effect when the deer had suddenly jumped up, shaken itself and raced away, carrying his gun firmly stuck in its horns.

Dumb-hunter stories are numerous. This story is from a textbook in the People's Republic of China: College English: Fast Reading, Book One, *Exercise #4, published by the Shanghai Foreign Language Press. The Chinese version of an American urban legend turns "The Deer Departed" into a tale-within-a-tale, drops the idea of taking a photograph of the trophy, and adds a hunting buddy to the cast of characters. The "Comprehension Exercise" following this story includes this interesting multiple-choice question: "What is the usual weapon in deer-hunting? a. Knives, b. Gun racks, c. Rifles, d. Pistols." Another question asks why the deer ran away, a detail that is not specifically explained in this version; the apparently correct answer choice is "because the hunter had missed his shot."*

"Horsing Around"

Men who went hunting with him learned that behind that stolid exterior was a sense of humor. Some of Coke's [Coke Stevenson, former Texas governor] "gags" would, in fact, become staples of Austin lore. During a hunting trip with several fellow-legislators and a lobbyist, for example, a rancher, an old friend called Stevenson aside and told him that in one of the back pastures where the men were to hunt was an aged horse—an old family pet—so infirm that it should be destroyed. The rancher asked Stevenson to do it for him. Stevenson agreed. As the hunters' car was passing the horse, he asked the driver to stop, and got out. "I think I'll just kill that ol' horse," he said, and, taking aim, shot it in the head.

His companions, unaware of the rancher's request, stared in amazement.

"Why did you shoot that horse?" the lobbyist finally asked.

"I just always wondered what it would feel like to shoot a horse," Stevenson drawled. Pausing, he stared hard at the lobbyist. "Now I'm wondering what it would feel like to shoot a man."

From The New Yorker, *January 15, 1990, p. 60, in Robert A. Caro's series titled "Annals of Politics." Governor Stevenson may actually have enacted this old hunting yarn; if so, he was lucky that things did not end the way the story often does—with the other hunters in panic shooting, or at least attacking and disarming, the perpetrator of the prank. In* The Baby Train *I titled this story "Shooting the Bull," since another version of the story has the fellow hunters shooting one of the farmer's prize bulls after the prankster has shot the old horse, mule, or cow as the farmer had asked him. This is evidently a favorite story among American professional athletes, a famous version having often been told by Billy Martin, who claimed that the prank was played on him by Mickey Mantle and Whitey Ford when the three baseball greats were deer hunting. David Young of Ore City, Texas, reported to me in 1991 that Dallas Cowboys coach Tom Landry told it that year as a true experience when he had taken coach Mike Ditka of the Chicago Bears hunting in Texas, but when asked about the incident, Landry confessed that he just liked to tell the story "to get things going." Versions of this legend appeared in Morton Thompson's 1945 book* Joe, The Wounded Tennis Player *and in H. Allen Smith's 1953 book* The Compleat Practical Joker. *Tobias Wolff based his story "Hunters in the Snow" on the shooting-a-man version of the legend that appears in his 1981 book* In the Garden of the North American Martyrs.

"The Hapless Water Skier"

In 1965 while I was stationed at Eglin AFB, Florida, I was invited to go water skiing with the family of a friend on a small reservoir in southern Alabama. Along the edge of the lake was an area of tree stumps and fences protruding from the water. As we were getting ready, the boat owner told us he would keep us well clear of the shoreline, because the summer before a skier had fallen and had been killed there.

According to him, as the boat went back, the skier started yelling for help, saying he was tangled in barbed wire and couldn't move his legs. When they pulled him from the water, he was dead. He had fallen into a nest of water moccasins and had died from over 100 snake bites.

Two years later I was at Barksdale AFB in northwestern Louisiana. Again, I was invited to go water skiing, this time in one of the local bayous. As we got ready to start—I'm sure you are ahead of me now—I was told we must stay away from the shoreline where all the dead trees were, because last summer a skier was killed when he fell into a nest of water moccasins there.

This version of a widespread southern story came in a 1991 letter from Lt. Col. Gary L. Dikkers, USAF. Dr. O. Finley Graves of the University of Mississippi, who published a 1978 article in Southern Folklore Quarterly *about snake stories, wrote to me pointing out occurrences of "The Hapless Water Skier" in southern literature, including Ellen Douglas's 1988* Can't Quit You, Baby, *which described it as "an apocryphal tale . . . that rolled like ball lightning through the Mississippi Delta during the late '60s." Could the story possibly be true? Douglas quipped that "It's always true. Always true that a tangle of water moccasins lies in wait for the skier. Always, always true." In 1990 the* San Antonio Light *discussed water moccasins, or "cottonmouths" as they are often called, in its "Who's Who at the Zoo" column, describing this species as "quiet and not easy to locate." The column mentioned as mere hearsay the story of a little girl who fell while water skiing on Lake Amistad and was "immediately killed by multiple moccasin bites when she landed in a 'nest' of these snakes." Naturalist Bruce Lee Deuley, writer of the column, commented, "There are no water moccasins in Lake Amistad, and I have found no record of these reptiles traveling or grouping in large colonies." Whether such a death ever happened, it's highly unlikely that virtually the same accident occurred in many different places and times, yet always escaped the notice of wildlife experts.*

"The Giant Catfish"

There are the stories about the divers who work for the U.S. Bureau of Reclamation and swim down to the bottoms of the Colorado River dams to clean the grates and make repairs.

Anglers say a diver saw a flathead [catfish] so big that, as Rich Beaudry of the Arizona Game and Fish Department puts it, "You'd have to have a

jack winch on a truck to pull him in. And the reason nobody has ever caught one is that they're so big they keep breaking the lines." And then Beaudry adds, sadly, "Trouble is, it's always 'my friend the diver' who's seen it, but you can never find the diver."

From Arizona Highways, *November 1991. Robert Miller of Richfield, Utah, who sent me this clipping, commented "for the past 25 years or so I have heard stories about huge catfish that were supposedly seen from Hite, Utah, all the way to Yuma, Arizona." Midwestern versions are discussed in John Madson's 1985 book* Up on the River: An Upper Mississippi Chronicle. *Stories of giant catfish have been told for generations throughout the South, Midwest, and Southwest, places where truly huge catfish do indeed grow, but never to quite the proportions claimed by legend, i.e., as big as calves or cows or even cars. In modern versions the fish is mistaken for a Volkswagen Beetle because its mouth is slowly opening and closing like a car hood lid being moved up and down in the current. In another variation on the theme, the body of a drowned passenger may be said to still be locked inside the VW, and several giant catfish are prowling outside trying to find a way in. Divers, seeing such horrible sights, emerge from the depths pale and shaking. They vow never to dive in murky rivers or reservoirs again, and overnight their hair turns white from the shock. A good collection of catfish facts and folklore is included in Jens Lund's entry "Catfish" in the 1996 work* American Folklore: An Encyclopedia.

"The Flying Cow"

Moscow, April 30 [1997] (Reuters)—A tale of Russian cows falling from the sky onto a fishing boat in the Pacific has been keeping German diplomats on their toes.

But the story, reported by the German Embassy in Moscow to the Foreign Ministry in Bonn and made public by a German newspaper, bears all the hallmarks of an urban legend—a fantasy, told and retold until it gains an air of authenticity.

It goes like this: Several weeks ago Russian rescue workers picked some Japanese fishermen out of the sea and detained them after they claimed their vessel had sunk after being hit by a cow.

Investigations by Russian authorities then uncovered a bizarre crime story, involving Russian soldiers and airborne cattle-rustling, the daily *Hamburger Morgenpost* wrote.

"Members of the Russian forces stole a couple of cows and transported them in a plane. During the flight the cattle got out of control. The crew felt forced to throw the cows out in order to avoid a crash," the paper wrote, quoting from an official embassy dispatch.

Sources in the German embassy told Reuters that there had indeed been such a wire and indeed, the quotes were authentic.

So far no clear source has emerged for the story and some people say it sounds very similar to an episode in a popular recent Russian film called *Osobennosti Natsionalnoi Okhoty* (Peculiarities of the National Hunt).

The film, also one of Russia's bestselling videos, depicts hunters stealing a cow and hiding it in a military jet.

Some six months ago the Moscow daily *Komsomolskaya Pravda*, inspired by the film, wrote a short report involving cows and planes in its column *Baiki*, one of the paper's journalists told Reuters.

Baiki translates as "invented stories" and covers yarns like the one about baby crocodiles flushed down toilets into the sewage system where they grow before creeping back into flats and houses.

Russians say the cow story even predates the film as a longstanding joke in which a Russian fisherman explains the loss of his boat with the falling cow yarn.

The joke ends with the communist authorities, clearly not amused, sending the fisherman to a psychiatric hospital.

In early April the story of the falling cows popped up on the Internet global computer network. . . .

A news story, bylined Susanne Hoell, forwarded to me as E-mail, thus continuing the transmission of this story via print, broadcast, and now electronic media. This Reuters story goes on to trace the passage of the story out of Russia via German and American embassy personnel and eventually to the Western press. The story concludes with a quotation by a spokesman from the Russian Defense Ministry, "This is sheer nonsense. Not a single word is true." Reuters, incidentally, often distributes stories of this kind reporting bizarre incidents that supposedly occurred abroad. The older "joke" version of the flying-cow story appeared in a Moscow News *column in the June 1–7, 1990, issue. I discussed this one as well as versions from Great Britain in* The Baby Train. *In the June 1997 issue of* Alaska Fishermen's Journal *the story was repeated again with the disclaimer that "We cannot verify the accuracy of the following story, but we are compelled to pass it along because it's too weird and wonderful to bury." This publication's source was an individual who found it on the Internet. Granted, "The Flying Cow" is pretty far from its roots as oral folklore, and a cow is not exactly wildlife, but the story is too weird and wonderful not to include in this chapter. Besides, the Reuters story calls it "an urban legend," and Reuters wouldn't lie, would they?*

"The Fatal Boot"

I remember a story told by my step-grandfather who was born in Kentucky. The eldest of three brothers bought a pair of boots. While the boots were still new he was in the woods and was struck by a rattlesnake. The snake bite caused his death. The next brother inherited the boots, began wearing them, and died. The youngest brother suffered a like fate.

When the property was put up for sale, someone, in examining the boots, found that the rattlesnake had broken off one fang in the heel of the boot. The venom on that fang had caused the death of the brothers.

That had to be a record for one snake!

This is the full text of the story sent to me in 1987 by Tom Riley of San Antonio, Texas, that I paraphrased in discussing "The Fatal Boot" in Curses! Broiled Again! *Like "The Wrong Rattler" story in the introduction to this chapter, this legend is an old rural tale that continues to be told in modern urban settings. Sometimes the boot is specified as a cowboy boot, a hiking boot, or a rubber boot worn while doing farm work. In 1991 David Young of Ore City, Texas, wrote to say that he recalled from a 1966 trip to Florida being shown the actual "fatal boot," except that it was a shoe this time. He wrote, "We stopped at a lot of tourist traps, and the shoe was in a lighted glass display case with the story posted next to it: shoe was passed on to brother, brother died. Fang discovered too late."*

"Snakes in the Amusement Park"

I heard this story several years ago, and I believe it to be an urban legend. You be the judge.

Some years ago at an Ohio amusement park called Cedar Point a husband, wife and son went to spend the day. Cedar Point is in northern Ohio on Lake Erie; it is an old area, overgrown with trees and vegetation, and very moist. The family arrived early in the morning, and they went on the "Log Ride" first. This ride involves single seating in a "log" that travels up through the trees, down a log chute, under waterfalls, and down a final hill before slowing to a stop. The ride supposedly follows the route a log would take after it is cut and sent down river.

The story goes that they had a whole "log" to themselves, and the little boy, eight years old, begged his parents to let him ride in the front seat alone while they rode in the back seating compartment.

The parents agreed, and they settled into their respective seats and began the ride. A short time into the ride, the parents noticed their son moving about wildly and flailing his arms. The mother and father assumed that their son was just having a really good time.

But when the ride stopped, the child was slumped over and dead! When the seat was examined, a small poisonous watersnake was found coiled in the floor where the boy's feet were. The snake had repeatedly bitten him several times during the course of the ride. He had been moving about wildly trying to escape the bites. Apparently the ride had not been checked out thoroughly when the park opened.

Sent to me in January 1992 by Deborah Bowman of Worthington, Ohio. This story is told about numerous rides—from the Tunnel of Love to roller coasters—at amusement parks coast to coast, especially in the South and Midwest. Often there are said to be watersnakes that bite the hand of a rider who has dangled it into the water. In other versions the snakes, or sometimes other creatures, have infested the ride cars, merry-go-round horses, etc., during manufacture abroad—usually said to be India—or during storage over the previous winter. Even modern, up-to-date amusement parks are plagued with stories like this, and similar tales are told about those bins full of plastic balls now found in the "playlands" of fast-food restaurants.

"The Snake in the Strawberry Patch"

Lorrie Ostrowski told a tale "the girl at work swore is true."

A woman with her 2-week-old infant beside her, was driving a pickup truck in the Tappahannock area. The woman decided to stop on the side of the road to pick strawberries and briefly left her son in the truck with a bottle of milk.

Returning to the truck a few minutes later, the woman noticed something black dangling from her newborn's mouth. The black object was the tail of a snake that had slithered down the baby's throat after the milk and killed the boy.

Now doesn't that story make you drop your fork?

But wait a minute. The story is loaded with holes. After all, who ever heard of a snake desperately seeking milk? FALSE! . . . Or, maybe, true?

The easiest trail failed. Mrs. Ostrowski asked her friend to talk with a reporter, but the friend refused.

Mrs. Ostrowski, 23, of 10340 Iron Mill Road, a secretary at Robertshaw Controls Co., then asked for the number of the coworker's aunt, supposedly the source of the story. The coworker refused to give out her aunt's phone number or name.

So, the next option was the Essex County Sheriff's Department, which covers Tappahannock.

Essex Sheriff Denwood W. Insley had heard the story.

"The source was just general gossip," Insley said. "I overheard, being mentioned in general talk, that it happened in . . . King and Queen County. Whether or not it happened, I don't know. But, I know it didn't happen in Essex County."

Sheriff Robert F. Longest of King and Queen County also knew of the story, but heard the snake incident happened in Chesterfield County.

"I heard rumors, and that's all I know. If it happened in my county, it was not reported to my department. I feel reasonably sure that it didn't happen in King and Queen County," Longest said.

"It didn't happen here," said Alan W. Thompson, an investigator for Chesterfield County, who had not heard of the incident. "I'm sure if it happened, we would have heard about it."

Susan Gilley, of the Virginia Department of Game and Inland Fisheries, had heard the story, but said it could not have happened because a newborn's mouth is too small for a mature black snake to enter.

However, she said a young black snake—which is gray and brown, not black—could fit.

She offered the name of a snake expert, Dr. Joseph C. Mitchell, a University of Richmond research biologist specializing in reptiles and amphibians. He laughed at the story.

"Snakes don't drink milk. They're carnivorous. Snakes wouldn't even be attracted to milk. That (tale) is crazy and totally beyond the known biology of snakes," Dr. Mitchell said.

OK, so this urban rumor unreasonably attributes powers to a snake!

The story appeared to be false, but where did it originate?

Faithful folklore followers pointed to the book *The Choking Doberman and Other New Urban Legends*, by Jan Harold Brunvand, to check the story's history.

Sure enough, a variation of the snake tale, attributed to an old Irish legend, is cited in the book. . . .

This is the first half of an article by Eileen Barnett published in the Richmond (Virginia) News Leader *on August 24, 1987. "The Snake in the Strawberry Patch," another updating of an old rural snake story, was very popular in North Carolina and Virginia that summer. The notion that snakes crave milk is the basis for many older legends, and the snake supposedly creeping inside someone's body is often the consequence of this craving.*

18

Pet Problems

I've included stories so far in this book about pets that are flushed, poisoned, crushed, roasted, microwaved, buried and exhumed, stolen on the way to burial, and subjected to various other dangers and indignities (including some unspeakable acts involving gerbils). So why do I need to add a separate chapter titled "Pet Problems"?

In part, I just like the alliteration of the title. Second, this chapter provides a nice balance to the previous one on wildlife. Mostly, though, it's because there are a few more exotic hazards to pets and pet owners not covered earlier, and I really hate to leave anything out.

Pet problems are a major theme in legends worldwide; every major pet legend I can think of that's popular in the United States seems to have its counterpart abroad, although occasionally I hear a pet story from overseas that hasn't yet shown up in the United States. Take "The Battered Cat," for instance, which I've collected only from England so far, where it is told something like this:

> A cat dashed into the road, and a motorist could not avoid running over it. There was a sickening thump, and the driver stopped as quickly as possible and ran back to examine the poor animal and to see if he could help it. He found the cat lying on the grass by the roadside, eyes closed, on its back, its feet in the air, but still breathing.
>
> Thinking that the cat was unconscious and dying after the accident, the driver ran back to his car and got his jack-handle out of the boot [the trunk of the car]. He gave the recumbent cat a quick strong blow to the head to put it out of its misery.
>
> Then an old woman ran screaming from a nearby house, exclaiming that this mad driver had killed her cat, which often liked to snooze there by the roadside.
>
> The driver tried to calm her, but the woman's screams aroused the neighbors, and they insisted that the police be called to investigate. They found the body of the cat that had been hit by the car still wedged underneath. The man had beaten the old lady's sleeping pet to death.

On this side of the Atlantic, "The Tranquilized Cat" is a story I have thus far heard only from the States. This one was first sent to me in 1994 by Vince Macek of Decatur, Georgia, and this time the problem is more with the pet owner than with the pet:

> A woman was planning to take her cat with her on a plane trip. At a doctor's appointment she asked her doctor if there was anything she could give her cat to keep it calm on the trip. After a moment's thought, the doc took a tranquilizer pill, broke off a portion that seemed about cat-dosage size, and told her to give it to the cat about an hour before take-off.
>
> Some time later the doctor related this to a veterinarian associate, and the vet said, "You didn't really do that, did you? Why on a cat that drug has the opposite effect as on a human. That cat will be a clawing wreck!"
>
> Later the doctor saw his patient again, and she told him, "I took your advice and gave my cat the pill, and on the plane he was out of control, about to jump out of his skin. It was all we could do to restrain him."
>
> The doctor didn't know what to say—luckily—and the woman continued, "I can't thank you enough for that pill, doctor. I just can't imagine how the cat would have behaved without it!"

Cats are the certified funniest animals in American urban legends, but overseas—especially in Britain and the former colonies—the clown prince of pets is the budgerigar (i.e., budgie; you still don't get it? Then how about parakeet?). I think it's partly the name of the bird involved that appeals, since "budgie" seems funny to me however you say it. Here's a budgie legend from New Zealand, which is easily recognized as a variation on the "Hare Dryer" story of Chapter 1:

> Some workmen were fixing the gas pipes leading into an old lady's house. She had to go out while they were working, and she kindly invited them to go inside and help themselves to tea and biscuits during their break.
>
> However, the workmen had a mishap with the repair, and some gas escaped into the house. They went inside to open some windows and

> doors, and there they found the lady's pet budgie lying on the floor of its cage, apparently gassed to death.
>
> None of the workmen could bear to tell the kind little old lady what happened, so they carefully propped the bird back up on its perch in a lifelike posture. When the lady returned home she immediately spotted the bird and shrieked, "But my little budgie was lying dead on the floor of his cage when I left this morning. Look! He's come back to life!"

I believe the all-time most popular British budgie legend was best told by folklorist Paul Smith in his 1986 *The Book of Nastier Legends*. I've got lots of variations of this story on file, but this particular telling definitely gains in effect from the stiff, dry style with which an Englishman narrates it:

> There are times when you can try just too hard. A young man was invited for the first time to visit his girlfriend's parents' home. As he was very keen for them to like him he was all set to make a good impression, whatever might happen.
>
> When he arrived at the house he was invited in only to discover immediately that his future mother-in-law was desperately fond of budgerigars. Unluckily the young man was allergic to such pets—a fact which he regrettably attempted to hide.
>
> They were all sitting together in the lounge when the conversation turned to pet birds, and the girl's mother let the budgie out of its cage to fly around the room. It flew round for a while and then settled on the young man's head. In desperation he tried to dislodge it but misjudged his actions and knocked the bird straight off his head into the roaring fire, where it burnt to death in front of everyone.

If you are keen on situational humor rather than funny language, you may prefer the version of this story in which the young man has no allergy and the bird does not actually land on his head. Instead, the bird keeps flying back and forth, and the young man, leaning back to relax and cross his legs, happens to catch the budgie in mid-flight, booting it neatly into that same roaring fire.

"The Captivating Kitty Collar"

As reported from Australia, a handyman friend of a friend rigged up a cat-door gadget so that a woman's pet feline would be able to gain entry to her house but other neighborhood strays would not. The friend attached a strong magnet, with the negative pole exposed, to the cat door, and then put another such magnet on the cat's collar. A latch held the door shut when stray cats tried to sneak in.

When the family cat approached the door, the two magnets repelled each other, tripping the latch, and the door swung open. It worked just fine, until . . . "One day puss disappeared. When he didn't turn up for dinner, the woman got worried and began to search the neighborhood. She eventually found her cat three streets away. It was stuck by its collar to a car's hubcap."

"The Bump in the Rug"

There's a story going the rounds that involves a carpet layer who had worked all day installing wall-to-wall carpeting. When he noticed a lump under the carpet in the middle of the living room, he felt his shirt pocket for his cigarettes—they were gone. He was not about to take up the carpet, so he went outside for a two-by-four. Tamping down cigarettes with it would be easy. Once the lump was smoothed, the man gathered up his tools and carried them to his truck. Then two things happened simul-

Born Loser © Distributed by United Feature Syndicate. Reprinted by permission.

taneously. He saw his cigarettes on the seat of the truck, and over his shoulder he heard the voice of the woman to whom the carpet belonged. "Have you seen anything of my parakeet?" she asked plaintively.

From the "Laughter, the Best Medicine" section of Reader's Digest, *May 1964, where it is credited to "Bob Casey, quoted by Frank Rhoades in San Diego* Union.*" I first heard this story from a University of Utah student in 1980, who said it was supposed to have happened to a coworker of his father some twenty-five years earlier. In 1987, a reader in Brooklyn, New York, wrote to say that his father told the story as a personal experience that happened to him in the late 1950s. On October 16, 1988, Dr. Patrick D. Shelley, minister of Plymouth Congregational Church in Lansing, Michigan, startled my parents in the congregation when he quoted "The Bump in the Rug" from my book* The Choking Doberman. *Dr. Shelley commented in his sermon, "I share this particular story today because it illustrates beautifully how tragic events often occur in life: sometimes with the best of intentions, sometimes with no intentionality at all; but always with traumatic consequences." In the April 23, 1990, issue of* People *magazine a profile of Don Aslett, a professional housecleaner, included this exchange:* "What are some of your most bizarre cleaning experiences? *Once, the lump under the carpet that we were beating on turned out to be a kid's hamster. . . ." In England, of course, the trapped pet is a budgerigar; I do love that word!*

"The Pet Nabber"

Valdez, Alaska—A bald eagle satisfied its hunger at a Valdez gas station when it snatched up a small dog and flew away, leaving the dog's owner screaming in horror.

The dog, identified in the Valdez Star as Chihuahua-like, had been let out of a motorhome to run around in the station's parking lot while the owners, an unidentified tourist couple from Georgia passing through last week, cleaned the windshield.

The woman owner clutched her hands to her face and cried, "Oh, my God," while station attendant Dennis Fleming tried to console her.

However, Fleming said as her husband walked around the side of the camper, out of sight of his wife, he began to grin and chopped his hands in the air and exclaimed, "Yeah! Yeah!"

This was a widely reprinted and much-discussed AP news story of June 19, 1993; it may, of course, be true, but the mention of an "unidentified tourist couple," and the husband's undisguised glee at the loss of his wife's pet are suspicious details. Besides, there is a history of unlikely and unverified stories about small pets carried off by large birds going back at least a decade. I first heard of an owl carrying off a pet cat from a backyard patio in Albuquerque in 1985, but Australian folklorist Bill Scott reported hearing about a pelican carrying off a chihuahua two years earlier. By 1996, when Scott published a book of urban legends, he had collected so many versions of the story that he titled his book Pelicans & Chihuahuas. *He reported on a baker's dozen such stories, some of them involving eagles carrying off miniature dachshunds, and a few reported from England, the United States, and Germany. So frequent were the reports from Down Under, however, that Scott commented, "unfortunate canines, in Australia at least, seem to need to spend their lives looking over their shoulders if they do not wish to be carried off and eaten by unlikely predators." The pet owners in the Australian stories are invariably tourists, and in some of them they cry out for their pet: "Pancho! Pancho!" A couple of the stories mention the wife's distress as greater than her husband's. My conclusion is that even if we have a real pet problem here, the accounts of the incidents have acquired a strong "folk" style.*

"The Flying Kitten"

Oldest truth of all: Hairdressers tell clients great—and true—stories. Here's one that qualifies on both counts, told by Carole Taylor of DiGiovanni Coiffures to Lynn Schrichte of Northwest.

A couple Carole knows found a darling kitten and decided to keep it. A few days later, the animal climbed to the top branch of a birch tree and refused to come down. After several hours of coaxing, with no results, the couple decided to toss a rope across the branch and pull it down to where the kitten was reachable.

Nice plan—except that when the cat was almost within reach, the rope broke suddenly, and the cat was catapulted out of sight.

Days of searching followed—all for naught. A week later, one of the former cat owners ran into a neighbor at the grocery store. The neighbor was stocking up on cat food.

"I didn't know you had a cat," said the former owner.

"You're not going to believe this," replied the neighbor, "but my husband and I were sitting in the back yard about a week ago, having a drink, when suddenly this kitten just dropped out of the sky and landed in Joe's lap."

No word on which woman got to keep the cat. Just glad he survived his airborne training. Eight lives to go. . . .

This is the full text of a story that I paraphrased in Curses! Broiled Again! *from the "Bob Levey's Washington" column in the* Washington Post, *June 1, 1987. I've heard several versions of "The Flying Kitten" since then, but none as well told as Levey's. A reader informed me that the same story appeared in Loyal Jones's and Billy Edd Wheeler's 1987 book* Laughter in Appalachia, *and another sent me a press account of a launched cat from Simi Valley, California, in 1991; this feline flier, however, landed safely on a nearby roof and was rescued by its owner.*

"The Missionaries and the Cat"

I've heard this from about five different returned Mormon missionaries, all of whom went to different mission locations. This missionary and his companion visited an elderly lady who had a prize cat that was the love of her life and her only companion. But this cat was obnoxious and always sharpening its claws on the missionaries' legs or getting fur on their dark suits, or whatever.

One day, while the elderly lady was getting the nice young elders some refreshments, one of the LDS elders reached down and flicked kitty on the nose. And as everybody supposedly knows, if you flick a cat on the nose you can kill it by driving its "nose bone" into its brain. This is exactly what happened.

The horrified missionary shoved kitty under the sofa and tried to act as though nothing had happened. On their next visit the missionaries were greeted by a distraught elderly lady mourning the demise of her beloved pet.

Sent to me by Allison Myers of Tucson, Arizona, in 1990. One year earlier I had received the story from Dr. Will Waterhouse, a U.S. Army ophthalmologist then stationed in Landstuhl, West Germany, who had heard it from a friend who had served a Mormon mission in Scotland; in his version the cat had been pawing at illustrations that the missionaries had attached to their low-tech teaching aid, a flannel-covered board. Other versions mention flip charts. Sometimes the cat's corpse is concealed by the missionaries, but in other versions they simply prop the dead kitty up and keep on petting it until it's time to leave. In 1991, Sharon Northern of Portland, Oregon, wrote me to ask if I had heard about the old lady in Germany who had slammed her front door in the faces of two Mormon missionaries, breaking the neck of her small dog, which had stuck its head out to see who was on the porch. And in 1993 Jennifer Lewandowski of Elmhurst, Illinois, sent me the story of a piano tuner who rapped a bothersome dog on the head with his tuning fork, accidentally killing the beloved pet. This time the pet's body was hidden under a bed.

"The Bungled Rescue of the Cat"

THE LEAST SUCCESSFUL ANIMAL RESCUE

The firemen's strike of 1978 made possible one of the great animal rescue attempts of all time. Valiantly, the British Army had taken over emergency firefighting and on January 14, they were called out by an elderly lady in South London to retrieve her cat which had become trapped up a tree. They arrived with impressive haste and soon discharged their duty. So grateful was the lady that she invited them all in for tea. Driving off later, with fond farewells completed, they ran over the cat and killed it.

Quoted from Stephen Pile's 1979 book The Incomplete Book of Failures. *There was, indeed, a British firefighters' strike in 1978, and this story—which may be true—began circulating the same year. However, different versions are told about both regular firemen and substitutes in the United States as well as in England.*

"The Eaten Pets"

Do Vietnamese residing in San Antonio carry on a well-known culinary practice of their native land—killing and eating dogs?

In the Remount Drive and Dinn Drive area, not far from Windsor Park Mall, strange cooking odors have led to a great deal of conscientious sniffing of late on the part of animal lovers.

"It's the smell of roasted or boiled puppy dog. Friends of mine living in the neighborhood near all those homes of newly arrived Vietnamese swear to it, and I agree," says Kathleen Hastings of 358 Savannah Drive, who elaborates:

"Puppies in the same residential blocks are seen for a few weeks, frisking and fattening up in their yards. Then, poof!, they're gone, never to be seen again, replaced by the aforementioned cooking odors."

Said Kathleen Walthall of the local Humane Society, "There's no Texas law against eating dogs so long as they are killed humanely. I wouldn't do it myself. But if the practice exists here, I have no power to stop it."

City veterinarian Dr. Annelda Baetz concurred, saying, "Why, the Chow dog was originally bred by the Chinese for purposes of 'good eating.' You can't legally throw dogs to lions or crocodiles in America, but killing them in a humane way in order to prepare a gastronomic delicacy is OK."

Grumps Kathleen Hastings, "If we don't have a law protecting defenseless dogs from the jaws of cannibals, we had better pass one—and fast!"

Lansing—It may be OK for man's best friend to whimper for scraps under the dinner table, but Fido had better not be the main course.

That's the message from a state lawmaker who has proposed closing a loophole in Michigan law that allows people to indulge in meals composed of dogs and cats.

The extent of the problem hasn't been gauged in Michigan, though there are documented cases in other states such as California.

The Michigan Humane Society has received a few complaints from residents in Detroit's southern suburbs and Lansing who fear their disappearing pets may have ended up on someone's dinner plate.

"There are some people taking people's pets off the street and killing them and eating them," said Eileen Liska, director of research and legislation for Michigan Humane Society.

"They're not documented cases; we can't justify undercover surveillance because there isn't anything in the law that specifically deters it."

She said officials suspect a few immigrants from southeast Asia, because in their native countries dog is considered a delicacy.

The first example is from Paul Thompson's column in the San Antonio Express-News *for April 13, 1988. In a follow-up column published three days later Thompson reported "a whole lot of sniffing . . . without concrete proof that anyone goes in for 'roast puppy.'" Four Vietnamese readers who called Thompson insisted that, since meat is plentiful in the United States "no Oriental will be tempted to seek out dogs as a culinary adjunct." The second example is an Associated Press story of October 8, 1990. Both of these items are typical of many similar articles that have appeared in the American press since Southeast Asian refugees began arriving in large numbers during the 1970s and '80s. Vague rumors about disappearing pets, strange cooking odors, and supposedly larger problems with pet-eating in another state—usually California—are standard features of such stories. The relationship of the dog breed "Chow" to anyone "chowing down" on dogs is tenuous at best, and the charge that dog eaters are "cannibals," although ludicrous, illustrates how people regard their pets. Two indisputable facts make the rumors seem credible; first, that pets do sometimes disappear for no apparent reason, and second, that in some Asian countries dogs are sometimes eaten. Efforts to pass laws outlawing the eating of cats and dogs have failed, usually because such legislation could pave the way for laws prohibiting the eating of* any *animals, as advocated by some animal-rights advocates. Stealing of pets and cruelty to animals are already crimes in most places, but there is no proof that either action is involved in whatever rare instances of dog-eating may have occurred in this country. Another eaten-dog story, "The Swiss Charred Poodle" appeared in Chapter 2, and there is a larger genre of stories about unusual meat dishes served in foreign or fast-food restaurants. Another persistent story tells about an immigrant buying a pet pony and, before the eyes of the horrified sellers, killing it to serve at an ethnic feast. I have heard this one over a period of several years in New York, Utah, and (of course) California. The killer is said to have used a two-by-four, a baseball bat, or a gun to kill the pony; the homeland of the killer is said to have been Samoa, Tonga, Vietnam, or "some island," but, significantly, never France, a country where horse meat is eaten. The prejudices displayed in American "eaten pet" stories are generally directed against Asians, and occasionally against immigrants from southern or eastern Europe.*

"The Pet and the Naked Man"

We are told, through the news media, to take extra precaution during this cold weather. One advice is to take care of our plants. Sometimes that can be hazardous, as evidenced by this article in the *Batesville (Arkansas) Daily Guard:*

Seems the weather turned cold in Houston, Texas, so one man brought an outside hanging plant into the house to keep it from freezing. Said plant contained a small green snake.

The snake warmed up, then slithered onto the floor and under the sofa. The man's wife screamed. The man, who was taking a shower, ran naked into the front room. He bent down to look for the snake. His dog cold-nosed him in the rear end. The man thought it was the snake, and fainted.

His wife figured it was a heart attack. She called the ambulance. When it showed up the attendants loaded the man on a stretcher. About this time, the snake reappeared scaring the attendants. They dropped the stretcher breaking the man's leg. And that's how he landed in the hospital.

From a letter to the editor signed Lydia Sisk, Pasco, Washington, in the Tri-City Herald, *sent to me in March 1989 by Ellen Schmittroth of Richland. (The third of the tri-cities is Kennewick.) Schmittroth commented that "This smells suspiciously like a myth. It was so funny that I made several copies and sent them all over the place. When I read it to my mother over the phone, she laughed so hard she dislocated her jaw. Maybe the surgeon general should do something about putting warning labels on such stories." The set-up for this slapstick story is usually a snake that gets into a house, sometimes hidden in the root ball of a living Christmas tree; non-snake versions begin with a clogged sink drain or a broken hot-water heater. The pet involved is either a cold-nosed dog or a curious cat that takes a swipe at the naked man's testicles. The inevitable conclusion to the story involves startled or laughing paramedics who drop the stretcher and further injure the victim. The above version and Ms. Schmittroth's note nicely illustrate the channels through which such stories move from person to person and place to place, both in print and by oral tradition.*

19

Slapstick Comedy

Back in 1970 columnist Al Allen of the *Sacramento Bee* devoted the very first of his "On the Light Side" columns to telling certain humorous, improbable and oft-repeated stories that he called "Mack Sennetts." He was referring to the kinds of slapstick scenes found in the old Keystone Kops movies directed and produced by Sennett. These farcical flicks were full of sight gags, chases, sudden reversals of direction, and all manner of loony mishaps and near misses. When I contacted Allen after learning of our mutual interest in such slapstick stories, we agreed that many of the comical urban legends were close relatives of "Mack Sennetts."

The term "slapstick" actually refers to the sound of two sticks slapping together, or to a sort of paddle, used to create a loud smacking sound that was cued to the climax of silly jokes on the vaudeville stage and in early film comedies. If you got the timing just right, the resounding SMACK! of the slapstick was supposed to give the pie-in-the-face routine or the dropped-drawers gag a bigger comedic punch. In fight scenes, actors might actually slap at each other with a hinged set of sticks so that the force of their feigned blows was underscored by the loud cracking sound. Later the term "slapstick" was applied to the nature of the humorous scene itself, rather than to the background audio. (At least this is what dictionaries say; the whole thing sounds like a theater legend to me.)

At any rate, obvious elements of slapstick comedy are found in some urban legends, especially the stories that involve what I call "hilarious accidents." Typically in such stories there is a series of mishaps, each worse than the last, all leading up to some kind of exposure of the victim before others' eyes. The comedy in these legends is simple, visual, physical, and farcical, yet it's just believable enough to seem convincing when told by a believer to whose friend's friend the incident happened. Sometimes a punch line destroys the pretense that the slapstick incident really happened, putting the story more into the genre of jokes than legends. Yet the incidents in slapstick legends usually are plausible enough to pass for truth in the minds of some people, especially when the stories get into print.

One of my favorite slapstick legends is about a woman who had to take her son's pet garter snake to him at school for show-and-tell. She put the snake into what she thought was a secure box, and started out in her car. Before long, however, she felt something tickling her ankle, and when she looked down she saw that the snake had escaped the box and was slithering up the leg of her slacks.

The woman frantically kicked her leg and brushed at it with one hand, trying to dislodge the snake, but it didn't work, and the snake kept creeping up. So she pulled over to the roadside, jumped out of the car, and began jumping around and even rolling on the ground trying to dislodge the snake.

A man driving by saw her contortions and thought "Oh, my God! That poor woman is having some kind of seizure!" So he stopped his car and ran over to help her. He tackled the woman and tried to hold her still, but she kept screaming and writhing around.

Another man driving by saw this scene and thought, "Oh, my God! That guy's attacking that poor woman!" So he too stopped his car, ran over, and punched the first man in the face. The woman was finally able to shake out the snake, and then she explained the situation to the two Good Samaritans. This "Snake-Caused Accident" story sometimes involves a gerbil in a box being transported to school or to a vet. Both of these bizarre scenarios may have been invented for use in law school exams, but they have passed on into urban legend tradition.

The concluding story in the preceding chapter, "The Pet and the Naked Man," is another good example of a slapstick urban legend. The sequence of mishaps there goes snake-in-house/naked-man's rescue/accident caused by curious pet/second accident caused by laughing paramedics. Few people hearing the story really stop to question *why* the man would try to find the snake while still naked from the shower or how likely it would be for the snake to reappear just as the paramedics are loading the stretcher. But if you start to question the elements of a farce too closely, it isn't funny anymore.

The "laughing paramedics" element of the story almost deserves to be classified as a separate legend, except that it always appears attached to an account of another mishap. In this chapter, for example, laughing paramedics enter the scene following an exploding toilet or another hilarious accident involving a man on a roof. When you think about it—except that nobody *does* think about these things—paramedics nowadays use wheeled gurneys, not hand-carried stretchers, and they surely must be trained to maintain a dignified professional reserve and to hang on to the patient, no matter how ludicrous the accident they are attending. But the "laughing paramedics" is a slapstick scene inserted into several comical legends.

Another nice thing about these laughing paramedics is that they clue listeners in to how they are expected to react. So if you're trying to get full effect from a funny story you're telling, just throw in an accident, followed by some paramedics who are laughing their heads off.

"Lost Denture Claim"

A clerk in an insurance company was processing a claim for a lost pair of dentures. He requested more information on how they were lost.

The policyholder explained that it all started when she ran out of toilet paper. She came home from buying some at the store and realized that now she had to answer a call of nature rather urgently. So she headed quickly for the bathroom while tearing open the package of toilet paper.

In her haste, as she entered the bathroom, she tripped and dropped the package of toilet paper. She lunged for the dropped package and simultaneously reached out with her arms to break her fall; her left hand hit the handle of the toilet just as her chin hit the edge of the bowl. Her dentures were jolted into the toilet bowl, and the swirling water flushed them down the drain.

"The Exploding Toilet"

GREAT MOTORCYCLING RUMORS

We have heard this story told and seen it printed half a dozen times in the last 30 years. It is always related as fact. Most recently, one of our editors

Robert Enriquez

heard it from a paramedic who was teaching a seminar on emergency medical care.

The story begins with a new owner cleaning his bike on the patio outside a plate glass door or window. When he finishes cleaning, he starts the bike. Somehow he manages to lose control, sending him and the bike through the plate glass window. In the process, he suffers multiple lacerations and paramedics are called. He is summarily rushed to the hospital for stitches. His wife is left to deal with the fallen bike, which is now dripping gasoline on the living room rug. Unable to lift the motorcycle, she uses toilet paper to soak up the gas. When the TP is saturated, she replaces it with more and puts the gas-soaked paper in the commode.

Finally, her husband returns home sporting stitches and bandages. He rights the bike, returns it to the patio and retires to the bathroom, where he seats himself on the commode and, inevitably, lights a cigarette. He drops the match into the commode, which is full of gasoline-soaked paper and fumes. The commode explodes, launching him through the glass shower door. The paramedics are called again, but they are laughing so hard as they try to remove him to the ambulance that they drop the stretcher.

The bike is sold the next day.

This is from Motorcyclist *magazine, September 1991. The same magazine also had published the story in February 1984. My colleague at the University of Utah Adrian "Buzz" Palmer spotted both stories. In a variation on the theme, the man is trying out a new mini-bike he has bought for his children when he spills the gasoline. In a version from New Zealand the man is working on his "leaky car petrol tank" and drains the tank into a toddler's potty, which his wife then pours into the toilet. Whatever the set-up, these variations invariably describe broken glass, spilled gasoline, the wife's involvement in the accident, and (of course) laughing paramedics. There are also many nonvehicular versions of "The Exploding Toilet" in which the volatile material put into the toilet is hair spray or insecticide. Yet other versions begin with a different accident that sends the husband to the hospital; in his absence, the wife paints the bathroom and pours paint thinner into the toilet, leading to the second mishap. In 1988 a version of "The Exploding Toilet" was reported as news from Tel Aviv and rapidly spread worldwide in the media until it was retracted by the newspaper in Israel that had first reported it. An analysis of this incident, plus a history of exploding-toilet stories back to the days of outhouses, is included in my book* The Truth Never Stands in the Way of a Good Story, *in the chapter "A Blast Heard 'round the World." The punch line in the rural prototype of the legend was, "It must have been something I et!"*

"Stuck on the Toilet"

This story was told to me many years ago by a friend of mine who said his father, a physician, was present at the hospital in California where it happened.

A young doctor had the day off and a pair of tickets to a concert. He puttered around the house, did some chores, then picked up a baby-sitter and took his wife out for the evening.

During the intermission they called home to check on things. There being no answer, they hurried back. Dashing into the house, they called the baby-sitter's name and heard her respond from the bathroom. There they found her stuck tight to the toilet seat, which the doctor had re-varnished that morning.

Unable to free her, they unbolted the seat, covered the girl with a blanket, and took her to the hospital emergency room. But even the specialists there were unable to detach the seat from the sitter. When all else failed, they put the poor girl on her hands and knees on an examination table and began to use a scalpel to slice away the varnish just a micron away from her skin.

As word of this strange predicament spread among the hospital staff, the emergency room attracted a crowd of doctors and interns. At this point, the chief of staff, who was making his rounds, walked in. An intern standing next to him, trying to act nonchalant, asked the chief, "Have you ever seen anything like that?"

The chief replied, "Yes, many times. But never with a frame around it."

Sent to me in 1989 by Cliff Thompson of Gahanna, Ohio. The punch line here—a feature more typical of a joke than a legend—is a sure sign of the farcical nature of this story. In other versions, injuries are multiplied when the doctor sits on the edge of the bathtub while trying to free the girl, slips, and either breaks a limb or suffers a concussion. Sometimes his accident is caused by his uncontrollable laughter, and occasionally, laughing paramedics enter the scene. Another contemporary stuck-on-the-toilet story describes a very fat passenger who becomes stuck fast onto the plastic seat of a toilet on a cruise ship or an airliner; there is some evidence that such accidents have actually occurred, although most retellings are strongly influenced by the stuck-toilet urban legends. These modern legends, in turn, may derive from older folk stories that described people becoming stuck to chamber pots.

"The Man on the Roof"

A 32-year-old roofer was jerked to the ground and dragged almost 200 feet when his wife drove away in the family car with his safety rope tied to the bumper!

David Willis was hospitalized with a broken leg, cracked ribs, concussion and numerous bumps and bruises after the bizarre accident.

But he told reporters in Cape Town, South Africa, that he's lucky to be around to talk about his close call.

"One second I was hammering the roof and the next I was plowing up tomato plants in the garden," he continued.

"Everything happened so fast it was like a dream. But I was in so much pain I knew that what was happening was real."

Willis said the drama unfolded a few minutes after he climbed onto the roof of his house to replace some weather-beaten shingles.

He tied one end of a safety rope to the chimney and pulled the loose end through the belt loop in his pants. He then dropped the rope down to his 9-year-old son and told him to attach it "to something secure."

The dutiful child promptly tied the rope to the bumper of his mother's car and scampered off to a nearby park to play.

"My wife and I spoke to each other as she got into the car to go shopping," said Willis.

"But neither of us noticed that the rope was tied to the bumper.

"I turned around and started hammering on a shingle just as she pulled away. I hit the ground hard and shot right through the garden fence.

"I figured I was dragged about 200 feet through the grass before the rope finally broke."

Willis' wife Michelle didn't realize what happened and drove off into the distance.

A neighbor found Willis writhing in his front yard and called an ambulance.

"I'm in no condition to spank my son even if I wanted to," said Willis.

"Actually, I don't think I need to. He knows his thoughtlessness almost killed his daddy."

Article by Irwin Fisher from the tabloid Weekly World News *on September 19, 1988. The named locale, plus the phrase "attach it to something secure," identify the story as being greatly expanded from a brief Reuters news item circulated in January 1980. Ladder humor is a staple of slapstick comedy, whether in films or folklore. "The Man on the Roof" story has been a popular urban legend both in the United States and abroad since at least the mid-1960s. The man sometimes climbs onto the roof to adjust his TV antenna or to shovel down a heavy accumulation of snow. Often the story merges into "The Exploding*

Toilet" when the wife decides to paint the bathroom during her husband's hospital stay. She pours used paint thinner into the toilet just as her husband is arriving home, and she neglects to flush, setting the poor man up for a second accident. Naturally, those laughing paramedics are waiting in the wings to enter this slapstick comedy during Scene Three. The man pulled from his roof becomes an airline pilot working at home in Greenwich, Connecticut, in a version included in Cabin Pressure, *a 1989 collection of flight attendants' anecdotes compiled by Elizabeth Harwell and Corylee Spiro. However, in another airline version a mechanic is working on the wing of a large aircraft while secured by a rope that is tied to a portable piece of large ground equipment. The modern legends may have originated with a popular European folktale about a farmer and his wife who decide to switch tasks. The husband makes a complete mess of the household tasks, even putting the cow to graze on the grass roof of the house while he cleans up from various mishaps he caused inside. To secure the cow, he ties a rope around its neck, drops the loose end down the chimney, and ties the other end around his waist. Naturally, the cow falls off the roof, dragging the man up the chimney upside down. I've searched for a variant of this folktale that includes laughing paramedics, but the ones I've found so far just have the wife laughing her head off.*

"The Exploding Bra"

This happened around 1960 to my aunt, who was at that time a very glamorous young lady. She wore a platinum beehive hairdo, gold spike heels, capri pants—and she wore an article of underclothing I have actually seen, an inflatable bra. This was briefly popular in the early '60s, and consisted of a plastic falsie which was blown up with a straw to the desired fullness and inserted into a special bra.

The story goes that my aunt and her husband were in an airplane when the decompression effect resulted in her bra expanding alarmingly. She raced for the restroom; in some versions she made it in time, but in others she was in the middle of the aisle when her frontage loudly exploded.

I showed your story of the inflatable bra exploding to a colleague who mentioned hearing similar stories 25 years ago in Western Colorado when he was in high school. The stories he heard were about girls wearing inflatable bras to the prom and having their dates pin a corsage on and the bras popping and/or deflating.

Eve Golden of Secaucus, New Jersey, sent me the first story in 1989; after I published a column on the topic, I received the second version from my friend Dan Lester, then living in Durango, Colorado. Jearl Walker, in his 1975 book The Flying Circus of Physics, *includes an even more slapstick version of the story. He reprints an undated Associated Press report of an airline stewardess whose inflatable bra "expands to about size 46," whereupon the stewardess uses a passenger's hatpin to pierce the bra, leading "a man of foreign descent" on board to grapple with her, intending to prevent the stewardess from injuring herself. More recently I have heard of breast implants rather than inflatable bras supposedly expanding when cabin pressure in an airliner changes suddenly.*

"The Nude Housewife"

The following incident took place in an apartment house near Homewood, Illinois, and for obvious reasons I shall use no names. A housewife washed her hair, put it in curlers, and then went to the basement laundry room with some dirty clothes. Soon she was waiting for one load to finish in the dryer as she put the second load into the washer.

At the last minute she decided that the dress she was wearing needed cleaning, too. She removed it and threw it into the washing machine,

knowing she would get a change from the dryer in a moment or two. Standing there in her shoes and brief undergarments, she noticed a cobweb in the corner. She decided to remove it. She didn't want to get her hair dirty, so she pulled a discarded football helmet over the curlers, and got ready to sweep down the cobweb. Just then the meter reader walked into the basement. The lady froze quietly in the corner, hoping to avoid his attention. She thought she had been successful, but as he departed he looked at her and said, "I do hope your team wins."

From Jerome Beatty, Jr.'s, "Trade Winds" column in Saturday Review, *July 4, 1964, where a discreet illustration is included. In the November 1970 issue of* Esquire, *Beatty described telling this story to friends as something that had happened to "a friend of a friend of mine in Illinois" and then having another version from the March 1961 issue of* Reader's Digest *pointed out to him. The* Digest *also illustrated the story, for modesty adding "an old raccoon coat" to the woman's attire. This oft-told slapstick story with a joke-like punch line is a favorite of Ann Landers, who has published it in her columns at least six times between 1975 and 1992 and who was also credited with it in a 1966 book called* Family Laugh Lines. *Landers described the housewife putting on her son's football helmet to protect her hair curlers from leaking pipes, but she mentioned no spider web, broom, or raccoon coat. Erma Bombeck modified the story yet again in her 1979* Aunt Erma's Cope Book *by having the housewife wearing her son's full football uniform when the washer repairman arrived. The best treatment of the plot I have seen appeared in Gerald Kloss's column "Slightly Kloss-Eyed" in the* Milwaukee Journal *in 1988. Kloss, in a parody of urban legend research, pretended to have collected several texts from his readers. From "Helena Handbasket" of "Dry Prong, LA" he quoted the story of a 275-pound defensive tackle for a pro football team who was surprised by a female meter reader while he tried to repair a leaky faucet while wearing only a football helmet. The meter reader quipped, "I hope you win the game Sunday, mister," and the player replied: "Thanks for your support. You can talk about all the money we make, but we're really playing for all you fans out there, and you can count on us to put out a 100-percent effort. Our running game's shaping up and if our pass defense holds up, I think we've got a good chance of going all the way." Beautiful!*

"The Nude in the RV"

This is not a funny book, but we'll begin it by telling a funny story. It's about a couple of veteran campers and we tell it only because (1) it happened needlessly, (2) it might have ended in tragedy, and (3) anything as silly as this won't happen to you if you follow our philosophy of restricting weekend camping to within easy driving distance of home.

It happened to John and Jane Doe (we call them that in order to protect them from the laughter and ribbing of the many friends they've made over the years in campgrounds throughout the United States, Canada, and Mexico) while homeward-bound after weeks on the road in their pickup-truck camper. And it happened on the last day.

Three hundred miles usually was the limit of a day's driving for John and Jane on any camping trip they ever had taken. But on the end of one of the most pleasant journeys of their lives, as day dawned they were 450 miles from home, and so they decided to press on until they got there.

Then, a good breakfast under their belts, coffee pot, frying pan, dishes and knives and forks washed and safely stowed away, campsite policed for stray scraps of debris they might have overlooked, John got behind the wheel of their camper and Jane on the seat beside him.

Nine hours later and still about 75 miles from home, John had had it. He pulled to the side of the road, turned to Jane and said: "You drive, I'm going to climb into the sack and take a nap." He got out of the cab, walked to the camper's rear door, climbed in, took off his shoes and stripped down to his BVDs, stretched out on a bunk, pulled a cover over him and within minutes was dead to the world.

Jane, totally out of sight and without means of communication with John in the back compartment, tooled merrily down the highway thinking nice thoughts of spending that night in the coziness of their long-unseen home—until suddenly she came to a fork in the road and did not know which to take, left or right.

She did what any driver would do under such circumstances—came to a stop to ponder the problem. But so abruptly that John was tossed from his bunk and onto the floor of the camper. His mind befogged by sleep, he jumped to his feet, plowed through the rear door and sockless, shoeless, shirtless and clad only in his shorts, leaped down into the road to find out what was going on.

And just then, having made up her mind, Jane took off again, oblivious to what was going on behind her. John shouted, screamed, cried, raced after her.

"Jane! Jane! Stop! Stop!"

But Jane did not hear nor did she stop, and as the camper faded into the distance, passing motorists slowed and stared at John, wondered what kind of nut was this, and sped off again.

To one or two he raised his thumb, wondering at the coldness, the cruelty, the animosity of drivers who would not give a man a lift. And then, for the first time, he came fully awake and aware of what little he wore. No socks, no shoes, no undershirt, only shorts. Quickly then he hopped behind some bushes hoping that a police car would come along that he could flag down.

But none came, the sun was fading and John was growing colder. So, stifling his embarrassment, he once more stepped to the side of the road and bravely signaled for a lift. Again car after car slowed, stared and sped off again until finally a truck came along and stopped.

"Buddy," the driver said, "you look like you're in trouble. Hop in."

John did, told his story, and the driver, a sympathetic man, stripped off his jacket and said "Here, buddy, you wear this and we'll go find your wife."

He stepped on the gas, tooled down the road to catch the long-gone camper and so an hour or more went by and they were at a cutoff 15 miles from John's home.

"She must be there by now," he said. "I'll get out here."

"Not on your life," the truck driver said. "I'll take you."

And he did. But when they got there, Jane was not.

John thanked him, invited him in for a drink, heard him decline, took his name and address so he could properly say thank you by mail and perhaps with a gift, climbed down from the cab, waved goodbye, walked up the walk to the front door, to the rear door and then to every window that he could reach. They all, of course, were locked.

But, luckily, the garage doors were not. So John opened them wide, unfolded a garden chair and sat down inside, safe from prying passing eyes, to wait for Jane.

He sat and he sat and slowly became aware that the lawn was parched, more brown than green, and badly in need of watering—this, John, an amateur gardener who took great pride in his grass and his flowers, could not stand.

John rationalized. They live in a sparsely settled area. Houses are few and far between. He'd worked in the yard before in bathing trunks. If any neighbors should see him maybe they'd think he was wearing bathing trunks once again.

Thus mentally fortified, he hooked up the garden hose, turned on the valve and proceeded to give the lawn a long-overdue watering.

And that was what he was doing when Jane, who thought him still asleep in the camper, came home several wrong turns later. She turned into the driveway, saw him, let out a shriek, rammed her foot down on the gas pedal instead of the brake, drove into the garage, through the rear wall and out again. Luckily she was unhurt.

And so our camping story ends.

Moral: Never drive more than 300 miles a day on a camping trip; 50 to 200 miles if on an overnight or weekend camping trip.

Moral: Study a road map and become familiar with every turn before starting each day's drive.

Moral: Never ride in the back of a camper or trailer; sit up front with the driver.

Moral: Have rear-vision mirrors on both sides of a recreational vehicle. And use them constantly. Know what's going on behind you as well as in front of you.

This much embellished and expanded version of a popular urban legend constitutes the preface of Dan and Inez Morris's 1973 book The Weekend Camper. *In* The Vanishing Hitchhiker *I quote a long oral text of the story collected by folklorist Ronald Baker in Indiana, and I trace the legend in published, filmed, recorded, and word-of-mouth sources back to the early 1960s. Some versions of the story from the South describe the husband finally catching up with his wife, putting on some pants, but neglecting to zip his fly; when they stop at a restaurant, he notices his error and hastily zips up, catching the tablecloth in the zipper, which leads to further slapstick results. In some English versions of the story it is the wife rather than the husband who is left behind, and in an Australian version sent to me in 1989 by Adrienne Eccles of Unley, South Australia, a character referred to as "Auntie," clad only in her panties, is accidentally left behind. She hitches a ride with a motorcyclist: "He put her on the pillion seat, and they gave chase. A short time later, Uncle was astounded to be overtaken by a motorcycle ridden by a leather-clad bikie and his nearly nude wife." All of these stories are similar to a legend of the 1940s about a scandalous incident that supposedly happened during an overnight train trip. In "The Cut-Out Pullman Car," a businessman clad only in bathrobe and slippers went from the club car after his nightcap to the sleeping compartment of a young woman whom he had met on the train. When the businessman woke up the next morning, he was in the wrong car and the wrong city; the woman was gone, and so was his billfold. His clothes were still in his own compartment in another Pullman car far away in the city to which he had been traveling. Possibly "The Cut-Out Pullman Car" was updated to fit our post-railroad era of travel.*

"The Stunned Deer—or Deer Stunt"

With the assistance of one of Quincy's finest, I have acquired a copy of the actual recording of an emergency call for help, as it was received by an ambulance service near Kansas City.

Remember, this is the transcript of a real call. Some of the more colorful words have been replaced in order to make it readable for the entire family.

Other than that, each word is as it was spoken that night. Believe it or not.

Dispatcher: Fire and ambulance, where do you need us?
Caller: Hello?
Dispatcher: Yes?
Caller: Who is this?
Dispatcher: This is the ambulance emergency line. Do you have an emergency?

Caller: I . . . I need an ambulance.

Dispatcher: Who is this?

Caller: Joe.

Dispatcher: OK, Joe, where do you need us?

Caller: I'm in the (stupid) phone booth.

Dispatcher: OK. What's the address there?

Caller: Hold on.

Dispatcher: OK. Sir, did you call through 911?

Caller: Uh . . . yeah . . . no.

Dispatcher: OK, Joe, I need a location. What street are you on?

Caller: Uh, I'm in a (stupid) phone booth at the Stop and Go. That's it. I'm at the (stupid) Stop and Go. On uh, on uh . . . wait a minute. Hucks . . . where's the (stupid) street? Hucksmith, Corville and something . . . at the (stupid) Stop and Go.

Dispatcher: Hucksmith, Corville and what?

Caller: Hold on . . . yo.

Dispatcher: uh huh.

Caller: Let me see . . . Carfee, Coofee . . .

Dispatcher: Coffee?

Caller: There you go. There you go. I'm in the (stupid) phone booth. Let me tell you what. I'm going down the (stupid) road, driving my car, minding my own (stupid) business, and a (stupid) deer jumps out and hit my car.

Dispatcher: OK, sir, are you injured?

Caller: Let me tell ya. I get out, and pick the (stupid) deer up. I thought he's dead. I put the (stupid) deer in my back seat, and I'm driving down the (stupid) road, minding my own business. The (stupid) deer woke up and bit me in the back of my (stupid) neck.

It bit me and done kicked the (stuffing) out of my car. Now I'm in the (stupid) phone booth.

The deer bit me in the neck. A big (stupid) dog came and bit me in the leg. I hit him with the (stupid) tire iron, and I stabbed him with my knife.

I got a hurt leg and the (stupid) deer bit me in the neck. And, the dog won't let me out of the (stupid) phone booth because he wants the deer.

Now who gets the deer? Me or the dog?

Dispatcher: OK, sir, are you injured?

Caller: Yeah! The (stupid) deer bit me in the neck. Hold on, the (stupid) dog is biting me. Hold on . . . (doggone it) get out of . . . hold on . . . the (stupid) dog is biting my (posterior). Hold on.

Unfortunately, the tape ends here. So, we never learn whether the driver gets the deer, the dog gets the deer, the deer gets the driver, or the dog gets the deer and the driver.

And, I don't know if anybody ever got an ambulance.

Have a good day outdoors.

From John Landis's "Outdoors" column in the Quincy (Illinois) Herald-Whig *for December 6, 1992. Elaine Viets, columnist for the* St. Louis Post-Dispatch, *in 1989 traced this story to an actual incident that occurred in 1974 in Poughkeepsie, New York. Viets even spoke to the officer who took the call. Numerous tapes circulate in police departments all over the United States, all purporting to be copies of the actual emergency-line call about the stunned deer. However, the tapes vary greatly in language and details. Landis's Kansas City version, for instance, tells essentially the same story as Viets's obtained from New York, but none of the wording matches. I discuss the entire tradition, including other stories about different stunned creatures awakening inside cars, in my book* The Truth Never Stands in the Way of a Good Story.

20

Bogus Warnings

"We live in a time besotted with Bad Information," wrote Joel Achenbach in the *Washington Post* (December 4, 1996). He continued, "It's everywhere. It's on the street, traveling by word of mouth. It's lurking in dark recesses of the Internet. It's in the newspaper. It's at your dinner table, passed along as known fact, irrefutable evidence, attributed to unnamed scientists, statisticians, 'studies.'"

I would add this to Achenbach's list: Bad Information is also found on thousands of copies of anonymously produced fliers that are handed around neighborhoods and workplaces, posted on bulletin boards, sent home with schoolchildren, scouts, and even preschoolers, and faxed, mailed, and E-mailed to a wider audience.

Most of these fliers are bogus warnings against some kind of dire threat. Such warnings were formerly typed or even handwritten, but all the warning fliers nowadays seem to be produced on computers and duplicated in copy shops. Often they are printed out in all capital letters sprinkled with spelling errors and other typos, and sporting a generous use of exclamation points. Sometimes these fliers are reproduced on the letterheads of companies or institutions or they may cite supposedly valid sources, lending them an authoritative look and feel. Routing information directing the fliers around the office is common, as are handwritten additions like "Warning!!!" or "Please Read and Circulate!!!" or "This Is Not a Joke!!!"

What makes such documents a part of *folklore*—technically "Xeroxlore" or "photocopylore," as folklorists dub them—is that they are anonymous, variable, unverifiable texts that are stereotyped in form and content. Like most urban legends, there's often a modicum of Good Information included, but unlike true legends, these warning notices contain no well-developed narrative content; in that respect, they are perhaps more like rumors (unverified reports) than legends (too-good-to-be-true "true" stories).

Patricia A. Turner of the University of California at Davis, in her landmark book of 1993, *I Heard It Through the Grapevine: Rumor in African-American Culture,* provides a good recent example of the interplay of oral and printed dissemination of Bad Information. One of the many rumors Turner col-

ATTENTION!!! ATTENTION!!! ATTENTION!!!

.50 CENT SODAS

BLACKS AND MINORITY GROUPS

DID YOU SEE (T.V. SHOW) 20/20???

PLEASE BE ADVISE, "TOP POP" & "TROPICAL FANTASY" ALSO TREAT SODAS ARE BEING MANUFACTURED BY THE KLU.. KLUX.. KLAN..

SODAS CONTAIN STIMULANTS TO STERILIZE THE BLACK MAN, AND WHO KNOWS WHAT ELSE!!!!

THEY ARE ONLY PUT IN STORES IN HARLEM AND MINORITY AREAS YOU WON'T FIND THEM DOWNTOWN....LOOK AROUND....

YOU HAVE BEEN WARNED
PLEASE SAVE THE CHILDREN

lected was this: "Tropical Fantasy [a fruit-flavored soft drink] is made by the Ku Klux Klan. There is a special ingredient in it that makes black men sterile." The same rumor of a sterilizing additive was spread concerning the Church's fried chicken franchise, and the same supposed KKK connection was made with both Church's Chicken and Troop, a once-popular brand of athletic wear. Besides word of mouth, this typical piece of Bad Information (*none* of these assertions is true) also circulated in New York City among the African-American community in an anti-Fantasy-soda flier that was headed "Attention!!! Attention!!! Attention!!!" and framed at the bottom margin with "You Have Been Warned. Please Save the Children." The main text of the flier referred to supposed validation of the claims on the "T.V. Show 20/20" and stated that Fantasy and two other brands were manufactured by "The Klu., Klux., Klan."

Here is another example of Bad Information in a similarly bogus warning flier, but in a completely different context. This example was taken from their company's bulletin board and sent to me by Laurie Catlender and Bruce MacIsaac of Scarborough, Ontario, Canada, in 1993:

CAUTION

HOME

OR

OFFICE

****

Subject: ATTENTION PAGER AND ANSWERING MACHINE USERS

==

WATCH OUT PAGER USERS AND ANSWERING MACHINE FOLKS!!!!!!

WE HAVE RECEIVED INFORMATION OF A VERY EXPENSIVE TELEPHONE FRAUD THAT IS DIRECTED AT PAGER AND TELEPHONE ANSWERING MACHINE OWNERS. SINCE OUR EMPLOYEES UTILIZE BOTH TYPES OF TARGETED EQUIPMENT, BOTH AT WORK AND AT HOME, IT IS FELT THAT THIS INFORMATION SHOULD BE PASSED ALONG AS SOON AS POSSIBLE.

OVER THE LAST SEVERAL MONTHS THERE HAS BEEN A GROUP OF PEOPLE IN THE NEW YORK CITY AREA CONDUCTING A SCAM DIRECTED AT PAGER USERS AND ANSWERING MACHINE OWNERS. THIS GROUP USES A COMPUTER TO GENERATE CALLS TO PAGER UNITS AND TELEPHONE ANSWERING MACHINES. THE COMPUTER IS ACTIVATED BY THE ELECTRONIC BEEP ON EITHER THE PAGER OR ANSWERING MACHINE MESSAGE UNIT. IF AFTER SEVERAL SECONDS IT DOES NOT RECEIVE THE ELECTRONIC BEEP, I.E., A REAL PERSON ANSWERS THE TELEPHONE, IT AUTOMATICALLY DISCONNECTS AND GOES TO THE NEXT NUMBER. THE NUMBER THAT IS LEFT IS 212-540-XXXX (XXXX CAN BE ANY FOUR NUMBERS). IF YOU GET A MESSAGE WITH THESE NUMBERS - DO NOT CALL IT. THE CALL WILL COST YOU $55.00 AND THERE WILL BE NO ANSWER. THE 212 AREA CODE IS FOR NEW YORK CITY AND THE 540 EXCHANGE ACTS THE SAME AS A 900 NUMBER -- THE TELEPHONE THAT YOU ARE CALLING FROM IS AUTOMATICALLY BILLED WHETHER YOU TALK TO SOMEONE OR NOT.

REMEMBER, IF YOU GET A MESSAGE ON YOUR PAGER OR ANSWERING MACHINE WITH 212-540-XXXX - DO NOT CALL IT. IF THEY GET YOU TO CALL, THEY CAN COLLECT THE $55.00 CONNECTION FEE THROUGH AUTOMATIC BILLING.

****

What lends this example some credibility is that there are some genuine and well-documented forms of telephone and pager fraud. But several things mark this warning as a likely piece of photocopied Bad Information. Consider, for example, the vague "We Have Received Information," the handwritten heading, the lack of source information, and especially the highly doubtful description of how such a scam might operate (especially the assertion that you would be billed whether the telephone is answered or not!).

Personally—warnings or no warnings—I never return calls to any long-distance numbers left on my answering machine unless I know the caller *and* really want to talk to him or her. If someone wants to notify me that I've won the lottery or inherited a fortune, then let them send me a letter, or better yet show me the money. And whenever anyone complains that I didn't return a call, I just say that my machine must have malfunctioned, which is true about half the time anyway. (This paragraph, I assure you, is *Good* Information.)

As I was writing this chapter I came across the following apt passage in Stephen Jay Gould's regular "This View of Life" column in *Natural History* magazine (December 1997/January 1998): "An odd principle of human psychology, well known and exploited by the full panoply of prevaricators, from charming barkers like Barnum to evil demagogues like Goebbels, holds that even the silliest of lies can win credibility by constant repetition. In current American parlance, these proclamations of 'truth' by xeroxing . . . fall into the fascinating domain of 'urban legends.'"

"Pushing Him Off the Wagon"

You know these chips, or tokens, that Alcoholics Anonymous gives out to mark your period of abstinence? I have one on a string around my neck: a yellow plastic poker chip with "9 months" printed on one side and "God grant me the serenity" on the reverse.

Well, I want to warn you that there are some bars that will give you free drinks for these chips—one drink per 30-day chip is the usual offer. They want to turn reforming alcoholics into good customers again.

"Blue Star Acid"

WARNING TO PARENTS

POST ALL CLASSROOMS

BH

484A

A form of tattoo called "BLUE STAR" is being sold to school children. It's a small piece of paper containing a blue star. They are the size of a pencil eraser and each star is soaked with LSD.

The drug is absorbed through the skin simply by handling the paper.

There are also brightly colored paper tabs resembling postage stamps that have the picture of the following:

Superman	Mickey Mouse	Disney Characters
Clowns	Bart Simpson	Butterflies

Each one is wrapped in foil.

This is a new way of selling acid by appealing to young children.

These are laced with drugs.

If your child gets any of the above, **DO NOT HANDLE THEM.** These are known to react quickly and some are laced with strychrine.

Symptoms: Hallucinations, severe vomiting, uncontrolled laughter, mood changes, change in body temperature.

PLEASE: FEEL FREE TO REPRODUCE THIS ARTICLE AND DISTRIBUTE IT WITHIN YOUR COMMUNITY AND WORKPLACE.

From: J. O'Connell - Danbury Hospital Outpatient Chemical Dependency Treatment Services.

Please copy and post at your work, give to friends, send a copy to your local schools.

This is very serious - young lives have already been taken.

This is growing faster than we can warn parents and professionals!!!!

WARNING TO PARENTS

A form of tattoo called "Blue Star" is being sold to school children. It is a piece of paper containing a blue star. They are the size of a pencil eraser and each star is soaked with LSD. The drug is absorbed through the skin simply by handling the paper.

There are also bright colored paper tattoos resembling postage stamps that have the picture of the following: SUPERMAN, MICKEY MOUSE, CLOWNS, DISNEY CHARACTERS, BART SIMPSON, and BUTTERFLIES. If your child gets any of the above, do not handle them. These are known to react quickly and some are laced with strychnine.

Symptoms: Hallucinations, severe vomiting, uncontrollable laughing, mood changes and change in body temperature.

Please feel free to reproduce this article and distribute it within your community and workplace. Get the word out about this danger to our children.

From: J. O'Donnell-Danbury Hospital Outpatient Chemical Dependency Treatment Service

Please copy and post at your work, give to friends, send a copy to your local schools. This is very serious--young lives have already been taken.

From my thick file of examples of this particular bogus warning I selected two, both sent to me in 1996. The first, which "hung for years in a prominent position in this school system," came from Isaac P. Espy, Jr., Athletic Director of the City Schools of Scottsboro, Alabama, who commented, "this bad boy has urban legend written all over it." The second example "turned up in a local bank" and was sent by Mary Mosley of Fulton, Missouri, who wrote, "I smelled an urban legend right away." Variations on this flier have been around since the early 1980s, possibly based on a garbled unauthorized reprinting of an actual police notice of that era, and they continue to proliferate. "Blotter acid"—absorbent paper soaked in LSD—has been produced since the 1960s, and all kinds of pictures, symbols, and texts have been printed on the paper, but these "tabs" have never existed in the form of tattoos. Investigative journalists and drug-enforcement officials have consistently denounced such fliers, and the reference to "J. O'Connell" (or "O'Donnell") is as bogus as the rest of the information. A 1991 press release from the Michigan State Police discounts all of the warning's claims: "While LSD does exist in paper form, it is NOT casually sold to children, it is NOT laced with strychnine, and it does NOT cause death in users. It is NOT a new drug, nor is it epidemic." A police narcotics supervisor quoted in the same release puzzled, "We don't know who generated the original letter or why it continues to recycle every year. It is like a chain letter that started 10 years ago and won't go away." What happens, I assume, is that whenever some well-meaning citizen comes across a copy of an older notice and believes it to be authentic, he or she decides to make duplicates on a photocopy machine and to send it circulating once again. Since the warning is dramatic, frightening, and quite convincing to an unaware reader, on and on it goes. Translations of essentially the same bogus warning have circulated internationally. What a long strange trip it's been!

"Lights Out!"

INTEROFFICE MEMORANDUM

DATE: 07-Oct-1993 02:26pm

To: See Below

Subject: SAFETY ALERT!!

Subject: Important Safety Alert

My Dear Friends:

The following alert from the Norfolk Southern Police was sent to all employees; please take a minute to read.

BULLETIN
!!!THERE IS A NEW GANG INITIATION!!!

This new "INITIATION" of MURDER is brought about by gang members driving around with their car lights off. When you flash your car lights to signal them that their lights are out, the gang members take it literally as "LIGHTS OUT", so they follow you to your destination and KILL you!!! That's their initiation.

Two families have already fallen victim to this initiation ritual in the St. Louis and Chicago, IL. areas.

This information should be given widespread distribution on your respective territories and posted on all bulletin boards. BEWARE and inform your families and friends.

***** DO NOT FLASH YOUR CAR LIGHTS FOR ANYONE!**

This is a serious matter and should not be taken lightly.

The above information was furnished by the Illinois State Police Department.

I thought this was especially important for all to read. Please, do be careful and have a great day!

Sue

THIS IS NOT A JOKE!!

FROM THE DESK OF
DEBBIE

This memo was distributed at my Mike's office- he works for juvenile probation. This is not a joke Please pass this info on to your families & friends

Debbie

08/24/93 13:28 ☎404 333 1748 ABITIBI-PRICE →→→ NY PBT EXCPT EG 001/001
404-399-5274 TITON INDUSTRIES 880 P02 SEP 24 '93 13:2
FAX NO: (404) 644-7856 N386 P01

FAX
TO: New York
Chicago
Dallas
FROM: Atlanta Sales Office
Note: Please spread the word just as a pre-caution. (Better safe than sorry)

Copy all

Per a fax received by the Sheriff's Department, the following is for your information. <u>This has not been confirmed, but please be aware of the following:</u>

Sacramento Police Dept., Grady Harn, saw a national alert poster for this weekend, September 25-26, 1993. Police Departments across the nation are being warned that this is "blood" initiation weekend. Their intent is to have all new bloods nationwide drive around on Saturday and Sunday nights with their headlights off. In order to be accepted into the gang, they have to shoot and kill all individuals in the first auto that does a courtesy flash to warn them that their lights are off.

Be cautious if encountering any autos with lights off this weekend.

Two typical examples of a bogus warning that circulated widely across the United States in literally thousands of copies from the summer of 1993 until about the end of that year. The interoffice memo, presumably based on a police report, moved from "Sue" on to "Debbie," who added a handwritten Post-it note explaining that she got it from her husband, who got it at his place of employment, on to "Kelley," who added a note—"This reeks of urban legend to me!"—and sent it on to me. The faxed warning mentions four major U.S. cities in the header. No such gang initiation—either planned or actually car-

ried out—could be found by any of the numerous journalists and law-enforcement officials who tried to investigate the warnings. "Blood Weekend" in September 1993 came and went without anyone being killed for flashing headlights. There is no "Grady Harn" in the Sacramento Police Department. The "Lights Out!" warning created intense fear and outrage among American motorists because the "courtesy flash" to warn other drivers that their headlights are off is a well-established custom that is regarded as a good turn, not a threat. Feeding into the scare were both the known increase in gang violence and publicity about a growing number of "road rage" incidents. I discuss this bogus warning in detail in my book The Truth Never Stands in the Way of a Good Story.

"The Good Times Virus"

DANGEROUS COMPUTER VIRUS 10:19 AM 5/3/95
PLEASE READ THE WARNING BELOW IF YOU USE THE INTERNET:

We were just been warned of a new computer virus that is being sent across the InterNet. If you receive an e-mail message with the subject line "Good Times" DO NOT READ THE MESSAGE - DELETE IT IMMEDIATELY!!!

Someone is sending e-mail under this title nation-wide. If you get anything like this, do not download the file! It has a virus that rewrites your hard drive, obliterating anything on it. What makes this virus so terrifying, according to the FCC, is that no program needs to be exchanged for a new computer to be infected. It can spread through the existing e-mail systems of the InterNet. One a computer is infected, one of several things can happen. If the computer contains a hard drive, that will most likely be destroyed. If the program is not stopped, the computer's processor will be placed in an nth-complexity infinite binary loop - which can severely damage the processor if left running that way too long.

There is one sure means of detecting what is now known as the "Good Times" virus. It always travels to new computers the same way in a text e-mail with the subject line reading simply "Good Times". Avoiding infection is easy once the file has been received - not reading it!

The act of loading the file into the mail server's ASCII buffer causes the "Good Times" mainline program to initialize and execute. The program is highly intelligent - it will send copies of itself to everyone whose e-mail addres[illegible]ained in a received-mail file or a sent-mail file[illegible]one. It will then proceed to trash the com[illegible]n.

Date: Fri, 3 Oct 199[illegible]
To: jan.brunvand@m.cc.u[illegible]
Subject: Fwd: Deadly ca[illegible]

Forwarded message:

NEW VIRUS WARNING
If you receive an e-mail with a [illegible]
delete it immediately WITHOUT re[illegible]most
dangerous E-mail virus yet.

It will re-write your hard drive. Not [illegible] that, but it will scramble any disks that are even close to your computer. It will recalibrate your refrigerator's coolness setting so all your ice cream melts and your milk curdles. It will demagnetize the strips on all your credit cards, reprogram your ATM access code, screw up the tracking on your VCR and use subspace field harmonics to scratch any CDs you try to play.

It will give your ex-wife your new phone number. It will mix antifreeze into your fish tank. It will drink all your beer and leave its dirty socks on the coffee table when there's company coming over. It will hide your car keys when you are late for work and interfere with your car radio so that you hear only static while stuck in traffic.

It will replace your shampoo with Nair and your Nair with Rogaine, all while dating your current boy/girlfriend (husband/wife) behind your back and billing their hotel rendezvous to your Visa card.

Badtimes will give you Dutch Elm disease. It will leave the toilet seat up and leave the hairdryer plugged in dangerously close to a full bathtub.

It will not only remove the forbidden tags from your mattresses and pillows, it will refill your skim milk with whole. It is insidious and subtle. It is dangerous and terrifying to behold. It is also a rather interesting shade of mauve.

The first example was an E-mail message printed out with the headers removed and found taped to a bulletin board in the Lake Washington School District in Kirkland/Redmond, Washington; Ross E. McCullough of Redmond sent it to me. The second example is a parody of "Good Times" that came to me via E-mail forwarded by a fellow folklorist. Parodies are a vital part of modern folklore, and other such computer virus parodies describe the "Bobbit Virus" (removes a vital part of your hard disk then reattaches it, but that part will never work again), the "Ted Turner Virus" (colorizes your monochrome monitor), and the "Adam and Eve Virus" (takes a couple of bytes out of your Apple), among many others. The New York Times, *in an article by Peter H. Lewis published on February 27, 1996, described the "Good Times" warning as "sufficiently dweeby to impress even experienced computer users." Lewis asserted that "the warning itself is infinitely loopy. And for the nth time, the Good Times Virus does not exist. It is a fraud, a cyburban legend." I couldn't have said it better myself. The "Computer Incident Advisory Capability" program of the U.S. Department of Energy has a Web site debunking this and several other virus warnings. See http://ciac.llnlgov/ciac/CIACHoaxes. The site is maintained by the Lawrence Livermore National Laboratory at the University of California, Berkeley.*

"The Kidney Heist"

Dr. Brunvand,
I thought I'd send this along to you. I haven't heard this one before, but I am sure you have.
Best.

Barry Karr
CSICOP/Skeptical Inquirer

<< Subj: Re: Kidney theft cartel legend
Date: 97-03-31 10:12:57 EST
From: madigan.
To: SkeptI.

I encountered this posting on a mailing service that goes out to about 1500 people. (I posted Alan Hale's plea on that same service) Do you have anything I can use to respond to this popular legend?

Subject: This will Blow Your Mind, or Kidney!
A big thanks, I think, to Michelle for bringing this to our attention. I heard this kind of story from Dr's when I worked at St. Lukes and didn't know what to make of it. Kidneys ARE expensive. So why not steal them like thieves steal possessions? The whole thing is quite do-able. -L

Dear Friends,
Although I'm skeptical of this story, let it not be said that I didn't try to protect your organs . . .

I wish to warn you about a new crime ring that is targeting business travelers. This ring is well organized, well fund-

Slug Signorino

ed, has very skilled personnel, and is currently in most major cities and recently very active in New Orleans. The crime begins when a business traveler goes to a lounge for a drink at the end of the work day. A person in the bar walks up as they sit alone and offers to buy them a drink. The last thing the traveler remembers until they wake up in a hotel room bath tub, their body submerged to their neck in ice, is sipping that drink. There is a note taped to the wall instructing them not to move and to call 911. A phone is on a small table next to the bathtub for them to call. The business traveler calls 911 who have become quite familiar with this crime. The business traveler is instructed by the 911 operator to very slowly and carefully reach behind them and feel if there is a tube protruding from their lower back. The business traveler finds the tube and answers, "Yes." The 911 operator tells them to remain still, having already sent paramedics to help. The operator knows that both of the business traveler's kidneys have been harvested. This is not a scam or out of a science fiction novel, it is real.

It is documented and confirmed. If you travel or someone close to you travels, please be careful.

Regards,
Jerry Mayfield
Austin Ops Engineering Manager
Telephone: 512-433-6855

Subject: Body Part Criminal
Author: LES U.
Date: 1/2/97 11:06 AM

Just when you thought it was safe in the airports. . . .Hard to believe, but I got this from a reliable source at Corporate.

For any of you doing any traveling, beware.
From: Patty R. on 12/16/96 10:33 AM
Yes, this does happen. My sister-in-law works with a lady that this happened to her son's neighbor who lives in Houston. The only "good" thing to this whole story is the fact that the people doing this horrible crime are very in tune to what complications can happen afterwards because of the details precautions they take the time to set up before leaving the room.

The word from my sister-in-law is that the hospital in Las Vegas (yes, Vegas) prior to transferring him back to Houston stated that these people know exactly what they are doing. The incision, etc. was exact and clean. They use sterile equipment etc. and the hospital stated that other than the fact that the victim loses a kidney there has not been any reports of other complications due to non-sterile, etc. tactics that were used.

From: Kathy W.

Sadly, this is very true. My husband is a Houston Firefighter/EMT and they have received alerts regarding this crime ring. It is to be taken very seriously. The daughter of a friend of a fellow firefighter had this happen to her. Skilled doctor's are performing these crimes! (which, btw, have been highly noted in the Las Vegas area)

The following is a warning to business travelers provided by America West Airlines.

Dear friends
I wish to warn you about a new crime ring that is targeting business travelers. This ring is well organized, well funded, has very skilled personnel, and is currently in most major cities and recently very active in New Orleans and Las Vegas. The crime begins when a business traveler goes to a lounge for a drink at the end of the work day. A person in the bar walks up as they sit alone and offers to buy them a drink. The last thing the traveler remembers, until they wake up in a hotel room bathtub, their body submerged to their neck in ice, is sipping that drink. There is a note taped to the wall instructing them not to move and to call 911. A phone is on a small table next to the bathtub for them to call. The business traveler calls 911 who have become quite familiar with this crime. The business traveler is instructed by the 911 operator to very slowly and carefully reach behind them and feel if their is a tube protruding from their lower back. The business traveler finds the tube and answer, "yes." The 911 operator tells them to remain still, having already sent paramedics to help. The operator knows that both of the business traveler's kidneys have been harvested. This is not a scam or out of a science fiction novel, it is real. It is documented and confirmable. If you travel or someone close to you travels, please be careful.
Additionally, the Military and Firefighters has received alerts regarding this bazaar crime. It is to be taken very seriously.

"Hold your kidneys" takes on a whole new meaning.

Barry Karr, executive director and public relations director of CSICOP—the Committee for the Scientific Investigation of Claims of the Paranormal—electronically forwarded me this query about "The Kidney Heist." I referred him to my discussion of the background of the story, going back to 1991, in The Baby Train. *The second version of the warning was circulated by travel agents as a cautionary message for business travelers. Earlier forms of this bogus warning were ridiculous enough, ignoring the necessity for tissue matches and organ registration for transplants, as well as the near-impossibility of recruiting any well-paid surgeons to perform such clandestine operations. The recent versions of the warning, usually set in Las Vegas or New Orleans, follow an even less likely scenario: how would the kidney thieves get all that ice down the hall into the bathtub without being noticed, and how could the victim live with* both *kidneys removed? Will Christopher Baer's 1998 novel* Kiss Me, Judas *opens with a scene drawn straight from the ice-in-the-bathtub version of "The Kidney Heist." A review in* Library Journal *(September 15, 1998) described the book as "dark, graphic, and twisted," cautioning that it is "not for the faint of heart." One wonders how effective the scene would be for readers who have already heard the urban legend or have seen it featured in the 1998 slasher film* Urban Legend. *For an excellent survey of the international tradition of such stories see Véronique Campion-Vincent, "Organ Theft Narratives,"* Western Folklore, *vol. 56 (winter 1997), pp. 1–37.*

"The Welded Contacts"

CONTACT LENSES

We would appreciate your calling the following hazard to the attention of all of your people immediately.

Two recent incidents have uncovered a previously unknown phenomenon of serious gravity.

At Dequeane Electric a worker threw an electrical switch into closed position which produced a shortlived sparking.

An employee at UPS flipped open the colored lense of his welding goggles to better position the welding rod. He inadvertantly struck the metal to be welded, producing an arc.

BOTH MEN WERE WEARING CONTACT LENSES. On returning home from work, they removed the contacts AND THE CORNEA OF THE EYE WAS REMOVED along with the lenses.
Result: PERMANENT BLINDESS!

The electric arc generates microwaves that instantly dry up the fluid between the eye and the lense, causing the cornea to be bonded to the lense. This trauma is painless and the operator never knows an injury has occurred until removing the contacts.

As this phenomenon was unknown, no Federal or State safety and health agency has regulations on this matter, but they are pursuing the investigation zealously and will respond according to findings.

In the meantime, until such regulations are established or until this matter can be brought before your safety committee, it is suggested that no contact lenses be worn by anyone who is potentially subject to an electrical sparking situation.

DANGER!!!!

-SHOULD BE POSTED EVERYWHERE-

The warning sheet, date-stamped April 8, 1983, was sent to me in 1985 by Mark Lutton of Malden, Massachusetts, who found it on a bulletin board of the company he was working for then. Nobody was able to identify where the notice came from, and the rest of the stamp is not legible, since the sheet has evidently been photocopied several times. Similar notices have been widely reported in the United States and Great Britain as recently as 1990. A 1983 Policy Statement from the American Academy of Ophthalmology, entitled

"The Effects of Exposure to Electric Arc Welding on Contact Lens Wearers," traced the rumors back to 1967 and discounted the possibility of such an accident. Officials of Pittsburgh's Dusquesne Electric Company and of United Parcel Service, both named (although sometimes misspelled) in these warnings, cannot identify any such case. In the January 1987 issue of Welding Journal, *editor Jeffrey D. Weber wrote that the welded-cornea story was "pseudo-science" and concluded, "The story is not true, it never happened and it never could." A Maryland physician asked about "The Welded Contacts" had the best response I've seen to questions about the possibility of such a horrible accident; he told a writer for the* Baltimore Sun, *"It is a physical impossibility to dry up the fluid in your eyes. You'd have to stick your head in a blast furnace to do that. Removing your cornea would be like pulling off your ear."*

"The Procter & Gamble Trademark"

Company Involved: PROCTOR & GAMBLE COMPANY Source of Information: Phil Donahue TV SHOW

The President of Proctor & Gamble Company recently appeared on the Phil Donahue TV Show. The subject of which he spoke, was his company's support of the Church of Satan.

He stated that a large portion of Proctor & Gamble's profit goes to the Church of Satan, also known as the Devil's Church.

When asked by Mr. Donahue if he felt that stating this on television would hurt his business, the president replied—"There are not enough Christians in the U.S. to make a difference."

The President of Proctor & Gamble was contacted by the President of the Church of Satan, and notified that if he was going to support the Church of Satan then Proctor & Gamble would have to place the emblem/symbol of the church organization on the labels of each Proctor & Gamble product. It is noted that since that time, the symbol of the Church of Satan has been placed on all their labels.

Recently, on the Merv Griffith Show, a group of cultists were featured, among them, the owner of Proctor & Gamble Corp. He said that as long as the gays and other cults have come out of their closets. He was doing the same. He said that he had told Satan that if he (Satan) would help him prosper then he would give his heart and soul to him when he dies. He gave Satan all the credit for his riches.

PROCTOR & GAMBLE CORP. MANUFACTURES THE FOLLOWING PRODUCTS AMONG OTHERS:
CAKE MIX: Duncan Hines Products, DIAPERS: Pampers-Luv's, MOUTH WASH: Scope CLEANING AIDS & DETERGENTS: Biz, Bold, Bounce, Cascade, Cheer, Comet, Dash, Dawn, Downey, Era, Gain, Joy, Mr. Clean, Oxydol, SpickNSpan, Tide, Top Job. COFFEE: Foulgers & High Point. COOKING OILS & SHORTNINGS: Crisco, Fluffo, Puritan PEANUT BUTTER: Jiffy, DEODRANTS: Secret & Sure LOTIONS: Wondra SHAMPOO: Head & Shoulders, Pert & Prell SOAPS: Camay, Coast, Ivory, Safeguard & Zest TOOTHPASTE: Gleem & Crest

If in doubt, watch for the SATANIC SYMBOL To be found on the front or back of all their products. The actual size is shown below with enlarged drawing below it. It is a tiny Ram's horn with three sets of stars placed in such a way that if the stars of each set are joined, they form the number 666, known as the devil's number.

Christians should always remember that if they buy any products with this symbol, they will be taking part in the support of the Church of Satan, or devil worship. We suggest that you use what you have on hand, but make sure you don't buy any more.

Please feel free to make copies of this letter and pass them out to anyone who you feel should be informed, so that as little business as possible will go to Proctor & Gamble. Then we can easily prove to their President that there are more than enough Christians and other believers in God to put a very large dent into his profits.

This example comes from literally hundreds that have landed in my files since 1982; it was not dated or otherwise identified. All such sheets urge readers to circulate copies of the warning, and it is evident from the photocopy "static" that this is already a multigenerational copy. No Procter & Gamble (P&G) official has appeared on any of the television talk shows named on such fliers to discuss the trademark or anything else. The offending detail of P&G packaging is the cryptic trademark showing a bearded man-in-the-moon facing thirteen stars. Some "proofs" of the trademark's alleged Satanic implication require the viewer to hold the logo up to a mirror and observe the 666 formed by the lines in the man's beard. It's interesting that people who examine the trademark so closely have not observed how to spell the company name correctly. The company has received hundreds of thousands of calls about its trademark, and issued explanations several times of its benign origin and innocent meaning, all to no avail in suppressing the rumor. In 1985 P&G stopped using the trademark on some of its products, retaining it only on letterheads and at the company's corporate headquarters in Cincinnati. Several times over the years P&G has brought lawsuits against individuals and companies for spreading the rumor. An article by Dana Canedy in the New York Times *of July 29, 1997, traced the history of the company's problems with the trademark rumors and described the latest suit being brought by P&G against the Amway Corporation and several of its distributors, accusing them of spreading the Satanism rumors as a business ploy. Earlier Satanism rumors bedeviled the McDonald's restaurant chain a decade earlier, but these eventually faded. P&G should be so lucky!*

"The Madalyn Murray O'Hair Petition"

IMPORTANT NOTICE

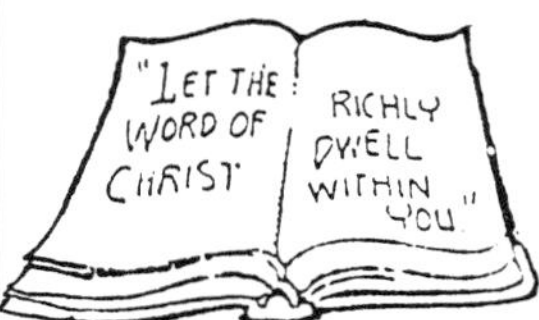

Madalyn Murry O'Hair, an atheist, whose efforts successfully eliminated the use of Bible reading and prayer from all public schools fifteen years ago, has been granted a federal hearing in Washington, D.C. on the subject of F.C.C. (Federal Communications Commission). The petition, R.H. 2493 would ultimately pave the way to stop the reading of the gospel on the air waves of America. She took her petition, with 27,000 signatures, to back her stand.

If her attempt is successful, all Sunday Worship Services being broadcast, either by radio or television will stop. Any elderly people and shut-ins, as well as those recuperating from hospitalization or illness, depend on radio and television to fulfill their worship needs every week.

Madalyn is also campaigning to remove all Christmas programs, Christmas songs, and Christmas Carols from Public schools. You can help this time!! We need 1,000,000 (one million) signed letters. This would defeat Mrs. O'Hair and show that there are many concerned Christians ...alive and well in our country.

Please sign, cut off and mail the form below.
Pleas do not sign Mr. and Mrs. Let each adult sign one separately and mail it in. Please be sure to put "Petition No. 2493" on the lower LEFT HAND OUTSIDE CORNER OF THE ENVELOPE when mailing your letter. PLEASE PHOTOCOPY this letter/form and send it to ten friends and relatives.

Federal Communications Commission
1919 "M" Street, N.W.
Washington, DC 20554

RE: Petition No. 2493

I am an American and proud of my heritage. I am also very much aware of the place religious faith has played in the freedom that we, as Americans, now enjoy. Therefore, I protest any human effort to remove from radio or television any programs designed to show faith, GOD as a Supreme Being, or to remove CHRISTMAS SONGS, PROGRAMS AND CAROLS FROM PUBLIC SCHOOLS.

Sincerely,

PRINT NAME: ______________________

SIGNATURE: ______________________

ADDRESS: ______________________

____

The millions of copies of this bogus warning and response form that have circulated in the United States since 1975 are nearly identical, except for variant spellings of Ms. O'Hair's name and different versions of the FCC address. This flier came from a church in Ohio. The FCC did indeed process a petition numbered RM-2493 submitted in 1974, which asked the commission to suspend the assignment of franchises for public television stations until the government could study the question of whether religious groups were getting too many of the channels. The FCC denied this petition the following year, and shortly afterwards letters and telephone calls began to come in from people who thought Madalyn Murray O'Hair had been involved. She was not, and she has never submitted any sort of petition to the FCC. The commission has no authority to prohibit religious broadcasting, and it certainly cannot regulate religious programs in the schools. Despite press releases and even a recorded explanation on the FCC voice-mail system, the petitions continue to flow in at the rate of thousands, even millions per year; the tide of letters ebbs and flows, but never stops. The FCC eventually received permission from the U.S. Postal Service to destroy all letters marked 2493 without opening them, and since most of the mail-in forms specify that the sender should write "Petition 2493" in the lower left-hand corner of the envelope, a great deal of time and effort has been saved. Considering the amount of postage sold to support this bogus campaign, it seems that the government has come out ahead on the deal. Rumors circulate among some Christian groups that atheists themselves are the ones printing and distributing the fliers about the fake petition just to make Christians look foolish. Atheist groups deny the charge. It's like a holy war of rumors and legends, with the FCC futilely trying to bring an end to the conflict.

"The Veterans' Insurance Dividend"

PLEASE PASS THIS ALONG TO YOUR PARENT, OR FRIEND,
IF NOT APPLICABLE TO YOURSELF

Insurance Refund For World War 2 Veterans

A Bill was passed in Congress (CSSB 102) recently which will give all World War 2 Veterans a dividend of 65 cents per $1,000 of their GI insurance for each month of service.

This refund is due regardless of whether or not the insurance is still carried. THE DIVIDEND CANNOT BE RECEIVED UNLESS IT IS REQUESTED.

The Veterans Administration is urging all WW 2 Vets to apply regardless of whether any insurance is held. The V.A. will check for eligibility. The refunds are not going to make anyone rich but a couple of hundred dollars is always nice. For example, a Vet who had $10,000 in insurance would be entitled to dividends of $79.00 for 12 months service. $156.00 for 24 months, $234.00 for 36 months, etc. The form below contains all the required information. Please use it and also pass on the information to friends. The bill has not been widely publicized so please help spread the word.

TO: VETERANS ADMINISTRATION
REGIONAL OFFICE AND INSURANCE CENTER
P.O. BOX 8079
PHILADELPHIA PA 19101

Dear Sir or Madam,

I, ______________ hereby apply for a dividend of 65 cents for each $1,000 of GI insurance for each month of service. Below is specific information.

Name ____________________

Address ____________________

City, State, Zip ____________________

Social Security # ____________________

Serial Number ____________________

Branch of Service ____________________

Date of Service ____________________

Date of Discharge __

____

Sincerely,

A frequently reappearing flier warning veterans not to miss out on a bonus allegedly owed to them by the government. Such bogus warnings have appeared at intervals since the mid-1940s, and each of the VA's 58 regional offices around the country has had to deal with the problem. During what the VA calls "active hoax periods" the Philadelphia center alone may get from 10,000 to 15,000 letters a week from vets hoping to cash in on the special insurance dividend. All they get in return is a postcard with the bad news. Here's the complete text of the VA's postcard, sent to me by Professor Thomas Foote at Evergreen State College in Olympia, Washington, who submitted a claim in 1992 just to see what would happen:

> *A false and misleading rumor sweeping the nation is plaguing us at the Veterans Administration and leading thousands of veterans such as you to write us requesting dividends on insurance that you had in force while on active duty in the U.S. Armed Forces.*
>
> *Congress did not pass any new law giving veterans a dividend based on the amount of months their insurance was in force while on active duty. The information you received regarding such a dividend is a hoax.*
>
> *Also false is the rumor that individuals who served in the military after 1965 and were insured under the SGLI (Servicemen's Group Life Insurance) program are entitled to a refund. There have never been any dividends, rebates or refunds due to surplus funds in the SGLI program.*
>
> *You can help us to eliminate these rumors by passing this information along to any of your friends or to any veteran's group to which you belong.*
> *Thank you.*
>
> *Veterans Administration*

The VA authorities really ought to correct their wording in the second paragraph of the debunking message. The phrase "the amount of months" should read "the number of months." I wonder if I could get a dividend for pointing this out.

21

Mistaken Identifications

An experience that happens to everyone at some time or other is mistaking a stranger for someone you know. For example, in my first couple of years teaching at the University of Idaho, there was a guy in another department who people seemed to think looked a lot like me. We even had some matching coats and ties in our wardrobes, plus similar short haircuts, so colleagues and students were constantly confusing us and starting conversations that made absolutely no sense, since we barely knew each other and our paths seldom crossed, even on that small, friendly campus. Friends kept telling me that I hadn't seemed quite myself when they saw me at such-and-such a place last week, and then I'd realize that once again it was my double from Poly Sci or wherever whom they had met, since I certainly had not been where they thought they had seen me at the time.

A variation on this theme is failing to recognize someone whom you ought to know. Again, as a young instructor, I was mistaken a few times in my opening class sessions for a fellow student instead of as the teacher in charge. It was gratifying in a way, but still mutually embarrassing for the parties involved. A friend on another campus told me that he had this conversation once with a young student to whom he happened to speak on campus early in the fall semester. She: "Well, have you seen your advisor yet?" He: "I don't have an advisor, I have advisees." (Their paths parted at this point, and he was not sure that she got his meaning.)

Such experiences are bound to inspire *anecdotes,* that is, personal stories of typical true experiences. And anecdotes sometimes grow into *legends,* that is, longer versions of such stories that become stereotyped in style and then travel from place to place and person to person. A typical personal anecdote of mistaken identities might be about failing to recognize the guest of honor at some event and then sticking one's foot in one's mouth. I read one time about a young investment banker who chatted with a distinguished older gentleman before a guest lecture at his company, even offering the stranger some investment advice. The stranger turned out to be the Nobel Prize winner in economics who had been brought in to address the group. Another story I've heard is about a guy who forgot to bring any kind of writing instrument or notepad to the meeting with government officials for which he had been scheduled by his company. He asked a "secretary" to fetch him what he needed, which she quietly did; later it turned out that she *was* a secretary—the Secretary of the (whatever) department in the government, who had been waiting in the conference room to address the visitor. As such stories are told and retold, new details are added, background and local color is elaborated, and the stories take on a life of their own. The classic in this genre is probably the one about the person at a reception in London who realizes that the woman to whom he is speaking has a familiar face, but he just cannot place her. So he asks, "And what are you doing nowadays?" She replies, "Oh, I'm still being the Queen of England's sister."

There are not many urban legends based on mistaken identities, but those that do exist are among the most widely told and believed "true" stories of our time.

"All My Children"

Every elementary-school teacher has probably heard the story about the teacher who, while on a bus, thought she recognized the man sitting a few seats in front of her.

"Hello there, Mr. Johnson," she said, but the man didn't respond.

She kept calling out until—with everyone on the bus now looking at them—the man finally turned around. Then she saw that she didn't know him after all.

"Sorry," she said. "I thought you were the father of one of my children."

"The Elevator Incident"

This may be one of those apocryphal stories that acquire credibility through its many retellings. But the fact that it's even circulating says something about the times.

The version that Joanne Stichman of West Los Angeles heard goes like this: Three women visiting Manhattan for the first time were invited to a bridge party in a high-rise building. With stories of muggings and rapes filling their heads, they were somewhat apprehensive about getting there safely.

The doorman admitted them and they entered the elevator, pushing the button for the 18th floor. But instead of going up, the elevator descended to the basement where, to their shock, a muscular, unsmiling man entered with a large dog.

The uneasy silence was suddenly broken when the man said, "Sit!" The women fell to the floor. He looked at them in amazement. "I meant the dog," he said.

Recently, a 54-year-old local Japanese woman from Lana'i left the [Hawaiian] Islands for the very first time to join relatives on a vacation in Las Vegas. The bright lights and big city didn't seem to faze her, but apparently she had some rather curious notions about Mainland blacks.

Boarding an unoccupied hotel elevator, on the way back to her room, she was startled to see the elevator doors suddenly reopen, allowing two black men on. The elevator stood motionless for a moment as she edged nervously toward the back. Finally, one of the men told the other to "Hit the floor," then stood laughing hysterically as the Lana'i grandmother spread herself prone on the elevator floor. Obviously, she thought this was the end, just like on TV. When the two men finally stopped laughing, they apologized and helped her up off the floor.

The next day, when the Lanaian went to check out, she discovered her bill had already been paid. A large bouquet of flowers was left for her with a note: "Sorry, and thanks for the best laugh I've had in a long, long time." It was signed: Lionel Richie.

A terrified tourist mistook Eddie Murphy for a mugger in a posh hotel, collapsed in fear at his feet and begged him not to hurt her.

But the kind-hearted comic felt so sorry for the jittery German visitor that he even paid her hotel bill.

Gisela Klein, 48, was waiting for the elevator to take her to the ground floor of Manhattan's luxurious Ritz Carlton where she was planning to meet her husband for dinner.

As she waited, Murphy and his bodyguards appeared from their rooms and stood next to her.

Klein was so nerve-wracked by New York's fearsome reputation as a hotbed of crime that she was convinced the Hollywood superstar and his burly security men were muggers.

And when Eddie asked her what floor she wanted, the petrified German fell to her knees sobbing, and begged them to spare her.

Murphy says: "At first I thought this lady was making a joke, but she was terrified."

Red-faced Gisela reveals: "After a few seconds I realized they weren't going to rob me.

"They were laughing and thought I was joking.

"I was so ashamed. Eddie Murphy is one of my favorites, but I didn't recognize him."

But easy-going Eddie wasn't fazed by the embarrassing mix-up.

When Gisela and her husband later checked out after their week-long stay, they found the highhearted comedian had paid their $3,500 hotel bill in full.

Eddie even left a note for her, saying: "Madam, our encounter was one of the nicest and funniest moments in my life. If only all women would fall at me [sic] feet like you did.

"But since you didn't have as much fun as we had, I have paid your hotel bill for you."

Perhaps most damaging to his reputation was what Murphy calls "The Elevator Story." He explained: "There's a story I was on an elevator with 10 bodyguards. An old lady was there. One bodyguard said, 'Hit the floor,' as in 'press the button.' The old lady got scared and dropped to the floor. And we were so embarrassed, and we helped her up, and I sent her flowers and paid her hotel bill, and *it never happened!* Here's the clincher: Whenever I go, 'No, it never happened.' they always say, 'Yes it did. My cousin was there.'"

"The Elevator Incident" is one of the most popular international urban legends of the 1980s and '90s, told in innumerable "true" versions, and repeated by countless broadcasters and columnists. The first example lacks the black celebrity that soon became a fixed detail in the

legend; it is from Steve Harvey's "Around the Southland" column published on July 10, 1981, in the Los Angeles Times. *Notice that already then Harvey alluded to "many retellings," identified the story as "apocryphal," and cited an oral source. In* The Choking Doberman *I traced Reggie Jackson versions of the legend that circulated in 1982 and 1983, eventually replaced by Lionel Richie versions, as in the second example quoted above from* Honolulu Magazine *for June 1989. The humor in most of these stories centers on the women—either foreign or from the boondocks—failing to recognize the celebrity. If a dog is present in the Richie versions, the singer may say "Sit Lady," which echoes the title of one of his popular songs, "Lady." In dogless versions of the story one of the black men may say "Hit fo'," meaning "Hit the button for the fourth floor." Other black celebrities named in American versions of the story include Wilt Chamberlain, "Mean Joe" Greene, Rosie Grier, Arsenio Hall, Lionel Hampton, Larry Holmes, Michael Jackson, "Magic" Johnson, Richard Pryor, Lou Rawls, O. J. Simpson, and Stevie Wonder (traveling with a Seeing Eye dog). Sometimes Harry Belafonte is mentioned in versions from abroad. But in recent years, Eddie Murphy has become far and away the most popular person to be mentioned in the story; the quoted example above is typical of reinvented and much-inflated tabloid versions; it was published in the* Star *for November 21, 1996. Murphy's denial of the story is quoted from an interview in* Parade *published on June 9, 1996. A characteristic detail of the Murphy versions is sending the victim a dozen long-stemmed roses with a $100 bill wrapped around each stem. In a column by black journalist Joseph H. Brown in the* Tampa Tribune *for July 14, 1996, a Lionel Richie version of "The Elevator Incident" was quoted from a lecture given by a black professor from the University of Miami. Brown identified the story as an "urban folk tale" and commented, "I hope the good professor didn't get his degrees with this kind of anecdotal research." Brown also mentioned the* Parade *interview with Eddie Murphy and added to the list of celebrities named in the story Denzel Washington, Bill Cosby, and Mike Tyson. The background of "The Elevator Incident" legend is probed further in the next two items.*

"It All Started with Neil (Or Did It?)"

I have picked up another version of the story that has nothing to do with racial stereotyping, urban paranoia, or dogs.

The story is told to me by Keith D. Young, who told it three years ago at a meeting of the Adventurers' Club. The setting is not an elevator but a corridor in the historic Houses of Parliament in London.

Young points out that the British are masters of pomp and ceremony. "Even innocent bystanders and spectators sometimes feel themselves involuntarily caught up in and reacting to the drama of the moment, though they may know little or nothing of the ritual itself. . . ." The innate desire to do the right thing on solemn occasions, he suggests, may explain this story:

In Parliament, the equivalent of our Speaker of the House is called the Keeper of the Woolsack; at the time of the story this gentleman was Sir Quentin Hogg, Lord Hailsham. Parliament had just adjourned, and his lordship, resplendent in the gold and scarlet robes of his office, topped by a ceremonial wig, emerges from the great hall into the corridor on the way to his chambers. The corridor is crowded with an American tour group, beyond which Lord Hailsham sees an old friend, the Hon. Neil Matten, MP, with whom he would like a word.

"Neil!" his lordship shouts. "Neil!"

"There followed an embarrassed silence," Young concludes, "as all the tourists obediently fell to their knees."

You never know what might crop up in—or near—the courts of justice. Consider this item that Kincardine lawyer Norman Shepherd snared and sent to me:

The Lord High Chancellor of England, who sits in the House of Lords, presiding over not only that august body but the entire British legal system, is a formidable figure.

Formerly plain Quentin Hogg, now Lord Hailsham, he was wandering down a corridor in the House of Parliament when he spotted an old friend, Conservative MP Neil Marten, emerging from a doorway.

"Neil!" he boomed out.

Just then a party of American tourists stopped to give way as the full-wigged elaborately-gowned and obviously important apparition cruised past, trying to get Marten's attention.

"Neil!" shouted Hailsham, even louder.

So the Americans duly obeyed, falling to their knees before the astonished, but amused, Lord Chancellor.

During our freshman year at Brown University in Providence, R.I., my friend Neil occasionally served as an altar boy at the Catholic Mass in the campus chapel. During one Mass he neglected to bring out all the things necessary for the consecration of the sacrament. Unnoticed, he slipped away to retrieve them, but was unable to return before the priest needed him.

The priest looked left and right, then out toward the congregation. "Neil?" he said with a frown. Immediately, the congregation dropped to their knees in prayer.

The first example of the Neil/kneel story is from Jack Smith's column in the Los Angeles Times *for September 1, 1983. I partially quoted this in* The Choking Doberman *as a possible prototype for "The Elevator Incident." I was informed by British readers that there were several flaws in this telling, including that: 1) Lord Hailsham was never knighted, so he should not be called "Sir," 2) his office was that of Lord Chancellor, and 3) the "Woolsack" is merely the Lord Chancellor's seat, and there is no "Keeper of the Woolsack." Mike Lawrence of Chichester, England, wrote me in 1988 reporting that "the story of Lord Hailsham calling to his friend Neil is an apocryphal tale which English politicians occasionally tell on chat shows." The second example of Neil/kneel is from Peter V. MacDonald's "Court Jesters" column in the* Toronto Daily Star *for August 13, 1989. Like Smith, MacDonald cites an oral source; his details of English government are accurate, so presumably he has the name "Neil Marten" right as well. The third example is from the November 1995 issue of* Reader's Digest, *where it is credited to "Matt Skinner." Scottish folklorist Sandy Hobbs of the Paisley College of Technology also sent me a variation of this story found in a book of classroom anecdotes published in Edinburgh in 1986. This one concerns a teacher who is showing two new students around the school. When the teacher shouts "Neil!" at an older student who is racing down a hallway, the two youngsters at his side kneel down. Possibly the British stories are the actual prototypes of the "Sit" versions of "The Elevator Incident"; this would mean that the American Neil/kneel story in* Reader's Digest *is either a separate offshoot of the older tradition, an independently occurring actual incident, or even a hoax perpetrated by someone who had heard the earlier story and saw a chance to sell it to the* Digest. *I'd be glad to send a bouquet of roses to anyone who could sort this out for me. Meanwhile, see the next item for yet another variation on the elevator-incident theme.*

"Sit, Whitey!"

In an episode from the *Bob Newhart Show,* Julius Harris, in the character of an insurance salesman seeking reasons for his poor sales record, calls his dog "Whitey" by name twice. The first time is during his counseling session with psychologist Bob, and the second is in the reception area after getting his dog a snack from a sandwich machine down the hall. "Whitey" is actually a *black* Great Dane, obedient but still intimidating. Harris, tall, bald, and black, is dressed in a colorful African-style outfit and wearing beads and sunglasses. Bob timidly suggests that perhaps he should change his image; following this advice, his client decides to stop wearing sunglasses.

After the interview with Bob, the insurance salesman goes around the corner and down the hall; meanwhile, all the other characters in the episode except Bob and Jerry leave on the office elevator. When the man and his dog return, Harris snaps "Sit, Whitey!" and Jerry reacts by sitting hastily but briefly on the edge of the receptionist's desk.

That's all there is to it—a quick punch line and sight-gag that leaves the audience in stitches.

From my notes from viewing the videotaped episode originally broadcast on December 1, 1973. Before seeing the tape, I had quoted some references to this episode in the section on "The Elevator Incident" in my 1984 book The Choking Doberman. *Based on what readers and columnists recalling the episode had written, I guessed that the dog was white, that the guest star may have been Isaac Hayes, that the incident happened on the elevator, and that more than one* Newhart *character had sat down on command. None of these things turned out to be true, illustrating how changes in folk stories occur as they are imperfectly remembered and repeated from person to person. Even Bob Newhart himself, who responded to my 1983 query about the episode, failed to recall the name of the guest star; however, when I sent Newhart a copy of my newspaper column discussing the episode, he replied in a note dated June 25, 1992, "regarding the Sit Whitey episode of the Bob Newhart Show, I think it was the longest sustained laugh we ever received. It's interesting the variations that have arisen over the years." Vince Waldron, in his 1987 book* Classic Sitcoms, *comments "the episode contains one of the series's most memorable throwaway gags," referring to this bit of action. Whether the sitcom episode spawned the urban legend is an open question. Certainly the televised gag added an elevator and a black man to the Neil/kneel story, but the "Sit, Whitey!"*

punch line is never echoed in the oral tradition and sounds like a joke-writer's clever invention. "The Elevator Incident" did not begin to circulate until nine years after the Newhart *episode, although reruns continued through most of that period. My guess is that one of the writers had heard a prototype of the elevator story circulating orally and then added details as he scripted it, some of which eventually fed back into the spoken tradition.*

"Black and White"

A speech on apartheid before the United Nations, a reception hosted by several foreign ambassadors, and finally dinner with Zimbabwe President Robert Mugabe and his wife at the home of Bill and Camille Cosby—the day's schedule promised to be a heady one, even for a man as prominent as the Rev. Jesse Jackson.

But as he stood outside of a hotel waiting for a limousine, it happened. Out of nowhere came the seemingly innocent yet ugly reminder that some people in this day and age still judge a person's station in life by the color of his skin. "This White lady walked up to me," Rev. Jackson recalls. "She said, 'Oh, I'm so glad to see you. You really saved me. If you hadn't helped me get those bags off the elevator, I couldn't have made it.'" Having said all that, she then gave him a dollar.

Startled, Rev. Jackson—a two-time candidate for the presidency of the United States—took the dollar, thanked the woman and climbed into his waiting stretch limousine, which was driven by a White chauffeur.

Michael Thurmond, a lawyer and former chairman of the Black Caucus in the Georgia Legislature, remembers the sting of leaving an elegant reception for lawmakers at the Ritz-Carlton hotel in Atlanta last year and being asked by an elderly white woman, and then her husband, to retrieve their car.

Thurmond, dressed in a $250 tailor-made blazer, white shirt and silk tie, was standing by the hotel door waiting for his car when the wife approached him. Thurmond says he politely told her he was not an employee.

But when her husband asked moments later, Thurmond angrily snapped at the man, who stammered an apology and nervously walked away.

"I was really ticked," Thurmond said. "Here I am being entertained upstairs as chairman of the black caucus with all these business people trying to shake your hand, and you come downstairs and get mistaken for a parking attendant."

Karl Malone went to Salt Lake International Airport Tuesday to pick up his inbound brother.

While standing in the baggage claim area, however, he was startled when a woman approached and made a strange request.

"She picked me out of the crowd," said the 6-foot-9 256-pound Malone. "She said she needed a porter-boy. You know, someone to help her with her bags. I said, "'OK, I'll help you.'"

Waiting for the woman's luggage to appear, Malone's new employer continued the conversation. He discovered she came from his home state and lived in Bossier City, Louisiana.

"She asked if that's what I did for a living," Karl said. "I told her I drove a truck during the day and I did this at night, for a few extra bucks. . . . Some of the Delta [Airline] people saw what was happening. They were dying laughing."

Bags in tow, Malone and the woman went outside.

"I asked her what kind of car we were looking for," he said. "She said a blue Mercedes. We found it—the guy inside was looking at me kinda funny—and I got the stuff put away."

Then, the moment of truth.

Said Malone, "She reached in her purse to tip me and I told her, 'No, thanks,' I said. 'It's O.K., I really play pro basketball.' She looked at me and hey, she turned another color she was so embarrassed. It was really funny. It was all in fun; I was having a good time."

After this, the Mailman might deserve a new nickname.

The Skycap, perhaps!

The Jesse Jackson anecdote is from Douglas C. Lyons's article "Racism and Blacks Who've 'Made It,'" in Ebony *for October 1989. Lyons also tells of the time David Wilmot, dean of admissions at Georgetown Law School was mistaken for a parking valet at a posh Washington hotel. The Michael Thurmond anecdote is from Robert Anthony Watts's article on racism distributed to newspapers by the Associated Press in September 1993. The Karl Malone anecdote is from Steve Luhm's "NBA Notes" column in the* Salt Lake (City) Tribune *for December 2, 1990. Mistaken identities of blacks by whites certainly do occur, but in their retellings details are selected for emphasis and the stories may enter the realm of folklore. In Salt Lake City, for example, variations on the Karl Malone story circulating by word of mouth that week involved the make of car, the conversation, what Malone was wearing, his reaction, etc. A similar incident is supposed to have occurred to U.S. Supreme Court justice Thurgood Marshall being mistaken for an elevator operator in the Supreme Court building. An older and even more legendary body of similar stories describes a black (or Hispanic) celebrity mowing his lawn and being mistaken for a gardener by a woman—always a woman—who asks how much he is paid for his work. "Well, Ma'am, they don't pay me nothin,'" the man replies, "but the lady of the house lets me sleep with her." This story has been told about blacks from George Washington Carver to Charley Pride, as well as about golfers Lee Trevino and Chi Chi Rodriguez.*

"The Ice-Cream-Cone Caper"

As told by Paul Harvey

Our For What It's Worth Department understands that actor Robert Redford is in Santa Fe, New Mexico, making a movie . . .

But the lady who encountered him in an ice-cream parlor on Canyon Street was determined to stay cool . . .

She pretended to ignore the presence of the movie star . . .

But after leaving the shop she realized that she did not have the ice-cream cone she'd bought and paid for.

She returned to the shop . . .

To ask for her ice-cream cone.

Overhearing, Robert Redford said, "Madame, you'll probably find it where you put it—in your purse."

Meltdown time

Paul Newman's blue eyes can make more than a heart melt.

Will Spanheimer of Kennewick was visiting his aunt, Madalaine Hart, in Phoenix, Arizona, when they decided an ice cream cone would be just the thing on a 110-degree day.

But walking into the shop just ahead of them were Newman and wife Joanne Woodward. After working up their nerve, Spanheimer and Hart walked inside, ordered cones and left.

Then Hart realized something was amiss. "Where's my ice cream cone?" she asked her nephew. They went back inside the store to look for it.

Then the magic moment—Hart felt a tap on her shoulder and turned to see those famous blue eyes gazing into hers.

And he had the answer to the missing cone caper. She had put it—a waffle cone with three scoops and whipped cream—in her purse.

In this legend the celebrity involved is recognized, but with embarrassing results for the civilian. Most versions are jam-packed with circumstantial details, none of which can be true, since all the celebrities supposedly involved in the incident have denied it ever occurred. Paul Harvey was one of many journalists and broadcasters who told and retold the cone-caper story in 1986; this is quoted from the 1991 book For What It's Worth, *as told on the air in Harvey's trademark breathless style. The Paul Newman version quoted is from the "FYI" column of the* Tri-City Herald *(published in Pasco, Washington) for October 11, 1993. Similar versions appeared in Lois Wyse's column "The Way We Are" in* Good Housekeeping *for April 1991, and in Robin Adams Sloan's "Gossip Column" distributed by King Features to newspaper television magazines in September 1992. Robert L. Kierstead, ombudsman for the* Boston Globe, *published a good account of his paper's initially falling for the story, plus a survey of the story's history, in a November 1986 column sent to me by Philip Moshcovitz of Brookline, Massachusetts. Kierstead commented, "The story was too good to be true and was not challenged soon enough." My own report on the popularity of the story in 1986—when it was also told about Jack Nicholson and Tom Brokaw—appeared in* Curses! Broiled Again! *where*

I suggested a possible Freudian reading of the cone-in-the-purse reaction to the presence of the handsome star.

"The Blind Man"

Dear Ann Landers: I greatly enjoyed the column about the housewife who did her housework in the nude. Perhaps you will get a laugh out of this story, which may or may not be true.

A woman picked a very warm day to begin her spring housecleaning. After an hour or two she thought, "This heat is unbearable. I can't stand these clothes another minute." She promptly took every stitch off and happily continued with her housework. Then the doorbell rang.

"Wouldn't you know it," she said to herself, and tiptoed to the window. She peered through the curtains and saw a man standing at the front door. The woman called out, "Who is it?"

"Blind man," was the reply.

"Are you sure," she shouted back.

"Of course I'm sure," was the answer.

"Since he's blind," she thought, "it won't make any difference." She ran down the stairs with a dollar bill in her hand, flung open the door and handed it to him. The man looked surprised, took the dollar bill and asked "OK, lady, where do you want me to hang these blinds?"

—P. T. Paducah, Ky.

From Ann Landers's column of August 10, 1986. She printed a shorter version sent by a reader, but not credited to a specific source, in her column of October 13, 1998. Again, it was prefaced by a reference to "The Nude Housewife." In a newspaper column of my own I traced this story back to the early 1970s, but readers quickly informed me that they had heard it in the 1950s when "Venetian blinds" were specifically mentioned. It was also a favorite joke told by Henny Youngman and other professional comedians. Probably "The Blind Man" would have fit just as neatly under "Jumping to Conclusions," or "Slapstick Comedy," but I placed it here because of the mistaken identity involved, plus the donated dollar, which reminds me of the measly tip given to the black celebrity in some of the "Black and White" stories.

22

Campus Capers

College and university life is full of folklore. You might not expect this, remembering that our Institutions of Higher Learning are devoted to Searching for Truth, Pushing the Frontiers of Knowledge, Preserving our Cultural Heritage, Educating the Cream of the Academic Crop, etc., etc., etc. (My computer automatically capitalizes all that kind of stuff, but leaves what I write about fraternities, food fights, or football games in plain lower case.) Maybe it's in part the dignity and aloofness of the academic tradition—symbolized best by the preservation of our anachronistic graduation ceremonies—that leads campus folk to respond at times with goofy customs, slang, parodies, superstitions, mock rituals, and—yes—even urban legends centered on campus capers.

The broad topic of academic folklore could fill volumes; in fact, it has already filled one remarkable collection entitled *Piled Higher and Deeper,* published in 1990 by folklorist Simon J. Bronner. (The title refers to a joke about the meaning of the degree abbreviation Ph.D.) Another scholar who has studied academic lore, Professor Barre Toelken, suggests that students, although obviously literate, when they interact as a *folk* group on campus could be called "communally aliterate." What Toelken means is that when students have something of immediate concern to communicate, they tend to do so by word of mouth and customary example rather than in writing. Out of that principle emerges a rich vein of academic folklore.

Take the recurring problem of what to do if an instructor fails to show up for class on time. Torn by their outrage at being stood up and their fear of being marked absent if the teacher does eventually arrive, students typically rely on the rule of "The Obligatory Wait" to settle their dilemma. This "rule," which is not to be found in any campus source of official regulations, supposedly holds that students in a class are expected to wait a specified number of minutes, depending upon the rank of the teacher. A typical formula is five minutes for an instructor, ten for an assistant professor, fifteen for an associate professor, and twenty minutes for a full professor. (Some students, confused by academic ranks, may include a separate waiting period for a "Doctor.") But you will not find this, or any other such rule, in published sources; it's strictly a folk idea circulating by word of mouth on most college campuses.

Another typical piece of campus lore is "The Suicide Rule"; notice here that we have another supposed regulation, as if the university has resolved every possible issue with a special statute. "The Suicide Rule," many students believe, requires that if your roommate commits suicide, the university must give you a 4.0 (straight A grades) for the semester. While you are looking for "The Obligatory Wait" in the rule books, just try finding that one as well! It's not there, I assure you.

I should mention here that I have had letters and calls from some extremely certain college students and administrators assuring me that regulations such as these *are* in the printed guidelines on their campus. These correspondents always promise to get back to me with a copy of the relevant regs as soon as they have found them. Not a single one of these people has ever come through with that proof, although it's true that some professors or departments may announce their own rules for attendance if a teacher is late. Also, there are a few examples of colleges awarding ad hoc grades to students who have suffered some kind of tragedy during a semester. (Usually this turns out to be giving the student an incomplete grade or else awarding the letter grade that he or she has earned so far in that semester.)

Many college newspapers have investigated such campus folklore as "The Obligatory Wait" and "The Suicide Rule," always concluding their reports with a debunking of such traditions. A campus news story taking another approach appeared in *New University,* the University of California at Irvine student paper, on June 3, 1991. The student journalist, staff writer Craig Outhier, ended his story thus:

> Why stop at simple death? Couldn't a long and protracted illness be just as emotionally traumatic on a roommate as a quick and painless exit? How about partial credit for broken limbs? A 3.8 for contracted venereal disease?
>
> Naw.
>
> For now, the only thing you'll get from your roommate's death is your own room.

The arrival of computers on campus, with easy access for faculty and students to E-mail and the World Wide Web, rather than decreasing the amount of college folklore, has instead spawned a whole new series of anonymous apocryphal texts. It's a sort of cyberlore for the on-line college generation. While not strictly speaking folklore in the classic sense—circulating orally and exhibiting constant variation—some of these electronic texts do read much like the oral legends of the past. Here's a recent example that purports to be a response to a professor's brain-twisting final exam topic. The E-mails that forwarded this item widely around the Net were generally headed "A true story":

> A thermodynamics professor had written a take-home exam for his graduate students. It had one question: Is hell exothermic or endothermic? Support your answer with a proof.
>
> Most of the students wrote proofs of their beliefs using Boyle's Law or some variant. One student, however wrote the following:
>
> First, we postulate that if souls exist, then they must have some mass. If they do, then a mole of souls can also have a mass. So, at what rate are souls moving into hell and at what rate are souls leaving? I think that we can safely assume that once a soul gets to hell, it will not leave. Therefore, no souls are leaving.
>
> As for souls entering hell, let's look at the different religions that exist in the world today. Some of these religions state that if you are not a member of their religion, you will go to hell. Since there are more than one of these religions and people do not belong to more than one religion, we can project that all people and all souls go to hell.
>
> With birth and death rates as they are, we can expect the number of souls in hell to increase exponentially. Now, we look at the rate of change in volume in hell. Boyle's Law states that in order for the temperature and pressure in hell to stay the same, the ratio of the mass of souls and volume needs to stay constant.
>
> 1) So, if hell is expanding at a slower rate than the rate at which souls enter hell, then the temperature and pressure in hell will increase until all hell breaks loose.
>
> 2) Of course, if hell is expanding at a rate faster than the increase of

souls in hell, then the temperature and pressure will drop until hell freezes over.

So which is it?

If we accept the postulate given to me by Therese Banyan during Freshman year, "that it will be a cold night in hell before I sleep with you" and take into account the fact that I still have not succeeded in having sexual relations with her, then 2 cannot be true, and hell is exothermic.

The student got the only A.

Another piece of recent cyberlore purports to be a witty applicant's response to the college admissions office that required each would-be student to respond to the question "Are there any significant experiences you have had, or accomplishments you have realized, that have helped to define you as a person?" The applicant responded with an essay that began:

> I am a dynamic figure, often seen scaling walls and crushing ice. I have been known to remodel train stations on my lunch breaks, making them more efficient in the area of heat retention. I translate ethnic slurs for Cuban refugees, I write award-winning operas, I manage time efficiently. Occasionally, I tread water for three days in a row.

And, after several more paragraphs of that sort of thing, the applicant ended his brag (similar to the frontier boast of a Davy Crockett or a Mike Fink) with this:

> I balance, I weave, I dodge, I frolic, and my bills are all paid. On weekends, to let off steam, I participate in full-contact origami. Years ago I discovered the meaning of life but forgot to write it down. I have made extraordinary four-course meals using only a mouli and a toaster oven. I breed prizewinning clams. I have won bullfights in San Juan, cliff-diving competitions in Sri Lanka, and spelling bees at the Kremlin. I have played Hamlet, I have performed open-heart surgery, and I have spoken with Elvis.
>
> But I have not yet gone to college.

My only question about this impressive performance is this: What's a "mouli?"

"Now Urine Trouble"

A doctor instructing a class of medical students tells them that it's possible to detect the presence of too much sugar in the urine by tasting it. He demonstrates by sticking his finger into a urine sample and then sticking his finger in his mouth. He pronounces the sample too sweet, and asks the students to try it for themselves.

Each student repeats the test, some of them agreeing on the diagnosis, others not quite getting it. None of them notices, until their teacher explains, that he had put his middle *finger into the sample but stuck his* forefinger *into his mouth. The test was of their powers of perception, not of their ability to taste sugar in urine.*

"The Dormitory Surprise"

This story was told by an upperclassman in my dorm at the University of Illinois at Urbana during the first few weeks of the semester in 1967:

This happened last year to a guy who lived here. It was homecoming weekend, and he was expecting his parents to come in and they would then go to the game together. His fiancee and her parents were also coming.

So this guy went to take a shower, and he was coming back to his room with only a towel wrapped around his hips. When he got to the door of his room, he heard voices inside, and he thought it was just some of the guys goofing around in his room. So he whipped the towel off, took his penis in his hand, threw the door open, and yelled "RAT-A-TAT-TAT, you're all dead."

And inside the room were his parents, his fiancee, and her parents!

Sent to me in an unsigned letter from Chicago in 1987. I discussed "The Dormitory Surprise" in The Mexican Pet *and* The Baby Train, *with examples from several different colleges and going back to the mid-1950s, proving that the legend existed even before the days of coed dorms on campus. Variations of this story describe the naked student wrapping his or her head in a towel to avoid recognition when forced to walk through a room with other people in it. All such stories—and there are several nonacademic counterparts—project the common caught-in-the-nude nightmare to a real-world situation.*

"The Gay Roommate"

I heard a story that sounds like a legend, but I want to know for sure. I heard this when I was in high school as a warning about what can happen at college.

Supposedly, a new student began developing respiratory problems and then noticed some rectal bleeding after a few weeks at school. When he visited the campus doctor, he was told that his respiratory condition came from breathing too much ether, but the bleeding came from anal sex.

The student immediately returned to his room and found a bottle of ether in his roommate's closet. As soon as his roommate returned, the patient beat him up and then moved out of the room. Apparently, at night, his roommate had been sedating him and then having sex with him.

I originally heard this story about the University of Wisconsin at La Crosse, but later I heard it about UW-Madison, and then a private school in Milwaukee. My roommate heard a variation involving chloroform, but without the bleeding.

So what's the word? Is this a legend?

From a letter sent to me by Todd Huhn of Watertown, Wisconsin, in October 1991. Internal evidence of variation and distribution clearly marks this as an urban legend, and the dozens of other versions of the story circulating on campuses all across the country confirm that identification. "The Gay Roommate" was a popular story at American col-

leges and universities from 1989 to 1991. I surveyed the tradition up to May 1991 in The Baby Train, *and the above example is one of a dozen further reports that came in later. A student writing from Michigan State University in 1992 quoted his own roommate, insisting, "This story is true; I know it's true. A friend of my roommate's in Freshman year, he knew the dude it happened to!" While these campus stories reflect homophobia, and possibly also some latent homosexual desire on the part of men who tell them, the basic story is not merely a product of recent American dormitory living. A similar story circulated in Australian (and probably other) military units in the 1940s describing young naval recruits victimized by older men who first supplied them with alcoholic drinks. In his 1886 edition of* The Book of the Thousand Nights and a Night, *the Victorian scholar Richard F. Burton mentioned an unscrupulous Middle Eastern official victimizing young European sailors in the same way.*

"The Roommate's Death"

This story takes place in a sorority house on this campus, during Christmas vacation when most of the girls had gone home.

There were two or three girls left in the sorority house. It was late at night and the girls decided that they were hungry, so two of the girls went downstairs to the kitchen. One of the girls went back to the room to rejoin the other girl, leaving one girl downstairs in the kitchen.

A little bit later on, say about a half hour later, the two girls in the room started wondering about the other girl 'cause she hadn't come back yet. So they went out on the landing and they heard something moving around downstairs. So they called down and nobody answered, the person or whatever it was moving around was still heard.

They were afraid to go downstairs, so they locked themselves in their room and waited for morning. They actually waited about an hour, when they decided to try it again. They were going to open the door when they heard a noise outside—like a scratching, so they got scared and didn't open the door. The scratching was like somebody dragging somebody down the steps. They were afraid to leave the room 'cause someone was out in the hall.

They stayed in their room till early the next morning until the mailman came around, and they hailed the mailman out the window. He came in, and [they told him] during the night, they had heard a scratching on their door. The mailman came in the front door and went up the stairs, and told the girls to stay in their room, that everything was all right but that they were to stay in their rooms.

But the girls didn't listen to him 'cause he had said it was all right, so they came out into the hall. When they opened the door, they saw their girlfriend on the floor with a hatchet in her head.

I heard this in 1983 told at West Georgia College, Carrollton, Georgia. It was supposed to have happened on the University of Illinois campus. This is the way it was told.

This girl got off work and went back to the dorm where she lived. It was late and she and her roommate had an agreement that if either one had brought a guy back to the room, she would put a rubber band on the doorknob. Well, sure enough, the girl gets to her room and there is a rubber band on the doorknob.

The girl had had a tough night and wasn't in the best of moods. She wasn't about to hang around in the hallway half the night, so she unlocks the door and goes in. Well, she gets in the room and hears all this heavy breathing and rustling around on her roommate's side of the room. The girl doesn't turn on the lights and being as quiet as possible slips out of her clothes, gets in bed and falls asleep.

The next morning the girl wakes up and it's light outside. She yawns and sits up and looks over on her roommate's side of the room. Sprawled on the bed is her roommate, gutted and torn apart. There's blood all over the wall and floor. The girl gets up and starts to dash out of the room. She reaches the door and stops in her tracks. There, printed neatly on the door in blood is, "Aren't you glad you didn't turn on the lights?"

The first version of this popular campus legend of the 1960s comes from Linda Dégh's article "The Roommate's Death and Related Dormitory Stories in Formation," in Indiana Folklore, *vol. 2, 1969; it was told by an Indiana University student who heard it in her dormitory in 1964, during her freshman year. I have added paragraphing to Dégh's ver-*

batim text. The broken taboo—"[he] told the girls to stay in their room"—and the male rescuer are typical of the earlier versions of the legend. The second example incorporating the handwriting-on-the-wall motif is more typical of versions told since the 1980s; this text was sent to me in 1992 by Todd Webb of Jonesboro, Georgia. In a variation on the wall-writing theme the message may be written in lipstick, reminiscent of the "AIDS Mary" legend. Students all across the country continue to tell this legend, often as a warning to freshmen by upperclass students or by resident advisers in the dormitories.

"Switched Campus Buildings"

I heard this story when I was a student at the University of Virginia in Charlottesville. It involves the University Chapel there, a small, squat, grey stone building which contrasts with the general red brick Georgian/classical design of virtually every other building on the central grounds.

The story goes that the architect of the chapel was also the architect of the chapel at Cornell University in New York. Somehow, his designs for these chapels were switched, so that Cornell received a red brick Georgian chapel while Virginia received its current chapel. I have never been able to ask anyone who has been to Cornell whether they have such a chapel or not.

Dear Professor Folklore: I graduated from Calif. State Polytechnic University, Pomona, in 1978. I heard a story that the architect who designed the red-brick dorm building had earlier designed prisons.

I quoted a variation of the chapel story with a switch between Virginia and Notre Dame in The Baby Train*; the above version was sent to me in 1989 by Daniel M. Covino of Rye Brook, New York. Numerous stories circulate on other campuses alleging that building plans were switched between institutions, usually those with radically different architectural styles or those in distant parts of the country that have completely opposite climates. The prisonlike nature of so many college living units prompts stories such as the* *second example above, which I quote from a postcard sent in 1995 by Richard T. Wylie of Torrance, California. Another common campus-architecture legend follows.*

"Sinking Libraries"

When I was an undergraduate at Northwestern University from 1977 to 1981, there was a story circulating on campus that the University Library was gradually sinking. The building had been constructed on a section of campus known as the "lakefill," which, as its name implies, was at one time under the waters of Lake Michigan.

As I remember it, the architects had neglected to include the weight of the books when making their necessary calculations. As a result, the library was sinking by a quarter of an inch each year. For all I know this may actually be true.

When I was a freshman in the early '80s at the University of Pittsburgh I heard about the Sliding Engineering Building. It seems that the engineers, when designing the foundations for this large building, had neglected to take into account some instability of the soil upon which it was built. This, coupled with the building's location at the top of a sloping street, resulted in a tendency for it to slide down the hill.

The only way to prevent it from sliding was to keep the building light enough, and the only way to accomplish this was to limit the amount of laboratory equipment in the basement labs. So it was only the judicious restraint of the experimenting professors that kept the building from sliding down to rest against the residence halls at the bottom of the slope, and then from sliding on through an elementary school immediately below them.

Northwestern University seems to have the most famous "sinking library" in the United States, judging from all the letters and articles I have received about it. Jenny Cline of Maynard, Massachusetts, sent me the above example in 1990. Another notorious sinking library is at Syracuse University. Essentially the same legend—sometimes without a mention of unstable subsoil—is told on many American college and university campuses, possibly encouraged by the students' noting that the shelves of the library are never completely full; some books are always checked out. The sliding-building story from Pittsburgh came to me from John F. Myers of Charleston, South Carolina, in 1993. Off campus there are similar legends about new buildings either leaning off-vertical or steadily sinking into the ground; the most common sinking buildings seem to be new shopping malls.

"The Acrobatic Professor"

Your campus stories prompted my husband to recall some about a chemistry professor at Mississippi State named Seeley, a terror to all the agriculture students.

Once students asked when they would have an exam. He replied, "The day you see me come into the classroom through the transom."

The next day he brought a ladder with him, set it next to the door, climbed in through the transom and gave them an exam.

When he retired, a cartoon of his head sticking through a transom was supposedly published in the campus newspaper.

I was surprised to learn while reading *The Mexican Pet* that a story I had taken as truth was probably an urban legend. As a freshman at Texas A&M University in 1968, I was told by older students that my introductory calculus professor had once answered the usual first-week question about pop quizzes by saying that the class could expect one when he entered the room via the back window.

He was a slight man with physical impairments that made it difficult for him to walk, so there was some nervous laughter at this announcement, especially since the class met in a second-floor classroom. There was no balcony off the room, but only a small ledge outside the rather large windows.

One day near the middle of the semester, the story went, the class was about to dismiss itself after waiting the then-standard fifteen minutes for the professor to arrive, when a window at the back of the room opened, and in crawled the professor. He stood up and distributed a stack of pop quizzes to the astonished class.

Marie H. Lewis of Baton Rouge, Louisiana, sent me her husband's recollection of the Professor Seeley story in 1991. This was probably the same Mississippi State University professor who was alluded to without name or field in the October 1961 edition of Reader's Digest. *I have heard similar stories about a German professor at the University of North Carolina, a mathematician at Union College in Schenectady, New York, a history professor at Tennessee Technological University, and—best known of all the acrobatic professors—about Professor Guy Y. ("Guy Wire") Williams, who taught at the University of Oklahoma from 1906 until his death in 1968. Campus folklore claimed that Williams had once been a circus acrobat, but an official history of the University only mentions that he was "a skilled gymnast and acrobat," without specifically describing the transom feat. Three published photos of Williams show him mixing chemicals, twirling a lariat, and "startling his class with an impromptu handstand on the corner of his desk." But there is no mention of climbing through a transom, nor are pop quizzes described. Transoms would be characteristic of only the very oldest classroom buildings; the variation of the story from Texas A&M with the professor simply entering through a window was sent to me in 1990 by John T. Yantis of Texas.*

"The Telltale Report"

It was in 1886 that "discretionary supervision" of attendance at scholastic exercises, as the Dean discreetly termed it, was adopted [at Harvard]. . . . "Discretionary supervision" meant in practice that upperclassmen could cut classes at will; and term-time trips to New York, Montreal, and Bermuda became all too common. The Faculty remained in blissful ignorance of this new definition of liberty until it was called to their attention by a careless student and his irate father. The lad had left Cambridge for the more genial climate of Havana, writing a series of post-dated letters, which his chum was supposed to mail to his parents at proper intervals. Unfortunately, his "goody" [housekeeper] placed the lot in the mail; the alarmed father came to Cambridge, and no officer of the University had the remotest idea where the son might be. Shortly after, the Overseers offered the Faculty the choice between holding a daily morning roll-call and checking attendance in classes. They chose the latter.

From Samuel Eliot Morison's 1936 book Three Centuries of Harvard: 1636–1936, *pp. 368–69. While the imposition and discontinuation of "discretionary supervision" at Harvard can be historically verified, the anecdote about the anonymous "lad's" postdated letters giving him away because of slipups by his "chum" and his "goody" sounds apocryphal. This story did not survive on the liberated campuses of the twentieth century, but a similar account of telltale reports written in advance and mailed by a landlady as a group, or in the wrong sequence, became a standard theme in twentieth-century folklore of Mormon missionaries who are required to file weekly activity reports and to stay on the job during their church-assigned two-year missions. Every Mormon missionary has heard the cautionary tale about the missionaries who strayed—to a World Series game, the Olympics, Disneyland, skiing, etc.—and were caught when those telltale reports arrived in the mail.*

"The Daughter's Letter from College"

When I was a university president, trying to deal with campus protests against the war in Vietnam, building a law school and a medical school and three community colleges, handling several budget crises a year, serving as a defendant in twenty lawsuits at a time, and even having to worry about three assassination threats, it was a condition of survival to take the longer and the wider view. On one particularly noisy day a kind and perceptive friend handed me a letter sent by an American college girl to her parents.

> Dear Mom and Dad: I'm sorry to be so long in writing again, but all my writing paper was lost the night the dormitory was burned down by the demonstrators. I'm out of the hospital now, and the doctor says my eyesight should be back to normal sooner or later.
>
> The wonderful boy, Bill, who rescued me from the fire kindly offered to share his little apartment with me until the dorm is rebuilt. He comes from a good family, so you won't be too surprised when I tell you we are going to get married. In fact, you always wanted a grandchild, so you will be glad to know that you will be grandparents next month.
>
> Please disregard the above practice in English composition. There was no fire, I haven't been in the hospital, I'm not pregnant, and I don't even have a boyfriend. But I did get a "D" in French and an "F" in chemistry, and I wanted to be sure you received this news in proper perspective.
>
> Love,
> Mary

From the foreword to Harlan Cleveland's 1985 book The Knowledge Executive: Leadership in an Information Society. *While not precisely a legend, this anonymous letter in several variations has circulated on many college and university campuses since at least the mid-1960s. Cleveland's version is somewhat sanitized and much shorter and less detailed than most texts. It omits the class-based or racist elements usually found in the letter. For example, the daughter may describe her new fiancé as of "a different race and religion than ours," or even as the son of "an important gunbearer in the village in*

Africa from which he comes." Other texts mention that the daughter has been diagnosed with syphilis as well as being pregnant, or that the fiancé cannot marry her until his "minor infection" allows him to pass the state's blood test. The photocopied sheets upon which the letters are distributed are often titled "Perspective—writer unknown."

"The Barometer Problem"

I heard this story while attending San Jose State University in 1975. One of the questions on a physics final exam asked the students to measure the height of a building using a barometer. Not having studied the chapter on pressure changes with altitude, one student thought for a moment and then wrote: "Take the barometer to the top of the building to be measured. Throw it off. Using a stopwatch, time its descent and from that data compute the height of the building."

The professor was not impressed, and graded the student's response as incorrect. The student protested to the teacher and was reluctantly given another chance to answer the question.

The second time he wrote, "Take the barometer to the basement of the building to be measured. Find the building superintendent or manager, and tell him you will give him the barometer if he tells you the correct height of the building."

It wasn't said whether the professor was impressed with this second response.

Sent to me in 1989 by Steve Butler of San Clemente, California. If the professor had failed to be impressed by the student's second effort, he might have liked one of the other "wrong answers" sometimes mentioned in this story. These alternate solutions involve lowering the barometer from the roof on a rope and measuring the rope, suspending the barometer on a string as a pendulum and calculating the height based on the pendulum's swing, measuring the shadows of the barometer and the building from the same base and calculating the height, or measuring the side of the building in units of "one barometer" as the student climbs the steps from bottom to top. College students tend to circulate this story in order to illustrate the arbitrary nature of testing, while faculty members may tell the story to demonstrate the possibilities of creative thinking.

"Term Paper Trickery"

In 1984 when I was a senior at Regis Jesuit High School in Denver my English teacher was a faculty member from the associated Regis College. On the first day he felt compelled to warn us about plagiarism, and he told us the following story, which we all believed to be true, as I assumed the teacher himself did.

He said there was a teacher who had an introductory college English class similar to the one we were in. This teacher gave the class a term paper assignment, and when the papers were graded and being returned to the class he asked to see one of the students after class. This particular student had bought a term paper through the mail, and then had submitted it as his own.

After class the teacher told the student flat out that he had plagiarized the paper. The student instinctively denied it, but the teacher insisted, and eventually the student admitted the truth and asked how the teacher had known that he had copied it.

The teacher replied, "Because it is a chapter out of my own master's thesis."

A grading story that was told as true at my high school in Oakland, California, in 1957–58. There was a legend about one of our biology teachers, that he never read the middle of a paper, only the beginning and the end. Supposedly, one student a few years ahead of my class had put the theory to the test by turning in a biology paper with a brilliant beginning, a fantastic ending, and the Gettysburg Address in the middle. It was graded F, with the comment, "Ha, ha; I do too read the middle part."

Stories of resubmitted term papers—inevitably recognized by the instructors—are common on college and high school campuses, even more so in these days of Internet sources of research papers. The first example above was sent to me by Matthew S. Christensen of Durham, North Carolina, in 1990. Variations on the theme include stories in which the paper receives a high grade, despite the teacher's awareness that it was not original, since, as he comments, "I like this paper better every time I read it," or "I got only a B-minus when I wrote this twenty years ago, but I thought it deserved an A." The second term paper story above was sent to me by Melanie Nickel of San Diego, California, in 1991. The student's attempted trickery represents what I call the "Gotcha!" ploy: the writer inserts a garbled sentence, a repeated paragraph, a meaningless footnote, or an upside-down page just to check whether his or her paper is actually read in full by the teacher. When I was editor of an academic journal some years ago I received a few manuscripts with one page upside down; my practice was to reverse a different page before mailing back a rejected manuscript.

"The Bird Foot Exam"

It seems that this college student needed a small two-hour course to fill out his schedule. The only one that fit was in Wildlife Zoology. He had some reservations, as he heard the course was tough and the teacher a bit different. But it seemed like the only choice, so he signed up.

After one week and one chapter the professor had a test for the class. He passed it out, and it was a sheet of paper divided into squares and in each square was a carefully drawn picture of some bird legs. Not bodies, not feet—just different bird's legs. The test simply asked them to identify the birds from the pictures of their legs.

Well, he was absolutely floored. He didn't have a clue. The student sat and stared at the test and got madder and madder. Finally, reaching the boiling point, he stomped up to the front of the classroom and threw the test on the teacher's desk and exclaimed, "This is the worst test I have ever seen, and this is the dumbest course I have ever taken."

The teacher picked up the paper, saw that the student hadn't even put his name on the paper, and said, "By the way, young man, what's your name?" At this the student bent over, pulled up his pants, revealed his legs and said, "You identify me."

Usually in this story the test does *reveal the birds' feet, sometimes using stuffed birds lined up under little bags rather than drawings. This example is from* Parables, etc.: A Monthly Resource Letter for Pastors/Teacher/Speakers, *vol. 4, no. 11, January 1985. An alternate punch line is "You tell me prof!" The "What's your name" theme also appears in the next story, yet another student commentary on the supposed arbitrary nature of college testing and grading.*

"Do You Know Who I Am?"

To the Editor: As an undergraduate studying folklore at Harvard-Radcliffe 10 years ago, I was naturally interested in tales of student excuses, true or untrue. To those you report in "Beyond 'Dog Ate My Homework'" (Education page, April 28), I add [this] from my informal fieldwork:

(1) During an exam, a proctor sees one student who is obviously cheat-

ing. When the exam is over and the students hand in their blue books, the proctor pulls the cheater aside: "I'll take that book, please. I saw you cheating."

The student stares the proctor right in the eye: "Cheating? I? Have you *any* idea who I am?" "No," says the proctor. "Good!" says the student—and grabs a stack of blue books, throws them into the air with his own and runs from the room. . . .

From a letter to the editor of the New York Times *by Ellen Schorr of New York City, published on May 14, 1993. Other versions of "Do You Know . . ." describe the officious proctor refusing to accept an examination paper because the student did not stop writing immediately when time was called. The clever student may simply stick his blue book into the pile of look-alike books, or, if the blue books are thrown in the air, the time may be just before winter vacation, and the student says "Merry Christmas, Prof.!" before waltzing out of the room, free and clear. Stephen G. Bates of Cambridge, Massachusetts, wrote me in 1989 saying that his father told a variation of this academic legend 25 years earlier, in which a young assistant professor complained to a woman next to him at a University of Chicago reception about President Hutchins's interminable faculty meetings. The woman asked, "Do you know who I am? I am Mrs. Robert Hutchins." The faculty member replied, "Do you know who I am?" and, of course, she did not. Comedian Buddy Hackett, among others, has told the military variation of the story in which a saucy private working in the motor pool inadvertently insults a general who has called to reserve a car. The general, infuriated, asks "Do you know who this is?" General so and so, of course. "Do you know who* this *is?" asks the private, and the rest is folklore.*

"Tricky Q & A"

A friend in Dayton, Ohio, told me a story that he had heard at work. His friend had heard it from another friend who swore it was true. There were these two seniors at Stanford University taking a chemistry class from a rather witty teacher named Professor Bonk. Students even called his popular class "Bonk-istry." The night before the final exam these two seniors on a lark decided to go to Lake Tahoe and gamble. Well, the worst happened, and they slept through their chemistry final exam the next day.

So they decided to tell Professor Bonk that they missed the class because they were out of town the night before, and while driving to the exam that day their car had a flat tire. Prof. Bonk took pity and scheduled them a make-up exam the next day.

The two students were administered the make-up exam in separate rooms. The first section of the test was simple chemistry true/false worth 10% of the test score. The second section was an essay worth 90% of the test, and the question was "Which tire was flat?"

I first heard this story at Oxford 1983 when I was studying for my "A" levels (entrance exam). Later at the University of Kent as an undergraduate, I heard it a couple more times.

A young woman, setting her sights on entrance into Oxford as an undergraduate, takes the Oxbridge exam after her "A" levels. This is considered to be the most difficult entrance exam in the Western world.

Her first examination paper is on philosophy, and the first question is "What is courage?" She quickly writes, "This is courage," picks up her bag and coat, and leaves the examination hall. She receives an "A" grade on her paper and is accepted to the college of her choice.

Ask Marilyn: Not long ago, you printed a letter from a girl who said her philosophy teacher gave a test that consisted of one question: "Why?" I liked your disapproving answer, but I'm surprised you didn't mention that the story is an urban myth.

—Trister Keane, Brooklyn, N.Y.

It's no myth—as you'd know if you read my mail. Many people wrote to relate their own distressing experiences taking this "test."

Some had answered "Because" and received no credit because the teacher said the correct answer was "Why not?" Others had answered "Why Not?" and received no credit because the answer was "Because." One person answered "Just because," earning only partial credit and a detailed explanation of why her reply fell short of the ideal. But all had one feeling in common: They hoped their teachers saw my column that week. (And a few were going to forward it to them, "just to be sure")

A final exam had just one question: "Write the best possible final exam question for this course, then answer it."

One student immediately wrote, "The best possible final exam question for this course is 'Write the best possible final exam question for this course, then answer it.'"

In the end, you really never know what they're looking for" [on graduate school entrance exam essays], the first woman said wearily. "There's this famous Yale application question, 'Ask something and then answer it.' So this guy writes, 'Do you play the tuba?' and he answers, 'No.' And he gets accepted."

"That," the second woman said dismissively, "is an urban myth."

Reprinted with special permission of King Features Syndicate

These are a sampling of the many stories about supposed tricky questions and answers among college faculty and students. The version of "Which tire?" came from David W. Stultz of Nineveh, Indiana, in 1995. Most versions that mention "Professor Bonk" set the story at Duke University where a chemistry professor by that name teaches and may actually have asked that question of two erring students. However, the story is widely told on many campuses about a variety of other subjects as well. My example of the "Why?" examination comes from Marilyn vos Savant's Parade *magazine column of March 29, 1992, but she originally discussed the story way back on May 26, 1991. I have heard of instances of professors using the "Why?" question, but never of any who based a course grade or final examination grade on the answer. In my humble opinion, these teachers were inspired by having heard this old campus legend during their own undergraduate days, and they asked the question more as a prank than a real test. The "What is courage?" example came from John Longenbaugh of Sitka, Alaska, in 1991; this is an international story that I've heard from New Zealand and Italy, as well as the United States and Canada. I'm told that the French version asks for a definition of* "L'audace," *with the entire winning answer being* "L'audace—c'ést ça!" *In yet another version of the story, the requirement is to write a five-page answer; a student writes "This is courage" and attaches five blank pages. The "Write your own question" topic is used occasionally on exams by some instructors, but the student's witty response quoted above, as I've heard it several times, is probably a legend. The story about the Yale application question is from "Interview Jitters at Graduate School," by Susan Schnur in the* New York Times, *April 10, 1994.*

"The Second Blue Book"

I did hear, just yesterday, of a student at an East Coast college who asked for two blue books during a final exam. When the test ended, he handed in only one. He had written a note on the first page and left the rest of the book blank. "Dear Mom," it said, "Just finished Psych 101 and want to tell you that I love you."

Taking the other blue book home, he completed the exam, with the help of his textbooks, and mailed it to his mother. His professor called to ask about the mixup. The student feigned astonishment, then dismay. Retrieving the mailed blue book from his mother, he turned it in and, yes, got an A.

Quoted from Jon Anderson's article on scams published in the Chicago Tribune *in December 1990 and reprinted elsewhere the same month. In most versions of this classic campus legend the student writes a longer letter to his mother, lavishly praising the professor and the course. Then he asks his professor to verify his story by calling or writing his mother and arranging a swap of the two blue books. There are other blue book scam stories, two of which I quote in* The Mexican Pet *from a 1970 article. Students should not try this ploy in their own examinations, since most professors have heard the stories before, and the rest are likely to figure out on their own what the student is up to. As for examinations in general, here's a well-known professorial principle: If you say "This is important" the A student writes it down. If you write it on the blackboard, the B student writes it down. If you say, "This is very important," and write it on the blackboard, the C student writes it down. And if you say, "This will be on the final exam," the D student asks you to repeat it.*

23

"True" Urban Legends

In a sense, *all* urban legends are at least partly true, for as folklorist Linda Dégh has pointed out, these stories inevitably include "two kinds of so-called reality factors." First, we find ample instances of what Dégh called "verifiable facts commonly known to be true" (like the existence of crime, pets, freeways, shopping malls, baby-sitters, college professors, embarrassing moments, sex scandals, and many other realistic details of everyday experience). Second, the legends incorporate "illusions, commonly believed to be true" (such as the operation of poetic justice, the likelihood of incredible coincidences, the possibility of someone mistaking a rat for a dog, the leaving behind of incriminating notes or photos by criminals, and the frequent flushing of unwanted reptile pets down the toilet). Put the facts and the illusions together with the skills of a good narrator, and you have believable, and even partly "true," urban legends.

However, the truth factor in urban legends is most often simply a matter of people not questioning the teller's details while trusting that narrator's supposedly reliable sources. People believe an urban legend because the plot stays within the realm of possibility—no alien invaders, psychic powers, or sea monsters—and the storyteller is someone "who would never lie" and who can cite the authority of that famous "friend of a friend" to whom this remarkable thing actually happened. Parodying this rather naive attitude, a Boulder, Colorado, humor periodical called the *Onion* (which has the audacity to bill itself as "America's Finest News Source") in March 1977 published this item:

"URBAN LEGENDS TRUE," SAYS FRIEND OF COUSIN'S ROOMMATE

Chicago—According to a study released Sunday by the friend of this one guy's roommate, contemporary word-of-mouth folklore, or "urban legends," are true. While not actually heard first-hand, the guy said, "Though typically met with skepticism, urban legends are almost always true. Like the one about the guy whose friends threw him a surprise party, but he was naked. I know for a fact that that's a true story—my sister's ex-boyfriend was at that party." The guy also said that a child actually did die from consuming Pop Rocks candy with Coca-Cola, claiming that "it was in the paper."

There are some who would respond to such a ludicrous statement that any comments about the truth or falsity of urban legends are moot, since legends are by definition untrue. Others would assert that since we are studying *stories,* not actual incidents, it makes no difference whether any of these stories—or parts of stories—happen to be true. In any case, in this chapter are discussed half a dozen stories that seem typically urban-legendary, but for which there is some actual truth component. Oddly, in most cases, it takes more length and detail to prove this point than it normally does simply to debunk a story.

"True Stories, Or At Least Good Urban Legends Dept."

From Steve Orthwein at The Edge: *A woman calls an import parts warehouse and asks for a 28-ounce water pump. "A what?" says the confused parts guy. "My husband says he needs a 28-ounce water pump." "A 28-ounce water pump? What kind of car does it fit?" "A Datsun." As he writes down "Datsun, 28 oz. water pump" the light in his head goes on. "Oh yes ma'am. We've got 28-ounce water pumps. We have 24-ounce and 26-ounce water pumps, too." "Finally," she says. "You're the first place I've called that knew what I was talking about." "Yes, ma'am. That's because we're a full-service parts warehouse. It's our job to have the parts you need, like a 28-ounce water pump," he says, smiling, as he jots down: customer pickup, Datsun 280Z water pump, part number. . . .*

(In Autoweek, *January 12, 1998.)*

"The Pregnant Shoplifter"

An Arlington [Virginia] woman has filed suit against a Seven Corners sporting goods store, claiming a store employee forced her to prove she was pregnant because he thought she was shoplifting a basketball.

Betsy J. Nelson, 33, who was nine months pregnant when she went shopping at Irving's Sport Shop last February, is seeking $100,000 in compensatory damages and $500,000 in punitive damages from the store, charging false arrest and negligence on the part of store employees, according to a suit filed in Arlington Circuit Court last week. . . .

From an article by Nancy Scannell, Washington Post, *July 19, 1985. I was pretty darn sure that this story was apocryphal when it started going around in 1985. Herb Caen of the* San Francisco Chronicle *likewise had commented, on September 12, 1985, "Too neat. Sounds like a fable." I included a skeptical reference to the story in* The Mexican Pet. *I immediately heard from readers who sent me newspaper clippings—such as the one quoted above—providing names, dates, places, and other authenticating information. I admitted my error in* Curses! Broiled Again! *and now it's time to close the books, so to speak, on this incident. Here's the rest of the story: the* Washington Post *reported on November 19, 1986, that a circuit court jury in Arlington had rejected the claim of false arrest and negligence brought by Ms. Nelson, and the judge dismissed her claim for punitive damages. That's the truth, but let me warn you that if you hear a story about the woman trying to steal a watermelon from a supermarket by hiding it under her dress and claiming to be pregnant, or the one about the frozen chicken hidden under the shoplifter's hat, I'm 99 percent sure these are just urban legends.*

"The Unsolvable Math Problem"

What happened to George B. Dantzig in 1940, in his own words:

During my first year at Berkeley I arrived late one day at one of [Professor Jerzy] Neyman's classes. On the blackboard there were two problems that I assumed had been assigned for homework. I copied them down. A few days later I apologized to Neyman for taking so long to do the homework—the problems seemed to be a little harder to do than usual. I asked him if he still wanted it. He told me to throw it on his desk. I did so reluctantly because his desk was covered with such a heap of papers that I feared my homework would be lost there forever. About six weeks later, one Sunday morning about eight o'clock, Anne and I were awakened by someone banging on our front door. It was Neyman. He rushed in with papers in hand, all excited: "I've just written an introduction to one of your papers. Read it so I can send it out right away for publication." For a minute I had no idea what he was talking about. To make a long story short, the problems on the blackboard that I had solved thinking they were homework were in fact two famous unsolved problems in statistics. That was the first inkling I had that there was anything special about them.

As reported by Rev. Robert H. Schuller in a 1983 book:

Let me tell you about myself. My name is George Danzig [*sic*], and I am in the physics department at Stanford University. I've just returned from Vienna as the American delegate to the International Mathematics Convention, appointed by the President. I was a senior at Stanford during the Depression; we knew when the class graduated, we'd all be joining unemployment lines. There was a slim chance that the top man in class might get a teaching job, but that was about it. I wasn't at the head of my class, but I hoped that if I were able to score a perfect paper on the final exam, I might be given a job opportunity.

I studied so hard for that exam, I ended up making it to class late. When I arrived, the others were already hard at work; I was embarrassed and just picked up my paper and slunk in to my desk. I sat down and worked the eight problems on the test paper and then started in on the two that were written up on the board. Try as I might, I couldn't solve either one of them. I was devastated; out of ten problems, I had missed two for sure. But just as I was about to hand in the paper, I took a chance and asked the professor if I might have a couple days to work on the two I had missed. I was surprised when he agreed, and I rushed home and plunged into those equations with a vengeance. I spent hours and hours, and finally solved one of them. I never could get the other. And when I turned in that paper, I knew I had lost all chance of a job. That was the blackest day of my life.

The next morning I was awakened by a pounding on the door. It was my professor, all dressed up and very excited. "George, George," he kept shouting, "you've made mathematics history!" Well, I didn't know what he was talking about. And then he explained. I had come to class late and had missed his opening remarks. He had been encouraging the class to keep trying, not to give up if they found some of the problems difficult. "Don't put yourself down," he had said. "Remember there are classic, unsolvable problems that no one can solve. Even Einstein was unable to unlock their secrets." And then he had written two of these unsolvable problems on the blackboard. When I came in I didn't know they were unsolvable. I thought they were part of my exam, and I was determined that I could work them properly. And I solved one! It was published in the *International Journal of Higher Mathematics,* and my professor gave me a job as his assistant. I've been at Stanford for forty-three years now. . . . Dr. Schuller, I'm just going to ask you one question. If I had come to class on time, do you think I would have solved that problem? I don't.

Schuller's version as presented to pastors in 1983:
Speaking of mathematics, Robert Schuller, of Chrystal [*sic*] Cathedral fame tells a story about sitting on a plane next to a fellow with his nose in a book. . . . Schuller said he wrote books on Possibility Thinking but admitted that they probably had nothing in common as "in mathematics it doesn't matter whether you are a possibility thinker or an impossibility thinker. Two plus two equals four regardless of whether you are a negative or a positive person."

"Well, I'm not so sure about that," his seat partner interrupted him. "Let me tell you about myself . . ." etc.

How Schuller's version got back to George Dantzig (again, in his own words):

The other day, as I was taking an early morning walk, I was hailed by Don Knuth as he rode by on his bicycle. He is a colleague at Stanford. He stopped and said, "Hey George—I was visiting in Indiana recently and heard a sermon about you in church. Do you know that you are an influence on Christians of middle America?" I looked at him amazed. "After the sermon," he went on, "the minister came over and asked me if I knew a George Dantzig at Stanford, because that was the name of the person his sermon was about."

The origin of that minister's sermon can be traced to another Lutheran minister, the Reverend Schuler [*sic*] of the Crystal Cathedral in Los Angeles. Several years ago he and I happened to have adjacent seats on an airplane. He told me his ideas about thinking positively, and I told him my story about the homework problems and my thesis. A few months later I received a letter from him asking permission to include my story in a book he was writing on the power of positive thinking. Schuler's published version was a bit garbled and exaggerated but essentially correct.

How a Texas churchgoer reported it:

My mother related this to me as she had heard it in a sermon in Fort Worth, Texas. A young man in college was working very hard to prove himself, studying 'til all hours to learn as much as was humanly possible. He was taking a course in upper-level math that he was very much concerned about for fear that he would not be able to pass. He studied for the final so long and so hard that he overslept on the morning of the final.

He ran into the examination room several minutes late and found three equations to solve on the blackboard. The first two went by rather easily, but the third one was impossible. He worked frantically on it until, ten minutes short of the deadline, he found a method that worked and finished the problem just as time was called. He was very disappointed in himself that such a seemingly easy problem had taken him so long to figure out.

Then, that evening he received a phone call from his professor. "Do you realize what you did on the test today?" he practically shouted at the student. "Oh, no," thought the student, "I didn't get the problem right after all."

"You were only supposed to do the first two problems," the professor continued. "The last one was just one that I wrote to show an equation that mathematicians since Einstein have been trying to solve, without success. And you just solved it!"

Although I traced the path of this academic story in Curses! Broiled Again! *I presented there only paraphrases of the various retellings of George Dantzig's experience. The full verbatim accounts quoted here are well worth comparing in order to note the numerous variations of detail that have occurred. Dantzig's accounts above of the class and of the meeting with Schuller are quoted from an interview published in the September 1986 issue of the* College Mathematics Journal. *Schuller's version, undoubtedly also included in at least one of his televised programs, is quoted from Michael and Donna Nason's 1983 book* Robert Schuller: The Inside Story. *In the same year, the Schuller story was presented to pastors in the September issue of the newsletter* Parables, etc. *The Texas minister's version of the story was sent to me in 1982 by Marc Hairston, then a student at Rice University in Houston. For the record, here are a few corrections and clarifications: 1. George Dantzig is in the Department of Operations Research at Stanford; 2. Schuller's "Crystal Cathedral" is in Garden Grove, California; 3. Dantzig's solution of the first problem was published in* Annals of Mathematical Statistics, *vol. 22, 1951; and 4. Dantzig, at the time of the incident, was a beginning graduate student at Berkeley. When I met Professor Dantzig—"the father of linear programming"—at Stanford in 1991, he explained several points in the story that were still vague to me even after receiving his 1987 letter in reply to my queries. The second problem he had solved, for example, was published jointly with Abraham Wald in 1951; Wald had arrived at a solution independently and by a different method. This whole incident provides a fine example of how a personal experience, repeated several times in different contexts, and circulating in both printed and oral sources, may eventually achieve a new life of its own as a folk story, although, as Dantzig gently pointed out to me, I should have titled it more correctly as "The* Previously *Unsolvable Math Problem." In 1989 Dean Oisboid of Los Angeles sent me this variation of the story that he heard in the early 1970s from a junior high school mathematics teacher:*

> *This gifted Indian student rushed in late to class and hastily scribbled down the 10 homework problems that were on the board. The next day the student approached the teacher and complained that the homework was too hard.*
>
> *"Homework? What homework?" asked the teacher.*
>
> *"The problems on the board," replied the student.*
>
> *"Those weren't homework problems. Those were 10 unsolvable problems of mathematics."*
>
> *"Oh!" said the student. Then giving his homework to the teacher, he continued, "I solved 9 of them."*

I wonder what the odds are of this as an independent invention versus being yet another version of the Dantzig story. That's a question far beyond my own mathematical ability, if you'll pardon my impossibility thinking. I enjoyed yet another version of the story when I saw the 1997 hit film Good Will Hunting.

"The Heel in the Grate"

A query from Seattle, 1986:

Dear Professor: My aunt told this story in the late 1950s:

She said that during a local wedding one of the bridesmaids got the spike heel of her shoe caught in a ventilation grate in the aisle. The next usher coming down the aisle tried to pick up the shoe; the entire grate came up, so he just took it with him.

Then the bride came down the aisle and fell in the hole. Was my aunt suckered by an urban legend?

Joyce D. Kehoe

A reaction to this story, from Dayton, Ohio, 1987:

Dear Professor: That story in your column today is an old tale indeed! The version I heard many years ago concerned a church choir processing down the aisle with the soprano losing her heel in a grate, the Tenor lifting the entire grate and the Minister falling into the hole.

Carol G. Alexander

Another reaction to the story, from San Diego, California, 1987:

I read that story in *Reader's Digest,* probably about 1950! In that case it was the choir making its processional: someone's heel caught in the grill, she kept on walking without her shoe, the man next in line picked up the grill, and the person behind him fell in. I recall getting an enormous kick out of the story at that time, as the incident was well written. The choir was solemn, never missing a beat until the last person fell in—you could just picture the scene.

Marlene Carey

From *Reader's Digest,* January 1958:

Chain Reaction

It started at the end of a Sunday morning service in an Ontario Church.

The Choir began the recessional, singing as they marched in perfect unison up the center aisle to the back of the church.

The last young lady in the women's section was wearing a new pair of shoes with needle heels—heels that are so slender they slip through any grating. And in the aisle was a grating that covered the hot-air register.

Without a thought for her fancy heels, the young woman sang and marched. And the heel of one shoe sank right through a hole in the register grate. Instantly she realized her predicament. She knew she couldn't hold up the whole recessional while she back-stepped to pull out her heel. She did the next best thing in the emergency. Without missing a step she slipped her foot out of her shoe and continued up the aisle. There wasn't a break in the recessional. Everything moved like clockwork.

The first man following that young woman noted the situation and, without losing a beat, reached down and picked up her shoe.

The entire grate came with it. Startled but still singing, the man continued up the aisle bearing in his hand one grate attached to one shoe.

Never a break in the recessional. Everybody singing. Everything moving like clockwork. And then in tune and in time to the beat, the next man stepped into the open register.

—*Kitchener-Waterloo (Ontario) Record,* quoted in *The Lutheran*

Comments by Marj Heyduck's *The Best of Marj: Favorite "Third and Main" columns (Dayton [Ohio] Journal Herald,* 1962):

This story not only produced outburts of laughter in *The Journal Herald*'s circulation area . . . but was reprinted in dozens of church publications in the United States and Canada . . . in *Reader's Digest* . . . it produced a sequel that has given me a sure-fire ending to any speech . . . and, a sure sign of humor, it's a story that bubbles up again and again as a new audience grows up to hear it . . . [this passage is punctuated with ellipses exactly as in the original].

[After re-checking with her source, "Woody" Jones, and retelling the story, Marj Heyduck concluded as follows, supposedly quoting the man who fell into the open register]:

"Well, we settled down and when the director was satisfied, he turned to the minister and nodded. That was the minister's cue to give the benediction. And the minister forgot what he was going to say. He opened his mouth but nothing came out. You could see his mind had gone blank. Then, he said the first thing that came to him.

"He said, 'And now unto Him who will keep us from falling. . . .' And he couldn't go on. He realized what he had said and he started to laugh. So did the choir. So did the congregation. And it was getting to be a happy day all around—except for the choir director. He was simply furious. His eyes blazed and smoke came out of his ears!"

A comment from Woodfin B. ("Woody") Jones of Tipp City, Ohio, 1987: Concerning "The Heel in the Grate" story, Mr. Brunvand, the incident occurred in the Hanover Presbyterian Church in Hanover, Indiana, home of Hanover College, during the 1948–49 school year.

I have a kind of proprietary feeling about the story. I told it to Marj Heyduck, but the story lay dormant until 1957 when she used it in her "Third & Main" column in *The* [Dayton] *Journal Herald,* the first time, to my knowledge, that it had been printed. Marj died several years ago [in 1969], but she is fondly remembered throughout the Miami Valley. This was one of the most requested stories when she made speeches in Dayton and the Valley.

I enclose the addresses of two of the principals in the incident, The Rev. James A. Stuckey and Edwin C. Steiner.

Testimonial from James A. Stuckey, originally written in 1980 and sent to me in 1987:

I, James Albert Stuckey, was a member of the Hanover College Choir in the spring of 1949 who, during the recessional, happened to spy the shoe of a female member of the choir (so I assumed) caught in the grate of the hot air register in the center of the aisle of the Hanover Presbyterian Church. Being the kind of courteous, thoughtful freshman so highly prized in those days, I, of course, stopped to retrieve the shoe. I got it, and the grate, tucked both under my copy of *The Hymnal* (1933), and continued down the aisle. The minister's wife, who had seen all this, guided the singer behind me around the pit (one Ed Bockstiegel), but Ed Steiner, the next bass in line, fell in. The minister (John Fox) did *not* pronounce, "Now onto Him who is able to keep us from falling . . ." as the benediction. Ruth Murphy was glad to get her shoe back.

Testimonial from Ed Steiner, 1987:

Yes, it certainly was I who fell into that hot air duct. . . . As we were recessing I happened to look over and see Mrs. Parker [wife of Hanover College president] singing in her pew. I started to smile at her when a very strange look came over her face, and she started to shake her head at me. I was trying to figure out what the problem was, and I was completely distracted from what was going on in front of me. Needless to say, before I figured things out, I had stepped in the hole! There was absolutely no physical warning; I hit the hole cleanly; I didn't even scrape my toe on the edge of the hole. It was like stepping off a gigantic stairstep, and I went into the hole all the way up to my thigh.

. . . I just dragged myself, completely unhurt, out of the hole, picked up my music and proceeded to the back of the church.

A final (?) comment from a reader, 1993:

Dear Professor: While the 1949–50 story told you by Rev. Stuckey concerning the "Heel in the Grate" (*Curses! Broiled Again!*) may have happened then, if so, it was the second occurrence. I can vouch for the fact that it happened in the fall of 1943 or '44 because I was the soprano in the Hanover, Indiana, Presbyterian Church choir whose shoe caught in the grate. One of the men behind me in the choir processional attempted to retrieve the shoe, but only succeeded in tipping the grate. (The grate was quite large and heavy.)

During the recessional one of the men stepped on the grate which tipped and sent him to his knees. He quickly recovered, which is more than I can say about the rest of us when the minister started the benediction, "And now to Him who is able to keep us from falling," etc.

Helen T. Ramsey
Denver, Colorado

The above selections comprise the most complete account of the history of this incident (or incidents?) and the resulting story versions. The letter from Helen Ramsey is published here for the first time, and it throws the question of this story's ultimate origin and history back into confusion. If nothing else, the story presented above—if, indeed, this is *finally the whole story—raises the question of why the Hanover Presbyterian Church did not fix its serious problem during the 1940s with a dangerous grate in the center aisle until years later. Perhaps they never did fix the grate, and similar accidents have continued to occur. Someday I hope to visit that church and check out the physical scene in person. Meanwhile, it is important to note, both in this "true" legend and the previous one, the important role played by the media in circulating and varying the stories. Finally, I must point out that the "heel-in-grate" incident appeared in a completely different context—that of a "clean room" of a space-travel center—in the 1966 film* The Glass Bottom Boat, *starring Doris Day (who lost her heel), Rod Taylor, Dick Martin (who stepped into the opening), and Arthur Godfrey.*

"Craig's World-Record Collection"

A memo circulated in Cambridge, Massachusetts, 1990:

I would be grateful if you and your organization could respond to this request to help Craig Shergold.

Craig is a seven year old boy who has a brain tumor and has very little time left to live. It is his dream to have an entry in the Guiness Book of World Records for the largest number of get well cards ever received by an individual.

If you are willing to help and also willing to share this note with your staff, you may sends [*sic*] cards to:

Craig Shergold
38 Shelby Road
Carshalton
Surrey SN8 1LD
United Kingdom

Please add to and send the attached pages to another ten school districts, companies, or organizations of your choice.

A letter sent to customers of a San Diego, California, company, 1991:

I am sure that you receive many requests for your time and energies and I realize that you get pulled in may [*sic*] different directions. However, I hope that you will find the time to help fulfill this somewhat simple request.

Craig Shergold is a seven year old child from Surrey, England, who is suffering from terminal cancer. It is his wish to be included in the Guinness Book of Records with the largest number of business cards collected by one person. Please help fulfill this request by sending one of your business cards to Craig at the address below and by sending this letter to ten other individuals. If only we could meet the needs of all children so simply . . .

Craig Shergold
36 Sherlby Road
Carshalton
Surrey SN 1 1LD, England
DO NOT MAIL THIS LETTER TO CRAIG

A leaflet faxed to a hospital in Bakersfield, California, 1996:

Children's Wish Foundation Request

Craig Shirgold is a 7 year old boy who lives in Keene, NH. He is dying from an inoperable brain tumor. He made a wish to Children's Wish Foundation that he wants one million get well cards sent to him by

August 15th 1996

so that he can make the World Book of Records before he dies. Cards can be made or bought. PLEASE send the cards to this following address:

Craig Shirgold
C/O Children's Wish Foundation
32 Perimeter Center East
Atlanta, Georgia 30346

REX USA LTD.

Please pass this on to anyone you feel might help make this little boy's wish come true. [The leaflet is framed by tiny outlines of a child, and at the bottom of the sheet is printed "Thanks, K. Lee," followed by a hand-drawn heart.]

Clipped from a school newsletter, date and place unknown:

Attention Students:

Craig Shirgold is a 14 year old boy who has a brain tumor and has no chance of getting well. His last wish is to receive 1 million letters or greeting cards. This is your chance to grant a very important wish. It won't take up too much of your time to write a few words.

Thanks a bunch!

[signed by two students]

Send to:

Craig Shirgold [followed by the Atlanta address in the above example]

PS: Please tell everyone you know (including adults).

True? How could it be, with all those variations in age, disease, and addresses? I have left off specific sources so as not to embarrass the many people who have sent cards to Craig and circulated appeals for more cards. The above items are just a tiny sample from my ten-inch thick file of letters, E-mails, faxes, leaflets, and clippings documenting the Craig Shergold story. Or is it the Craig "Sherhold," "Shargold," or "Shirgold" story? And does he live on "Shelby," "Sherlby," "Selby," or "South Selby Rd." at number 26, 35, 36, 37, 38, 56, or 90? Is it "Surrey," "Surry," or "Surreny"; and is the town "Carshalton," "Charshalton," "Carshaulton," "Carshelton," "Carshaltonn," or even "Cahchalton," England? The English postal codes listed also vary greatly. One version of the address even has him living in "Surry, British Columbia" in Canada, and then there's that reference to Keene, New Hampshire. While some letters simply ask for cards or letters to be sent via an agency in Atlanta, Georgia, other letters claim that Craig himself lives in Atlanta. There's also some variation on the address in Georgia, whether "Perimeter" or "Parameter" Avenue (or "Center") and whether at number 32, 3200, or 321. So what's the truth behind it all?

Craig Shergold's supposed appeal for postcards, greeting cards, get-well cards, or business cards is a case of life imitating legend. What started as a fictional, but heartwarming, story about bringing happiness to a sick child turned into a nightmare when the flood of mail became overwhelming. Craig's card collection eventually reached 33 million pieces, as reported in the December 24, 1990, issue of Time *magazine, and his family has been trying for months to shut off the flow.*

The saga began in 1982 when a mythical child known as "Little Buddy" was rumored to be pursuing a nonexistent record. Supposedly, this leukemia patient in Paisley, Scotland, wanted to break the record for number of postcards received as listed in the Guinness Book of World Records. *There was no such record, yet millions of cards flooded in from well-wishers around the world, swamping the Paisley post office. There was no "Little Buddy" to whom the mail could be delivered.*

The appeal circulated by word of mouth, mail, CB radio, and in the press. Then, in 1988, attention shifted to Mario Morby, a young English cancer patient. Mario announced that he wanted to beat the record he had heard about, and hordes of people sent him cards, either directly or through foundations that adopted his cause.

Mario's name and his record of 1,000,265 postcards appeared in the 1989 Guinness book under the category "Collections." But the flood of cards kept coming, and computer networks began to publicize the appeal. The postcards kept on arriving in ever-increasing numbers, much to the distress of everyone who had to deal with them. Before this stage of the card appeal slacked off, a rumor surfaced that Mario had died when a huge pile of mail sacks fell on him. Even the 1991 Old Farmer's Almanac *printed this story.*

Enter Craig Shergold of Carshalton, England, then a seven-year-old cancer patient, who in September 1989 set out to beat Mario's postcard record. People enthusiastically shifted their efforts to Craig, and by November he had received over 1.5 million cards, a new record certified by Guinness.

Besides mail and computerized circulation of Craig's appeal, a chain letter began to be faxed through business channels, each letter asking recipients to forward ten more copies. Craig's surname, address, illness, and collecting goal all varied in these letters, but they quite consistently described him as seven years old and dying. In the United States some companies set up collection boxes in which employees were invited to leave cards to be sent to Craig, and at least one store printed the Craig appeal on its cash-register receipts in 1990.

Thanks to American billionaire John W. Kluge, in March 1991 Craig was brought to the University of Virginia medical center and operated on to remove a benign brain tumor. The June 10, 1991, issue of People *magazine spread the good news with a picture of a smiling Craig surrounded by sacks of unopened mail.*

At that point his family wanted Craig simply to recover, live a normal life, and stop receiving massive card collections from well-meaning but misinformed people. The cards did lift Craig's spirits, and there was another good side to the story: Kluge had heard about Craig and was moved to aid him when he received an appeal to help Craig get into the record book.

Among the scores of articles discussing and debunking the Craig Shergold card appeal are these: John Pekkanen, "The Boy and the Billionaire," Reader's Digest, *March 1991; Charisse Jones, "A Dream Comes True and Comes True . . . ,"* New York Times, *September 1, 1993; and the Phoenix-based Make-A-Wish Foundation Web site at http://www.wish.org/wish/craig.html.*

"Green Stamps"

From Ohio, 1988:

This story was told to me by a friend several years ago; the incident supposedly happened to her aunt.

A woman went for her annual gynecological exam, and she was

extremely nervous, since it was a new doctor whom she had never been examined by before. As usual, she was instructed to go to the bathroom and provide a urine sample.

However, there was no toilet paper in the dispenser, so she reached into her purse and pulled out a tissue to use. Once she was undressed in the examining room the doctor entered and began his exam. When the woman was lying back with her feet in the stirrups the doctor pulled off a couple of S&H Green Stamps that had apparently been stuck to the tissue she used to wipe with, and he held them up and asked, "Excuse me, do you save these?"

This can't possibly be true . . . can it?

Published in 1983:
Giving Away Green Stamps

Dr. Burrand tells the following experience. "I had a lady come in for her annual physical examination.

My nurse had her remove all her clothes and get up on the examination table.

Almost at once she asked to be excused to go to the toilet. Unfortunately the paper holder was empty and instead of calling the nurse for a new roll she removed some tissues from her purse and used them."

"The patient returned to the examining room and got back on the table, then called the nurse who called me," said Dr. Burrand. The nurse kept the patient draped with the sheet but had her put her feet up in the stirrups for a vaginal examination. When I lifted the sheet to examine the patient, I was amazed and then amused to see a block of green trading stamps stuck to her butt. Apparently when she took the kleenex tissues from her purse, some green stamps clung to the tissues and were transferred to the patient's skin without her knowledge," said Dr. Burrand.

"Well, Mrs. Patient," I said, "I know many people have a gimmick for various items for sale, but I don't know what you're using green stamps as a gimmick for, as I don't know what you're selling!" laughed the doctor.

Published in 1988:
And double coupons, too?

A patient told me recently about her trip to the gynecologist for a routine Pap smear. Sent to the lavatory to provide a urine sample, she found no tissue, so she dug around in her purse and came up with a Kleenex. Later, during the exam, her doctor remarked, "Well, I've been paid a lot of unusual ways, but this is the first time anyone's offered Green Stamps." The stamps, it seems, had been stuck to the Kleenex.

—Lee A. Fischer, M.D.

A letter from Montana, 1985:

I first heard the Green Stamps story in 1977 or 1978. It was told by a nursing supervisor of a hospital in Champaign, Illinois, who claimed it actually happened to her aunt. I loved the story when I first heard it, and I repeated it to everyone I knew.

About six months later, the same nursing supervisor and I were having lunch with several other people from the nursing office. The nursing supervisor told the Green Stamp story again, but one woman said, very matter of factly, "That story is not true."

The nursing supervisor assured her that it was true, that it had really happened to her aunt. But the other woman insisted that she had heard the same story in Milwaukee some years before. The lunch party broke up with the nursing supervisor firm in the conviction that it had indeed happened to her aunt. The other woman told me later that she was furious with the nursing supervisor because she had so wanted to believe that the story she heard in Milwaukee was true. When she heard the tale repeated, she knew in an instant that the tale was apocryphal.

The first example above came to me from a reader of my newspaper column, then published in the Columbus (Ohio) Dispatch, *who signed the letter only "J.W." Of the 34 items in my Green Stamp file, most are like this version—vague as to place or date and attributed to a FOAF. Specifically, 28 of my filed versions refer only to a FOAF, and they come from all across the United States: from New York to California, New Mexico to Michigan, and Maryland to Texas. Two versions mention "Blue Chip" stamps, and one an Elvis postage stamp; I also have one version from London in which a postage stamp is mentioned. So far, then, the Green Stamp story would appear to be a typical urban legend, but what about these two published versions above, one of which purports to be told directly by the examining physician? The first of these (punctuated exactly as in the original) comes from a small self-published booklet entitled* Medical Mini-Shockers *by Stanley H. Macht, a retired radiologist in Hagerstown, Maryland. Dr. Macht says in his foreword, "These stories are true. They were reported by my colleagues." The second published example comes from the trade magazine* Medical Economics *for October 17, 1988. When I wrote to the editor inquiring about the source, I learned that "the story was simply submitted as an anecdote—a humorous filler. We ask doctors to send us these 'amazing, amusing, embarrassing' little experiences, and we publish some of them." Evidently the story is well known among medical personnel, as the last quoted example above suggests; it came in a letter from Anthony Wellever of Helena, Montana. While neither of the two published versions offers an airtight proof of the incident's truth, I published two detailed accounts that claim to be first-person in* The Mexican Pet. *One was from a woman named Donna Cellar, who described exactly this incident as having happened to her, in the fall of 1963 in Dallas, Texas, and the other was from a woman whom I know very well who looked me straight in the eye and said the incident absolutely had happened to* her *in the late 1950s! This publication led to a number of further reports being sent to me, one of which was dated in the 1950s, and the others in the early 1960s. A typical example: "I heard the Green Stamp story in Glenview, Illinois, a suburb of Chicago, from a woman named Ann Cole that I worked with from December 1, 1962 until May 31, 1963, that is, some time before your Mrs. Celler's experience of Fall, 1963." Another: "I heard the Green Stamp story told as current news from two friends at Charlie Taylor's drug store in Perryton, Texas, in the summer of 1962. It happened to a former high school beauty queen whose maiden name was . . ." (Well, perhaps it's best I do not quote the name). Frankly, at this point, I am not certain whether the Green Stamp story is an actual repeated experience, a mere legend that some women have adopted as "their own story," or, perhaps, even a gynecologist's prank. A final note: The 1990s version of the story circulating orally and on the Internet describes a woman who uses a "feminine hygiene deodorant" from a spray can just before her appointment for a physical exam. But she gets hold of a can of spray-on glitter instead, without noticing her mistake. The doctor comments something like, "Well, aren't we fancy today." Now that one has to be true, right?*

"The Bullet Baby"

From the *American Medical Weekly,* Louisville, Kentucky, November 7, 1874, vol. I, no. 19, pp. 233–34:

Attention Gynæcologists!—Notes from the Diary of a Field And Hospital Surgeon, C.S.A.
By L. G. Capers, M.D., Vicksburg, Mississippi
[Two paragraphs of general discussion of "wonderful stories about 'the war'"]

On the 12th day of May, 1863, the battle of R. was fought. Gen. G.'s brigade met the advance of Grant's army, under Gen. L., about one mile from the village of R. About three hundred yards in rear of my regiment was situated a fine residence, the occupants being a matron, her two daughters, and servants (the host being absent in another army). About 3 o'clock P.M., when the battle was raging most furiously, the above-mentioned lady and her two daughters (aged respectively fifteen and seventeen), filled with interest and enthusiasm, stood bravely in front of their homestead, ready and eager to minister to their wounded countrymen should they fall in the dreadful fray.

Our men were fighting nobly, but pressed by superior numbers, had gradually fallen back to within one hundred and fifty yards of the house. My position being near my regiment, suddenly I beheld a noble, gallant young friend staggering closer, and then fall to the earth. In the same moment a piercing scream from the house reached my ear! I was soon by the side of the young man, and, upon examination, found a compound fracture, with extensive comminution of the left tibia; the ball having ricochetted from these parts, and, in its onward flight, passed through the scrotum, carrying away the left testicle. Scarcely had I finished dressing the wounds of this poor fellow, when the estimable matron came running to me in the greatest distress, begging me to go to one of her daughters, who, she informed me, had been badly wounded a few minutes before. Hastening to the house, I found that the eldest of the young ladies had indeed received a most serious wound. A minnie ball had penetrated the left abdominal parietes, about midway between the umbilicus and anterior spinal process of the ilium, and was lost in the abdominal cavity, leaving a ragged wound behind. Believing there was little or no hope of her recovery, I had only time to prescribe an anodyne, when our army fell back, leaving both field and village in the hands of the enemy.

Having remained with my wounded at the village of R., I had the opportunity of visiting the young lady the next day, and interruptedly, for a period of nearly two months, at the end of which time she had entirely recovered, with no untoward symptoms during treatment; save a severe peritonitis, she seemed as well as ever!

About six months after her recovery, the movements of our army brought me again to the village of R., and I was again sent for to see the young lady. She appeared in excellent health and spirits, but her abdomen had become enormously enlarged, so much so as to resemble pregnancy at the seventh or eighth month. Indeed, had I not known the family and the facts of the abdominal wound, I should have so pronounced the case. Under the above circumstances, I failed to give a positive diagnosis, determining to keep the case under surveillance. This I did.

Just two hundred and seventy-eight days from the date of the receipt of the wound by the minnie ball, I delivered this same young lady of a fine boy, weighing eight pounds. I was not very much surprised; but imagine the surprise and mortification of the young lady herself, her entire family. This can be better imagined than described. Although I found the hymen intact in my examination before delivery, I gave no credence to the earnest and oft-repeated assertions of the young lady of her innocence and virgin purity.

About three weeks from the date of this remarkable birth, I was called to see the child, the grandmother insisting there was "something wrong about the genitals." Examination revealed an enlarged, swollen, sensitive scrotum, containing on the right side a hard, roughened substance, evidently foreign. I decided upon operating for its removal at once, and in so doing, extracted from the scrotum a minnie ball, mashed and battered as if it had met in its flight some hard, unyielding substance.

To attempt to picture my astonishment would be impossible! What may already seem very plain to my readers, as they glance over this paper, was, to me, at the time, mysterious. It was only after several days and nights of sleepless reflection that a solution flashed before me, and ever since has appeared as clear as the noon-day sun!

"What is it?" The ball I took from the scrotum of the babe was the identical one which, on the 12th of May, shattered the tibia of my young friend, and in its mutilated condition, plunged through his testicle, carrying with it particles of semen and spermatozoa into the abdomen of the young lady, then through her left ovary, and into the uterus, in this manner impregnating her! There can be no other solution of the phenomenon! These convictions I expressed to the family, and, at their solicitations, visited my young soldier friend, laying the case fully before him in its proper light. At first, most naturally, he appeared skeptical, but concluded to visit the young mother. Whether convinced or not, he soon married her, ere the little boy had attained his fourth month.

As a matter of additional interest, I may mention having received a letter during the past year, reporting a happy married state and three children, but neither resembling to the same marked degree, as the first—our hero—Pater familias!

November 6, 1982

Dear Abby: You said it is possible for a woman to become pregnant and still remain a virgin. It sounds impossible, but I know it's true, which reminds me of a similar story I read in a reputable magazine some years ago.

It seems that during the Civil War (May 12, 1863, to be exact), a young Virginia farm girl was standing on her front porch while a battle was raging nearby. A stray bullet first passed through the scrotum of a young Union cavalryman, then lodged in the reproductive tract of the young woman, who thus became pregnant by a man she had not been within 100 feet of! And nine months later she gave birth to a healthy baby!

You don't believe it? If it hadn't been published in the very reliable American Heritage magazine (December 1971, page 99, in a story titled "The Case of the Miraculous Bullet"), I wouldn't have believed it either.

—Leland E. Smith, Nashville, Tennessee

Dear Mr. Smith: Several years ago I ran that item in this space, which brought me a letter from a 90-year-old South Dakota Indian. He said he heard a different version of the same story. Only the girl wasn't a Virginia farm girl, she was an Indian maiden who claimed she had been impregnated by a bow and arrow.

I reprint Dr. Capers's entire report above because the source is not easy to find, and it has been so often summarized and paraphrased incorrectly or incompletely. By the time the story reached American Heritage, *for example, the incident had moved from Mississippi to Virginia and the participants had become Union supporters. Also, the detail of the minnie ball lodging in the infant's scrotum was not mentioned. I, like "Dear Abby," distrusted the story; I discussed it in* The Choking Doberman, *guessing it to be either "an old wartime legend or perhaps a nineteenth-century doctor's or editor's hoax." The story did, indeed, prove to be a hoax, as I learned when I located this retraction published in vol. I, no. 21 (November 21, 1874), pp. 263–64, of the* American Medical Weekly:

> *Dr. L. G. Capers, of Vicksburg, Miss., disclaims responsibility for the truth of that remarkable case of impregnation by a minnie ball as reported in No. 19 of this Journal. He tells the story as it was told to him. He does not say it is untrue, but is disposed to appositely remember the truth of the old adage, that "accidents may happen in the best regulated families." The joke is, that the Doctor reported the case without any signature, but as the editor is indisposed to be made the victim of* canards, *and recognized the writing sent, he was unwilling to deprive the author of the contemplated fun, and allowed him to enjoy even more of this than was anticipated. The readers have enjoyed the story much, but not enough "to cut capers" after reading it.*

Professor James O. Breeden of Southern Methodist University deserves credit for authoritatively debunking the story in his article "'The Case of the Miraculous Bullet' Revisited" in Military Affairs, *vol. 45, no. 1(1981), but neither Abby nor I were aware of his article when we expressed our own disbelief.*

Epilogue

Urban Legend Parodies

"The Report of My Death . . ."

From: several.internet.pals@hereandthere.com
To: jan.brunvand@m.cc.utah.edu
Subject: Is Prof. Jan Brunvand dead?

Heard on Univ. of Oregon campus that Prof. Jan Brunvand (author of "Vanishing Hitchhiker," "Choking Doberman,") was found dead at his office desk at the Univ. of Utah. He was found by freshman student after he failed to appear for a scheduled class lecture.

My reply:

Report true. This comes from the other side. I still have Internet access, and the fly fishing is fantastic.

Cheers,

—Jan

Folklorists have long recognized the existence of "metafolklore"—folklore *about* folklore. (Example: "Knock." "Who's there?" "Opportunity.") Similarly, there is a body of folklore about *folklorists*, for instance, did any scholar ever actually give up in the definitions game and simply describe our subject in these terms, "Folklore is what folklorists study?" Or did tale-type and -motif guru Stith Thompson ever really tell folktales at an academic conference merely by reciting their numbers from his classification systems?

Given such self-referential in-group traditions, it's not surprising that urban legend parodies have proliferated in our postmodern age. The Internet is loaded with good examples, such as this one that was forwarded to me recently:

Michelle Desperately Needs Your Help!!

Please forward this to everyone you know. This is not a chain letter. It is a little girl's dying wish. Her name is Michelle Brandt, and early this year she was diagnosed with congenital halitosis nervosa (CHN), a disease for which there is no cure. Michelle fell under the influence of a homeopathic doctor who promised to cure her condition if she only ate garlic.

How she could have fallen for such a quack is easy. People in desperate situations will do anything; they will grasp at straws. Perhaps you've known someone who, faced with desperate circumstances, took a path that might seem foolish or misguided. The fact is that Michelle and her parents are now broke; having spent their life savings and mortgaged their home, they are broke.

In fact, they are now in desperate circumstances. When they had a little bit of money left, they decided to treat Michelle to one fine meal. As a final treat for their beloved daughter, the Brandts ordered her favorite dessert, which was pound cake. Michelle, bless her heart, so enjoyed the pound cake that her parents asked the waiter for the recipe. The waiter told them that the recipe would cost them "two fifty," and the Brandts immediately agreed.

Later, when they got their credit card bill, they realized that they were charged $250.00, not the $2.50 they had expected. This bill devastated the Brandts, for it was the last of their money, and they no longer could afford the treatment for Michelle's incurable condition.

What the Brandts have done is decided to get revenge. They are passing along the recipe to you, free of charge. They got this idea from their next-door neighbors, the Gorskys. They figure that if they paid $250 to [name of restaurant deleted pending results of lawsuit], they're going to make sure everyone gets their money's worth.

Rather than plea for money or try to charge people for this recipe, the Brandts are trying to make one final gesture against corporate greed. They hope that this gesture will help wake up corporate America and let it know that the "little people" will not be pushed around, especially those with a daughter afflicted with CHN.

On the eve of the composition of this letter, Michelle wanted to add something. Michelle, already traumatized because of her CHN, had suffered another shock recently. She had been to her older sister's wedding. At the banquet, the groom (Michelle's new brother-in-law) told the guests to look under their seats, where manila envelopes were stowed. Inside the envelopes were pictures of Michelle's sister and the best man in a compromising position.

The wedding, of course, was ruined, even though the Brandts had made a lovely pound cake for the wedding. Poor Michelle realized that nothing is certain (except that she never will recover from CHN) and wanted to try to stake her claim for immortality. She is only asking one thing: That each of you pass along this letter so that she will remain alive, at least in the magic of E-mail.

Even the ACHNS (American Congenital Halitosis Nervosa Society) has chipped in. The ACHNS has pledged to donate three cents for every person who receives this letter, to the fight to cure Michelle's incurable condition. Keep in mind that this will cost you nothing to forward this. Just a few moments of your time is all it takes.

This letter has already been around the world eight times, and it would be a shame if you broke the link now. (Remember, though, this is not a chain letter.)

How can any decent person refuse a dying girl's last wish, especially when the ACHNS is pledged to devote money to Michelle's cause? Can you, in good conscience, just delete this? All it takes is for you to hit the "forward" key, add a few names, and send it along.

In a world of over 5 billion people, how often do you get the chance to make a difference in someone's life? Not too often, I bet. But your effort can help Michelle's family to regain its faith in people. You see, they lost their faith when Michelle's favorite uncle, Walter, took a trip to Las Vegas. Walter, who always thought himself a bit of a lady's man, met an attractive woman in a casino there, and the two seemed to hit it off. Eventually, she suggested that they go back to her hotel room. The next thing Walter knew, he woke up in a bathtub. The woman was gone, but there was a phone on a chair and a note. The note said that he should not get out of the tub but should call 911 immediately. Walter did this, and the operator knew just what to ask him. When the operator found out he was in a tub, she told him, "Both of your kidneys have been removed by a band of black-market organ sellers. Don't move. Help is on its way." Fortunately, the person who stole Walter's kidneys was a skilled surgeon, but the Brandts' faith in humanity was very much shaken.

Here's your chance! Just forward this non-chain letter to as many people as you know. Remember that for every person you forward this to, the ACHNS will donate three cents to the effort to cure Michelle's incurable CHN affliction. If you forward it to 10 people, that's 30 cents. And if each of them forwards it to 10 people, that's $3.00. And if each of them forwards it to three people, that's $30.00! And, if all of those people forward it to everyone, that's $300.00 (which is only 20 percent more than [restaurant name deleted pending results of lawsuit] charged the Brandts when that money could have gone to making Michelle comfortable in her final days.)

After all you've read, can you possibly say "no" to poor little Michelle? This is one brave little girl. She has suffered so much. [This note attached by the Brandts' lawyer: After much litigation consumed the last of the Brandts' funds, they lost their suit to the restaurant. Under the terms of the settlement, I am not allowed to tell you the name of the restaurant, how much the Brandts have agreed to pay the restaurant because of this letter, or the ingredients of the recipe. It is my hope that this disclaimer will put an end to the litigation that has taken so much of the Brandts' energy, devoted merely to asserting their rights.]

Here's another parody along the same lines, also from the Internet:

Craig Shergold is a 10-year-old boy who is dying of cancer. Before he dies, he would like to set the world record for receiving the most Neiman-Marcus Cookie Recipes. You can help Craig by sending an irate fax to LEXIS-NEXIS demanding that they remove all traces of your mother's maiden name from their executive washroom wall. They will respond by sending E-mail labeled "goodtimes" to the computer controlling Craig's life-support equipment. When Felippe Linz, the technician operating the computer opens this mail, his hard drive will be overwritten with thousands of credit card invoices for $250.00, erasing the last bit of evidence that Hilary was seen on the grassy knoll when JFK was shot, thus allowing world domination by Bill Gates, and his tri-lateral commission cronies who are eating fried peanut butter and banana sandwiches in the black helicopters with Elvis.

Humorist Dave Barry got into the UL parody mode in his column of November 25, 1990, which was devoted to hair-care stories:

> In the early 1960's, when I was in high school, the primary form of feminine hair care was spraying it with what appeared to be fast-drying marine shellac. Women needed industrial hair sprays back then to maintain the popular and attractive "beehive" hairstyle, which was a tall dense mound of hair that had been teased, then sprayed until it achieved the same luxurious natural softness as a traffic stanchion and could not be penetrated by a hatchet, let alone a comb.
>
> In fact there was one high-school girl who had a major beehive, and after several months she decided to wash it, so she broke it open, perhaps using power tools, and inside she found a NEST OF SPIDERS. Yes! At least that's the story I heard at Pleasantville High School. I checked this story out recently with the highest possible authority, a woman I know named Susan, and she confirmed that it was true, only she heard it was cockroaches. My wife, who is also very well-informed, says she heard it was BIRDS. I'm confident that if I kept asking around, I'd find somebody who heard that the woman opened up her hairdo and out crawled an albino alligator from the New York City sewer system.

Another form of legend parody is the fake college course description, as in this example of an "urban myth" and its interpretation published in the The Harvard Lampoon's *A Harvard Education in a Book.* You can tell this course is fake, because I never call them urban "myths."

> Myth: "My hairdresser told me about this lady who was walking her dog one rainy day in New York. As she strolled down Fifth Avenue, she looked in shop windows and didn't pay much attention to her wet dog. Just as she was about to head home, she felt a dragging. She looked down, and there at the end of the leash was a microwave oven."
>
> Brunvand's interpretation: This myth reflects society's fear of the potential evils of technology.

And, finally, this:

****

Warning, Caution, Danger, and Beware!

Gullibility Virus Spreading over the Internet!

****

Washington, D.C.—The Institute for the Investigation of Irregular Internet Phenomena announced today that many Internet users are becoming infected by a new virus that causes them to believe without question every groundless story, legend, and dire warning that shows up in their inbox or on their browser. The Gullibility Virus, as it is called, apparently makes people believe and forward copies of silly hoaxes relating to cookie recipes, e-mail viruses, taxes on modems, and get-rich-quick schemes.

"These are not just readers of tabloids or people who buy lottery tickets based on fortune cookie numbers," a spokesman said. "Most are otherwise normal people, who would laugh at the same stories if told to them by a stranger on a street corner." However, once these same people become infected with the Gullibility Virus, they believe anything they read on the Internet.

"My immunity to tall tales and bizarre claims is all gone," reported one weeping victim. "I believe every warning message and sick child story my friends forward to me, even though most of the messages are anonymous." Another victim, now in remission, added, "When I first heard about Good Times, I just accepted it without question. After all, there were dozens of other recipients on the mail header, so I thought the virus must be true." It was a long time, the victim said, before she could stand up at a Hoaxees Anonymous meeting and state, "My name is Jane, and I've been hoaxed." Now, however, she is spreading the word. "Challenge and check whatever you read," she says.

Internet users are urged to examine themselves for symptoms of the virus, which include the following:

> The willingness to believe improbable stories without thinking. The urge to forward multiple copies of such stories to others. A lack of desire to take three minutes to check to see if a story is true.

T. C. is an example of someone recently infected. He told one reporter, "I read on the Net that the major ingredient in almost all shampoos makes your hair fall out, so I've stopped using shampoos." When told about the Gullibility Virus, T. C. said he would stop reading e-mail, so that he would not become infected.

Anyone with symptoms like these is urged to seek help immediately. Experts recommended that at the first feelings of gullibility, Internet users rush to their favorite search engine and look up the item tempting them to thoughtless credence. Most hoaxes, legends, and tall tales have been widely discussed and exposed by the Internet community.

This message is so important, we're sending it anonymously! Forward it to all your friends right away! Don't think about it! This is not a chain letter! This story is true! Don't check it out! This story is so timely, there is no data on it! This story is so important, we're using lots of exclamation points! Lots!! For every message you forward to some unsuspecting person, the Home for the Hopelessly Gullible will donate ten cents to itself. (If you wonder how the Home will know you are forwarding these messages all over creation, you're obviously thinking too much.)

ACT NOW! DON'T DELAY! LIMITED TIME ONLY! NOT SOLD IN ANY STORE!